Pope Francis and the
Event of Encounter

Global Perspectives on the New Evangelization

Volume 1

Series Introduction

Then he sat down and taught the crowds from the boat. After he had finished speaking, he said to Simon, "Put out into deep water and lower your nets for a catch." Simon said in reply, "Master, we have worked hard all night and have caught nothing, but at your command I will lower the nets." When they had done this, they caught a great number of fish and their nets were tearing.

Luke 5:3–6

"How beautiful upon the mountains are the feet of the one bringing good news, announcing peace, bearing good news, announcing salvation, saying to Zion, 'Your God is King!'" (Isaiah 52:7). Evangelization is something beautiful. Derived from the Greek word, *euaggelion*, evangelization means to bear a "happy/blessed message." It is safe to say that every human being longs for good news, and the entire drama of salvation history, as revealed especially in Scripture and Tradition, hinges on a claim to the best news there is. In a word, salvation through divine intimacy—Emmanuel, God with us (see Isaiah 7:14; Matthew 1:23). And as for the essence of this salvation? Isaiah's witness makes it clear: a return to goodness, peace, and the lordship of God.

The bridge of meaning between Isaiah's text and the life and teachings of Jesus of Nazareth is unmistakable: "After John had been arrested, Jesus came to Galilee proclaiming the gospel (*euaggelion*) of God: 'This is the time of fulfillment. The kingdom of God is at hand. Repent, and believe in the gospel'" (Mark 1:14–15). Jesus not only proclaims the good news indicated by Isaiah—"Your God is King!"—he manifests and embodies it. Jesus is the good news of God in person: "And the Word became flesh and made his dwelling among us" (John 1:14). In Jesus's humanity united with his divinity, the good news of God becomes sacrament through the perpetual liturgy of incarnation. Yet the totality of God's revelation in Jesus is laced with paradox. He is a servant king. His royal garments are stark nakedness. His crown is woven of thorns. His ministry is unconcerned with the accumulation of material wealth but, to the contrary, is about giving all away. His queen is a vestal virgin, the Church, *in persona Mariae*, and he reigns from a wooden throne of suffering.

In the twenty-first century, the paradoxical message of the Gospel is no less shocking than it was two thousand years ago. If anything, it is even more riveting to scientific sensibilities and to a surging expansion of secularism taking root in virtually every cultural setting of the world. As Pope Paul VI put it in his 1975 apostolic exhortation, *Evangelii nuntiandi*, we have entered definitively "a new period of evangelization (*feliciora evangelizationis tempora*)" (2). In other words, today we find ourselves in a happy and profitable season to evangelize.

This book series, *Global Perspectives on the New Evangelization*, aims to contribute to the mission field of this "New Evangelization." By offering fresh voices from a diversity of perspectives, these books put Catholic theology into dialogue with a host of conversation partners around a variety of themes. Through the principle of inculturation, rooted in that of incarnation, this series seeks to reawaken those facets of truth found in the beautiful complementarity of cultural voices as harmonized in the one, holy, catholic, and apostolic Church.

John C. Cavadini and **Donald Wallenfang,** *Series editors*

Pope Francis and the Event of Encounter

EDITED BY

John C. Cavadini

AND

Donald Wallenfang

☙PICKWICK *Publications* · Eugene, Oregon

POPE FRANCIS AND THE EVENT OF ENCOUNTER

Global Perspectives on the New Evangelization 1

Pickwick Publications
An Imprint of Wipf and Stock Publishers
199 W. 8th Ave., Suite 3
Eugene, OR 97401

www.wipfandstock.com

PAPERBACK ISBN: 978-1-62032-196-6
HARDCOVER ISBN: 978-1-4982-4337-7
EBOOK ISBN: 978-1-4982-4336-0

Cataloguing-in-Publication data:

Names: Cavadini, John C., editor. | Wallenfang, Donald, editor.

Title: Pope Francis and the event of encounter / edited by John C. Cavadini and Donald Wallenfang.

Description: Eugene, OR : Pickwick Publications, 2018 | Series: Global Perspectives on the New Evangelization 1 | Includes bibliographical references and index.

Identifiers: ISBN 978-1-62032-196-6 (paperback) | ISBN 978-1-4982-4337-7 (hardcover) | ISBN 978-1-4982-4336-0 (ebook)

Subjects: LCSH: Francis, Pope, 1936–. | Phenomenology. | Catholic Church and philosophy.

Classification: BX1378.7 P6510 2018 (print) | BX1378.7 P6510 (ebook)

Manufactured in the U.S.A.   01/18/18

The editors would like to dedicate this volume to the memory and legacy of St. Joseph, the Worker, and the Husband of Mary. It was devotion to St. Joseph that brought the editors together as kindred spirits under the shelter and protection of this heroic witness to fatherhood.

"In human history the 'rays of fatherhood' meet a first resistance in the obscure but real fact of original sin. *This is truly the key for interpreting reality.* Original sin is not only the violation of a positive command of God but also, and above all, a violation of *the will of God as expressed in that command. Original sin attempts, then, to abolish fatherhood.*"

John Paul II, *Crossing the Threshold of Hope*, 227–28.

"When Joseph awoke, he did as the angel of the Lord had commanded him and took his wife into his home."

Matthew 1:24

Contents

Doctrinal Encounters

Cultural and Political Encounters

Contributors

Melanie Susan Barrett, PhD, STD, is Chairperson and Professor in the Department of Moral Theology at University of St. Mary of the Lake / Mundelein Seminary. She holds both a doctorate (PhD) in Religious Ethics from the University of Chicago Divinity School, and a doctorate (STD) in Moral Theology from the University of Fribourg in Switzerland. She is the author of *Love's Beauty at the Heart of the Christian Moral Life: The Ethics of Catholic Theologian Hans Urs von Balthasar*, and a second (forthcoming) book on suffering and the moral life in the work of Thomas Aquinas. She serves on the editorial boards for the *Journal of Moral Theology* and *Chicago Studies*. She is a member of the Society of Christian Ethics and the Academy of Catholic Theology.

John C. Cavadini, PhD, is a Professor in the Department of Theology at the University of Notre Dame, having served as Chair of the Department from 1997–2010 and led the Department to a top 10 ranking in the NRC rankings of doctoral programs. He is also the McGrath–Cavadini Director of the McGrath Institute for Church Life. His main areas of research and teaching are in patristic and early medieval theology, with special interests in the theology of Augustine and in the history of biblical exegesis. In 2009, he was appointed by Pope Benedict XVI to a five-year term on the International Theological Commission and was also created a member of the Equestrian Order of St. Gregory the Great, *classis civilis*, by Pope Benedict. He has served as a consultant to the USCCB Committee on Doctrine since 2006.

Leonard J. DeLorenzo, PhD, is Associate Professional Specialist in the McGrath Institute for Church Life with a concurrent appointment in the Department of Theology at the University of Notre Dame. He is author of *Witness: Learning to Tell the Stories of Grace that Illumine Our Lives* (Ave Maria Press, 2016), *Work of Love: A Theological Reconstruction of the Communion of Saints* (University of Notre Dame Press, 2017), and co-editor with Vittorio Montemaggi of *Dante, Mercy, and the Beauty of the Human Person* (Cascade, 2017/18). He lives in South Bend, Indiana, with his wife, Lisa, and their five children.

Fr. Terrence Ehrman, CSC, PhD, is the Assistant Director for Life Science Research and Outreach at the Center for Theology, Science, and Human Flourishing, and concurrent professional specialist in the theology department at the University of Notre Dame. He investigates the relationship between theology and science, particularly the life sciences of ecology and evolution. His interests include understanding who God is as Creator, who we are as creatures, and what our relationship is to God, ourselves, and the natural world. He teaches a course in the theology department entitled *Science, Theology, and Creation*.

Joseph S. Flipper, PhD, is Assistant Professor of Theology and Assistant Director of the Ethics and Social Justice Center at Bellarmine University, Louisville, KY. He is the author of *Between Apocalypse and Eschaton: History and Eternity in Henri de Lubac* (2015). His current research focuses on the experience of time and space in theological and cultural modernisms.

Andrew Kim, PhD, is Assistant Professor of Theology at Marquette University. He received his MA from Union Theological Seminary and his doctorate from The Catholic University of America. His primary area of research concentrates on virtue ethics in the work of Thomas Aquinas. He has published articles in *Studies in Christian Ethics* and the *Journal of Moral Theology*, and he is the author of *An Introduction to Catholic Ethics Since Vatican II* (Cambridge University Press, 2016).

Jennifer Kryszak, PhD, is Assistant Professor of Theological and Ministerial Studies at St. Thomas University, Miami Gardens, Florida. She received her doctorate in Religion and Modernity from Duke University and her MA from the Graduate Theological Union. Her research focuses on the intersection of ecclesiology, ethnography, and visual culture. She is the author of articles in *Ecclesial Practices* and *Thinking About Religion*.

Timothy P. O'Malley, PhD, is Director of the Notre Dame Center for Liturgy in the McGrath Institute for Church Life. He teaches in the Department of Theology at the University of Notre Dame in the area of liturgical-sacramental theology, spirituality, and catechesis. He is the author of *Liturgy and the New Evangelization: Practicing the Art of Self-Giving Love* (Liturgical Press, 2014) and *Bored Again Catholic: How the Mass Could Save Your Life* (Our Sunday Visitor, 2017).

Brian Pedraza, PhD, is Assistant Professor of Theology at Franciscan Missionaries of Our Lady University (formerly Our Lady of the Lake College). He earned his doctorate at The Catholic University of America with a dissertation on the philosophical and theological anthropology of Pope St. John Paul II and its implications for the New Evangelization. He has published articles in the *Josephinum Journal of Theology*, *Church Life*, the *Catechetical Review*, and *First Things*.

Glenn B. Siniscalchi, PhD, is Assistant Professor of Theology at Notre Dame College, South Euclid, OH. He received his doctorate in systematic theology from Duquesne University (2013). His interests in theology and philosophy are centered on Thomistic natural theology, the historicity of the resurrection of Jesus, and the doctrine of the Church as the universal sacrament of salvation. His book, *Retrieving Apologetics*, was recently published by Pickwick Publications (2016).

R. Jared Staudt, PhD, serves as Visiting Associate Professor at the Augustine Institute and in the Office of Evangelization and Family Life Ministries at the Archdiocese of Denver. He earned his doctorate in systematic theology from Ave Maria University and his BA and MA in Catholic Studies from the University of St. Thomas in St. Paul, MN. He served previously as the Director of Religious Education in two parishes, as Director of Catholic Studies at the University of Mary, and acted as the managing and co-editor of the theological journal, *Nova et Vetera*. Staudt's primary interest is the relationship of religion and culture. He has explored this theme through research on the works of the historian Christopher Dawson, writing his dissertation of the virtue of religion in St. Thomas Aquinas, and teaches regularly on St. John Paul II's vision for the evangelization of culture.

Sister Mary Madeline Todd, OP, STD, is a Dominican Sister of Saint Cecilia Congregation in Nashville, Tennessee, and currently serves as Assistant Professor of Theology at Aquinas College in Nashville. She earned a doctorate in Sacred Theology from the Pontifical University of Saint Thomas Aquinas in Rome and an MA in English Literature from the University of Memphis. Her published writings include: "Two Women and the Lord: The Prophetic Vocation of Women in the Church and the World," in *Promise and Challenge: Catholic Women Reflect on Feminism, Complementarity, and the Church* (Our Sunday Visitor, 2015); "Enduring Mercy" in *Beautiful Mercy: Experiencing God's Unconditional Love So We Can Share It With Others* (Beacon Publishing, 2015); and the article "From Absence to Presence" in the Italian, English, and French editions of the Vatican's newspaper, *L'Osservatore Romano*.

Anh Q. Tran, SJ, PhD, is Assistant Professor of Historical and Systematic theology at Santa Clara University's Jesuit School of Theology at Berkeley. His research interests include world Christianity, religious pluralism, intercultural/interreligious dialogue, Asian spirituality and theology, and Christian missions in Asia. He is the author of *Gods, Heroes, and Ancestors: An Interreligious Encounter in Eighteenth-Century Vietnam* (Oxford University Press, 2018), and is a contributor and co-editor of *World Christianity: Perspectives and Insights* (Orbis, 2016).

Donald Wallenfang, OCDS, PhD, Emmanuel Mary of the Cross, is a Secular Discalced Carmelite and Coordinator of Undergraduate Studies in Theology and Associate Professor of Theology at Walsh University in North Canton, Ohio. He received his MTS from St. Norbert College and his doctorate from Loyola University Chicago. Wallenfang specializes in phenomenology, hermeneutics, and philosophical theology. His research concentrates on the work of Edith Stein, Emmanuel Levinas, Paul Ricoeur, Jean-Luc Marion, and Carmelite Spirituality. His articles have appeared in several journals and book compilations. He is the author of *Dialectical Anatomy of the Eucharist: An Étude in Phenomenology* (Cascade, 2017) and *Human and Divine Being: A Study on the Theological Anthropology of Edith Stein* (Cascade, 2017). Wallenfang is co-editor for the book series, *Global Perspectives on the New Evangelization*, with Pickwick Publications, and is a member of the Edith Stein Circle, *Société Internationale de Recherche Emmanuel Levinas*, and the North American Levinas Society.

Daniella Zsupan-Jerome, PhD, is Professor of Pastoral Theology at Notre Dame Seminary in New Orleans, LA. She holds a bachelor's degree in theology from the University of Notre Dame, a master's degree in liturgy from St. John's University in Collegeville, MN, a master's degree in religion and the arts from Yale Divinity School, and a doctorate in theology and education from Boston College. Her research focuses on social communication and ministry, especially digital culture and its potential for faith formation. She serves as a consultant for the United States Conference of Catholic Bishops' Committee on Communication and is author of the books *Connected toward Communion: The Church and Social Communication in the Digital Age* (Liturgical Press, 2014) and *Evangelization and Catechesis: Echoing the Good News through the Documents of the Church* (Twenty-Third Publications, 2017.) She has also published a number of articles and practical and devotional resources, including Liturgy Training Publication's *Daily Prayer 2013*, *Arts and Faith Advent and Lent* from Loyola Press, and regularly contributes to Liturgical Press's *Give Us This Day* series.

Acknowledgments

So many wonderful people make it possible for a project such as this one come to fruition. At the risk of failing to mention some who have contributed to the realization of this book, nevertheless the editors would like to mention a few essential benefactors. First, thank you to the McGrath Institute for Church Life at the University of Notre Dame and, in particular, to Robert and Joan McGrath for their legacy of generosity. Thank you to President Richard and Terie Jusseaume of Walsh University for their constant support and passion for the New Evangelization. Thank you to the United States Conference of Catholic Bishops, especially the Committee on Doctrine, as well as the Knights of Columbus, for sponsoring and hosting the "Intellectual Tasks of the New Evangelization" conferences in 2011, 2013 and 2016. Finally, thank you to all of the contributors to this first volume of the *Global Perspectives on the New Evangelization* book series. Altogether, these essays form a symphony of textual timbres and tonalities that reflect the plurivocity yet singularity of truth as revealed in the one, holy, catholic, and apostolic Church.

Introduction

For the opening volume of the *Global Perspectives on the New Evangelization* series, we have selected a topic that is most central for today: the peculiar papacy of Francis and his clarion emphasis on the event of encounter. Since being elected as successor to Pope Emeritus Benedict XVI on Wednesday, March 13, 2013, Francis has set the tone for the next chapter of the New Evangelization as inaugurated by Pope Paul VI in 1975, and crystalized by Pope John Paul II in 1979. What is the New Evangelization? From the time of its inception as a distinct ecclesial term through the pontificates of Paul VI, John Paul II and Benedict XVI, the New Evangelization has come to signify several things.

First, it implies a new universal cultural context in which to communicate the Gospel. This context is characterized well by J. Brian Bransfield in his 2010 book, *The Human Person: According to John Paul II*. He argues that three so-called revolutions have taken place over the past two-hundred years on a global scale: (1) the industrial revolution, (2) the sexual revolution, and (3) the technological revolution.[1] In sum, the effects of these saturating waves of social change have been drastic. Though the distinct movements may have their primary genesis in Europe and North America, they have spread throughout the world in cultural colonizing fashion. One by one, they have truncated the meaning of life to a narrow set of temporal values. The industrial revolution defines the human being as "you are what you produce/acquire." The sexual revolution defines the human being as "you are what you feel." And the technological revolution exacerbates the hermeneutic according to the value of expedience: "you are the pleasure you produce/acquire as quickly and efficiently as possible." Altogether, this has resulted in a prevailing social milieu of secularism, materialism and self-referential individualism.[2]

---

1. See Bransfield, *Human Person*, 17–43.
2. See Wuerl, *New Evangelization*, 26–27.

Consider the widespread phenomena of "selfies" and Snapchat—virtual worlds of meaning in which the self is featured center-stage without fail. It seems to be the return of Narcissus, but this time, instead of drowning in the pool reflecting his image, he works to commodify it and to proliferate it in as many virtual corners as possible. In his 2007 encyclical, *Spe salvi*, Benedict XVI writes of the twenty-first-century citizen: "Perhaps many people reject faith today simply because they do not find the prospect of eternal life attractive. What they desire is not eternal life at all, but this present life, for which faith in eternal life seems something of an impediment" (10). St. Paul's charge to the church at Colossae, "think of what is above, not of what is on earth" (3:2), has been reversed: "think of what is on earth, not of what is above." A radical skepticism has set in concerning matters of God and faith. As the new default epistemological paradigm, skepticism distrusts any alleged revelation "from on high" and instead puts all confidence in the whims of the self, regardless of consequence or of history's harbingers.

More than ever before, once-fortified cultural centers have atrophied, giving way to the ideological dictatorship of relativism. For all of their positive features, democracies inevitably have reinforced the notion that truth is a shifting target for thought. Majority vote is prescriptive of truth rather than the other way around. We have been left with the impression that we can invent the truth as we go and Nietzsche's "will to power" has certified that we can get away with it. The social atmosphere in which to manifest and to proclaim the Gospel today is ambiguous and disenchanted at best, and apathetic and zombie-like at worst. As an evangelist, the most despairing predicament is when your audience really has no "ears to hear" or "eyes to see."[3] It is next to impossible to dismantle the strongholds of ideology, whether conservative or liberal, wherein every word is received by the listener through predetermined filters of acceptance or rejection.

While describing this new universal cultural context paints a rather grim picture of the present, at the same time it must be admitted that there remains much promise for the Gospel to be received with joy. As a second point, what is meant by the New Evangelization is a radical shift as to who is evangelizing who. In his two-volume work, *The Story of Christianity*, Justo González argues persuasively that Christianity is now "a polycentric reality, where many areas that had earlier been peripheral have become new centers."[4] In other words, for most of Christianity's history, the Mediterranean region and Europe were its geographical center. Today, however, the populations of Europe and North America are waning in Christian

---

3. See Isa 6:10; Jer 5:21; Ezek 12:2; Matt 13:15; Acts 28:27; Rom 11:8.

4. González, *Story of Christianity*, 525.

faithful, but the population of Christians living in the southern hemisphere is swelling in number. According to the principle of inculturation, stemming from the event of Incarnation, the Gospel takes root in the variety of cultures throughout the world. This is how we can claim the catholicity of the Church: a veritable unity of faith in and through a diversity of cultural expressions of the same faith.

The New Evangelization, therefore, signifies a geographic and cultural reversal of missionary activity, generally speaking. Instead of European missionaries exclusively setting out to evangelize territories south of the equator, missionaries from the southern hemisphere now are called upon to re-evangelize those former centers of Christendom in the northern hemisphere. Moreover, a new approach to evangelization has been inaugurated with Vatican II, especially as signaled in documents such as *Ad gentes divinitus*, *Unitatis redintegratio*, and *Nostra aetate*.

Peter Phan puts it well, that "Christian mission can no longer be what it was, a one-way proclamation of a message of salvation to a world of 'pagans' totally bereft of God's self revelation and grace. Rather, it is first of all a search for and recognition of the presence and activities of the Holy Spirit among the peoples to be evangelized, and in this humble and attentive process of listening, the evangelizers become the evangelized, and the evangelized become the evangelizers."[5] A great spirit of humility must prevail over the task of evangelization today. It is no longer to be understood according to a dichotomy between the "faithful" on one hand and the "pagans" on the other. *Ad gentes divinitus* relates that "just as Christ penetrated to people's hearts and by a truly human dialogue led them to the divine light, so too his disciples, profoundly pervaded by the Spirit of Christ, should know and converse with those among whom they live, that through sincere and patient dialogue they themselves might learn of the riches which a generous God has distributed among the nations."[6] Even for Jesus of Nazareth, evangelization was/is a two-way street inasmuch as "the kingdom of God is among you" (Luke 17:21). Throughout the Gospels, we observe Jesus validating and affirming the love and the goodness already dawning in people's hearts, only to make it grow even more. As some preachers put it today, "God loves us right where we're at, but too much to leave us there." According to the way of Jesus, listening to the other is an essential part of evangelization as an indispensable act of mercy and hospitality. Jesus's missionary itinerary and style exhibits what Pope Francis has come to call "the art of accompaniment," as Jesus "remov(ed) (his) sandals before the sacred ground of the

---

5. Phan, *In Our Own Tongues*, 43.

6. *Ad gentes divinitus*, 11.

other" and washed their feet.[7] Authentic evangelists are to be "shepherds, with the 'odour of the sheep,' mak(ing) it real, as shepherds among (their) flock, fishers of men."[8]

Finally, a third meaning of the New Evangelization is the placing of the accent on proclamation within the Catholic context. For most of its practices and focal points of activity, the Catholic Church is inclined toward the sacramental dynamism of manifestation.[9] For many Catholics, it can seem enough for the life of faith to frequent the sacraments and to engage in some social justice initiatives. Because of the primacy of the sacraments in Catholic belief and practice, and in light of the history of the Protestant Reformation with its emphasis on Scripture and preaching, Catholics may tend to shy away from the missionary task of evangelization. With the call of the New Evangelization comes the reawakening to the missionary mandate to "make disciples of all nations . . . teaching them to observe all that I have commanded you" (Matt 28:19–20). The New Evangelization is inspired by the conviction of *Dei verbum*: "The church has always venerated the divine scriptures as it has venerated the Body of the Lord, in that it never ceases, above all in the sacred liturgy, to partake of the bread of life and to offer it to the faithful from the one table of the word of God and the Body of Christ. It has always regarded and continues to regard the scriptures, taken together with sacred tradition, as the supreme rule of its faith."[10] Scripture, in a definitive way, has reentered as one of the centerpieces of the New Evangelization.[11] Admittedly, the term "evangelization" is associated more readily with Protestantism or Evangelical theology. It is something new for the Catholic ethos to open to the entire world with evangelical zeal, even taking note of effective Protestant practices in evangelization, such as vibrant preaching, the savvy use of technology, and the art of hospitality and fellowship. It has been an ironic phenomenon that not a little of Protestant evangelization and outreach has been aimed at Catholics and that the terms "Catholic" and "Christian," for many people, are not regarded as synonymous. From the Catholic perspective, however, the New Evangelization announces a universal call to conversion – a return to Christ and to the one, holy, catholic, and apostolic Church.

---

7. See Francis, *Evangelii gaudium*, 169–73; John 13:1–20.

8. Francis, *Chrism Mass Homily*, March 28, 2013.

9. For more on the crucial distinction, yet complementarity, between manifestation and proclamation, see Ricoeur, *Figuring the Sacred*, 48–67; Tracy, *Analogical Imagination*, 193–229; Wallenfang, *Dialectical Anatomy of the Eucharist*.

10. *Dei verbum*, 21.

11. See, for example, *Compendium of the New Evangelization*, 402, 967, 1092–93.

Finally, with its emphasis on proclamation, the New Evangelization reverses the traditional paradigm of catechesis. Instead of taking for granted warm bodies in the seats of churches and religious education programs, both clergy and laity realize the need for the Church to go out of itself into all sectors of society and culture. The concept of outreach is indispensable for the missionary mandate of the Church. People must be invited to belong and to participate fully. The Church is not so much a set of buildings, an organization, or an institution, as it is the "living stones . . . built into a spiritual house" that comprise her essence (see 1 Pet 2:4–5).[12] Pastoral efforts of evangelization must avail themselves to the wide range of technologies and social media platforms available to reach people wherever they are. Today it is essential that the Church go out of herself in order that she be built up. It is not so much about tallying up new members, coercing converts, or proselytizing would-be initiates, as it is about inviting anyone and everyone to "taste and see that the Lord is good" (Ps 34:9).

This new book series, *Global Perspectives on the New Evangelization*, was inspired in particular by the first three "Intellectual Tasks of the New Evangelization" conferences held at the St. John Paul II Shrine in Washington, DC, in 2011, 2013, and 2016, all generously sponsored by the Knights of Columbus. The editors of this series were in attendance together at the second and third conferences, during which the idea for the book series emerged. In addition to these conferences, other more recent gatherings have lent inspiration as well, such as "The New Evangelization Conference" held at St. Vincent College in May of 2016. The first volume of this book series, *Pope Francis and the Event of Encounter*, has enlisted the vision, talent and expertise of a select group of young Catholic American theologians around its designated theme. This volume marks the beginning of a conversation to be continued throughout the series. We wanted to create an ongoing venue for theological reflection that was unrestrained by academic red tape, publishing politics, or scholarly elitism. The essays in this volume represent a fairly diverse chorus of voices, all of which speak from the vital intersection between theological theory and pastoral practice.

The collection of essays are divided into four distinct families: "Merciful Encounters," "Ecological Encounters," "Doctrinal Encounters," and "Cultural and Political Encounters." The first family, "Merciful Encounters," begins with Jesuit, Anh Tran's, consideration of Pope Francis's unique identity as an Argentinian Jesuit. By probing the Jesuit foundations of the pope's missionary-oriented charism, Tran artistically calibrates the optic that will be in force throughout the entire book. Tran characterizes the "Francis

---

12. Also, see Dulles, *Models of the Church.*

effect," in relation to the task of evangelization, according to the key terms: joy, mercy and discernment. This analysis culminates in a recapitulation of Ignatian spirituality in which "love manifests itself more in deeds than in words."

Second in the family of "Merciful Encounters" is Mary Madeline Todd's poetic reflection on "embodied mercy." Given her Dominican formation, steeped as it is in the hylomorphism of Thomas Aquinas, Todd is attuned to the centrality of the Incarnation in Pope Francis's blueprint for evangelization today. Through the Word made flesh, divine mercy is communicated to the highest degree. Todd traces the *via pulchritudinis* ("way of beauty") of divine love as it makes its circuit from the spiritual heart, in and through the flesh, to the body and soul of the other. She shows how mercy accomplishes its greatest achievement in its embodied performance of gracefulness through word, deed and sacrament.

Following upon the heels of Todd's intuition of "embodied mercy" is Jennifer Kryszak's mosaic of its concrete instance among the Congregation of St. Joseph. Taking cues from *Laudato si'*, she notes the integral relationship between ecological and anthropological healing. By highlighting the locus of self-gift within the culture of encounter, Kryszak puts praxiological flesh on the theoretical bones of ideas by attending to the peculiar charism of the Sisters of St. Joseph: to serve, to sanctify and to save "the dear neighbor." Recollecting the "Generous Promises" of the Congregation of St. Joseph, this essay lifts the essential message of *Laudato si'* off the page and into the streets and market squares of society.

To continue with the theme of merciful encounters as experienced "in the flesh," Donald Wallenfang depicts Pope Francis as a phenomenologist par excellence. With his attentiveness to the in-the-flesh givens within common human experience, Pope Francis emulates the contemplative empathy of the missionary disciple of Christ. Wallenfang suggests a common genus between the generous pastoral approach of Pope Francis and the hermeneutics of generosity on display in the method of phenomenology. In the end, Wallenfang recommends the serious study of phenomenology as a means to cultivate an openness to *encuentro*, that is, a disposition of wonder and gratitude before the face of the other and all that gives itself abundantly.

Two essays in the volume concentrate their analyses on *Laudato si'* and thus are twinned as "Ecological Encounters." Brian Pedraza creatively makes the connection between the spiritual itinerary of Bonaventure and Pope Francis. Illuminating the Franciscan sensibility at work in each, Pedraza distills the network of interpersonal and interspecies communion between creatures and Creator. He underscores Pope Francis's call to an integrated vision of earthly life and being by relating the created order to its

Trinitarian prototype. Pedraza unearths the "Gospel of Creation" articulated by Pope Francis in order to set the stage for proclaiming the self-revelation of the Trinitarian God. For his part, Terrence Ehrman challenges the irascible accusation that Christianity is to blame for the present-day ecological crisis. In response, Ehrman seizes on Pope Francis's potent notion of "serene attentiveness" as instrumental for ecological conversion. Tapping into the charism of the Congregation of the Holy Cross, by venturing "across borders of every sort," Ehrman fortifies the possibility of dialogue between natural science and theology to serve as fertile ground for evangelization. He portrays Pope Francis as a modern-day Basil of Caesarea inasmuch as the pope suggests that a guided encounter with creation facilitates a propitious rendezvous with the Creator.

Leading off the third set of familial essays, "Doctrinal Encounters," is Melanie Barrett's tome on the complementary relationship between doctrine and praxis as advised by the pontiff. Barrett contends that Pope Francis's approach does not merit its criticism of replacing moral teachings with situation ethics. Instead, Barrett demonstrates how Pope Francis defines the intrinsic mutuality between ecclesial doctrine and mission. Barrett moves in careful systematic steps from assessing cultural challenges, to developing strategies for pastoral care, to emphasizing certain doctrinal moments as advantageous for effective evangelization. On the whole, we are led to remember that attention to doctrine hones pastoral practice, and experience in pastoral practice enlivens otherwise banal doctrines.

One pressing question for evangelization today is the credibility of Christian witness. Can the apologetics of the follower of Christ be trusted, even after an intensified surge of demythologization in a post-Enlightenment world? Locating Pope Francis as the preeminent Christian witness, Glenn Siniscalchi argues in the affirmative. Siniscalchi deems it necessary to inventory the pope's primary motives of credibility that thread together the doctrinal cohesion of his writings. Observing the integrity between the pope's teachings and lifestyle, Siniscalchi capitalizes on the power of a witness whose words and actions find no point of contradiction. By accenting the positive features of interreligious dialogue, and the pivotal role of charity within all dialogue, Siniscalchi reminds us of the promise of hope that goes before and behind every genuine evangelical encounter.

Concomitant with the summons to credibility within the Christian witness is the vocation to virtue. Andrew Kim develops his own apologetic in defense of the unity of the virtues thesis that likewise is upheld by Pope Francis in *Evangelii gaudium*. Kim perceptively notices the role of a morality animated by the unity of the virtues within the election of the "missionary option" of evangelization. Against the critics of the unity of the virtues thesis, Kim cogently argues along with the pope that it is counterintuitive to believe that one can cultivate select virtues while neglecting others. In sum, Kim asserts the plausibility of the unity of the virtues thesis, in light of the Augustinian notion of scalar virtue, in order to reinforce the vitality of virtue as the guiding star of the New Evangelization.

To round out the collection of "Doctrinal Encounters" is Timothy O'Malley's provocative reflection on the sacramental realism of *Amoris laetitia*. Juxtaposing Pope Francis's post-synodal apostolic exhortation with Pope John Paul II's *Theology of the Body* corpus, O'Malley stresses the power of the mundane as expressed in the treatment of marriage and family life by the Jesuit bishop of Rome. With delicate nuance and conviviality, O'Malley acknowledges the harmony between both pontiffs' works and yet, in the end, throws light on the subtle peril of placing too much emphasis on the conjugal act within a theological reflection of marriage. O'Malley enlists the work of Marc Ouellet to recuperate the sacramental and liturgical meaningfulness of the everyday domestic church.

Finally, we reach the last family of essays in the volume, "Cultural and Political Encounters." Rather than fall prey to some facile ideological reductionism, as the name "political" might seduce one to think, the last five essays give voice to the Catholic intuition of the both/and. Collectively, they show the truthful nature of truth as dialectical. The first essay in the batch is Leonard DeLorenzo's account of what he calls Pope Francis's "low-stakes form of encounter." DeLorenzo relates the consistent style of Pope Francis's pastoral strategy: leading with simple gestures that open unanticipated spaces for personal encounter with God. At once meeting people where they are and leading them to new horizons of being-in-the-world, Pope Francis shows preference for the "concrete Catholic thing" through the practice of intercessory prayer. DeLorenzo showcases how the pope offers the paradigmatic model for meaningful intercessory prayer, always in relation to popular piety and the communion of saints.

Reminiscent of Tran's opening essay of the volume, Joseph Flipper delves into the hidden life and work of Jorge Mario Bergoglio in order to discover the early theological form that now is revealed on the world's stage in Pope Francis. Mining theological gems such as dialectical thought, critical engagement with theologies of liberation, and the critique of the spatialization of Christian social life, Flipper delivers in-depth and original scholarship on the ministerial history of Bergoglio in order to shed light on his pontifical acts and inscriptions. Flipper does not shy away from the context of political unrest that hovered over Bergoglio's pastoral work in Argentina, especially during the tumultuous civic politics of the 1970s. Rather, Flipper exhibits how Bergoglio's theological reflection was shaped by his unique socio-political situation in which he was called upon to shepherd the flock of the faithful, under the hope that "time is greater than space."

For evangelization to occur, effective communication is needed within every particular cultural environment. Daniella Zsupan-Jerome unveils the intentionality of communication developed by Pope Francis. With the onset of Internet and mobile technologies within the past twenty years, a plethora of questions arise concerning the responsible use of such tools of communication. Zsupan-Jerome provides a thorough treatment of the pope's guidance for approaching these questions. Going beyond practical considerations, Zsupan-Jerome accompanies the reader toward contemplation of the theological foundations of communication as a principal interpersonal phenomenon. This essay gives clarity about how to harness the power of social media as instruments of the New Evangelization.

One essential topic relating the work of Pope Francis to the New Evangelization is inculturation. R. Jared Staudt's essay on the evangelization of culture speaks to the process of inculturation with assiduity and nuance. Recounting the trajectory of magisterial teaching that deals with the issue of culture, Staudt asserts the continuity yet uniqueness of Pope Francis's deliberations on the topic. Francis is seen diagnosing cultural ills with precision and following up his diagnoses with tenable remedies. For example, he proposes a movement from a throw away culture to one of personal encounter. If evangelization is to take root among people, it must be a cultural phenomenon whereby culture is transformed by the healing balm of the Gospel. Staudt's analysis greatly assists the evangelist as a serious student of culture.

John Cavadini's essay on John A. O'Brien and the renewal of lay leadership in the Church brings the volume to a close, even if by way of making a new opening for evangelization. At the end of the day, it is necessary to ask the question anew: What is the goal of evangelization? Cavadini's essay reminds us that the ultimate fruit of evangelization is the redeeming experience of conversion—both for the evangelizer and the evangelized. Every act of authentic evangelization involves renewed and/or first-time conversion. After all, it has been said that the Gospel of Jesus Christ "comforts the afflicted, and afflicts the comfortable." By remembering the fervent evangelical zeal of John A. O'Brien, Cavadini challenges the would-be evangelist to embark on new terrain in sharing the Gospel with so many people who have yet to encounter it in the vibrancy of its message. It is not enough to talk about good strategies for evangelization, it must be embodied, performed and proclaimed "in-the-real." It is the scandal of the cross, as embodied in the Christian witness, that serves as the crux of encounter with the living Christ. To round out his essay, Cavadini proposes an extension of lay leadership beyond mere "collaboration" with the clergy, but rather to the degree of taking "co-responsibility" for the mission of the Church.

Altogether, these fifteen essays comprise an ode of praise and adoration for not only Pope Francis, but for the entire cadre of pontiffs of the twentieth and twenty-first centuries who have brought the mission of the New Evangelization to light and life. So far in his pontificate, Francis has served as a beacon of enduring hope through a historical time experiencing seismic waves of cultural shifting. In the midst of great uncertainty about the future, and temptations to resign from the summons to evangelize the world, *Evangelii gaudium* stands as a flagship user's guide for engagement in authentic and sincere evangelization. With his realist hermeneutics and earthy approach to ministry, Francis sets the Church on its courageous course toward the shores of salvation. This is, in the end, the driving impetus for sharing the good news of Jesus Christ: "I came so that they might have life and have it more abundantly" (John 10:10). Our hope is that you, the reader, find in these pages fuel for yourself to be a part of igniting the New Evangelization throughout the world today. May these essays be a constant conversation partner to remind you that you are not alone in your labor of love.

Ex voto suscepto,
John C. Cavadini and Donald Wallenfang

Bibliography

Bransfield, J. Brian. *The Human Person: according to John Paul II*. Boston: Pauline, 2010.

Dulles, Avery. *Models of the Church*. New York: Image, 2002.

Flannery, Austin, ed. *Vatican Council II: The Basic Sixteen Documents: Constitutions, Decrees, Declarations*. Northport, NY: Costello, 1996.

Francis, Pope. *Chrism Mass Homily*. March 28, 2013. http://w2.vatican.va/content/francesco/en/homilies/2013/documents/papa-francesco_20130328_messa-crismale.html.

Francis, Pope. *Evangelii gaudium*. 2013. http://w2.vatican.va/content/francesco/en/apost_exhortations/documents/papa-francesco_esortazione-ap_20131124_evangelii-gaudium.html.

González, Justo L. *The Story of Christianity*. Vol. 2, *The Reformation to the Present Day*. New York: HarperOne, 2010.

John Paul II, Pope. *Crossing the Threshold of Hope*. Edited by Vittorio Messori. Translated by Jenny McPhee and Martha McPhee. New York: Knopf, 1994.

Phan, Peter C. *In Our Own Tongues: Perspectives from Asia on Mission and Inculturation*. Maryknoll, NY: Orbis, 2003.

Ricoeur, Paul. *Figuring the Sacred: Religion, Narrative, and Imagination*. Edited by Mark I. Wallace. Minneapolis: Fortress, 1995.

Tracy, David. *The Analogical Imagination: Christian Theology and the Culture of Pluralism*. New York: Crossroad, 1981.

United States Conference of Catholic Bishops. *Compendium on the New Evangelization: Texts of the Pontifical and Conciliar Magisterium: 1939–2012*. Washington, DC: USCCB, 2015.

Wallenfang, Donald. *Dialectical Anatomy of the Eucharist: An Étude in Phenomenology*. Eugene, OR: Cascade, 2017.

Wuerl, Donald. *New Evangelization: Passing on the Catholic Faith Today*. Huntington, IN: Our Sunday Visitor, 2013.

Merciful Encounters

A Church of Mercy and Hope

Pope Francis and the New Evangelization

—Anh Q. Tran, SJ

Abstract:

This essay examines Pope Francis's ecclesial disposition and evangelist outlook, exemplified in his first exhortation, *Evangelii gaudium*. I will attempt to connect the pope's background as a Jesuit and a person from the Global South to explain his view on New Evangelization as an awakening of faith—stressing the encounter of a merciful God with his people in their particular circumstances. This is consistent, I argue, with his predecessors' (John Paul II and Benedict XVI) views of conversion and missionary outreach, though it is often done in a fresh (and sometimes unconventional) approach. I will then draw out the pope's insights for missiological and interreligious applications.

A New Wind in the Church

The election of Cardinal Jorge Mario Bergoglio of Bueno Aires on March 13, 2013, as the Successor of Peter, was a surprise. Who would predict that a seventy-seven-year-old man, a Jesuit from Latin America, would be the universal shepherd of the Catholic Church? Soon after his election, Francis electrified people from all walks of life, believers and non-believers alike by his humility and his avowed stance on solidarity with the common people, the poor, and the marginalized. Critical voices are not absent either. Reservations, open and oblique criticisms by way of comparing him to his predecessors, have increased in some church circles. It should not be a surprise, since Francis has broken all expectations and protocols set by the Vatican regarding the papal lifestyle.

While we can agree that Francis's words are not always measured, and his spontaneous interviews could be distorted by media reports, I am convinced that Francis is not a theological lightweight. He is a serious thinker and an effective evangelist—no less effective than John Paul II and Benedict XVI. He could be rightly called "theologian of the people" for his many down-to-earth homilies and speeches given in the Vatican and other places.

This essay examines Francis's ecclesial disposition and evangelical outlook, by way of a close reading of his apostolic exhortation *Evangelii gaudium*. I will attempt to connect the pope's background as a Jesuit and a person from South America to explain his view on New Evangelization as an awakening of faith—stressing the encounter of a merciful God with his people in their particular circumstances. This is consistent, I argue, with his predecessors' (John Paul II and Benedict XVI) views of conversion and missionary outreach, though it is often done in a fresh (and sometime unconventional) approach. I will then draw out the pope's insights for missiological and ecclesial applications.

Who Is Jorge Mario Bergoglio?

In order to understand Pope Francis's attitude toward the Church and its evangelizing mission, it is important to see the man in his context. As soon as Cardinal Bergoglio was elected to the papacy, he captured the hearts of many people by his simplicity. He spoke of himself not as pope but as bishop of Rome. His chosen name, Francis, is also unprecedented. Biographies about him began to multiply.[1] Everyone was eager to know more about this pope who is a member of a religious order, the first one in recent history to be such since the election of the Camaldolese monk Gregory XVI in 1831.

Six months after his election, the world learned about the person who became the Roman Pontiff from the pope himself. When asked by Antonio Spadaro, editor in chief of *La Civiltà Cattolica*, "Who is Jorge Mario Bergoglio?" the pope gave a simple, no less puzzling, answer:

---

1. Among many early biographies of Cardinal Bergoglio in English, several are worthy of note: Vallely, *Pope Francis: Untying the Knots*; Anguilar, *Pope Francis: His Life and Thought*; Rubin and Ambrogetti, *Pope Francis: Conversations with Jorge Bergoglio: His Life in His Own Words*; Ivereigh, *Great Reformer*; Deck, *Francis, Bishop of Rome*. Ivereigh's and Deck's works take into account Bergoglio's Jesuit background.

I do not know what might be the most fitting description . . . I am a sinner. This is the most accurate definition. It is not a figure of speech, a literary genre. I am a sinner . . . Yes, perhaps I can say that I am a bit astute, that I can adapt to circumstances, but it is also true that I am a bit naïve. Yes, but the best summary, the one that comes more from the inside and I feel most true is this: I am a sinner whom the Lord has looked upon.[2]

This remark by Francis about himself fits the standard description of a Jesuit since the order's 32nd General Congregation.[3]

In 1975, Jesuit major superiors from five continents gathered in Rome to discuss the impact of Vatican II on the identity and mission of the Society of Jesus. Among many decrees the General Congregation—the highest authority and ultimate governing body of the Jesuits—had passed, Decree 2, entitled "Jesuits Today," clearly spelled out the identity of a modern Jesuit:

What is it to be a Jesuit? It is to know that one is a sinner, yet called to be a companion of Jesus as Ignatius was: Ignatius, who begged the Blessed Virgin to "place him with her Son," and who then saw the Father himself ask Jesus, carrying his cross, to take this pilgrim into his company. What is it to be a companion of Jesus today? It is to engage, under the standard of the Cross, in the crucial struggle of our time: the struggle for faith and that struggle for justice which it includes.[4]

Elsewhere in the same decree are these inspirational words: "The service of faith and the promotion of justice cannot be for us simply one ministry among others. It must be the integrating factor of all our ministries; and not only of our ministries but also of our inner life as individuals, as communities, and as a world-wide brotherhood."[5] These words must have impacted the young Argentinian Jesuit provincial, who participated in that historic moment of the Society's re-orientation toward "the service of faith and the

---

2. Spadaro, "A Big Heart Open to God."

3. A General Congregation (GC) is a worldwide meeting of Jesuit provincial superiors and their delegates, summoned on the death or resignation of the Superior General to choose his successor. Occasionally, it is also convoked when the General decides action is needed on serious matters that he cannot or does not want to decide alone. The latest one, General Congregation 36, was convened in Rome on October 2, 2016.

4. General Congregation 32, Decree 2, 1–2. See text in Padberg, *Jesuit Life & Mission Today*, 291.

5. General Congregation 32, Decree 2, n9. Padberg, *Jesuit Life & Mission Today*, 292. Also see Decree 4.

promotion of justice." The Jesuit commitment to faith and justice became the thrust of Jesuit mission in the contemporary world.[6]

As a young provincial, chosen in 1973 at the age of 36, Bergoglio had to face many pressures from the complexity of the Argentinian political and ecclesial world. Some Jesuits saw Bergoglio's style of leadership as "authoritarian" during his tenure as provincial, and later as rector of the Jesuit Colegio Máximo of Philosophy and Theology at San Miguel (1980–1986).[7] Others found him a charismatic leader. Argentina, in the 1970s, had a military dictatorship and its bishops were quite conservative. On the one hand, Bergoglio was a staunch defender of the Jesuit embrace of social justice against a right-wing military regime that conducted a "dirty war" against those who tried to create a more equitable Argentinian society.[8] On the other hand, he had to deal with Jesuits who were traditional and conservative, as well as with liberal—and sometimes—radical Jesuits.[9] When two Jesuits—Francisco Jarics and Orlando Yorio—were kidnapped and tortured by the military in 1976 for being subversive, Bergoglio took the heat for failing to secure their release and being silent against military repression. Perhaps a sense of personal failure reminds the future pope of his own fragility and sinfulness in the face of tremendous suffering.[10]

After a short time in Germany pursuing doctoral studies, Bergoglio returned to Argentina and taught part-time at Colegio Máximo while taking on parish duties.[11] In 1990, he was assigned to the Jesuit church in Córdoba as spiritual director and confessor. As requested by Cardinal Antonio Quar-

6. General Congregation 32, Decree 4. Cf. Padberg, *Jesuit Life & Mission Today*, 298–318. This decree was quite controversial at the time, since many people in the Church linked it with the Latin American's Liberation Theology movement. Nevertheless, it has become *a magna carta* for the Jesuit way of proceeding.

7. Pope Francis admitted that his authoritarian way of making decisions that created problems: "I did not always do the necessary consultation. And this was not a good thing. My style of government as a Jesuit [provincial] at the beginning had many faults . . . I had to deal with difficult situations, and I made my decisions abruptly and by myself . . . [B]ut I have never been a right-winger . . . Over time I learned many things. The Lord has allowed this growth in knowledge of government through my faults and my sins." See Spadaro, "A Big Heart Open to God."

8. On Bergoglio and the "Dirty War," see Aguilar, *Pope Francis*, 67–82

9. This was the CIAS group in Argentina, mainly more upper-class Jesuits ascribing to liberation theology, while Bergoglio's approach was much more open to popular religion, cultural expression, and without the Marxist elements. I am indebted to Tom Rausch, SJ for this insight.

10. Bergoglio really went out of his way to secure the release of these Jesuits. On the complexity of Jarics and Yorio's affairs, see Ivereigh, *The Great Reformer*, 131–64.

11. It was not clear why Bergoglio interrupted his studies and returned to Argentina before completing his doctorate.

racino, Primate of Argentina, Pope John Paul II appointed him to the position of auxiliary bishop of Buenos Aires in 1992. Six years later, he became the archbishop of Bueno Aires, a position he held until the 2013 conclave. As a member of the Council of Latin American Bishops (*Consejo Episcopal Latinoamericano*, CELAM), Bergoglio was an active and influential participant in their meetings.[12] In fact, Bergoglio was responsible for drafting the final document of the Fifth General Meeting of Latin American bishops at Aparecida, Brazil, in 2007.

It would not be an exaggeration to claim that even as a bishop, Bergoglio remained a true son of Ignatius of Loyola, who made himself available to all and any ministries that the Church required of him. One should not be surprised at his action and way of thinking if one knows that he was a former novice master just before becoming a provincial. The influence of the Ignatian heritage, especially in his *sentire cum ecclesia* and the openness to listening to the Spirit through the process of discernment, marks his theological and pastoral approach.

From *Evangelii nuntiandi* to *Evangelii gaudium*

On November 24, 2013, Pope Francis issued his first major text, the apostolic exhortation *Evangelii gaudium*.[13] Readers of Francis's writings notice a sense of his indebtedness to Paul VI and John Paul II on the matter of evangelization. Written as a response to the 2012 meeting of the Synod of Bishops, *Evangelii gaudium* is Francis's *magna carta* for evangelization in the 21st century. This exhortation demonstrates the seamless continuity between Francis and his predecessors' interpretations of Vatican II: evangelization should be placed as the center of the Church's concern. In depth and in breath, the exhortation can be seen as an updating of *Evangelii nuntiandi*, an expansion of *Redemptoris missio*, and a program of Pope Francis's pontificate. It makes frequent use of *Evangelii nuntiandi* as well as other papal and episcopal writings.[14]

Following the thrust of Vatican II, Pope Paul VI refocused the attention of the Church on evangelization as the primary expression of ecclesial vocation and existence. In 1967, he renamed the *Propaganda Fidei*, an

12. Bergoglio was no stranger to CELAM meetings. He had been part of the preparation for the third CELAM in Pueblo in 1979 when he was still a Jesuit provincial.

13. One can argue that the encyclical *Lumen fidei* (June 29, 2013) is the first papal writing released by Francis, but it was penned largely by Pope Benedict XVI before his retirement.

14. *Evangelii nuntiandi* was cited thirteen times. Other citations come from *Redemptoris missio* and the 2007 Aparecida meeting of CELAM.

institution founded in 1622, as the Congregation for the Evangelization of Peoples. Paul VI was the first modern pope to make apostolic visits in other continents. As part of the commemoration on the Vatican II missionary decree *Ad gentes*, he asked the world-wide bishops to focus their synodal meeting on the theme of "Evangelization in the Modern World" (1974), to which he responded with the apostolic exhortation, *Evangelii nuntiandi* (1975). In this exhortation, Paul VI asserted that the church "exists in order to evangelize."[15] Evangelization, according to the pope, is a complex and dynamic process by which the Church "brings the Good News into all the strata of humanity, and through its influence transforming humanity from within and making it new."[16]

The missionary impulse was developed further by Pope John Paul II as a "new evangelization" during his pontificate. It was not the message that was new; what was to be new was the approach of proclamation. In the encyclical *Redemptoris missio*, John Paul II wrote: "Today the Church must face other challenges and push forward to new frontiers, both in the initial mission *ad gentes* and in the new evangelization of those people who have already heard Christ proclaimed."[17] For John Paul II, as for Paul VI, the recipients of the Gospel message include not only those who never have heard of Christ but also those who lived in a de-Christianized world, the faithful as well as non-practicing Christians, who might find the mode of proclamation outdated and ineffective. The new evangelization is not just repeating the past. The Church must find a way to authenticate and present, or rather, re-present faith in Jesus Christ in a refreshed way for these people.[18]

Evangelization should involve the whole Church, and not just clergy and religious. In a 1983 address to the bishops of Latin America, John Paul II said: "The commemoration of this half millennium of evangelization will have full significance if, as bishops, with your priests and faithful, you accept it as your commitment; a commitment not of re-evangelization, but rather of *a new evangelization*; new in its ardor, methods, and expression."[19] Understood in this manner, the idea of a "new" evangelization was taken up in the continental synods of bishops between 1994 and 1999 in preparation for the Jubilee Year of 2000. A new evangelization is synonymous with renewed efforts in the life of faith within various local churches, starting with a process to discern the changes in various social, cultural, economic,

15. Paul VI, *Evangelii nuntiandi*, 14.

16. Ibid., 18.

17. John Paul II, *Redemptoris missio*, 30.

18. See *Evangelii nuntiandi*, 52–56.

19. John Paul II, *Discourse to the XIX Assembly of CELAM*.

political, and religious settings that impact Christian life, and then to undertake new responsibilities and creativity to convincingly proclaim Christ and his message with joy.[20]

Pope Benedict XVI followed the same trend by giving impetus to the new evangelization in the context of globalization. In 2007, the Congregation for the Doctrine of the Faith sought to clarify the meaning of new evangelization by proposing a definition: "In its precise sense, evangelization is the *missio ad gentes* directed to those who do not know Christ. In a wider sense, it is used to describe ordinary pastoral work, while the phrase *new evangelization* designated pastoral outreach to those who no longer practice the Christian faith."[21] In September 2010, he established a new Pontifical Council for the Promotion of the New Evangelization. Its main task was to prepare for the Thirteenth Ordinary General Assembly of the Synod of Bishops (October 7–28, 2012) on the theme of "The New Evangelization for the Transmission of the Christian Faith."

As understood by the 2012 Synod of Bishops, the "new" evangelization, aimed at "distant Christians" (in particular, those Catholics who in many cases have become effectively secularized in Europe and North America), is not about missionary campaigns of proselytism, nor is it about promoting church attendance, nor simply to fight secularism, relativism, consumerism, fundamentalism, and other "-isms" that have plagued the Christian West. Rather, the new evangelization is also a spiritual awakening and the reanimation of an ecclesial conversion in which the Church asks of herself individually, communally and institutionally how to respond fully to Christ's mandate. It is an effort to renew the Church from within, by looking at the church's own capacity to become a real community, a true fraternity and a living body, capable of nurturing and transmitting the Christian faith.[22]

The new evangelization, therefore, does not mean a "new Gospel" but an adequate response to the signs of the times, and to the needs of individuals and people of today. In the final paragraphs of the synodal document, the bishops speak of the "joy of evangelizing" to give reason for the Christian faith, to communicate the words of hope to a world which

20. See John Paul II, *Ecclesia in Africa, Ecclesia in America, Ecclesia in Asia, Ecclesia in Oceania,* and *Ecclesia in Europa. Evangelii gaudium* makes frequent references to these documents.

21. Congregation for the Doctrine of the Faith, *Doctrinal Note on Some Aspects of Evangelization,* 12.

22. *Instrumentum laboris,* working document for the Synod on the New Evangelization and the Transmission of Christian Faith, 47–50.

seeks salvation, and to show the face of God in Jesus Christ who loves humanity until the end.[23]

The influence from Latin American theological insights on *Evanglii gaudium* is seen in passages relating to missionary outreach, discipleship, the option for the poor, and popular religiosity, drawn from the 2007 Aparecida document of the CELAM. In his theological outlook, Bergoglio espoused the Argentine *teología del pueblo*, or "theology of the people," which emphasizes the crucial "preferential option for the poor" tenet of liberation theology, but differs from it by not focusing on the "class struggle" but the notions of "people" and "anti-people." In terms of method, it rejects Marxist and rationalist elements, and instead focuses on popular religion and culture in Latin America. It holds that globalization has alienated and excluded the common people from meaningful economic and social participation. The "preferential option for the poor" should be expressed as "preferential option for the excluded." And popular religiosity, not ideas and theory, is taken as the primary point of entrance for theological reflection.[24]

A Summons to Evangelize

Evangelii gaudium is all about recovering the missionary vocation of everyone. The work of evangelization should not only to be carried out only by professionals, while others "simply remain passive recipients." On the contrary, every Christian should be an active agent, by virtue of their baptism, in the new evangelization. "[A]nyone who has truly experienced God's saving love does not need much time or lengthy training to go out and proclaim that love. Every Christian is a missionary to the extent that he or she has encountered the love of God in Christ Jesus."[25] Francis's term for this is "missionary disciples."[26]

Citing the 2012 Synod of Bishops, the pope affirms that the new evangelization is a summons to be carried out in three principle settings: "ordinary pastoral ministry" for the faithful, or those who preserve a deep sincere

23. Ibid., 167–69.

24. The Argentine school of liberation theology known as *teología del pueblo*, or "theology of the people," was developed in the 1970s by Lucio Gera and Rafael Tello, and advanced by Carlos Maria Galli, the Jesuit Juan Carlos Scannone, and Archbishop Victor Manuel Fernandez. For a brief discussion of *teología de pueblo* and how it influenced Bergoglio, see Ivereigh, *The Great Reformer*, 180–86; Deck, *Francis*, 32–60. On a general assessment of different Latin American schools of liberation theology, see Ellacuría and Sobrino, eds., *Mysterium Liberationis*.

25. Francis, *Evangelii gaudium*, 120.

26. Ibid., 119.

faith but seldom take part in the worship; "the baptized whose lives do not reflect the demands of baptism," who lack a relationship to the Church and no longer experience the consolation born of faith; and "those who do not know Jesus Christ or who have always rejected him," even though many quietly seek God.[27]

At the heart of evangelization—whether *missio ad gentes*, pastoral care for the faithful, or "new" evangelization—is about proclamation of a person, Jesus Christ, in words and in actions to make him relevant in today's world. A personal encounter with Jesus Christ was already insisted by Paul VI and John Paul II as central to the work of mission.[28] Paul VI insisted that the Church may engage in forms of socio-economic or libertarian platforms for human development, but these programs cannot substitute for a direct proclamation of Christ and his message.[29]

Evangelization, or re-evangelization, normally takes one of two forms: verbal proclamation of the good news of Jesus Christ and non-verbal witness of the life-giving actions of Christ in *imitatio Christi*. The first approach of evangelization has been done throughout Christian history by teaching, preaching, and catechizing about Jesus Christ and God's plan of salvation for the world. But the second form of proclamation is one embraced by the majority of people—Christians and non-Christians alike. Our world needs more exemplars and fewer preachers, as Pope Paul VI keenly observed:

> Modern man [*sic*] listens more willingly to witnesses than to teachers, and if he does listen to teachers, it is because they are witnesses. [. . .] It is therefore primarily by her conduct and by her life that the Church will evangelize the world, in other words, by her living witness of fidelity to the Lord Jesus—the witness of poverty and detachment, of freedom in the face of powers of this world, in short, the witness of sanctity.[30]

In 2007, the Congregation for the Doctrine of the Faith re-iterated the same point: "*to evangelize* does not mean simply to teach a doctrine, but to proclaim Jesus Christ by one's words and actions, that is, to make oneself an instrument of his presence and action in the world."[31] Pope Francis makes a similar point in a 2014 homily:

27. Ibid., 14–15.

28. See Pope Paul VI, *Evangelii nuntiandi*, 24, and Pope John Paul II, *Redemptoris mission*, 7–8, respectively.

29. See Pope Paul VI, *Evangelii nuntiandi*, 24, 35.

30. Ibid., 41.

31. Congregation for the Doctrine of the Faith, *Doctrinal Note on Some Aspects of Evangelization*, 2.

> If you happen to be with an atheist who tells you that he does not believe in God, you can read him the whole library, where it says that God exists, and where it is proven that God exists, and he will not believe. [However] if in the presence of this same atheist you witness to a consistent, Christian life, something will begin to work in his heart . . . It will be your witness that brings him the restlessness on which the Holy Spirit works.[32]

This advice is much in line with the often-quoted dictum attributed to St. Francis of Assisi: "preach the Gospel all the times, and use word when necessary."

Pope Francis evangelizes by example. Rather than talking about solidarity with the poor, Bergoglio, the archbishop of Buenos Aires, chose to commute by public buses to share the lot of his people. Even after being elected pope, Francis chooses to forego certain papal privileges and leads a simple life at the St. Martha residence. Rather than only speaking about mercy, he visits prisoners, shut-in elderly people, refugees, homeless people, broken families, and other people from the margins to give a human face to the virtues of compassion and mercy. Rather than just talking about the reform of the Roman curia, he appointed a group of eight cardinals from the five continents who remain on their post outside of the Vatican and will advise him on church affairs from the trenches. In 2014, Pope Francis called the Extraordinary General Assembly of the Synod of Bishops to help him discern how to deal with the complexity of marriage and family life in the modern world. Actions speak louder than words.

Shepherds and the Smell of the Sheep

Some of the most compelling passages in *Evangelii gaudium* challenge the Church to reform for mission, for "missionary outreach is paradigmatic for all the Church's activity."[33] Convinced that this renewal does not concern only individuals but the whole Church, Francis dreams of "a missionary impulse capable of transforming everything, so that the Church customs, ways of doing things, times and schedules, language and structures can be suitably channeled for the evangelization of today's world"; otherwise there is

---

32. Pope Francis, "Homily at Domus Sanctae Marthae," February 27, 2014. The Pope's daily homilies are available on the Vatican website. A number of them during his first year of papacy (2013–2014) have been collected and published by Orbis Books as Pope Francis, *Morning Homily, Morning Homilies II, Morning Homilies III,* and *Morning Homilies IV.*

33. Pope Francis, *Evangelii gaudium,* 15.

the danger of "ecclesial introversion," as John Paul II warned.[34] That means every structure and institution of the Church—parishes, small church communities, movements, and associations, dioceses, and even the papacy itself—needs to undergo conversion.[35]

In terms of Church governance, Pope Francis seeks "a sound decentralization," that is, a return to collegiality and synodality. We should not expect the pope "to offer a definite or complete word on every question which affects the Church and the world. It is not advisable for the Pope to take the place of local bishops in the discernment of every issue which arises in their territory."[36] Francis wants to see the juridical status of episcopal conferences strengthened, including having "genuine doctrinal authority."[37]

The way the Church proclaims her message is also in need of updating. Gone past are the days when the Church had a monopoly of moral authority on the conscience of believers. "In today's world of instant communication and occasionally biased media coverage," the Pope observes, certain issues of the "Church's moral teaching are [often] taken out of the context which gives them their meaning," distorted or reduced to secondary aspects.[38] The message must refocus on the essentials, simplifying them without losing depth or truth, instead of "disjointed transmission of a multitude of doctrines."[39] The Pope reminds Catholics that there is a hierarchy of truths, not only in the dogmas of faith but also in the Church's moral teachings.[40] We must avoid the risk of over-emphasizing certain aspects of truths, such as speaking more about temperance than charity and justice, "more about law than about grace, more about Church than about Christ, more about the Pope than about God's word."[41] In doing so, the Gospel is no longer preached but rather is reduced to doctrinal or moral points based on specific ideological option; the message would lose "the fragrance of the Gospel."[42]

In order to make the tasks of evangelization more relevant, the Church needs to engage with different currents of thought in philosophy, theology

34. Ibid., 27.

35. See ibid., 28–32.

36. Ibid., 16.

37. Ibid., 32. Francis's frequent citation of other episcopal conferences, as done in *Evangelii gaudium, Laudato si'*, and *Amoris laetitia,* gives them a distinctive attribute compared to other such texts.

38. Pope Francis, *Evangelii gaudium,* 34.

39. Ibid., 35.

40. See ibid., 36–37.

41. Ibid., 38.

42. Ibid., 39.

and pastoral practice. Such engagements might raise alarms among those who hold on to a "monolithic body of doctrine guarded by all and leave no room for nuance"; but on the contrary, such encounters serve to flesh out the inexhaustible riches of the Gospel.[43] The "greatest danger," the Pope warns, is seeking to "hold fast to a formulation while failing to convey its substance."[44] Furthermore, certain church practices must be stream lined. Pope Francis urges the Church not to be afraid to re-examine "certain customs not directly connected to the heart of Gospel," beautiful as they are and some may well have deep historical roots, but they "no longer serve as means of communicating the Gospel." The same can be said with regards to certain rules or precepts which "no longer have the same usefulness for directing and shaping people's lives."[45]

Church renewal requires of us the courage "to reach all the 'peripheries' in need of the light of the Gospel" and to **get out of our comfort zone: "I** prefer a Church which is bruised, hurting and dirty because it has been out on the streets, rather than a Church which is unhealthy from being confined and from clinging to its own security."[46] In particular, "the poor and the sick, those who are usually despised and overlooked" should be our primary audience of evangelization.[47]

Toward a Joyful, Merciful and Discerning Church

If one is to look for a way to understand Francis and his vision for the Church, there are three constant themes that appear regularly in his numerous homilies, speeches, writings, and actions, as well as in *Evangelii gaudium*: joy or consolation, mercy or compassion, and discernment.[48]

The first theme is "joy," or consolation. Joy is omnipresent in the opening paragraphs of *Evangelii gaudium*. The title says it all. We rejoice because "the joy of the Gospel fills the hearts and lives of all who encounter Jesus."[49] Francis is convinced that joy comes from a true personal encounter with

43. See ibid., 40.

44. Ibid., 41.

45. Ibid., 43.

46. Ibid., 20, 49.

47. See ibid., 48, 186–215. In a 2014 address to the participants in the "Meeting of Pontifical Mission Societies," Francis reiterated his point: "Evangelization, which must reach everyone, is nevertheless called to begin with the least, with the poor, with those who are weighed down by the burden and strain of life."

48. In my opinion, these are also the concerns that Pope Francis tells his Jesuit confreres at the Jesuit 36th General Congregation in Rome on October, 24, 2016.

49. Pope Francis, *Evangelii gaudium*, 1.

Jesus, who waits for us with opened arms to forgive us so that we can "lift up our heads and start anew."[50] Even in the midst of suffering, Christians can still rejoice because they are "infinitely loved" by God.[51] Though the tasks of evangelization are demanding and challenging, one should maintain a spirit of joy since it is "a source of authentic personal fulfillment": a minister of the Gospel cannot be gloomy or dejected "like someone who has just come back from a funeral!"[52] Instead they should be "people who can warm the hearts of people, who walk through the dark night with them, who know how to dialogue and to descend themselves into their people's night, into the darkness, but without getting lost."[53]

The enthusiasm for Jesus Christ and his good news has been present in Francis's life. During the early days of his pontificate, the pope told his Wednesday audience:

> May we live the Gospel with humility and courage! May we witness the novelty, the hope, the joy that the Lord brings to life. Let us feel within us "the delightful and comforting joy of evangelizing."[54] Because evangelizing, announcing Jesus, brings us joy! It energizes us. Being closed up within ourselves brings bitterness. Proclaiming the joy and hope that the Lord brings to the world lifts us up![55]

Renewed by the joy of Christ, Pope Francis calls all Christians to become "spirit-filled evangelizers."[56] Christians need to speak boldly about Christ and the Gospel and follow it with joyful lives, engaging the world.

The second theme of "mercy" is characteristic of Francis and the title of a book dedicated to the Extraordinary Jubilee year of Mercy (2016).[57] It is how he feels his papal vocation to be—to show the face of a merciful God. When asked to explain his episcopal motto, *miserando atque eligendo* ("by having mercy and by choosing him"), Francis said the motto was taken from a homily of Bede the Venerable on the story of the calling of Matthew. The pope adds: "I think the gerund miserando is impossible to translate in both

---

50. Ibid., 3.

51. Ibid., 6.

52. Ibid., 10.

53. Spadaro, "A Big Heart Open to God."

54. Pope Francis, *Evangelii gaudium*, 9.

55. Pope Francis, "General Audience," Wednesday, May 22, 2013.

56. Pope Francis, *Evangelii gaudium*, 259–61.

57. Pope Francis, *The Name of God Is Mercy*.

Italian and Spanish. I like to translate it with another gerund that does not exist: *misericordiando* ['mercy-ing']."[58]

Pope Francis sees mercy as a fundamental Christian element that can help the Church to face many challenges in the twenty-first century. For the pope, mercy means allowing and promoting a personal encounter with God, especially through the sacraments. The person stands not as a condemned person but as "beloved sinner" in need of God's mercy and the Church's compassionate accompaniment. An evangelizing Church should open her doors to the down-trodden, to remain with someone who has faltered along the way: "the Church is not a tollhouse" but the house of the Father of the prodigal son, "where there is a place for everyone, with all their problems."[59] Evangelizing communities take on the "smell of the sheep" by being supportive of people at "every step of the way, no matter how difficult or lengthy this may prove to be."[60]

The third theme, "discernment," frequently appearing in Francis's writings and speeches, is a way of proceeding or a method of acting under the guidance of the Holy Spirit. As understood in the Ignatian tradition, discernment is not a decision-making process by weighing abstract principles. It is a reading of the "signs of the times." In other words, it begins with taking a real-life situation, examining it under its social-historical contexts, and formulating a response to a specific circumstance. In an early interview, Francis says: "Discernment is always done in the presence of the Lord, looking at the signs, listening to the things that happen, the feeling of people, especially the poor . . . Discernment in the Lord guides me in my way of governing."[61] Discernment is also about sifting the interior movements of the Spirit and our interior reactions to that which we experience.

The process of evangelization thus becomes a process of discernment. Proclamation first requires moments of listening, understanding and interpretation (or the "see-judge-act" approach of pastoral theology). Only when we put ourselves in the complex and real situations of life, open to the voice of God and allow God to lead the way, concrete plans and procedures can follow. Francis remarks: "God is always a surprise, so you never know where and how you will find him. You are not setting the time and place for the encounter with him."[62] For the pope, discernment is a matter of personal

---

58. Spadaro, "A Big Heart Open to God."

59. Pople Francis, *Evangelii gaudium*, 47.

60. Ibid., 24.

61. Spadaro, "A Big Heart Open to God."

62. Ibid.

responses to the love and salvation of Jesus Christ that we have received. This is a radical trust in the primacy of the Spirit who directs the Church.[63]

What is one to make of Francis and his pontificate? If one wants to speak of Francis as theologian and church leader, he is more like John XXIII and Paul VI, who were doctrinally conservative but pastorally sensitive. Pope Francis is a pastoral theologian who is more kerygmatic than didactic, and who is more fascinated by concrete individuals and situations before him than ideologies. The differences between Francis and his immediate predecessors, John Paul II and Benedict XVI, are not in doctrinal matter, but certainly in style, in methodological concerns and emphases.

"Love manifests itself more in deeds than in words," the advice Ignatius of Loyola gave in his Spiritual Exercises,[64] is embodied by Pope Francis in his words and actions. As a Christian leader, Francis's actions—and not only his message—command respect from millions of people around the world, friends and foes. Even if one disagrees with him, one cannot help but see the irresistible "Francis effect."

Bibliography

32nd General Congregation of the Jesuits. http://www.sjweb.info/sjs/documents/CG32_D2_eng.pdf.

32nd General Congregation of the Jesuits, Decree 4. http://onlineministries.creighton.edu/CollaborativeMinistry/our-mission-today.html.

36th General Congregation of the Jesuits. http://www.gc36.org/.

Anguilar, Mario. *Pope Francis: His Life and Thought*. Cambridge: Lutterworth Press, 2014.

Congregation for the Doctrine of the Faith. *Doctrinal Note on Some Aspects of Evangelization*. December 3, 2007. http://www.vatican.va/roman_curia/congregations/cfaith/documents/rc_con_cfaith_doc_20071203_nota-evangelizzazione_en.html.

Deck, Allan Figueroa. *Francis, Bishop of Rome: The Gospel for the Third Millennium*. Mahwah, NJ: Paulist, 2016.

Ellacuría, Ignacio, and Jon Sobrino, eds. *Mysterium Liberationis: Fundamental Concepts of Liberation Theology*. Maryknoll, NY: Orbis, 1993.

Francis, Pope. *Evangelii gaudium*. 2013. http://w2.vatican.va/content/francesco/en/apost_exhortations/documents/papa-francesco_esortazione-ap_20131124_evangelii-gaudium.html.

———. *Morning Homilies*. Translated by Dinah Livingstone. Maryknoll, NY: Orbis, 2015.

63. Refer to chapter 8 of *Amoris laetitia* for Francis's elaboration on discernment beyond *Evangelii gaudium*.

64. First paragraph of "Contemplatio ad amorem," *Spiritual Exercises*, 130. Cf. 1 John 3:8: "Let us love, not in word or speech, but in deed and truth" (NAB).

————. *Morning Homilies II*. Translated by Dinah Livingstone. Maryknoll, NY: Orbis, 2016.

————. *Morning Homilies III*. Translated by Dinah Livingstone. Maryknoll, NY: Orbis, 2016.

————. *Morning Homilies IV*. Translated by Dinah Livingstone. Maryknoll, NY: Orbis, 2017.

————. *The Name of God Is Mercy*. New York: Random House, 2016.

Ivereigh, Austen. *The Great Reformer: Francis and the Making of a Radical Pope*. New York: Holt, 2014.

John Paul II, Pope. *Ecclesia in Africa*. 1995. http://w2.vatican.va/content/john-paul-ii/en/apost_exhortations/documents/hf_jp-ii_exh_14091995_ecclesia-in-africa.html.

————. *Ecclesia in America*. 1999. http://w2.vatican.va/content/john-paul-ii/en/apost_exhortations/documents/hf_jp-ii_exh_22011999_ecclesia-in-america.html.

————. *Ecclesia in Asia*. 1999. http://w2.vatican.va/content/john-paul-ii/en/apost_exhortations/documents/hf_jp-ii_exh_06111999_ecclesia-in-asia.html.

————. *Ecclesia in Europa*. 2003. http://w2.vatican.va/content/john-paul-ii/en/apost_exhortations/documents/hf_jp-ii_exh_20030628_ecclesia-in-europa.html.

————. *Ecclesia in Oceania*. 2001. http://w2.vatican.va/content/john-paul-ii/en/apost_exhortations/documents/hf_jp-ii_exh_20011122_ecclesia-in-oceania.html.

————. *Redemptoris missio*. 1990. http://w2.vatican.va/content/john-paul-ii/en/encyclicals/documents/hf_jp-ii_enc_07121990_redemptoris-missio.html.

————. *Discourse to the XIX Assembly of CELAM* (March 9, 1983), cited in *L'Osservatore Romano* (English edition). April 18, 1983.

Padberg, John, ed. *Jesuit Life & Mission Today: The Decrees & Accompanying Documents of the 31st–35th General Congregations of the Society of Jesus*. St Louis: Institutes of Jesuit Sources, 2009.

Pope Paul VI. *Evangelii nuntiandi*. 1975. http://w2.vatican.va/content/paul-vi/en/apost_exhortations/documents/hf_p-vi_exh_19751208_evangelii-nuntiandi.html.

Rubin, Sergio, and Francesca Ambrogetti. *El Jesuita: Conversaciones con Jorge Bergoglio* (2010). ET: *Pope Francis: Conversations with Jorge Bergoglio: His Life in His Own Words*. New York: Penguin, 2014.

Spadaro, Antonio. "A Big Heart Open to God: Interview with Pope Francis." *America*, September 30, 2013. http://americamagazine.org/pope-interview.

Vallely, Paul. *Pope Francis: Untying the Knots*. London: Bloombury, 2013.

CHAPTER 2 ——————————————————

Embodied Mercy

The Centrality of the Incarnation in the Thought of Pope Francis

—Mary Madeline Todd, OP

Abstract:

This essay will explore "incarnation" as the keystone linking Pope Francis's twofold emphasis on Christ as the revelation of the tenderness of the Father's mercy and the call of every follower of Christ to live mercifully in concrete service to others. The mercy communicated through the Incarnation of the Son of God, mediated by encountering him in word, sacrament, and along the road of daily life is, in the pope's theology, the source of grace that enables believers to reach out in mercy. Although mercy, as the Latin *misericordia* expresses, begins in the heart, it is made flesh in the gaze of the eyes, the outstretched hand, and the load-bearing shoulders not only of Jesus Christ, but of every person of faith moved to take up the call to mirror the compassion of the Good Samaritan. Encountering the merciful Christ transforms a person from within to enable that person to extend mercy, not as a vague sentiment but as a humanly rich and divinely graced action of love incarnate. The essay will trace the development of this theme in the pastoral writings before his election to the pontificate through the texts of Pope Francis for the Jubilee Year of Mercy.

"Jesus Christ is the face of the Father's mercy . . . Mercy has become living and visible in Jesus of Nazareth, reaching its culmination in him."[1] With

———
1. Pope Francis, *Misericordiae vultus*, 1.

these words, Pope Francis opens the document calling for an Extraordinary Jubilee of Mercy. Mercy, the pope notes, is an attribute of God, but it has not remained enclosed within the divine heart or hidden as a mystery veiled from the understanding of humanity. As written in the gospel, "The Word became flesh and dwelt among us, full of grace and truth" (John 1:14). The truth that the Word made flesh reveals to us by his Incarnation is precisely the truth that we are embraced by the Father's mercy, that there remains "the hope of being loved forever despite our sinfulness."[2] The reality of "incarnation" is, in the theological reflections of Pope Francis, key to the experience of divine mercy.[3] God the Son freely chose to take on human nature, and by assuming human flesh, he encountered and touched people in their human needs. Likewise, for all called to extend to others the mercy received, the interior desire to give must be embodied. The incarnational gift of the divine coming to meet us and of our going out to others is the two-fold dynamic of mercy received and mercy given which is central in the teaching of Pope Francis.

Even before the coming of Jesus Christ among us as man, God revealed himself as one full of patience and mercy for his Chosen People. Pope Francis observes that, especially in the Psalms, the mercy of God shines forth. God is praised by the psalmist as one who forgives sin and heals (see Psalm 103), as well as the one who liberates prisoners and restores sight to the blind (see Psalm 146). God is acclaimed as a loving Father who provides for the poor, the strangers, widows, and orphans (see Psalm 146). God is the one who remains close to the broken in spirit and in body; he draws close to all who suffer. In light of these attributes of divine love, Pope Francis considers the heavenly Father's love as one analogous to the compassion human parents experience when moved by the suffering of their children. He writes: "In short, the mercy of God is not an abstract idea, but a concrete reality with which he reveals his love as of that of a father or a mother, moved

---

2. Ibid., 2.

3. This observation does not imply novelty in the theological tradition coming from the New Testament itself, but rather continuity, as well as strength of emphasis on the link between the incarnation and the revelation of mercy. This continuity is not only with the earliest Christian theology, but also within the contemporary papacy. Pope John Paul II in *Dives in misericordia* writes: "Christ—the very fulfillment of the messianic prophecy—by becoming the incarnation of the love that is manifested with particular force with regard to the suffering, the unfortunate and sinners, makes present and thus more fully reveals the Father, who is God 'rich in mercy'" (3). Pope Benedict XVI in *Spe salvi* identifies the fruit of the incarnation with the link between justice and grace (here used as the equivalent of mercy): "The incarnation of God in Christ has so closely linked the two together—judgement and grace—that justice is firmly established: we all work out our salvation 'with fear and trembling' (Phil 2:12). Nevertheless grace allows us all to hope, and to go trustfully to meet the Judge whom we know as our 'advocate,' or *parakletos* (cf. 1 Jn 2:1)."

to the very depths out of love for their child. It is hardly an exaggeration to say that this is a 'visceral' love. It gushes forth from the depths naturally, full of tenderness and compassion, indulgence and mercy."[4]

The mercy flowing from the Father toward his creatures at all times was expressed uniquely in "the fullness of time" by the Incarnation of Jesus Christ, the Son of God made man. Pope Francis points to the revelation of God's merciful love as the basis of the mission of Jesus in the world: "The mission Jesus received from the Father was that of revealing the mystery of divine love in its fullness . . . This love has now been made visible and tangible in Jesus' entire life."[5] In the pope's comments and reflections, he describes this revelation of divine love as mediated through the many bodily encounters of Jesus with those in need: through his gaze, his touch, his words, and the signs he worked to feed, heal, and liberate those in bondage, all of which were acts rich in compassion.

In the book *The Name of God Is Mercy*, Pope Francis distinguishes between mercy as a divine attribute and the human experience of compassion. This distinction highlights the manner in which the Incarnation allowed God to enter into human suffering. He explains, "Mercy is divine and has to do with the judgment of sin. Compassion has a more human face. It means to suffer with, to suffer together, to not remain indifferent to the pain and the suffering of others."[6] The compassion of Jesus, whose Incarnation allowed him to become "like us in all things but sin" (Heb 4:15), moved him to teach and to feed the hungry crowds, and to restore to life the only son of the mourning widow in Nain. As Jesus encountered people in sorrow, the pope notes, "God Incarnate let himself be moved by human wretchedness, by our need, by our suffering."[7] This entering into the pain of human existence is a reflection of the Father's love made manifest in the life of the Son, and it shows us the call we receive to enter into the needs and suffering of our brothers and sisters in Christ. "Jesus," the pope states, "does not look at reality from the outside, without letting himself be moved, as if he were taking a picture . . . This kind of compassion is needed today to conquer the globalization of indifference. This kind of regard is needed when we find ourselves in front of a poor person, an outcast, or a sinner."[8] God took on flesh to communicate mercy to humanity. He did not remain indifferent; nor must we. This essay will trace the dynamic at

4. Ibid., 6.
5. Ibid., 8.
6. Pope Francis, *Name of God*, 91.
7. Ibid., 92.
8. Ibid.

work in the encounter with divine mercy experienced in the word, sacraments, and abiding presence of Christ, which impart both the grace and the call to extend the mercy received.

Encountering Mercy Incarnate in the Word

One way Jesus reveals the merciful love of the Father is directly through his spoken words, especially through his preaching of the parables. Perhaps the richest and most commented upon parable of divine mercy is that of the prodigal son. At his first public Mass as Bishop of Rome, Pope Francis preached on mercy, commenting on this story as the "parable of the merciful father." After considering the son, who after leaving home reaches his lowest point and comes to miss the "warmth of the father's house," the pope turns to the father who is utterly incapable of forgetting the son. The father is ever waiting, ever hoping for the son's return, ever keeping the son in his heart. This explains the father's response when he first catches sight of his returning son. As the pope paraphrases, "As soon as he sees him still far off, he runs out to meet him and embraces him with tenderness, the tenderness of God, without a word of reproach: his son has returned! And that is the joy of the father. In that embrace for his son is all this joy: he has returned!"[9] Jesus intended this parable not simply as a touching story, but as a lesson about the heart of God who is rich in mercy and ever hoping for us to return to our home and to our filial relationship with him. As Pope Francis reflects, "God is always waiting for us; he never grows tired. Jesus shows us this merciful patience of God so that we can regain confidence, hope—always!"[10] In the face of human weakness, the Father's unfailing patience and unconditional love are constant sources of hope.

In the parables of Jesus, mercy is not only a grace received but also a call to "be merciful, even as your Father is merciful" (Luke 6:36). The parable of the Good Samaritan illustrates God's response to human need. The Samaritan reflects the love of God, who seeing suffering humanity, did not simply pass by. Taking to himself a human nature, the Son of God came to broken humanity left beaten on the path of life by sin. During his years as Archbishop of Buenos Aires, Cardinal Bergoglio often pondered Christ's choice to participate in human pain by his Incarnation. He reflected on the freedom and the power of this choice, "The Word made flesh redeems our sinful flesh through his passion, that is, by taking on himself the pain of all flesh. Jesus draws close to all tormented flesh and with his own flesh

9. Pope Francis, "Embrace of God's Mercy," 4.
10. Ibid., 4–5.

cancels the legal claims against us."[11] Throughout the future pope's writings the merciful love of the heart of Christ serves as a model and a measure of our love for one another.

After his election to the papacy, Pope Francis, again reflecting on the parable of the Good Samaritan, affirms the need to remember the great mercy God has shown to us. Recalling the ways God continually comes to us to bandage our wounds of body and soul opens us to tend others' wounds. The pope states, "Every one of us, looking at our own lives as God does, can try to remember the ways in which the Lord has been merciful towards us, how he has been much more merciful than we imagined. In this we can find the courage to ask him to take a step further and to reveal yet more of his mercy in the future."[12] Speaking to priests at the Chrism Mass at Saint Peter's Basilica, the pope highlights this divine willingness to draw near to suffering humanity as the model of priestly service: "This was the way of the Good Samaritan, who 'showed mercy' (cf. Lk 10:37): he was moved, he drew near to the wounded man, he bandaged his wounds, took him to the inn, stayed there that evening and promised to return and cover any further cost. This is the way of mercy."[13] He points to the superabundant tenderness of the Heart of God as the font and the model for living mercifully, and he challenges his hearers to dare the risk of living mercifully rather than remaining constrained by patterns of human consideration and calculation. Receiving superabundant tenderness from God, we too can meet the needs of others with tender compassion.

Encountering Mercy Incarnate in the Sacraments

In his homily for the first public Mass of his papacy, Pope Francis spoke about God's mercy as an "unfailing love, one that always takes us by the hand and supports us, lifts us up, and leads us on."[14] By Christ's incarnate presence among his apostles, he revealed to them the Father's mercy and instituted the sacraments as channels of saving mercy, a mercy that they and their successors could extend to the children of God in every generation. Raniero Cantalamessa, preacher to the papal household, proposes that a "leap in quality" in the understanding of divine mercy is mediated by the Incarnation of the Word and his giving of the sacraments. In *The Gaze of Mercy* he writes, "With the coming of the Word into our midst, the forgive-

11. Pope Francis, *Open Mind*, 214.

12. Pope Francis, *Homily for Holy Chrism Mass*, March 24, 2016.

13. Ibid.

14. Pope Francis, "Embrace of God's Mercy," 3.

ness of God is also 'made flesh'; it is manifested through concrete words and actions, first in Christ's life and then in the Church's sacraments. It is no longer proclaimed 'through the prophets' but is directly given to us in first person by God himself."[15]

Building on the truth expressed by Father Cantalamessa, Pope Francis traces the continuity of the revelation and bestowal of mercy between the public life of Jesus and the life of the Church today. The pope detects in the graced encounters between Jesus and his disciples a foreshadowing of the sacramental ministry of the Church. He points out that seeing the risen Lord before his eyes and being invited to touch his wounds, Thomas the apostle moved from unbelief to faith. In the tenderness of the gaze of Jesus, Peter discovered the mercy that healed his denial of Jesus. The discouraged disciples on the road to Emmaus were reborn and nourished in faith when Jesus shared the Scriptures and the breaking of bread with them. He walked beside them on their journey and restored their hope by his merciful presence. These encounters with the mercy of God in the presence, words, and deeds of Jesus were not only for those who lived during his years of public ministry. As Pope Francis notes, people today can encounter Jesus risen and sacramentally present among us: "We too can enter the wounds of Jesus; we can actually touch him. This happens every time we receive the sacraments with faith."[16]

The sacraments derive their efficacy, their capacity to give and restore supernatural life and friendship, through the Paschal Mystery—the death and resurrection of Jesus made possible by his Incarnation. This mercy manifest in the flesh of Christ, this willingness to suffer and die in body, is the pattern of self-giving love and a cause for profound gratitude on the part of all the redeemed. In a Lenten letter written while he was still serving as Archbishop of Buenos Aires, then Cardinal Bergoglio wrote, "As Christians, our conversion must flow from a grateful response to the marvelous mystery of God's love, which he accomplished through the death and resurrection of his Son."[17] He explicitly linked our sharing in the grace of mercy to the sacraments, writing, "This marvelous mystery is present to us in every new birth to the life of faith, in every act of forgiveness that renews us and heals us, in every Eucharist that sows within us the same sentiments as those of Christ."[18] By Baptism we become the adopted children of the Father by the merits of the eternal Son of God made man. Every time we are cleansed anew in the

---

15. Cantalamessa, *Gaze of Mercy*, 117.

16. Pope Francis, "Embrace of God's Mercy," 5.

17. Pope Francis, "Freely You Have Received," 79.

18. Ibid., 79.

sacrament of Reconciliation and made one with God in the Eucharistic sacrifice, we encounter divine mercy incarnate in Jesus Christ and made flesh in the Eucharist by the unfathomable gift and mystery of God.

This emphasis on the mercy of God poured out on the cross and handed on in the sacramental ministry of the Church continues to be a key theme in the writing and preaching of Pope Francis. In his call for the Jubilee Year of Mercy, he highlights the Eucharist as the perpetuation of the self-gift of Jesus on the cross. He reflects that Jesus prayed Psalm 136 as he ascended the Mount of Olives before his passion, meditating on God's mercy throughout salvation history. The pope reflects, "To repeat continually 'for his mercy endures forever,' as the psalm does, seems to break through the dimensions of space and time, inserting everything into the eternal mystery of love. It is as if to say that not only in history, but for all eternity man will always be under the merciful gaze of the Father."[19] At the Last Supper and on the cross, Jesus instituted the Eucharist, thus immersing his free gift of himself in the eternal mercy of the Father. The pope states, "While he was instituting the Eucharist as an everlasting memorial of himself and his paschal sacrifice, he symbolically placed this supreme act of revelation in the light of his mercy. Within the very same context of mercy, Jesus entered upon his passion and death, conscious of the great mystery of love that he would consummate on the Cross."[20]

Aware of the great struggle we face in remaining focused on the love God has for us and the call to live as the children of God, Pope Francis also highlights the ongoing gift of mercy offered to us by God in the sacrament of Reconciliation. As with the Eucharist, Reconciliation derives its strength from the merciful love of God manifest in the passion, death, and resurrection of Jesus. Pope Francis affirms, "God's forgiveness knows no bounds. In the death and resurrection of Jesus Christ, God makes even more evident his love and its power to destroy all human sin. Reconciliation with God is made possible through the paschal mystery and the mediation of the Church."[21] Even if, humanly speaking, we find it hard to ask repeatedly for mercy, God never tires of granting it. The pope reiterates the inexhaust-

---

19. Pope Francis, *Misericordiae vultus*, 7.

20. Ibid., 7. Throughout the mystical tradition of the Church, the link between Jesus as Word incarnate shedding his blood on the cross and the outpouring of divine mercy has been explicit. For example, in *The Dialogue* Saint Catherine of Siena records the Father's revelation to her in prayer: "So now all the faithful can walk without hindrance and with no cringing fear of the reign of divine justice, because they are sheltered by the mercy that came down from heaven through the incarnation of this Son of mine. And how was heaven opened? With the key of his blood" (66).

21. Ibid., 22.

ible nature of divine mercy: "Thus God is always ready to forgive, and he never tires of forgiving in ways that are continually new and surprising . . . In the Sacrament of Reconciliation, God forgives our sins, which he truly blots out."[22] The encounter with God and his mercy is ever possible, and the power of this encounter, once mediated by the bodily presence of Jesus among the people, is now made tangible in the sacramental signs Christ instituted in and through his Church.

Encountering Mercy Incarnate along the Road of Daily Life

If even before the coming of Christ, God drew people to speak with him and walk with him, from Adam to Moses, from Abraham and Sarah to Enoch, all the more did the coming of Christ as man reveal the desire of God to be near to his people. In a Christmas Eve homily given in Buenos Aires, the future pope noted the radical transition the birth of Christ marks in God's self-revelation within salvation history: "He had broken in with his word; now he breaks in with his real Word—Jesus Christ, who is the Word of God. He bursts in, and he who had been accompanying us on our journey, for the first time plants himself right in the middle of our path."[23] Preaching on another occasion, Cardinal Bergoglio reminded his listeners that this divine desire to walk with us did not end two millennia ago, as he stated: "Our God is a God who is near, a God who makes himself present to us, a God who began to walk with his people and then became one of his people in Christ Jesus so that he could be close to us."[24]

Both before and after his election to the papacy, Pope France repeatedly emphasizes that the encounter of the eternal God with his creatures is not accidental, but intentional and concrete, especially evident in the ways Jesus reached out to the people he met. Commenting on the Scriptural statement that Jesus "went about doing good and healing," Cardinal Bergoglio saw in the manner of Jesus an evangelical way of accompaniment: "Jesus did not proselytize; he accompanied his people. The conversions he achieved were due precisely to his approach of accompanying, teaching, and listening . . . He is the God who is nearby, who is close to us in our flesh. He is the God who goes out to meet his people."[25] The accompaniment of others is

---

22. Ibid.

23. Pope Francis, "Look for Him," 30.

24. Pope Francis, "God Makes Us His Children," 91.

25. Ibid., 92.

essential to true evangelization, to spreading the gospel among and beside people as Jesus did.

One aspect of the tangible mercy extended by Jesus to those he encountered was his gaze upon them in truth and in love. Pope Francis often speaks of the mercy of God communicated in the gaze of Jesus. Reflecting on the encounters between Jesus and Peter, the pope considers the gaze of Jesus as a call to vocation, a stirring unto remorse, and an entrusting of mission. When Andrew brought his brother Simon to Jesus, claiming him as the awaited Messiah, Jesus gazed intently at Simon and renamed him Peter. Of this gaze, Pope Francis writes, "This is 'the first gaze, the gaze of the mission' which will be explained 'further ahead in Caesarea Philippi.' There, Jesus says: 'You are Peter, and on this rock I will build my Church': this will be your mission."[26] This gaze of love and call to apostleship filled Peter with enthusiasm and gratitude, but it was followed by a second gaze. The second gaze of Jesus met Peter's after his enthusiasm had been obscured and fear had moved him to deny the Lord. On Holy Thursday, after Peter denied Jesus three times, Jesus gazed again at him, and this gaze reduced Peter to bitter tears. Although the first gaze planted enthusiasm in Peter, the second, the pope posits, was more profound. The pope writes of the power of the merciful, forgiving gaze of Jesus: "The first transformation is the change of name and of vocation. Instead the second gaze is a gaze that changes the heart and is a change of conversion to love."[27]

The third gaze between Jesus and Peter marked a mutual exchange on the shores of the Sea of Galilee after the resurrection. Jesus asked Peter three times to confirm his love for him, and after this three-fold renewal, Jesus mercifully reaffirmed the mission he had entrusted to Peter to tend his flock. Jesus communicated not only a share in his pastoral mission, but also a share in his sacrificial gift of self. Revealing to Peter that when he had grown old another would lead him where he would rather not go, Jesus entrusted to the repentant Peter a share in his cross. Pope Francis interprets Jesus's words to Peter, "You too, like me, will be in that courtyard where I fixed my gaze on you, near the cross."[28] The pope concludes that we are all under the gaze of Christ, experiencing the merciful love of God. He notes, "He always looks at us with love, asks us for something, forgives us for something and gives us a mission."[29] In this experience of the gaze of Jesus upon us, we can

---

26. Pope Francis, "Three Manners of Gaze."

27. Ibid.

28. Ibid.

29. Ibid.

become more aware of and respond more fully to the mercy that not only heals us, but also sends us to be instruments of healing for others.

Another way Jesus extended mercy was in the touch of his hands. As the Father led the Chosen People with an outstretched hand to the Promised Land, so Jesus met people in their needs and reached out to touch and heal them. Commenting on the encounter between Jesus and a man with leprosy, Pope Francis reflects on the connection between faith, touch, and healing. Before Christ's coming, leprosy seemed to be a condition that barred one from divine and human mercy, as the pope notes, "Indeed, leprosy was considered a form of a curse of God, of profound uncleanliness. A leper had to stay away from everyone; he could not access the temple nor any divine service. Far from God and far from men."[30] Yet even though the man with leprosy lived as one accursed, he did not surrender to despair. On the contrary, he had preserved faith and hope in God's mercy that gave him boldness. Pope Francis admires this strength of soul, noting, "In order to reach Jesus, he was not afraid to break the law and enter the city . . . All that is done and said by this man, who was considered unclean, is an expression of his faith! This faith is the force that allows him to break every convention and seek the encounter with Jesus."[31]

As in many of the miracles of healing that Jesus performs, the faith of the man with leprosy provides an opening to the outpouring of divine mercy mediated by the touch of Jesus. Jesus is not distracted by the letter of the law that forbids this man to approach him and that would render Jesus himself unclean if he were to touch him. The pope notes that the retelling of this event in Mark's gospel focuses on the compassion that stirs Jesus: "The Gospel of Mark emphasizes that 'moved with pity, he stretched out his hand and touched him' . . . Jesus' gesture accompanies his words and renders the teaching more explicit. Contrary to the dispositions of the Law of Moses, which prohibited a leper from drawing near (cf. Lev 13:45–46), Jesus extends his hand and even touches him."[32] This touch is the physical expression of the divine mercy that is unafraid to meet humanity in its uncleanness. By the Incarnation, Jesus took on human nature. He reached out with his human hands to convey the mercy of God. In fact, the grace of mercy flowed so powerfully from him that even one who reached out to touch the hem of his garment could be healed in body and soul, as the encounter with the woman with a hemorrhage showed. She, like the man

30. Pope Francis, *General Audience*, June 22, 2016.

31. Ibid.

32. Ibid.

with leprosy, received by a touch full of faith a mercy that moved her from being an outcast to being a person restored to communion.

Jesus not only touched those he encountered, but he also willingly bore upon his shoulders the sheep and all their burdens as the truly Good Shepherd. Here the ultimate mercy of God—the mercy that goes to the final limit of giving all for the beloved—was revealed as Jesus took up the cross by which he bore the weight of the sins of all people on his own shoulders. Meditating on the parable of the Good Shepherd who seeks and carries the lost sheep, recounted in Luke 15, Pope Francis notes, "This icon has always been an expression of Jesus' care for sinners and of the mercy of God who never resigns himself to the loss of anyone."[33] The pope notes that the parable is paradoxical in its seeming impracticality. If the shepherd abandons the flock, it seems they will not survive. The shepherd that Jesus describes does, however, leave the ninety-nine to find the one lost sheep, and he bears the lost one on his shoulders, rejoicing.

Pope Francis notes that the point of the parable of the Good Shepherd is not the neglect of the flock, but the radical concern the shepherd has for each sheep. The parable, explains the pope, is an illustration of the personal mercy God has for each soul: "The Lord cannot accept the fact that a single person can be lost. God's action is that of one who goes out seeking his lost children and then rejoices and celebrates with everyone at their recovery. It is a burning desire: not even ninety-nine sheep could stop the shepherd and keep him enclosed in the fold."[34] He reflects that it is not possible for our merciful God to overlook one lost sheep because many are not lost. The lost one moves his heart most because of its desperate need. He states regarding the one lost, "Every one is very important to him and that one is in the most need, is the most abandoned, most discarded; and he goes to look for it."[35] This is the mystery of the incarnate Son of God who could not remain passive seeing humanity lost in its sin. He came among us and took up the cross of our sins, and by his resurrection assured the day when he will present the whole redeemed flock within the sheepfold of the Father's kingdom (see 1 Cor 15:24).[36] As one encounters Christ who gave His life for

33. Pope Francis, *General Audience*, May 4, 2016.

34. Ibid.

35. Ibid.

36. Pope Benedict XVI expressed this idea eloquently in *Jesus of Nazareth*, writing: "The Shepherd who sets off to seek the lost sheep is the eternal Word himself, and the sheep that he lovingly carries home on his shoulders is humanity, the human existence that he took upon himself. In his Incarnation and Cross he brings home the stray sheep, humanity; he brings me home, too. The incarnate Logos is the true 'sheep-bearer'—the Shepherd who follows after us through the storms and deserts of our life. Carried on his

us and whose resurrection is our hope of newness of life, such an encounter with mercy incarnate is utterly transforming. As Saint Thomas Aquinas teaches, grace has the power to both heal and elevate human nature.[37] By encountering Christ and receiving grace in the word and sacraments, we become, as St. Paul testified, "ambassadors for Christ" (2 Cor 5:20), living vessels of divine mercy.

Extending Mercy by Proclaiming the Word

Having encountered and been healed and transformed by God's mercy in the Incarnate Word, believers are sent to extend mercy to others. In his apostolic exhortation *Evangelii gaudium*, Pope Francis highlights the need to encounter the Word Incarnate in prayer so that the gospel becomes a living word—first personalized, then proclaimed. Although acknowledging the value of study of the written word, he notes the greater importance of engagement with the Word at the relational level, the capacity to listen to God. He affirms of the one called to preach, "He needs to approach the word with a docile and prayerful heart so that it may deeply penetrate his thoughts and feelings and bring about a new outlook in him."[38] He reminds the faithful that Jesus was not pleased with the teachers of the law who were not first transformed from within themselves. Pope Francis exhorts, "Whoever wants to preach must be the first to let the word of God move him deeply and become incarnate in his daily life."[39] This incarnating of the word in the life of the one who shares God's word with others proposes prayerful witness as the basis of evangelization. Those who see the gospel lived will be more open to hear the word that has been made flesh in the words and deeds of believers. Pope Francis points out that one can only proclaim the love God has for each person if one first experiences that love, the mercy of God spoken in the saving deeds of Jesus Christ.

Pope Francis observes that the lack of a first-hand encounter with the saving word of God feeds rejection of the message one attempts to preach. The pope's insistence on the incarnational principle of communicating divine mercy shapes his view of effective proclamation: "The Lord wants to make use of us as living, free and creative beings who let his word enter their own hearts before then passing it on to others. Christ's message must truly penetrate and possess the preacher, not just intellectually but in his entire

shoulders, we come home" (286).

37. See Thomas Aquinas, *Summa Theologica* I-II, Q. 109, a. 9, resp.

38. Pope Francis, *Evangelii gaudium*, 149.

39. Ibid., 150.

being."[40] Citing the words of Pope Paul VI in *Evangelii nuntiandi*, Pope Francis notes that the penetration of one's being by the word is possible only by the grace of the Holy Spirit: "The Holy Spirit, who inspired the word, 'today, just as at the beginning of the Church, acts in every evangelizer who allows himself to be possessed and led by him. The Holy Spirit places on his lips the words which he could not find by himself.'"[41] Just as in the historical Incarnation, in which the Word of God was made flesh in the womb of Mary by the power of the Holy Spirit, so also today God's word can become enfleshed in the hearts and lives of believers by the indwelling Holy Spirit.

Addressing catechists, Pope Francis employed a vivid metaphor for the dynamic of proclaiming divine mercy. He compared the two-fold experience of receiving and giving to the beating of the heart. He said, "The heart of a catechist always beats with this systolic and diastolic movement: union with Christ, encounter with others. Both of these: I am one with Jesus, and I go forth to encounter others. If one of these movements is missing, the heart no longer beats; it can no longer live."[42]

Extending Mercy through the Sacraments

Pope Francis, who continually calls all to be merciful as the Father is merciful, especially invites priests to live mercifully in fidelity to the grace of their ordination. This grace, flowing from God's choice of them and their free acceptance of their priestly vocation, makes of them ministers of the mercy of God through the sacraments. The ministerial priesthood is, in the pope's thought, another mode of incarnating the tender mercy of God for His people. He exhorts his brother priests: "As priests, we are witnesses to and ministers of the ever-increasing abundance of the Father's mercy; we have the rewarding and consoling task of incarnating mercy, as Jesus did, who 'went about doing good and healing' (Acts 10:38) in a thousand ways so that it could touch everyone."[43]

Reflecting on Jesus's healing of the man suffering from deafness and muteness, Pope Francis notes that divine mercy heals our capacity for communion. God's grace and mercy are first communicated in the sacrament of Baptism, which enables those baptized to be adopted children of God through the grace of the Son, whose Incarnation shows God's desire for union with us. Pope Francis states, "In his immense mercy, he overcomes

40. Ibid., 151.

41. Ibid.

42. Pope Francis, "Being with Christ," 17.

43. Pope Francis, *Homily for Holy Chrism Mass*, March 24, 2016.

the abyss of the infinite difference between him and us, and comes to meet us. To bring about this communication with man, God becomes man. It is not enough for him to speak to us through the law and the prophets, but instead he makes himself present in the person of his Son, the Word made flesh."[44] The pope links Jesus's healing of the deaf man to the healing of a soul in the sacrament of Baptism, a healing that bestows openness unto belonging: "However, at the beginning of our Christian life, at baptism, it is precisely this gesture and word of Jesus that are present: 'Ephphatha! Be opened!' And behold the miracle has been worked. We are healed of the deafness of selfishness and the impediment of being closed in on ourselves, and of sin, and we have been inserted into the great family of the Church."[45] God's merciful communication to us enables us to enter into communion not only with him, but also with the Church.

In June of the Year of Mercy, on the Solemnity of the Sacred Heart of Jesus, Pope Francis celebrated a Jubilee Mass for Priests. In his homily, he called priests to burn with the fire of charity in the Heart of Jesus by receiving his love and mercy. This merciful love received impels them to seek out the lost, to include all, and to rejoice as people are drawn into deeper communion with God and one another. Not only does the pope affirm the need to open wide the doors of the Church, but he also calls pastors to seek out those who need encouragement to approach the sacraments. He exhorts, "Unless a shepherd risks, he does not find . . . Indeed, he is *stubborn in doing good*, anointed with the divine obstinacy that loses sight of no one. Not only does he keep his doors open, but he also goes to seek out those who no longer wish to enter them."[46] Calling the shepherds of Christ's Church to foster inclusion, he encourages them to build communion, both generally and sacramentally, as he states, "As a minister of the communion that he celebrates and lives, he does not await greetings and compliments from others, but is the first to reach out, rejecting gossip, judgements and malice. He listens patiently to the problems of his people and accompanies them, sowing God's forgiveness with generous compassion."[47] The sacraments are the points of encounter where this communion and forgiveness are given freely.

Pope Francis further elaborates how the priest is called to be transformed by receiving divine mercy from Christ so that he rejoices to be at the service of the healing and restoration of the lost sheep of the Good Shepherd's flock. The pope explicitly links the joy of the Heart of Jesus to that of

44. Pope Francis, *Angelus*, September 6, 2015.

45. Ibid.

46. Pope Francis, *Homily for Jubilee of Mercy for Priests*, June 3, 2016.

47. Ibid.

the priest: "The joy of Jesus the Good Shepherd is not a joy *for himself* alone, but a joy *for others and with others*, the true joy of love. This is also the joy of the priest. He is changed by the mercy that he *freely* gives."[48] The source of this communion in joy is the priest's life of prayer and his own experience of God's mercy. The pope explains, "In prayer he discovers God's consolation and realizes that nothing is more powerful than his love. He thus experiences inner peace, and is happy to be a channel of mercy, to bring men and women closer to the Heart of God."[49] The most significant experience of this receiving and giving of mercy is in the celebration of the Eucharist, the privileged entering into the self-giving love of Jesus. Within the Eucharistic celebration is where Pope Francis invites priests to "rediscover each day our identity as shepherds."[50]

Extending Mercy along the Road of Daily Life

Pope Francis tirelessly reminds all who seek to live in union with Christ that love is not a concept or feeling divorced from the choices and actions of our daily lives. In Jesus we see the realization and the model of incarnate love. Pope Francis writes, "Love shares everything it has and reveals itself in communication . . . love is not Christian love if it is not generous and concrete . . . When we care for the needs of our brothers and sisters, like the Good Samaritan did, we are proclaiming the Kingdom and making it present."[51] Not only is the Incarnation of Christ the model of love's desire to draw near to the beloved, but it is also the source of the unity we share with others in the Body of Christ. This unity points to the need to incarnate our love for the people we encounter each day, as the pope notes in *Evangelii gaudium*: "God's word teaches that our brothers and sisters are the prolongation of the incarnation for each of us: 'As you did it to one of these, the least of my brethren, you did it to me' (Mt 25:40)."[52] As evident in the life of Jesus, merciful love does not ignore the needs of others, but rather reaches out to serve them. The pope observes, "We incarnate the duty of hearing the cry of the poor when we are deeply moved by the suffering of others."[53] As it moved Jesus, this heartfelt compassion moves us to look upon others with a

---

48. Ibid.
49. Ibid.
50. Ibid.
51. Pope Francis, "Freely You Have Received," 79.
52. Pope Francis, *Evangelii gaudium*, 179.
53. Ibid., 193.

gaze of mercy, to reach out to touch them in their suffering, and to take their burdens on our own shoulders.

Reflecting on the writings of Saint John that call us to abide in the Lord and let him abide in us, Pope Francis points out that this abiding is always manifest in concrete realities, whose criterion for authenticity is the Incarnation, the Word of God made flesh. He writes, "There is a basic criterion for truly living in love . . . The criterion is to abide in the Lord and the Lord in us, and the criterion of Christian concreteness is the same, always: The Word came in the flesh. The criterion is the Incarnation of the Word, God made Man and Christianity without this foundation is not true Christianity."[54] The fruits of a spirituality rooted in incarnational realism are, according to the pope, that love is found more in deeds than in words, and that in love, it is more important to give than to receive. The pope notes that the liturgical season of Christmas, with its focus on the gift of the Incarnate Word of God, renews our faith, which then must be expressed in loving deeds: "As we gaze on the Child in these final three days of the Christmas Season . . . let us renew our faith in Jesus Christ, who is true God and true Man. And let us ask for the grace to be granted this concreteness of Christian love so that we might always abide in love and that he might abide in us."[55]

The gaze that rests on Christ and receives his gaze of love is strengthened to turn with mercy toward those in need. In his homily for the beginning of Lent, Pope Francis invites those present to keep their "gaze fixed on [Jesus on] the Crucifix. He, loving us, invites us to be reconciled with God and to return to him, in order to find ourselves again."[56] This finding of oneself in the merciful gaze of God prepares one to be a missionary of mercy, the pope proclaims, not only as an ordained priest but also as one who shares in the common priesthood of the baptized: "May your hands bless and lift up brothers and sisters . . . through you may the gaze and the hands of God rest on his children and heal them of their wounds!"[57]

As Jesus showed his incarnate love in the touch that reached out to the sick and the poor, so the followers of Christ are called to be unafraid to touch those who suffer. Pope Francis boldly reminds the faithful that it is not enough to provide material relief to the poor and the sick while remaining at a distance from them. This is not the way of our God, who not only

54. Pope Francis, "Love Is Not a Soap Opera."

55. Ibid.

56. Pope Francis, *Homily for the Sending Forth of the Missionaries of Mercy*, February 10, 2016.

57. Ibid.

gives us our daily bread, but also becomes our Food to become one with us. The pope laments the charity that remains aloof, writing, "How often do we encounter a poor person who comes to meet us! We can also be generous, we can have compassion, but usually we do not touch him. We offer him coins, we toss them there, but we avoid touching his hand. And we forget that that person is the Body of Christ!"[58] Reaffirming that all are members of the Body of Christ, the pope challenges us to see the words and actions of Jesus as more than a mere model. He invites us to ponder the deeper incarnational principle that by becoming man, Christ united humanity to and in himself, a union lived in the real incorporation we receive in the Body of Christ by Baptism. He concludes his reflection, "Jesus teaches us not to be afraid to touch the poor and the excluded, because He is in them. Touching the poor can cleanse us from hypocrisy and make us distressed over their condition."[59] If we are to be merciful as our Father is merciful, we must be ready to touch the wounds of our brothers and sisters and to allow the merciful love that has healed our many wounds to be communicated by that contact.

Like Jesus, the Good Shepherd, who bears the burden of our sins and carries us to the Father, each of us is called to bear the burdens of others. Pope Francis notes that the parable of the Good Shepherd "is told by Jesus to make us understand that his closeness to sinners should not scandalize us, but on the contrary it should call us all to serious reflection on how we live our faith."[60] Jesus tells the parable in the presence of the scribes and Pharisees who murmur about his choice to eat and socialize with public sinners. The pope sees this parable as both an invitation to extend mercy and a warning that condemning others cannot be reconciled with the righteousness of God. The Lord's teaching is not merely to rebuke the pride and hypocrisy of people living in a past era, but it remains a challenge to people in every time and place to resist the ongoing tendency to reject those who are deemed unworthy of note or care. The pope points out, "God does not share our current throw-away culture; it doesn't count to God. God throws no one away; God loves everyone, looks for everyone: one by one! He doesn't know what 'throwing people away' means, because he is entirely love, entirely mercy."[61] He insists that we cannot impose our "structures and strategies" on the Lord. If we desire to be with the Shepherd, we must go where he goes—in search of the lost and the needy, rejoicing at their homecoming.

58. Pope Francis, *General Audience*, June 22, 2016.

59. Ibid.

60. Pope Francis, *General Audience*, May 4, 2016.

61. Ibid.

The Incarnation at the Heart of Pope Francis's Theology of Mercy

Pope Francis invites the members of the Church to receive God's mercy in a life-changing encounter with Jesus, who is mercy incarnate. This encounter impels believers to be missionaries of mercy to others, to embody the task of the New Evangelization. Pope Francis uses vivid language and strong challenges to point out the urgency of this task. With evangelical boldness he calls the faithful beyond thinking about God's mercy to living it. He writes in *Evangelii gaudium* of a need to incarnate God's word: "Realities are greater than ideas. This principle has to do with incarnation of the word and its being put into practice . . . The principle of reality, of a word already made flesh and constantly striving to take flesh anew, is essential to evangelization."[62] He pointedly states that the failure to live what the word of God proclaims leads us "to remain in the realm of pure ideas and to end up in a lifeless and unfruitful self-centredness and gnosticism."[63] Likewise, he warns against a spirituality that claims to be Christian but fails to satisfy spiritual hunger because it offers only "alienating solutions or . . . a disembodied Jesus who demands nothing of us with regard to others."[64] The pope concludes that this so-called Christianity, devoid of the Incarnate Word of God and the truth he embodies will ultimately prove unsustainable.

Pope Francis's incarnational realism awakens us to the truths that Christian works of mercy are not mere social projects, and that evangelization is not mere indoctrination. Those who encounter the living Christ not only enter into a relationship of love with him, but they also are moved by that union to seek the good of those he loves. As Pope Francis reminds the faithful, one cannot love Christ without loving the members of the Body of Christ. He writes, "True faith in the incarnate Son of God is inseparable from self-giving, from membership in the community, from service, from reconciliation with others. The Son of God, by becoming flesh, summoned us to the revolution of tenderness."[65] For the person alive with faith working through love, the Incarnation is not limited to an event of the past, but rather includes the reality of a Presence with and in us today. Pope Francis explores the many facets of this reality of Jesus's presence, writing, "A true missionary, who never ceases to be a disciple, knows that Jesus walks with

---

62. Pope Francis, *Evangelii gaudium*, 233.

63. Ibid.

64. Ibid., 89.

65. Ibid., 88.

him, speaks to him, breathes with him, works with him. He senses Jesus alive with him in the midst of the missionary enterprise."[66]

Pope Francis continues to invite all to encounter the mercy of God in a dynamic relationship of love with Jesus, the Word made flesh. He calls us to renewed hope in the face of obstacles, reminding us that trust in divine mercy has never been absent from the face of the earth since the coming of Christ, as he states, "In every epoch and in every place blessed are those who, on the strength of the word of God proclaimed in the Church and witnessed by Christians, believe that Jesus Christ is the love of God incarnate, Mercy incarnate."[67] Despite the evidence that seemingly points to the triumph of darkness, each person can encounter in Christ a merciful love so strong that it moved him to take on our humanity, embrace the cross even unto death, and rise again. This merciful love continues to draw us to the Father's embrace. As Pope Francis says near the conclusion of *Evangelii gaudium*, for the believer in Christ, there is in the good news of the gospel a cause for true joy and an answer to our pain: "We have a treasure of life and love which cannot deceive, and a message which cannot mislead or disappoint. It penetrates to the depths of our hearts, sustaining and ennobling us. It is a truth which is never out of date because it reaches that part of us which nothing else can reach. Our infinite sadness can only be cured by an infinite love." [68] The infinite love that can heal our infinite sadness is, as has been explored here, the mercy of the Father made manifest in the words of Christ, in the sacramental means through which he imparted mercy, and in the fidelity of his accompaniment of others on their journey to the Father's house. As the gospels proclaim and Pope Francis continually reminds his hearers, allowing ourselves to be embraced by the mercy of God changes us from within and makes us able to be merciful to others. Mercy encountered becomes mercy extended. Jesus Christ is infinite Love made visible, Mercy made flesh, that we might be healed and uplifted to become merciful as the Father is merciful.

Bibliography

Aquinas, Saint Thomas. *Summa Theologica*. 5 vols. Translated by the Fathers of the English Dominican Province. New York: Benziger Bros., 1948.

Benedict XVI, Pope. *Jesus of Nazareth: From the Baptism in the Jordan to the Transfiguration*. New York: Doubleday, 2007.

———. *Spe salvi*. Vatican City: Libreria Editrice Vaticana, 2007.

66. Ibid., 266.

67. Pope Francis, *Regina caeli*: April 7, 2013.

68. Pope Francis, *Evangelii gaudium*, 265.

Cantalamessa, Raniero. *The Gaze of Mercy: A Commentary on Divine and Human Mercy*. Translated by Marsha Daigle-Williamson. Frederick, MD: Word among Us, 2015.

Catherine of Siena, Saint. *The Dialogue*. Translated by Suzanne Noffke. New York: Paulist, 1980.

Francis, Pope. "Angelus: September 6, 2015." http://w2.vatican.va/content/francesco/en/angelus/2015/documents/papa-francesco_angelus_20150906.html.

————. "Being with Christ: Address to the Participants at the International Congress on Catechesis, September 27, 2013." In *The Church of Mercy: A Vision for the Church*, 15–20. Chicago: Loyola, 2014.

————. "The Embrace of God's Mercy: Homily for the Mass of Possession of the Chair of the Bishop of Rome, April 7, 2013." In *The Church of Mercy: A Vision for the Church*, 3–6. Chicago: Loyola, 2014.

————. *Evangelii gaudium* (Apostolic Exhortation). Vatican City: Libreria Editrice Vaticana, 2013.

————. "Freely You Have Received, Freely Give: Lenten Letter of Cardinal Jorge Mario Bergoglio, S.J., Archbishop of Buenos Aires, February 22, 2012." In *Only Love Can Save Us: Letters, Homilies, and Talks of Cardinal Jorge Bergoglio*, translated by Gerard Seromik, 77–80. Huntington, IN: Our Sunday Visitor, 2013.

————. "General Audience: May 4, 2016." http://w2.vatican.va/content/francesco/en/audiences/2016/documents/papa-francesco_20160504_udienza-generale.html.

————. "General Audience: June 22, 2016." http://w2.vatican.va/content/francesco/en/audiences/2016/documents/papa-francesco_20160622_udienza-generale.html.

————. "God Makes Us His Children and His Brothers and Sisters, Not Members of an Agency: Homily of Cardinal Jorge Mario Bergoglio, S.J., Archbishop of Buenos Aires, September 2, 2012." In *Only Love Can Save Us: Letters, Homilies, and Talks of Cardinal Jorge Bergoglio*, translated by Gerard Seromik, 91–95. Huntington, IN: Our Sunday Visitor, 2013.

————. "Homily of His Holiness Pope Francis: Holy Chrism Mass, March 24, 2016." http://w2.vatican.va/content/francesco/en/homilies/2016/documents/papa-francesco_20160324_omelia-crisma.html.

————. "Homily of His Holiness Pope Francis: Jubilee of Mercy for Priests, June 3, 2016." https://w2.vatican.va/content/francesco/en/homilies/2016/documents/papa-francesco_20160603_omelia-giubileo-sacerdoti.html.

————. "Homily of His Holiness Pope Francis: Sending Forth of the Missionaries of Mercy—Holy Mass, Blessing and Imposition of the Ashes, Feb 10, 2016." https://w2.vatican.va/content/francesco/en/homilies/2016/documents/papa-francesco_20160210_giubileo-omelia-invio-missionari-misericordia.html.

————. "Look for Him Where No One Else Would: Homily for Christmas Eve, Buenos Aires, December 24, 2010." In *Encountering Christ: Homilies, Letters, and Addresses of Cardinal Jorge Bergoglio*, 30–33. New Rochelle, NY: Scepter, 2013.

————. "Love Is Not a Soap Opera: Morning Meditation in the Chapel of the Domus Sanctae Marthae, January 9, 2014." http://w2.vatican.va/content/francesco/en/cotidie/2014/documents/papa-francesco-cotidie_20140109_love-soap-opera.html.

————. *Misericordiae vultus*: Bull of Indiction of the Extraordinary Jubilee of Mercy. Vatican City: Libreria Editrice Vaticana, 2015.

————. *The Name of God Is Mercy*. Translated by Oonagh Stransky. New York: Random House, 2016.

————. *Open Mind, Faithful Heart: Reflections on Following Jesus*. Translated by Joseph V. Owens. New York: Crossroad, 2013.

————. "Regina Caeli: April 7, 2013." http://w2.vatican.va/content/francesco/en/angelus/2013/documents/papa-francesco_regina-coeli_20130407.html.

————. "Three Manners of Gaze: Morning Meditation in the Chapel of the Domus Sanctae Marthae, May 22, 2015." https://w2.vatican.va/content/francesco/en/cotidie/2015/documents/papa-francesco-cotidie_20150522_three-manners-of-gaze.html.

Holy Bible. Revised Standard Version, Catholic Edition. Oxford: Oxford University Press, 2004.

John Paul II, Pope. *Dives in misericordia*. Vatican City: Libreria Editrice Vaticana, 1980.

CHAPTER 3 _____

From Encounter to Justice

Pope Francis, Catholic Sisters, and the Culture of Encounter

—Jennifer Kryszak

Abstract:

This essay argues that the event of encounter inspires action for social and ecological justice. First, I examine the writings and actions of
Pope Francis as a model for how Christians are called to embody the
kingdom of God in response to the encounter with the other, especially the poor. Francis asserts an integral ecology that recognizes the
interrelatedness of all creation and humanity's responsibility for all
of creation. Second, I place Francis's writings and actions in dialogue
with historical and ethnographic research on the Congregation of St.
Joseph, a Roman Catholic women's religious community. As the history and current practices of the sisters reveal, the encounter with the
other impacts the way religious communities have emphasized first
social and then ecological justice. I conclude that Francis's writings
affirm the turn to an integral ecology that continues to be embodied
in the lives and ministries of women religious.

> "If the present ecological crisis is one small sign of the
> ethical, cultural and spiritual crisis of modernity, we
> cannot presume to heal our relationship with nature and
> the environment without healing all fundamental hu-
> man relationships." Pope Francis, *Laudato si'*, 119.

A Catholic bishop kneeling to wash the feet of a Muslim woman, embracing a disabled man, cradling a young child—all of these images
witness to the power of the encounter with another person. In these ac-

tions, Pope Francis models a culture of encounter that evidences the human dignity of all people. Media abounds with images of Francis engaging those at the periphery of society as well as seemingly unlikely candidates for a pope's attention and care. These encounters often appear with sound-bites of Francis's pastoral approach to evangelization and his challenges to people who seek to separate themselves from those of different faiths, ethnic backgrounds, sexual identities, or abilities. While we can question how many Catholics and other individuals engage Pope Francis's writings, many people encounter Francis through the media. These encounters urge people to reflect more deeply on the encounter with this pastoral pope and to consider how they too can evangelize in the contemporary context. How does the event of encounter, the encounter with Francis that prods us to encounter others, challenge us to live out the Gospel message? What role does the event of encounter play in the Church's mission?

This essay argues that the event of encounter inspires action for social and ecological justice. I examine the writings and actions of Pope Francis as a vision of the kingdom of God that necessarily begins by encountering the other, especially the poor. Encountering Pope Francis, people are called to discern their own values and actions in order to promote the kingdom of God. Nonetheless, this encounter does not originate with Francis but rather runs throughout the history of Catholicism. Consequently, I place Francis's writings and actions in dialogue with historical and ethnographic research on the Congregation of St. Joseph, a Roman Catholic women's religious community. The Congregation focuses on serving "the dear neighbor," those who are most in need in society. Recognizing the impact of the environmental crisis on the poor, the sisters have extended the emphasis on the dear neighbor to all of creation. Their personal encounter with the poor compels them to care for Earth; this ministry in turn educates and inspires others to embody social and ecological justice. I conclude that Francis's writings offer a pivotal moment that affirms the turn to an integral ecology even as the sisters practice an embodied integral ecology in their ministries and religious life.

Encountering Francis

At the beginning of the twenty-first century, Francis's writings affirm the turn to ecological justice and an ecology that recognizes the interrelatedness of all creation. His presence and writings call people to enter into the encounter with the other and embody values that will attend to the social and environmental crises. This is in part because Francis not only articulates the

Gospel message and Church teaching, clearly affirming human dignity and promoting justice based on an encounter with Christ, but also demonstrates the encounter with the other in his own life. Thus, as individuals encounter Francis, they too are challenged to question their behaviors and attitudes and potentially respond to elicit the justice of the kingdom of God.

Pope Francis's writings possess more power when seen in light of his personal commitment to attending to those in front of him, recognizing their human dignity, and responding in God's love. Photographs and video of Francis confirm this lived reality for the pontiff. Images of Francis embracing a disabled man or holding a child call the viewer to connect his words and actions. Francis has clearly embraced the technological age in his use of media. While he challenges a thoughtless approach to technology, he demonstrates an acute awareness of the power and presence of the media and its potential influence on global society.[1] While some might argue that Francis simply uses the media to promote his self-image, I interpret his relationship with the media as being guided by the goal of evangelization.[2] The power of these images of Francis should not be understated. Even if individuals do not engage Francis's writings, many encounter him through these images of a compassionate leader. The images themselves thus prompt people to consider the role of the papacy as well as Christians in society. Encountering an image of Francis, a person potentially questions, "Why does the Pope act in this way? Would I do that? How then should I respond?"[3]

At a time in the United States and in global society where individuals and groups degrade and reject others' human dignity, Francis calls us to acknowledge how the encounter with the other calls us out of ourselves and challenges us to respond through joyous evangelization in order to bring about the kingdom of God. In *Evangelii gaudium*, Francis maintains, "To evangelize is to make the kingdom of God present in our world."[4] But what is this kingdom and how should we make it present? Francis asserts, "The Gospel is about the kingdom of God (cf. Luke 4:43); it is about loving God who reigns in our world. To the extent that he reigns within us, the life of society will be a setting for universal fraternity, justice, peace and dignity.

---

1. Francis articulates this challenge to technology in *Laudato si'*. See Francis, *Laudato si'*, 20, 46–47, 54, 60, 102–114, 128, 131, 136.

2. In *The Francis Effect*, Gehring similarly observes Francis's engagement with the media and how the image of Francis potentially affects the Church and global society (Gehring, *Francis Effect*, 2–4).

3. For an analysis of the image and its power in society, see Morgan, *Embodied Eye*, 3–6, 67–70. For an assessment of visual practices in the lives of religious communities, see Kryszak, "A Theology of Transformation," 70–93.

4. Francis, *Evangelii gaudium*, 176.

Both Christian preaching and life, then, are meant to have an impact on society."[5] In this vision, the kingdom of God is not merely a future reality in which we will encounter God; rather, the kingdom of God is already present among us and calls each Christian to preach the Gospel in order to manifest the kingdom more fully on earth.[6] As Christians are called to manifest the kingdom of God in the world, they are challenged to embody the values of the kingdom, to demonstrate fraternity, justice, peace, and dignity in their daily actions. This necessarily requires reflections on one's thoughts, attitudes, and actions. Accordingly, Francis challenges all people to reflect deeply on their beliefs and actions in order to bring about the conversion of humanity to the Gospel message.

In order to embody this kingdom and its values of fraternity, justice, peace, and dignity, Christians cannot manifest a privatized faith; rather, we must live in right relationship with God, others, and ourselves.[7] Christian faith must call a person out of herself to fully live the Trinitarian relation of love. In his address to the International Congress on Catechesis, Francis argues that this begins by focusing on Christ which then draws one into relationship with others: "This is the true dynamism of love; this is the movement of God himself! God is the center, but his is always self-gift, relationship, love that gives itself away . . . and this is what we will become if we remain united to Christ."[8] Encountering Christ in one's life does not isolate an individual but rather encourages the gift of self to others. Speaking to this gathering of catechists, Francis contends, "The heart of the catechist receives the gift of the *kerygma* and in turn offers it to others as gift . . . That is the nature itself of the *kerygma*: it is a gift that generates mission, that compels us to go beyond ourselves."[9] For catechists and all Christians, receiving the *kerygma* inspires one to share the Gospel message with others.

This self-gift models the values of the kingdom as embodied in the life of Christ. Consequently, our lives should be affected by Christ's example: "Moved by his example, we want to enter fully into the fabric of society, sharing the lives of all, listening to their concerns, helping them materially and spiritually in their needs, rejoicing with those who rejoice, weeping with those who weep; arm in arm with others, we are committed to building a

---

5. Ibid., 180.

6. Emphasizing the mission of the church to transform society, John Fuellenbach similarly offers the church as a contrast society in which Christians are called to engage secular society and embody the kingdom (Fuellenbach, *Church*, 208–12).

7. *Laudato si'* challenges this privatized spirituality. See Francis, *Laudato si'*, 216–17, 231, 240.

8. Francis, *Church of Mercy*, 17.

9. Ibid.

new world."[10] Francis calls Christians to joyfully embody the love they have received from Christ. This love should inspire our participation in the lives of others and guide our actions to manifest the kingdom of God. Thus, the self-gift to the other should transform society in light of the Gospel values. Accordingly, Francis calls Christians to manifest the values and actions of the kingdom, to be peacemakers, and to challenge culture and societal policies that degrade the dignity of humanity and creation.[11] Christians need to be aware of injustice and respond in light of the Gospel. Speaking at the Astalli Centre, the Jesuit Refugee Service in Rome, Francis connected service to the encounter with another and solidarity that elicits justice: "Serving means recognizing and accepting requests for justice and hope, and seeking roads together, real paths that lead to liberation."[12] Because the encounter with Christ draws us out of ourselves in self-gift to others, we are called to manifest love for others—love that should promote justice in society.

It is in the encounter that this self-gift can be made. In the modern world where technology, social media and consumerism distract us from the presence of others, the Church necessarily must meet people where they are—engage them in their everyday lives amid their joys and struggles. Francis exhorts Christians to move beyond our daily distractions and to engage the poor. As an integral part of the Body of Christ, the poor embody the kingdom in their daily lives. Consequently, engagement with the poor should shape the Church: "This is why I want a Church which is poor and for the poor. They have so much to teach us. Not only do they share in the *sensus fidei*, but in their difficulties they know the suffering Christ. We need to let ourselves be evangelized by them. The new evangelization is an invitation to acknowledge the saving power at work in their lives and to put them at the center of the Church's pilgrim way."[13] Accordingly, Francis challenges Christians to be shaped by this encounter with the poor. While Francis also argues that we need to assist the poor and work for structural changes to eliminate poverty, he implores us to truly open ourselves up to the wisdom and faith of the poor as a way to learn more about the Gospel. Because the poor are part of the Church, their lives and our encounter with the poor should shape our understanding of Christ, how to live as Church, and the ways in which we seek to evangelize. This encounter should alter our attitudes and behaviors by moving our focus from only charity to the interplay of charity and justice. Encountering the poor—learning about and

---

10. Francis, *Evangelii gaudium*, 269.

11. Ibid., 238–39.

12. Francis, *Church of Mercy*, 106.

13. Francis, *Evangelii gaudium*, 198.

experiencing their joys and struggles—should challenge us to embody the Gospel message as Christ did.

Nonetheless, it is not only the poor who affect us with this encounter. It is our neighbors, co-workers, young people, and the stranger in the grocery store. Each encounter with another person calls us to evangelization. How can we best articulate the kingdom of God in each encounter? How can Christians proclaim the Gospel in secular society? As Christians we are called to proclaim the Gospel throughout the world; yet, knowing how and where to undertake this activity can be difficult, especially in modern times when we engage those of different or no faith. As Francis asserts, "Each Christian and every community must discern the path that the Lord points out, but all of us are asked to obey his call to go forth from our own comfort zone in order to reach all the 'peripheries' in need of the light of the Gospel."[14] Within the contemporary context, these "peripheries" are at the edges of society where the majority of the Church typically does not engage those who are marginalized or discarded by society. Additionally, these peripheries can be in our workplaces and neighborhood where the Gospel message is silenced or privatized. Christians are called to proclaim and embody the Gospel in these contexts. How can Christians bring fraternity, justice, peace, and dignity to these peripheries? Sometimes we are called to verbally express our belief; more often we embody belief in our actions and decisions.

Thus, Francis models the Gospel for those who encounter him. Francis's life of living in simplicity and engaging the poor, ill, immigrants, and refugees, challenges people to consider how they can likewise reach out to the "peripheries." As Archbishop of Buenos Aires and Pope, his actions have embodied the Gospel values he articulates in his preaching and writings. By living simply, engaging diverse people, speaking honestly and candidly, Francis manifests justice and dignity. Moreover, he challenges us likewise to model our beliefs in our daily choices and actions. Again and again, Francis urges Christians to encounter those who are different than them—immigrants, refugees, the poor, those of different faiths, races, and sexual identities. These deep encounters should elicit continued presence and action for others. As Francis asserts, "True faith in the incarnate Son of God is inseparable from self-giving, from membership in the community, from service, from reconciliation with others. The Son of God, by becoming flesh, summoned us to the revolution of tenderness."[15] But what is this "revolution of tenderness"? How can or should Christians respond to this

---

14. Ibid., 20.

15. Ibid., 88. See also ibid., 177.

call? Francis points us to service to and relationship with others as parts of this revolution, but people might easily brush aside these words or not take up the challenge that they do not believe is embodied by the speaker. Nonetheless, Francis continually demonstrates his own joyous evangelization in his encounter with others and challenges humanity to this same depth of encounter and presence.

A simplistic response will not do for Francis. One's response cannot be to acknowledge Francis's actions, insight or role within the Church; rather, our response likewise must be to embody our expressed beliefs. He urges us through his writings and his actions to manifest the kingdom of God and to joyfully evangelize the world. Francis challenges the "culture of waste" evident in contemporary society: "We live in a culture of conflict, a culture of fragmentation, a culture in which I throw away what is of no use to me, a culture of waste."[16] This culture prevents people from truly being present to others and from being affected by people's daily struggles and tragedies. As Francis notes, poverty, violence, and death become normal, and this normalcy prevents modern people from responding to the concrete situations that degrade human dignity.[17] Often directed at people living in the Western world, this challenge can pointedly express how we continue to live self-content lives without being changed by the encounter with Francis, the poor, or any other human being. As Francis contends, "The dignity of the human person and the common good rank higher than the comfort of those who refuse to renounce their privileges. When these values are threatened, a prophetic voice must be raised."[18]

Francis raises this prophet voice against the culture of waste in *Laudato si'*. Strongly connecting the social and environmental crises, Francis calls people to discern their course of action: "We need to strengthen the conviction that we are one single human family. There are no frontiers or barriers, political or social, behind which we can hide, still less is there room for the globalization of indifference."[19] In *Laudato si'*, Francis challenges all people to recognize their inherent connections to everything in the universe. He examines the contemporary context in order to demonstrate how human action affects the environment which can impact humanity. For example, industry and daily human action such as transportation create pollutants which affect air and water quality. These adverse conditions in turn affect

16. Francis, *Church of Mercy*, 99–100. Francis also challenges contemporary culture's emphasis on efficiency and pragmatism (ibid., 60–61).

17. Francis addresses how these negative aspects come to be normal in ibid., 113.

18. Francis, *Evangelii gaudium*, 218.

19. Francis, *Laudato si'*, 52.

humanity—those often living in close proximity to industry and waste: "Industrial waste and chemical products utilized in cities and agricultural areas can lead to bioaccumulation in the organisms of the local population, even when levels of toxins in those places are low. Frequently, no measures are taken until after people's health has been irreversibly affected."[20] Human action creates these pollutants which affect the entirety of the ecosystem.

Consequently, Francis urges humans to recognize how their individual and corporate behavior affects the whole of creation. For humans, that must mean that we become aware of our impact on other people and societies, especially the poor: "Disregard for the duty to cultivate and maintain a proper relationship with my neighbour, for whose care and custody I am responsible, ruins my relationship with my own self, with others, with God and with the earth. When all these relationships are neglected, when justice no longer dwells in the land, the Bible tells us that life itself is endangered."[21] Francis asserts the unity of these relationships with God, others, and the created world; harming one relationship affects the others and prevents justice and dignity from being realized in society.

Moreover, Francis argues that people cannot recognize the value of creation if they do not recognize the value of another human being.[22] As Francis contends, "A sense of deep communion with the rest of nature cannot be real if our hearts lack tenderness, compassion and concern for our fellow human beings."[23] Recognizing the beauty of a flower or sunset becomes hollow if you cannot articulate the beauty, the dignity of another person. Our treatment or lack of concern for other human beings mirrors a pragmatic approach to the created world. Those with power in society make decisions and act in ways that reject the dignity of people at the margins of society and the environment itself. Likewise, the culture of waste numbs people from recognizing how their daily actions affect those who live in poverty.[24] From this foundation, Francis asserts humanity's responsibility for the care of creation because the plights of the environment and the poor are intricately connected.

20. Ibid., 21.

21. Ibid., 70.

22. "When we fail to acknowledge as part of reality the worth of a poor person, a human embryo, a person with disabilities—to offer just a few examples—it becomes difficult to hear the cry of nature itself; everything is interconnected" (ibid., 117).

23. Ibid., 91.

24. Throughout *Laudato si'*, Francis challenges this pragmatic approach to creation, demands businesses and nations to attend to human dignity and care for creation, and urges all humans to combat a culture of waste. For this critique, see ibid., especially chapters 1 and 3.

Because of this, Francis argues for an integral ecology, which recognizes the unity of the created world and the potential impact humanity has on all aspects of the whole.[25] This integral ecology requires a conversion of humanity: "Many things have to change course, but it is we human beings above all who need to change. We lack an awareness of our common origin, of our mutual belonging, and of a future to be shared with everyone. This basic awareness would enable the development of new convictions, attitudes and forms of life. A great cultural, spiritual and educational challenge stands before us, and it will demand that we set out on the long path of renewal."[26] Accordingly, Francis calls humanity to remember their dignity, change their practices, and to care for others and the environment.[27] He implores us to create new habits in our daily lives that challenge the culture of waste and promote justice.[28] Instead of rejecting technology and science, Francis recognizes the creativity and power in aspects of modern society and challenges individuals, businesses, and nations to use their creativity, knowledge, and inspiration to protect and value life.[29]

Thus the encounter that inspires evangelization is both the encounter with the environment and with people. These encounters demonstrate the interconnection of the social and environmental crises. Accordingly, Francis challenges people to recognize these connections: "Today, however, we have to realize that a true ecological approach *always* becomes a social approach; it must integrate questions of justice in debates on the environment, so as to hear *both the cry of the earth and the cry of the poor*."[30] Seeking to transform society in order to manifest the kingdom of God, Francis urges all of humanity to undertake this conversion, a conversion to encountering the other, recognizing dignity, and promoting justice.

Encountering the Dear Neighbor

While Pope Francis currently challenges all people to be changed through the encounter with the other, this experience of encounter has grounded previous and current evangelization and ministry in the Church. In particular, apostolic communities of religious women and men have developed in

25. For a description of this integral ecology, see ibid., chapter 4.

26. Ibid., 202.

27. Ibid., 205–8.

28. Ibid., 211.

29. Ibid., chapter 5.

30. Ibid., 49. Francis notes the multiple sources for the knowledge of this interconnection including Scripture and science (ibid., 63, 66).

response to how God calls individuals and communities to serve those they encounter. As Christ sent the apostles to spread the kingdom of God, apostolic communities embody this call to bring the kingdom into secular society. Often specific ecclesial or social needs or crises confronted the founding members of these communities and urged them to attend to individuals and groups marginalized by secular or religious society. Each apostolic community continues to respond to the founding narrative that inspired their formation.[31] One such community is the Congregation of St. Joseph, a community of the Sisters of St. Joseph. The history and ministries of these women religious parallel the histories of other apostolic communities and demonstrate the continued power of encounter in inspiring and shaping a mission for justice in society. Thus, I draw on historical and ethnographic research of the Congregation of St. Joseph to elucidate the movement from encountering the other to embodying an integral ecology.[32]

The Sisters of St. Joseph arose from the encounter of six women with the poor working class in seventeenth century France.[33] During that time, poverty was rampant and social structures could not attend to the needs of people surviving plagues and wars. The community arose to serve those most in need in society, those they called the "dear neighbor." These women had encountered Fr. Jean-Pierre Médaille, SJ in his missionary activities. In his interactions with them, Médaille recognized their desire to serve God through their neighbor and supported the formation of their religious community to manifest God in secular society.[34] The charism of the commu-

31. This demonstrates the way in which apostolic communities responded to the call of the Second Vatican Council to return to their founders and their charism (Second Vatican Council, *Perfectae caritatis*, 2). The engagement with their founding documents continues to shape the ways in which the communities embody their charism in society.

32. Between May 2011 and May 2013, I conducted ethnographic research with the Congregation of St. Joseph. I interviewed 117 sisters and 17 individuals who were CSJ Associates (non-vowed members of the Congregation) and/or employees of the Congregation. My research employed semi-structured interviews and participant observation.

33. For information on these women, see Vacher, *Nuns Without Cloister*, 8–18; and Coburn and Smith, *Spirited Lives*, 24–25.

34. For information on Jean-Pierre Médaille, see Vacher, *Nuns without Cloister*, 18–30; and Coburn and Smith, *Spirited Lives*, 20–24. The Sisters of St. Joseph did not accept the title of "nun" because they recognized that their charism necessarily conflicted with the restrictions of enclosure. Following the Council of Trent, the sisters as well as other groups of women sought to respond to their call within the boundaries of church teaching. This meant that the women could not identify as cloistered nuns and still leave the monastery to minister to people. For an assessment of the Council of Trent and the development of new forms of religious life, see Vacher, *Nuns without Cloister*, xvii–xxiii, xxix–xxxix.

nity, the gift by which they embody their spirituality and mission, directed the sisters to pursue the double union: the union with God and the union with neighbor.[35] Thus, the Sisters of St. Joseph pursued their ministries not only to address social ills but also for religious reasons. As their founding Constitution contends, the sisters dedicate themselves to the salvation and sanctification of their dear neighbors: "It seeks first to establish and maintain in very high virtue all of its members. Second, to practice all the holy works of mercy, spiritual and corporal, of which women are capable, and at the same time, by means of these works to benefit many souls of the dear neighbor."[36] Their ministries, the works of mercy, attended to people's educational, financial, and healthcare needs in relation to their spiritual needs.[37] Originally in the context of France, the sisters educated women and girls and taught them the skill of lace-making.[38] These ministries enabled the sisters to focus on skills that would provide the women with a source of income as well as spiritual readings which could affect their salvation.

The experiences of these women and their founding documents demonstrate the centrality of others to their charism. Historical documents attest to the power of the sisters' presence in these towns and cities.[39] Their dedication to women and girls offered hope and stability in an uncertain time. The rapid growth of the religious community further evidences the power of encounter as more women chose to join the community.[40] Because

35. In *The Eucharistic Letter*, Médaille describes the foundation of this double union in the relation of the Trinity and directs the sisters to embody this unity in their own lives and promote it in the lives of others (Médaille, *The Eucharistic Letter*, in *Documents of the Little Design St. Flour*, paragraphs 21–24).

36. Vacher, *Nuns without Cloister*, 69. In *Origins: The Sisters of St. Joseph*, Marius Nepper argues that the Constitutions clearly show the influence of Ignatius of Loyola and the constitutions of the Jesuits: "Especially would the congregation be following the Ignatian concept by the insistence of Father Médaille upon the apostolic zeal, the concern for organization, the orientation toward the most needy and toward those who one can hope will benefit the most, spiritually and apostolically" (Nepper, *Origins*, 31).

37. Furthermore, their Constitutions and *The Eucharistic Letter* direct the sisters to balance their spiritual and ministerial lives (Médaille, *The Eucharistic Letter*, in *Documents of the Little Design St. Flour*, paragraph 20).

38. For an analysis of lace-making and its impact on the sisters' religious motivations, see Kryszak, "Imaging Church," 35–41.

39. Vacher includes some of these documents in *Nuns without Cloister*. In one document, Lanthenas recounts how the sisters employed ribbon-making to justify their presence in Le Puy. Two other documents reflect the decisions of towns to request letters of patent for the Sisters of St. Joseph. These record the positive impact the sisters had on the local population. For these documents, see Vacher, *Nuns without Cloister*, 326–27, 334–36, and 348–50.

40. In the seventeenth and eighteenth centuries, the Sisters of St. Joseph included a variety of ways of being a sister including three groups within the Congregation that

the community was not founded with a particular mission of education or healthcare, the sisters were able to attend to the needs of each particular context. The flexibility of their charism enabled the Sisters of St. Joseph to respond to each encounter in order to promote unity with God and neighbor.

Suppressed during the French Revolution, the Sisters of St. Joseph were reformed to respond to the needs of the population after the war.[41] Overtime as the congregation grew, the sisters answered calls to missionary territories responding to the needs of the local people. In the context of the United States, the sisters organized to provide education and healthcare. Initially missioned to serve the Catholic population of St. Louis, Missouri and Cahokia, Illinois, the sisters focused on education, originally ministering to the immigrant population.[42] Recognizing the needs of the African American population, the sisters opened a school in 1845 for free blacks and prepared the children of slaves for the reception of the sacraments. While the sisters sought to respond to the obvious need for education, the white population of Missouri threatened the sisters and forced the closure of the school.[43]

The religious community spread throughout the United States responding to the request of local bishops and other Catholics. Called to the Western frontier, the Sisters of St. Joseph served the immigrant population as well as the Native Americans. In particular, the sisters' ministry on the Indian reservations challenged them in the daily encounter with the poor. Poverty plagued those on the reservations as well as in the schools. As Coburn and Smith argue, "The CSJs reported some religious conversions and intercultural successes, but their greatest contribution may have been in their humanitarian activities—the spiritual, material, and medical sustenance they provided for children and adults, particularly on the poverty-stricken reservations."[44] While we can critique the educational practices of

---

depended on social class and determined the amount of time dedicated to works of charity or work for pay. The Congregation also included the *agrégées* who took a vow to the Congregation and lived in small communities in various towns and the *associeés* who worked with the Congregation while not living with the community (Vacher, *Nuns without Cloister*, 67). Contemporary moves toward associates of religious communities have come to mirror these earlier forms of religious life.

41. Vacher, *Nuns without Cloister*, 317–19; and Coburn and Smith, *Spirited Lives*, 35–38.

42. For information on the lives and ministries of the Sisters of St. Joseph, see Coburn and Smith, *Spirited Lives*, 43–53.

43. Ibid., 53–54. Additional groups of the Sisters of St. Joseph answered the call from Bishop Augustin Verot to educate the newly freed slaves in Georgia and Florida (Byrne, "Sisters of St. Joseph," 260).

44. Coburn and Smith, *Spirited Lives*, 114.

the nineteenth century and the prejudice against Native American culture and beliefs, it is also clear in the context they were serving that the sisters attempted to secure food and clothing and provide spiritual guidance. Indeed some of the sisters allowed themselves to be challenged by those they were educating. The lives and beliefs of the Native Americans consequently influenced how the sisters envisioned their role as educators and missionaries.[45]

Over time, these communities of the Sisters of St. Joseph shifted and rearticulated their mission to attend to the needs of the local population or to answer previously unacknowledged issues. As the women religious responded to the context of the twentieth century and the Second Vatican Council, they came into increased contact with the poor and minorities. These encounters challenged the sisters to reconsider how they lived and ministered and to reflect further on the meaning of their religious consecration and the future of their religious community. Moreover, as their religious communities changed over time, they negotiated how their individual communities of the Sisters of St. Joseph related to one another and how they envisioned their future ministries.[46]

For seven communities of the Sisters of St. Joseph, this included reconfiguring the communities into the Congregation of St. Joseph. In 2007, the Sisters of St. Joseph united the communities of LaGrange Park, Illinois; Tipton, Indiana; Wichita, Kansas; Nazareth, Michigan; Cleveland, Ohio; Wheeling, West Virginia; and the Médaille community with sisters in Ohio, Louisiana, and Minnesota.[47] This reconfiguration consequently brought the women religious into relationship with others whom they had not previously known. This encounter with women religious in different geographic areas further challenged the sisters to reflect on how they were being called to live as a Congregation and how they should minister. In interviews conducted by the author, sisters from diverse states noted that while they shared a charism and a commitment to religious life, they had experienced life differently and felt challenged and inspired by the new relationship with those from other areas. Their different life narratives influence how the women religious understand themselves, their mission, and relation to the Church.

45. Ibid., 113–15.

46. For an assessment of how women's religious life has changed, see McNamara, *Sisters in Arms*, especially 565–644. For analysis of contemporary religious life, see Hereford, *Religious Life at the Crossroad*); Johnson et al., *New Generations of Catholic Sisters*; and Schneiders, *Buying the Field*.

47. The individual communities of the Sisters of St. Joseph voted between December 2005 and January 2006. The formation of the Congregation of St. Joseph received Vatican approval on March 19, 2007 (Congregation of St. Joseph, "LaGrange Park, Illinois: Our History").

Nonetheless, they each recall one or several individuals who embodied the joy of the Gospel and invited them—sometimes verbally but more often through their lives—to consider religious life. Encountering these individuals, whether they were laity, religious, or clergy, encouraged the women to dedicate their lives to Jesus and the dear neighbor.[48]

This encounter with others consequently affects their attention to their Congregation in order to inspire and guide their religious lives and ministries. In order to nurture these relationships, the sisters participate in prayer circles that cross state lines. They commit to being present to one another both physically and via technology for congregational meetings and celebrations. These practices of presence assist the Congregation in uniting the women religious in prayer and ministry as well as offering support to ministries in other locations. Thus, encounter and presence shape their communal lives.

As a Congregation, the women religious rearticulated their mission statement and crafted four Generous Promises through which to direct the resources of the Congregation. They maintain, "Our mission flows from the purpose for which the congregation exists: We live and work that all people may be united with God and with one another. It is rooted in the mission of Christ, the same mission which continually unfolds in His church, '*That all may be one as You, Father, are in Me, and I in You; I pray that they may be one in Us.*' (John 17:21)."[49] Connecting their mission to the mission of the Church, the Congregation promotes unity in society. Paralleling the activities of their founders, the sisters do not limit themselves to conventional ministries of education and healthcare. Rather, the sisters seek to evangelize people where they are; thus, they pursue diverse ministries to Catholics, other Christians, those of other religions, and of no faith. Among their many ministries, the Congregation presently focuses on human trafficking in order to educate the public and to abolish human trafficking.[50] These

---

48. The sisters recalled the influence of many individuals on their decision to join religious life. Often they commented on the impact of parents, older siblings, aunts who were Sisters of St. Joseph or members of other religious communities, and the women religious who educated them. These personal encounters with Sisters of St. Joseph as educators stood out among my interview participants. In light of the decreasing numbers of religious women and men in elementary and secondary education, the women religious echoed the concerns of scholars and religious leaders as they reflected on the future of their community. If they are not involved in education, will they have ways to invite others to join their community? As I note later in this essay, their other ministries offer the sisters new ways to encounter the other, evangelize, and model a joyous dedication to the gospel.

49. Congregation of St. Joseph, "Our Mission."

50. Human trafficking is currently the emphasis of the Federation of the Sisters of

efforts rely on the encounter with the other to change attitudes, increase awareness, and alter societal policies.

In their Generous Promises, the Congregation commits themselves to manifest this unity in local and global society as well as in their community:

> We, the Congregation of St. Joseph, promise to take the risk to surrender our lives and resources to work for specific systemic change in collaboration with others so that the hungers of the world might be fed.
>
> We, the Congregation of St. Joseph, promise to recognize the reality that Earth is dying, to claim our oneness with Earth and to take steps now to strengthen, heal and renew the face of Earth.
>
> We, the Congregation of St. Joseph, promise to network with others across the world to bring about a shift in the global culture from institutionalized power and privilege to a culture of inclusivity and mutuality.
>
> We, the Congregation of St. Joseph, promise to be mutually responsible and accountable for leadership in the congregation.[51]

These Generous Promises challenge the Congregation to step outside of their perspective and context in order to transform society. This goal of transformation urges the sisters and those they encounter to reconsider how they perceive and interact with others. Promoting a "culture of inclusivity and mutuality" the Congregation articulates the necessity of self-gift to protect the dignity of others and the care of the environment. In words that foreshadow *Laudato si'*, these Generous Promises demonstrate the connections between the crises of the poor and the environment and the responsibility of all, including the Congregation, for changing behaviors and attitudes. Indeed, these promises anticipate the call of Pope Francis to attend to structural sin in order to benefit people's lives.

In particular, the turn to ecological justice demonstrates the Congregation's mission for unity with God and others. Within their own experiences with people and in their ministries, the sisters came to recognize the relation between the state of the environment and the fate of the poorest members of society. Accordingly in their ministries and financial support of non-profit organizations, the Congregation attends to the natural environment in order

---

Saint Joseph, the national organization of the Sisters of St. Joseph. Consequently, the Sisters of St. Joseph as well as other communities of women religious promote awareness and educate individuals and businesses to end human trafficking. For information on their commitment to ending human trafficking, see U.S. Federation Sisters of Saint Joseph, "Human Trafficking."

51. Congregation of St. Joseph, "Our Mission."

to assist the poor. For example, their Generous Promise Grant funded the work of Grow Ohio Valley, increasing food production for low-income areas.[52] Likewise in Wheeling, West Virginia, the sisters perceive the potentially devastating effects mining and fracking can have on the local population. The beauty of the land and their love of the people urge the sisters to challenge business practices and societal structures that disregard the lives of the poor and the value of the land. During interviews, the sisters referenced the USCCB's pastoral letters on Appalachia in light of the experiences of the local population. Thus, the sisters' knowledge of the people and Catholic social teaching guides their ministerial decisions and activities.

The sisters' encounters with people further encourage them to attend to the specific ways communities interact with their environment in order to embody an integral ecology. Take, for example, the Congregation of St. Joseph's relationship with the Hilltop neighborhood in Wichita, Kansas. Built as temporary housing during WWII, the Hilltop neighborhood now consists of low-income housing with a transient population. Between the sisters' property and Hilltop, a plot of land on the edge of the neighborhood was used as a dump yard. Reflecting on the land and the people, the sisters and Hilltop residents decided to use the land to create a community garden in 1997. The goal was not simply to reclaim and maintain the land, but rather to provide an area for the neighborhood to garden, gather together, and find value in creation.[53] The project promoted the health of the residents as they engaged the land, grew healthy food, and nurtured relationships.[54]

Moreover, one of the Congregation's employees noted that there is little beauty in the Hilltop neighborhood. Yet, the garden provides an outlet for creativity and adds to the beauty of the area.[55] As scholars such as Susan Ross and Patrick McCormick have argued, beauty draws us out of ourselves and potentially leads to justice.[56] By engaging this land as a Community Garden, people reshaped their vision of each other and Earth. In other words, a better relationship with the land and resources promoted

52. Congregation of St. Joseph, "How One Ministry Led to Changing the Lives of Many" (n.p.).

53. They have also created a peace garden: "The idea there was to socialize, mingle, and gather. We have had one couple use it to renew their wedding vows . . . They were from the neighborhood" (George [pseudonym], August 2011). Thus, people have transformed the land into a place of encounter and care for creation and humanity.

54. Sarah McFarland Taylor likewise recognizes this relationship between community gardens and the physical and spiritual health of communities (Taylor, *Green Sisters*, 183–209).

55. One of the employees noted, "The eclectic art in the garden—the bowling balls—that was done by a gardener . . . we had nothing to do with that" (August 2011).

56. See Ross, *For the Beauty of the Earth*; and McCormick, *God's Beauty*.

the well-being of the local community and positively influenced the ways people interacted with each other and the environment.[57]

In all of these ministries, the Congregation of St. Joseph embodies what their founders recognized. They serve people's societal and spiritual needs. In doing so, they express the Gospel message in diverse ways and bring Christ into the lives of Christians and non-Christians. These encounters are foundational to their self-understanding as Sisters of St. Joseph serving the dear neighbor. While the neighbor shifts and changes over time and space, they serve the person in front of them: the poor women and girls in France, the immigrant, black, and Native American families in the United States, and the neighbor now recognized in the poor, marginalized, the immigrant, and the Earth. Their charism directs their ministries, opening them to more encounters, which in turn further impacts the shape and direction of their ministries. Moreover, this encounter with the other potentially inspires other people likewise to pursue ministry and evangelize in their secular lives. This is indeed evident in the CSJ Associates who often encounter the sisters in various ministries and commit to manifesting their mission for unity. These individuals demonstrate the power of encounter and how the life, actions, and words of a Christian can influence others.

Responding to the Gospel

Because of his life experiences and present status within the Church and global society, Pope Francis possesses the ability to articulate a culture of encounter in a way that reaches people across the globe. His access to and use of media demonstrates his desire to impact the greatest number of people. Moreover, his willingness to address diverse topics and issues manifests his desire to attend to the present state of the Church and society and to challenge a prevalent culture of waste. Furthermore, he pushes people to consider issues in greater depth, which urges people to be converted by the encounter with another and to embody the dignity and justice of the kingdom of God. Francis's care and empathy for those he encounters

57. Because of their commitment to manifesting unity with God and others, the sisters seek to embody an integral ecology which recognizes humanity's interconnections with creation and asserts the moral responsibility individuals and communities have to caring for the created world. As Pope John Paul II asserted, "When the ecological crisis is set within the broader context of *the search for peace* within society, we can understand better the importance of giving attention to what the earth and its atmosphere are telling us: namely, that there is an order in the universe which must be respected, and that the human person, endowed with the capability of choosing freely, has a grave responsibility to preserve this order for the well-being of future generations" (John Paul II, *Message for the World Day of Peace*, 15).

challenges others to respond in a similar manner. Thus, through his writings and presence, Pope Francis continues to inspire others to care for humanity and creation.

Each person potentially has this impact on individuals and the society as a whole. We must remember that we each have the responsibility to respond to those whom we meet. This response should affirm their human dignity. Moreover, we should be taken out of our own limited experiences in the encounter with the other. This encounter should move us to attend to people's needs, care for creation, and attempt to change societal structures and policies that devalue the environment and humanity. Indeed, our encounter with Francis and with those involved in this ministry, such as the Congregation of St. Joseph, should compel us to join this mission and commit ourselves to living in such a way as to value each person and aspect of creation we encounter.

Bibliography

Byrne, Patricia. "Sisters of St. Joseph: The Americanization of a French Tradition." *U.S. Catholic Historian* 5, nos. 3–4 (1986) 241–72.

Coburn, Carol K., and Martha Smith. *Spirited Lives: How Nuns Shaped Catholic Culture and American Life, 1836-1920*. Chapel Hill: University of North Carolina Press, 1999.

Congregation of St. Joseph. "How One Ministry Led to Changing the Lives of Many: Sister Judy Teufel and the Generous Promise Grant Fund." *Serving the Dear Neighbor: News From Mount St. Joseph* (2016) n.p.

———. "LaGrange Park, Illinois: Our History." http://www.csjoseph.org/lagrange_illinois.aspx.

———. "Our Mission." About Us. http://www.csjoseph.org/our_mission_vision.aspx.

Francis, Pope. *The Church of Mercy: A Vision for the Church*. Chicago: Loyola, 2014.

———. *The Joy of the Gospel: Evangelii Gaudium*. New York: Image, 2013.

———. *Laudato si': Encyclical letter on the Care for Our Common Home*. Vatican Website. http://w2.vatican.va/content/francesco/en/encyclicals/documents/papa-francesco_20150524_enciclica-laudato-si.html.

Fuellenbach, John. *Church: Community for the Kingdom*. Maryknoll, NY: Orbis, 2002.

Gehring, John. *The Francis Effect: A Radical Pope's Challenge to the American Catholic Church*. Lanham and London: Rowman and Littlefield, 2015.

Hereford, Amy. *Religious Life at the Crossroads: A School for Mystics and Prophets*. Maryknoll, NY: Orbis, 2013.

John Paul II, Pope. *Message for the World Day of Peace*, 1 January 1990. Vatican Website. https://w2.vatican.va/content/john-paul-ii/en/messages/peace/documents/hf_jp-ii_mes_19891208_xxiii-world-day-for-peace.html

Johnson, Mary, et al. *New Generations of Catholic Sisters: The Challenge of Diversity*. New York: Oxford University Press, 2014.

Kryszak, Jennifer. "Imaging Church: Religious Practices, Ecclesiology, and the Ministry of Art." PhD diss., Duke University, 2014.

—————. "A Theology of Transformation: Catholic Sisters and the Visual Practice of Church." *Ecclesial Practices: The Journal of Ecclesiology and Ethnography* 3 (2016) 70–93.

McCormick, Patrick. *God's Beauty: A Call to Justice.* Collegeville, MN: Liturgical, 2012.

McNamara, Jo Ann Kay. *Sisters in Arms: Catholic Nuns through Two Millennia.* Cambridge, MA: Harvard University Press, 1996.

Médaille, Jean-Pierre. *Documents of the Little Design St. Flour.* Translated by M. Nepper and the Intercongregational Research Team. N.P.: N.P., 1973.

Morgan, David. *The Embodied Eye: Religious Visual Culture and the Social Life of Feeling.* Berkeley: University of California Press, 2012.

Nepper, Marius. *Origins: The Sisters of Saint Joseph.* Translated by the Federation of the Sisters of Saint Joseph, U.S.A. Erie, PA: Villa Maria College, 1975.

Ross, Susan A. *For the Beauty of the Earth: Women, Sacramentality, and Justice.* New York: Paulist, 2006.

Schneiders, Sandra M. *Buying the Field: Catholic Religious Life in Mission to the World.* Religious Life in a New Millenium 3. New York: Paulist, 2013.

Second Vatican Council. *Perfectae caritatis*: Decree on the Adaptation and Renewal of Religious Life, Promulgated by Pope Paul VI, 28 October, 1965. Documents of the II Vatican Council. Vatican Website. http://www.vatican.va/archive/hist_councils/ii_vatican_council/documents/vat-ii_decree_19651028_perfectae-caritatis_en.html.

Taylor, Sarah McFarland. *Green Sisters: A Spiritual Ecology.* Cambridge, MA: Harvard University Press, 2007.

U.S. Federation Sisters of Saint Joseph. "Human Trafficking." http://www.sistersofsaintjosephfederation.org/justice-peace/human-trafficking.

Vacher, Marguerite. *Nuns without Cloister: Sisters of St. Joseph in the Seventeenth and Eighteenth Centuries.* Translated by Patricia Byrne and the United States Federation of the Sisters of St. Joseph. Lanham, MD: University Press of America, 2010.

CHAPTER 4

Pope Francis and His Phenomenology of *Encuentro*

—Donald Wallenfang, OCDS

Abstract:

Every man elected pope has big shoes to fill and Jorge Mario Bergoglio is no exception to this rule. His two predecessors, John Paul II and Benedict XVI, were prolific academics before ascending to the Chair of Peter. While Francis may not be the blazoned scholar that his forerunners were—his doctoral dissertation begun on the work of Romano Guardini remains unfinished to this day—he nevertheless exhibits an approach to life and ministry that could be described as phenomenological. Above all, Francis has intimated a definite theology of encounter (*encuentro*) with the living God and with one's neighbor. Appearing no less than thirty-four times in his recent apostolic exhortation, *Evangelii gaudium*, the word "encounter" may be one of the best expressions of Francis's ministerial vision for the Church. The notion of encounter is highly phenomenological because the method of phenomenology is structured around conscious encounter with any and all phenomena, whether they be God, the other, or a plate of spaghetti. In this essay, I will examine the implicit connection between the method of phenomenology and Francis's theology of encounter. Further, I will argue that instruction in phenomenology fosters an attitude of encounter about which Francis not only speaks, but personally lives. Just as phenomenology helped to unlock hidden insights about human personhood and sexuality in the work of John Paul II—such as his

Theology of the Body corpus—likewise will phenomenology continue to disclose the cloistered gems of divine mystery that saturate the created order.

Why Phenomenology?

G iven the daunting task of the New Evangelization today—a task to be shared by all of the faithful—new methods and approaches are required to adapt to the radical change in cultural context on a global scale.[1] At a time in which one's personal experience is set as the supreme arbiter of truth, effective evangelization has no other route than to appeal to the real-life experiences of its audience. And there is no better method at accessing the essential of human experience than phenomenology.

However, we must begin with the question, what is phenomenology? Because there are virtually no textbooks or easy synopses on the method, it is difficult to pin down exactly what phenomenology is.[2] Once I asked the prolific phenomenologist, Jean-Luc Marion, if it were possible to write a textbook for phenomenology. He said that it would be a difficult enterprise because "phenomenology is not a set of doctrines, but a toolbox." With limited literature on the easy-to-understand fundamentals of the method, we must rely on those who have studied phenomenology extensively to communicate its most basic points. This is precisely what I propose to do to begin this essay.

As the word suggests, phenomenology is the science of phenomena. Derived from the Greek verb, *phainomai* ("to be visible, to appear, to seem"), phenomenology examines that which gives itself to meaningful perception. It not only asks, what gives?, but more importantly, what does it mean? Because it investigates meaning and signification specifically, phenomenology is bound up inextricably with interpretation. In his book, *Plurality and Ambiguity*, David Tracy writes that "any act of interpretation involves at least

1. See the Introduction of this volume.

2. Some helpful primers on the method of phenomenology include Husserl, *Idea of Phenomenology*; Sokolowski, *Introduction to Phenomenology*; Moran, *Introduction to Phenomenology*; Käufer and Chemero, *Phenomenology*; and Marion, *Being Given*. But even these are rather limited in scope and in their accessibility for the average person. It is important to note that the method of phenomenology has undergone expansive development since its inception with the work of Husserl in the early twentieth century. At present, two distinct trajectories of phenomenology have been set: (1) phenomenology of givenness and (2) hermeneutic phenomenology. For more on this distinction, see Wallenfang, *Dialectical Anatomy of the Eucharist*.

three realities: some phenomenon to be interpreted, someone interpreting that phenomenon, and some interaction between these first two realities."[3] These are the basic building blocks of phenomenology: (1) the human subject, (2) the phenomenon that gives itself to conscious perception, and (3) the interaction between the human subject and the phenomenon. Following Edmund Husserl's original intention, Tracy goes on to say that "in order to avoid the temptations to pure subjectivity, it is better to start not with the interpreter but with the phenomenon requiring interpretation."[4] Husserl, the founder of phenomenology, would insist on returning to "the things themselves," as he put it.[5] Instead of allowing experience to swim in a sea of subjectivity and in relative approximations of the real, phenomenology reverses the typical approach to reality: it is not so much I who determines the world, it is more so the world that determines me. In other words, it is not up to me to dictate what gives itself to me, but what gives itself to me gives itself by itself, without my permission and apart from any arbitrary parameters that I would enforce. My role simply is to receive the phenomenon as it gives itself. It is toward this self-givenness of phenomena that phenomenology turns its attention.

In order to access this pure and uncompromised self-givenness, the method of phenomenology begins with its most important step: the reduction. The phenomenological reduction works to bracket and to set aside any and all biases, presuppositions and prejudices that may interfere with receiving the pure self-givenness of a phenomenon. In a word, judgment is what phenomenology always tries to avoid. Judgment is what must be reduced in order to access the pure data, or givens, of conscious perception. Let us consider an example of exercising the reduction. I'm at a special dinner with colleagues at a nice restaurant in town. It comes time to order our meals. I lean over to my friend and ask him what he knows about the dish

3. Tracy, *Plurality and Ambiguity*, 10.

4. Ibid., 10.

5. See Husserl, *Logical Investigations*, 1:168: "Meanings inspired only by remote, confused, inauthentic intuitions—if by any intuitions at all—are not enough: we must go back to the 'things themselves'"; Husserl, *Ideas*, 1:35–36: "But to judge rationally or scientifically about things signifies to conform *to the things themselves* or to go from words and opinions back to the things themselves, to consult them in their self-givenness and to set aside all prejudices alien to them . . . The essential fault in empiricistic argumentation consists of identifying or confusing the fundamental demand for a return to the 'things themselves' with the demand for legitimation of all cognition by *experience*. With his comprehensible naturalistic constriction of the limits bounding cognizable 'things,' the empiricist simply takes experience to be the only act that is presentive of things themselves"; and Heidegger, *Being and Time*, 58: "Thus 'phenomenology' means . . . to let that which shows itself be seen from itself in the very way in which it shows itself from itself."

called *Bouillabaisse*. He says that it's a kind of seafood stew and that he has tended to have disappointing experiences with it. I order it, nevertheless, taking a chance as to what I might encounter.

In a little while the dish is served amidst a kind of fanfare with its unusual iron pot, the server removing its lid with a hot pad, and its ladle and extra bowl. So far my colleagues are impressed with the culinary accoutrements, and so am I. I then scoop the stew into the bowl with the ladle. The waitress asks if I would like grated cheese over the stew and I say yes, please. Suspending all judgment, I dip my spoon into the stew and taste. Such warmth, such flavor, such gratitude. All is lighting up in this restaurant. Another friend says, "He must like it, he's making noise over there." Indeed, "Mmmmm." Not only am I enjoying the *Bouillabaisse*, I am enjoying the company of my friends, of the many other people in the restaurant—the sounds, the beauty, the wonder, the life, the goodness. Everything is lighting up in the way it gives itself to me with such decisiveness.

Because of the phenomenological reduction, I am able to access the saturation of givenness that floods my perception. If I were to remain in the so-called natural attitude, I would be perceptually arrested, oblivious to the wonders giving themselves to me all around. To go on perceiving with the natural attitude, I may assume that "there's nothing new under the sun" (see Ecclesiastes 1:9) and I may conduct myself according to self-interests or according to social conventions and manners that I think I should be observing in order to appear socially acceptable to others. Instead, phenomenology casts aside inhibition and those kinds of peer pressures that stifle the uncanny, the wonderful, the surprising. For phenomenology, the only expectation is to be surprised. It is most helpful to give an example of the phenomenological attitude at work with its hermeneutic of generosity and magnanimity, rather than to try to define the host of terms involved in its analytics. Phenomenology is more about an approach to life than it is about a set of terms, rules or doctrines. It leads to contemplation of the cosmos as question, as opening, as possibility. As Martin Heidegger writes in *Being and Time*, for phenomenology, "higher than actuality stands *possibility*. We can understand phenomenology only by seizing upon it as a possibility."[6] Phenomenology protects and promotes possibility as the only absolute. If "the proof is in the pudding," after all, phenomenology is so persuasive since it gives the fullest access to the "pudding" of experience.

Phenomenology is a champion of encounter. All is encounter: the encounter between the self and the phenomenon, even regarding the many phenomena that comprise the self, such as consciousness, perception, the

6. Heidegger, *Being and Time*, 63.

will, feeling, etc. Considering the Latin etymology of the word encounter, *in-contra* ("against, contrary, opposite, adverse"), every encounter involves contact with another—with an other-than-the-self, an otherwise-than-the-self. The very method of phenomenology is fashioned around this encounter between the self and the other. Phenomenology's sole task is to describe this encounter with as much detail as possible—a description which has no boundaries and no end, and its beginning perpetually lags behind the event of encounter toward which it returns to describe. Phenomenology comes to terms with experience like no other method can. It is master of experience because it knows how to yield to the givens of experience rather than manipulate, dominate or exploit them. In other words, phenomenology teaches one to yield to the imposition of the phenomenon—to be dispossessed by becoming possessed by what gives itself according to its own jurisdiction. The self is called to give way to the sway of the gift of the given. Judgment must be inverted so that I am no longer judge of the phenomenon, but its witness.

We find something similar in Jesus of Nazareth and the testimonies that surround his life and message: "Stop judging and you will not be judged. Stop condemning and you will not be condemned. Forgive and you will be forgiven. Give and gifts will be given to you; a good measure, packed together, shaken down, and overflowing, will be poured into your lap. For the measure with which you measure will in return be measured out to you" (Luke 6:37–38); "If any one hears my sayings and does not keep them, I do not judge him; for I did not come to judge the world but to save the world" (John 12:47 [RSV]); "For God did not send his Son into the world to condemn the world, but that the world might be saved through him" (John 3:17); "For the Son of Man did not come to be served but to serve and to give his life as a ransom for many" (Mark 10:45); "For the Son of Man has come to seek and to save what was lost" (Luke 19:10). If there is one thing that can be said about divine love as revealed to the end in Christ, it is that it is merciful. In other words, it gives. It never ceases to give. And in order to give without ceasing, it demands that obstacles to its giving be bracketed and set aside.

Divine love bears with the other patiently, suspending the time of judgment in order to give room for the time of conversion: "The Lord does not delay his promise, as some regard 'delay,' but he is patient with you, not wishing that any should perish but that all should come to repentance" (2 Peter 3:9). Akin to the method of phenomenology, Jesus appears over and over again to suspend judgment on sinners in order to open the possibility of their conversion upon encounter with his relentless love. Perhaps Jesus could be portrayed as phenomenologist par excellence in the way that his gaze and attuned hearing perceive with endless wonder and generosity, "mak(ing) what is totally unloveworthy into something worthy of love. And (he) does that by loving it."[7] As circulation of gift, love demands patience and forbearance. The greatest acts of love are those that cannot be rushed: raising a child, sitting at a person's bedside when death is imminent, sharing a meal with family and friends, bearing a son or daughter in the womb over the course of months, crafting or performing a work of art. Time belongs to love inasmuch as there is much loving to be done. Retrospectively, it is not inconceivable for the Gospel to be read as a phenomenological score in the key of mercy.

Pope Francis the Phenomenologist

Since March 13, 2013, mercy has been the posture of the pontificate of Francis. Bernard of Clairvaux expresses the essence of divine mercy in these words, "It is true that the creature loves less [than God] because she is less. But if she loves with her whole being, nothing is lacking where everything is given."[8] Similarly, Francis quotes an *abuela* who came to him for confession: "If the Lord didn't forgive everything, our world would not exist."[9] It is because of the extravagance and exorbitance of divine (for-)givenness, that is, grace, that nothing is lacking—that everything is possible through God in whom "all things are possible" (Matthew 19:26). Over the past three years, Francis never has tired of singing this refrain of mercy to the Church, especially in proclaiming 2015–2016 an Extraordinary Jubilee Year of Mercy.[10] Like Jesus, Francis insists that "the Church does not exist to condemn people but to bring about an encounter with the visceral love of God's mercy. I often say that in order for this to happen, it is necessary to go out."[11] To

7. Jüngel, *God as the Mystery of the World*, 329.

8. Bernard of Clairvaux, *Sermo* 83.4–6, as quoted in Paul VI, *Liturgy of the Hours*, 4:1334.

9. Francis, *The Name of God Is Mercy*, 25.

10. See Francis, *Misericordiae vultus*; and Francis, *The Name of God Is Mercy*.

11. Francis, *The Name of God Is Mercy*, 52. Also, see ibid., 92: "As Luke writes in the Gospel: 'When the Lord saw her, he was moved with pity for her' (7:13). God Incarnate let himself be moved by human wretchedness, by our need, by our suffering. The Greek verb that indicates this compassion is σπλαγχνίζομαι [*splanchnízomai*, ed.], which derives from the word that indicates internal organs or the mother's womb. It is similar to the love of a father and mother who are profoundly moved by their own son; it is a visceral love. God loves us in this way, with compassion and mercy. Jesus does not look at reality from the outside, without letting himself be moved, as if he were taking a picture. He lets himself get involved. This kind of compassion is needed today to conquer the globalization of indifference. This kind of regard is needed when we find ourselves in

encounter the visceral love of God's mercy, the Church must go out of itself, the self must go out of itself en route toward the other. A daily exodus must take place as the self evacuates itself in becoming responsible for the other over and over again.[12] This is the universal summons of love and mercy. Love is attentive to the other and mercy is the inscape of empathy. Mercy signifies solicitude—an incessant visceral provocation by the boundless needs of the other who faces me.

With his affinity for a "culture of encounter," Francis, like Christ, can be regarded as phenomenologist par excellence.[13] Using the word "encounter" nine times in a 2013 homily delivered to the Brazilian bishops, priests, religious and seminarians, Francis declared that,

> We are called by God, called to proclaim the Gospel, and called to promote the culture of encounter . . . 'Being with' Christ does not mean isolating ourselves from others. Rather, it is a 'being with' in order to go forth and encounter others . . . Encountering and welcoming everyone, solidarity—a word that is being hidden by this culture, as if it were a bad word—solidarity and fraternity: these are what make our society truly human. Be servants of communion and of the culture of encounter! I would like you to be almost obsessed about this. Be so without being presumptuous, imposing 'our truths,' but rather be guided by the humble yet joyful certainty of those who have been found, touched and transformed by the Truth who is Christ, ever to be proclaimed (cf. Luke 24:13–35) . . . God calls us, by name and by surname, each one of us, to proclaim the Gospel and to promote the culture of encounter with joy.[14]

---

front of a poor person, an outcast, or a sinner. This is the compassion that nourishes the awareness that we, too, are sinners"; and Francis, *General Audience*, October 16, 2013: "I insist on this missionary aspect, because Christ invites all to 'go out' and encounter others, he sends us, he asks us to move in order to spread the joy of the Gospel!"

12. See Levinas, *On Escape*.

13. See Francis, *Message for the 48th World Communications Day*: "A culture of encounter demands that we be ready not only to give, but also to receive"; Francis, *Homily*, May 22, 2013: "[T]he 'culture of encounter' that is the foundation of peace . . . Today is [the feast of] Saint Rita, Patron Saint of impossible things—this seems impossible: let us ask of her this grace, this grace that all, all, all people would do good and that we would encounter one another in this work, which is a work of creation, like the creation of the Father. A work of the family, because we are all children of God, all of us, all of us! And God loves us, all of us! May Saint Rita grant us this grace, which seems almost impossible. Amen"; and Francis, *Evangelii gaudium*, 171: "We need to practice the art of listening, which is more than simply hearing. Listening, in communication, is an openness of heart which makes possible that closeness without which genuine spiritual encounter cannot occur." Cf. Francis, *Encountering Truth*, 81–82.

14. Francis, *Homily for Mass with Brazilian Bishops, Priests, Religious and Seminarians*, July 27, 2013.

Just as phenomenology clears an opening to receive a phenomenon in its pure givenness, promoting a culture of encounter fosters at atmosphere of hospitality to welcome the other in his or her mysterious totality. A genuine solidarity and communion of persons is formed as the fruit of a culture built on the priority of encounter. A culture of encounter awakens the vigilance to be on the lookout for the other with loving anticipation, just as Christ was on the lookout for those he came to save.[15] Francis even characterizes the meaning of holiness as constantly being open to encounter with Christ: "Holiness is not just a collection of virtues. Indeed, such a conception of holiness causes great harm; it stifles our hearts, and after a while it fashions us into Pharisees. Holiness means 'walking in the presence of God and being perfect'; holiness means living in constant encounter with Jesus Christ."[16] Holiness is not the work of exclusion, but of hospitality, healing and inclusion. Holiness does not set oneself apart from others according to some misguided supremacy complex, but rather empowers the other to be set apart for God as well.

For his papal motto, he elected that which had been his motto as Archbishop of Buenos Aires: *miserando atque eligendo* ("to be shown mercy and to be chosen").[17] Taken from a homily of Bede the Venerable on the calling of Matthew, this motto signifies that "it was not you who chose me, but I who chose you" (John 15:16). In phenomenological fashion, God's mercy, as phenomenon, crashes upon the human subject from without—even from a without within the self. The self does not choose or determine the phenomenon of mercy, but vice versa. To experience God's mercy is to surrender, to give in to the chase. Edith Stein says it this way, "The person 'keeps himself' on the higher level . . . to a large extent by merely 'letting it happen,' by not deliberately stopping it."[18] Letting grace happen is the disposition of mercy.

15. See Francis, *Open Mind, Faithful Heart*, 10: "The Lord himself recommends that we be vigilantly on the lookout for this encounter. Jesus searches for me. He does not view us as part of a crowd but seeks us out one by one, searching our hearts. Vigilance means being receptive to the wisdom that will help us discern Jesus and truly find him. Sometimes the Lord passes by our side and we don't even see him—or else we 'know him so well' that we don't recognize him. Our vigilance is the prayerful attitude that makes us want to keep him with us when he seems to want to 'continue on his way' (Mark 6:48–50; Luke 24:28–30)."

16. Francis, *Open Mind, Faithful Heart*, 8.

17. See Francis, *The Name of God Is Mercy*, 11.

18. Stein, *Potency and Act*, 409. Cf. Francis, *Way of Humility*, 47: "It is possible for someone to be a great sinner and yet never fall into corruption. That may have been the case of Zacchaeus, Matthew, the Samaritan woman, Nicodemus, and the Good Thief, who had something in their sinful hearts that saved them from corruption. The clinging to self-containment that is characteristic of corrupt people had not yet taken shape in them; they were still open to forgiveness. Their deeds were born of a sinful heart; many

The essence of grace is not something that I can produce, but something that I first receive and then circulate. Wounds of the heart can be healed only if they are laid bare before the divine Heartmender.

In his signature apostolic exhortation, *Evangelii gaudium*, Francis positions encounter with divine mercy at the forefront of his message. He understands it to be the raison d'être of ministry and of the Church. Francis recalls the Thomistic elevation of mercy as the fountainhead of all virtues: "Thomas thus explains that, as far as external works are concerned, mercy is the greatest of all the virtues: 'In itself mercy is the greatest of the virtues, since all the others revolve around it and, more than this, it makes up for their deficiencies. This is particular to the superior virtue, and as such it is proper to God to have mercy, through which his omnipotence is manifested to the greatest degree.'"[19] Mercy reigns supreme among the virtues because of its generosity and redoubled potency. In other words, mercy is never finished or finalized. It is gift in action—given in advance and re-actualized in the aftermath of a misdeed as forgiveness. This is expressed well in the words of Shakespeare's Portia to Shylock in *The Merchant of Venice*:

> The quality of mercy is not strain'd,
>
> It droppeth as the gentle rain from heaven
>
> Upon the place beneath: it is twice blest;
>
> It blesseth him that gives and him that takes:
>
> 'Tis mightiest in the mightiest: it becomes
>
> The throned monarch better than his crown;
>
> > His sceptre shows the force of temporal power,
> >
> > The attribute to awe and majesty,
> >
> > Wherein doth sit the dread and fear of kings;
> >
> > But mercy is above this sceptred sway;
> >
> > It is enthroned in the hearts of kings,
> >
> > It is an attribute to God himself;
> >
> > And earthly power doth then show likest God's

---

of them were evil deeds, but at the same time the heart that produced them could feel its own weakness. And that was where God's strength could find a way in"; and Francis, *Encountering Truth*, 73: "The problem is not in being sinners; the problem is when we do not repent of our sins, when we are not ashamed of what we have done. That is the problem. And Peter has this shame, this humility, doesn't he? The sin, the sin of Peter, is something that with the great heart that Peter had, led him to a new encounter with Jesus, to the joy of forgiveness."

19. Francis, *Evangelii gaudium*, 37.

> When mercy seasons justice. Therefore, Jew,
>
> Though justice be thy plea, consider this,
>
> That, in the course of justice, none of us
>
> Should see salvation: we do pray for mercy;
>
> And that same prayer doth teach us all to render
>
> The deeds of mercy.

As the very definition of eloquence, this Shakespearean passage indicates the graciousness of mercy that is never strained, is twice blessed, and is the might of mightiness. It is the divine attribute that makes salvation possible for all those who are implicated in the compromise of justice, due both to natural weakness and finitude, and to voluntary transgression of justice's demands. Rooted in the biblical terms חֶסֶד (hesed), רַחֲמִים (rahamim), ἔλεος (eleos), and misericordia, the term "mercy" connotes several shades of meaning, including "kindness, compassion, goodness, piety, fidelity, clemency, forbearance, humility, abundance, godliness, brotherhood, sisterhood, motherly feeling, love." It is revelatory to observe that one of the Hebrew terms for "mercy," רַחֲמִים (rahamim), is related closely to the Hebrew term for "womb," רֶחֶם (rehem/raham). This suggests that to be merciful to someone means to care for her as in one's womb. Moreover, the English word "mercy" is derived from the Latin word merces, which means "the price to be paid for something." Mercy, therefore, signifies that which is paid in remission of a debt owed. Mercy involves the logic of the double negative in which a debt cancelled is a credit earned.[20] Suffering redeems suffering and the transfer of gift supplies what is lacking in its recipient.

Throughout the course of his pontificate, Francis has been calling the Church back to its most foundational vocation: to facilitate the encounter with God's mercy. This is a constant theme in all of his interviews, messages and writings. Because mercy is such a delicate and precarious procedure, Francis is careful to articulate its paradox. Mercy happens to the measure that those involved in its circuit yield to the advent of its unpredictable encounter. It is a procedure that neither can be coerced nor contrived. It is an encounter not with an idea, but with the incarnate Person, Jesus Christ. This encounter occurs in many ways, but always begins with the call of Christ:

> The encounter with Jesus always involves a call; the call may be
> a great one or a small one, but it is always there (Matt 4:18–19;
> 9:9; 10:1–4). The encounter may happen at any time, and it is
> pure gratuity, totally unmerited (Matt 20:5–6). Sometimes the

20. See Wallenfang, Human and Divine Being, chapter 2, for further details on "the logic of the double negative."

encounter must be sought out (Matt 8:2–3; 9:9); it may require heroic persistence (Matt 15:21–40) or loud shouts (Matt 8:24–25). The seeking may even entail painful confusion and doubt (Luke 7:18–24; Matt 11:2–7). However it happens, the encounter with Jesus Christ leads us toward ever greater humility (Luke 5:4–10). His invitation can be rejected or half-heartedly accepted (Matt 13:1–23). When it is rejected, pain pierces the heart of Christ (Matt 23:37–39; Matt 11:20–30). Seeking out Christ and finding him is not the anodyne exercise of a Pelagian spirit; rather, it assumes that there is sin and repentance (Matt 21:28–32). The encounter with Jesus Christ takes place in our daily lives, in the direct contact of prayer, in the wise discernment of the signs of the times (Matt 24:32–33; Luke 21:29–32), and in our brothers and sisters (Matt 25:31–46; Luke 10:25–37).[21]

Humility and vigilance are the conditions for the possibility of encounter with divine mercy. It begins with the call of Christ, but the call must be perceived in order to respond to it. It is not an anodyne and bland experience, but involves pain, suffering and disorientation in order for transformation to occur. The testimonies of the saints are unanimous on this point concerning the spiritual life: no pain, no gain. One must be grieved over one's sins in order to turn away from them and to embark on the way of spiritual perfection. Just as in the method of phenomenology, one must be able to identify the "natural attitude" in order to bracket it and to set it aside.

For its first step, phenomenology requires conversion of the natural attitude. Similarly, the first step of the New Evangelization is the call to conversion.[22] Encounter with a phenomenon, with the phenomenon of Christ and the phenomenon of the other, always involve something new.[23] Mercy is the name for the inclination and intentionality toward openness and generosity before the other—the other which is never identical to the self. Phenomenology fosters this openness that is exhibited by Christ and all the saints in their outlook toward the world. In his teaching and pastoral ministry witness, Pope Francis has proved himself to live with a kind of phenomenological approach to things, whether he would call it that or not. With his Jesuit hermeneutic involving all of the senses and a vivid imagina-

21. Francis, *Open Mind, Faithful Heart*, 9–10.

22. See USCCB, *Compendium on the New Evangelization*, 505, 1060, 1074, 1176, 1179.

23. See Isa 43:18–19: "Remember not the events of the past, the things of long ago consider not; see, I am doing something new! Now it springs forth, do you not perceive it? In the wilderness I make a way, in the wasteland, rivers"; 2 Cor 5:17: "So whoever is in Christ is a new creation: the old things have passed away; behold, new things have come."

tion for the sake of meditation and contemplation, Francis embodies a phenomenological approach to life and ministry. Perhaps his past experience in teaching psychology and literature during the 1960's in Santa Fé and Buenos Aires attuned him to the *sitz im leben* of generosity and receptivity to the other. Perhaps his love for dancing the tango, listening to opera, playing soccer and the piano helped to form his proclivity for possibility and wonder.[24] Undoubtedly, his extensive ministerial experience as a parish priest, as a confessor, as a Rector, and as Provincial of the Jesuits in Argentina shaped his attention to real-life experience as the beginning and end of theology. In any case, from the point of view of phenomenology, Francis is someone who demonstrates its fruits in a paradigmatic way.

Why Study Phenomenology?

In an essay entitled, "Christian Living Formerly and Today," Karl Rahner writes that "the devout Christian of the future will either be a 'mystic,' one who has 'experienced' something, or he will cease to be anything at all."[25] At the same time, in the opening sentence of his 2013 article on the artwork of James Turrell entitled, "Contemplative Recovery," Jeffrey Kosky writes that "one way to understand modernity is as the age in which contemplation is repressed, marginalized, or otherwise forgotten."[26] How can one become a contemplative mystic today in an age in which the demands of technology outstrip the universal human vocation to contemplate the cosmos? This very well may be the greatest challenge of our times. Seriously. We have forgotten how to listen to the songs of the birds and the trickle of the stream. We have forgotten how to gaze at the stars as they bequeath their testimony of creativity. We have forgotten how to sow seeds by hand and to await with patience their miraculous metamorphosis. We have forgotten. We are a people that has become more transient than we are stable, more distracted than we are attentive, more preoccupied than we are occupied. We are living in a hidden crisis of a proportion unmatched in human history—as hidden as the silent victims in their mother's wombs, as hidden as the children trafficked as objects with price tags for perverse consumption, as hidden as all of the conversations not had in families that are fragmented to pieces and glued to pixels. The unmistakable irony is that the beautiful and creative hiddenness of contemplation has been usurped by the ugly and destructive hiddenness of consumption. Contemplation creatively gives. Consumption

24. See Piqué, *Pope Francis*, 46–47.
25. Rahner, *Theological Investigations*, 7:15.
26. Kosky, "Contemplative Recovery," 44.

destructively takes. Given this bleak picture of human existence, what are we to do?

Contemplate. Yet how are we to contemplate if we never have "experienced" something—if we have lost the art form of encounter?[27] We must rediscover it. We must be taught it once again. And who are the great pedagogues of the art form of encounter and the métier of contemplation: Christ, the saints, the Church. Yes, these are enough. However, holistic education is paramount for developing an intellect able to withstand the talons of technology that threaten to choke out any remaining impetus for contemplation's gaze of wonder. Technological hype infiltrates the natural and supernatural sources of contemplation, hypnotizing first the senses and second the spirit. An intellectual antidote is required that cultivates perception attuned to mystery and that discovers again and again transcendence disclosed through immanence. A deconstruction of technology is needed to prevent a collapse of the soul into the dictatorship of technocracy. Phenomenology is that method positioned to rejuvenate the soul's yearning for the beautiful, the true, and the good. As indicated above, phenomenology is the method with the competence to call a thing what it is and to identify with precision all unwarranted biases and prejudices that blur the revelation of givenness.

My hypothesis is that training in phenomenology, especially as the method has evolved up to the present, promotes an attitude of wonder and the openness necessary for true encounter to take place. While classic metaphysics forever will remain the backbone and anchor of the truth of being, phenomenology may serve as a stimulating ancillary to the stark soberness of metaphysics. Because it appeals to real-life experience in all its rawness and detail, phenomenology is poised to act as a bridge between the givenness of experience itself and contemplation of that same experience. Whereas metaphysics approaches truth "through the front door," phenomenology approximates truth "through the back door." In the game of American football, this is what's called an "end-around." Surprise. Phenomenology, as a method, unveils the dynamism of surprise and wonder necessary to enter the arena of authentic encounter. Francis writes of the religious experience that "if (it) doesn't have this measure of astonishment, of surprise, if this compassion is not sprung upon you—then it's cold, it

---

27. Cf. Rom 10:14–15, 17: "But how can they call on him in whom they have not believed? And how can they believe in him of whom they have not heard? And how can they hear without someone to preach? And how can people preach unless they are sent? As it is written, 'How beautiful are the feet of those who bring [the] good news!' . . . Thus faith comes from what is heard, and what is heard comes through the word of Christ."

doesn't draw us in completely; it's a different kind of experience that doesn't bring us to a transcendental plane . . . oases are very important to the religious experience."[28] If Pope Francis is right to place the accent on encounter within the process of evangelization, which I think he is, phenomenology may be a potent contributor to building this culture of encounter by shaping the soul to contemplate once again.

Bibliography

Francis, Pope. *Encountering Truth: Meeting God in the Everyday.* Translated by Matthew Sherry. New York: Image, 2015.

———. *General Audience.* October 16, 2013. https://w2.vatican.va/content/francesco/en/audiences/2013/documents/papa-francesco_20131016_udienza-generale.html.

———. *Homily.* May 22, 2013. http://w2.vatican.va/content/francesco/en/cotidie/2013/documents/papa-francesco-cotidie_20130522_to-do-good.html.

———. *Homily for Mass with Brazilian Bishops, Priests, Religious and Seminarians.* July 27, 2013. http://w2.vatican.va/content/francesco/en/homilies/2013/documents/papa-francesco_20130727_gmg-omelia-rio-clero.html.

———. *Message for the 48th World Communications Day.* 2014. https://w2.vatican.va/content/francesco/en/messages/communications/documents/papa-francesco_20140124_messaggio-comunicazioni-sociali.html.

———. *Misericordiae vultus.* 2015. https://w2.vatican.va/content/francesco/en/apost_letters/documents/papa-francesco_bolla_20150411_misericordiae-vultus.html.

———. *The Name of God Is Mercy: A Conversation with Andrea Tornielli.* Translated by Oonagh Stransky. New York: Random House, 2016.

———. *Open Mind, Faithful Heart: Reflections on Following Jesus.* Translated by Joseph V. Owens. New York: Crossroad, 2013.

———. *The Way of Humility: Corruption and Sin; On Self-Accusation.* Translated by Helena Scott. San Francisco: Ignatius, 2013.

Gubser, Michael. *The Far Reaches: Phenomenology, Ethics, and Social Renewal in Central Europe.* Stanford, CA: Stanford University Press, 2014.

Heidegger, Martin. *Being and Time.* Translated by John Macquarrie and Edward Robinson. San Francisco: HarperCollins, 1962.

Husserl, Edmund. *Cartesian Meditations: An Introduction to Phenomenology.* Translated by Dorion Cairns. The Hague: Nihoff, 1960.

———. *The Idea of Phenomenology.* Translated by L. Hardy. Boston: Kluwer, 1990.

———. *Ideas Pertaining to a Pure Phenomenology and to a Phenomenological Philosophy.* Translated by F. Kersten. Boston: Nijhoff, 1982.

———. *Introduction to the Logical Investigations.* Translated by Philip Bossert and C. H. Peters. The Hague: Martinus Nijhoff, 1975.

———. *Logical Investigations.* Vols. 1–2. Translated by J. N. Findlay. New York: Routledge, 2001.

28. Rubin and Ambrogetti, *Pope Francis*, 41–42. Cf. Francis, *Encountering Truth,* 7, 305–6.

Jüngel, Eberhard. *God as the Mystery of the World: On the Foundation of the Theology of the Crucified One in the Dispute between Theism and Atheism.* Translated by Darrell L. Guder. Grand Rapids: Eerdmans, 1983.

Käufer, Stephan, and Anthony Chemero. *Phenomenology: An Introduction.* Cambridge: Polity, 2015.

Kosky, Jeffrey L. "Contemplative Recovery: The Artwork of James Turrell." *Cross Currents* 63, no. 1 (2013) 44–61.

Levinas, Emmanuel. *On Escape.* Translated by Bettina Bergo. Stanford, CA: Stanford University Press, 2003.

Marion, Jean-Luc. *Being Given: Toward a Phenomenology of Givenness.* Translated by Jeffrey L. Kosky. Stanford, CA: Stanford University Press, 2002.

Moran, Dermot. *Introduction to Phenomenology.* New York: Routledge, 2000.

Paul VI. *The Liturgy of the Hours according to the Roman Rite.* 4 vols. Translated by the International Commission on English in the Liturgy. New York: Catholic Book, 1975.

Piqué, Elisabetta. *Pope Francis: Life and Revolution, a Biography of Jorge Bergoglio.* Translated by Anna Mazzotti and Lydia Colin. Chicago: Loyola, 2014.

Rahner, Karl. *Theological Investigations.* Vol. 7. Translated by David Bourke. New York: Herder & Herder, 1971.

Rubin, Sergio, and Francesca Ambrogetti. *Pope Francis: Conversations with Jorge Bergoglio.* Translated by Laura Dail Literary Agency, Inc. New York: Putnam's Sons, 2013.

Sokolowski, Robert. *Introduction to Phenomenology.* New York: Cambridge University Press, 2000.

Stein, Edith. *Potency and Act: Studies Toward a Philosophy of Being.* Translated by Walter Redmond. Washington, DC: ICS, 2009.

Tracy, David. *Plurality and Ambiguity: Hermeneutics, Religion, Hope.* Chicago: University of Chicago Press, 1987.

United States Conference of Catholic Bishops. *Compendium on the New Evangelization: Texts of the Pontifical and Conciliar Magisterium: 1939–2012.* Washington, DC: USCCB, 2015.

Wallenfang, Donald. *Dialectical Anatomy of the Eucharist: An Étude in Phenomenology.* Eugene, OR: Cascade, 2017.

———. *Human and Divine Being: A Study on the Theological Anthropology of Edith Stein.* Eugene, OR: Cascade, 2017.

Wuerl, Donald. *New Evangelization: Passing on the Catholic Faith Today.* Huntington, IN: Our Sunday Visitor, 2013.

Ecological Encounters

CHAPTER 5 _____

"Everything Is Related"

Laudato si' and the Ascent from Creation to God

—BRIAN PEDRAZA

Abstract:

Pope Francis's encyclical *Laudato si'* undoubtedly contributes to the body of modern Catholic Social Teaching and encourages urgent action concerning the environment. Less attention, however, has been paid to its implications for the New Evangelization. By reading the document through a Franciscan and particularly Bonaventurian lens, this chapter argues that the pope's call for an integral ecology is simultaneously a way of proclaiming the Gospel. Francis's vision of the interrelatedness of all creation thus acts as a pathway by which the Church can proclaim the Trinitarian God. Indeed, for Francis, the attainment of an integral ecology requires not only the communion of human beings with the environment and with each other, but with God who, as the source of creation, is a communion in himself.

No less than nine times does Pope Francis declare in his encyclical, *Laudato si'*, that "everything is related" or words of a similar nature.[1] The constant refrain might sound needless in the ears of a western culture that seemingly prizes the relatedness of beings: election years bring calls to solidarity; globalization is a dominant paradigm in such disparate fields as

---

1. See Francis, *Laudato si'*, 70, 91, 92, 117, 120, 137, 138, 142, and 240. Clearly, as Francis states in 138, "it cannot be emphasized enough how everything is interconnected."

education and economics; the emergence of the so-called "sharing economy" trades on the experience of personal involvement; and who could deny the nearly ubiquitous use of social media and its massive web of interconnectivity, no doubt a hallmark of this period of history?

And yet, in a document aimed at the reversal of environmental degradation, Francis's diagnosis is precisely this: we are individualistic and disconnected, not only from each other but from the world. Because we do not recognize the dignity of other persons nor perceive the created world as a gift, we use the first and seek to dominate the second. Thus, when we put on the clothing of solidarity, we often do so to advance more properly individualistic motives. When we immerse ourselves in the alternate universe of social media, we often do so to escape our own reality. Reading the "signs of the times" today, we might say that our culture is gripped by the tension between longing for relationship and clasping to individualism.

In this chapter I would like to explore Francis's call for a return to relationship—what he calls an "integral ecology"—and its implications for the New Evangelization. Ecology (from the Greek, *oikos*, meaning "household"), Francis notes, concerns the relationship of living organisms and their environment. In his view, an *integral* vision of our common home is one that is multifaceted: it is social and environmental. It includes the broad sweep of human cultures and the intimate details of quotidian life.[2] At its heart is the human person, for "there can be no ecology," Francis notes, "without an adequate anthropology."[3] In its approach to the environment, it does not exclude the religious dimension (creation), and it likewise considers the development of human beings both religiously and morally.[4] Such a definition of ecology may seem so broad as to escape practicality, but behind it lies the same simple refrain: "everything is related."

Early on in the encyclical, the pope recalls the figure of his namesake, St. Francis, and the words St. Bonaventure spoke of him: "From a reflection on the primary source of all things, filled with even more abundant piety, he would call creatures, no matter how small, by the name of 'brother' or 'sister.'"[5] One could easily pass over this affirmation of the man who inspired the pope's name, but Francis explains that this description captures why the saint of Assisi is the "example par excellence of . . . an integral ecology lived

---

2. Francis analyzes each in chap. 4, "Integral Ecology," of *Laudato si'*.

3. Francis, *Laudato si'*, 118.

4. Francis undoubtedly is drawing upon the notion of the "integral development" of the human person proposed by Pope Paul VI in his 1967 encyclical *Populorum progessio*.

5. Francis, *Laudato si'*, 11, quoting the *Major Legend of St. Francis* 8.6.

out joyfully and authentically."[6] For the pope, Bonaventure's description of his order's founder is a key to understanding the integral vision one must cultivate to properly love persons and care for the earth.

Because of this, Bonaventure's words provide a path for my own reflections on Pope Francis's teaching, though I appropriate Bonaventure's words in the reverse order. For if it was the poor man of Assisi's encounter with God in Jesus Christ that allowed him to see the fraternal bond he had with all of creation, then perhaps, in our own time, cultivating a vision of the interrelatedness of all things can act as a sort of *praeambula fidei* for the human encounter with God. Perhaps our recognition of dependence on the environment and on each other can prepare the way for the proclamation of the Trinitarian God, who not only is a relationship of divine persons but likewise is the ultimate communion at which the human heart is aimed. In sum, I propose that we read *Laudato si'* not only as a call to all people of goodwill to take care of the environment, but as a part of the pope's pastoral efforts—a "missionary option"—aimed at bringing men and women into communion with God.[7]

In retracing this path, I loosely follow a Bonaventurian "itinerary." In Bonaventure's well-known masterpiece, *The Soul's Journey into God*, he meditates upon St. Francis's vision of the seraphic Christ. In accord with the six wings of the seraphic figure, the soul makes its journey in six stages, though these can be broadly categorized into three: contemplating God through his vestiges found in creation, contemplating God in his image that is the human person, and contemplating God in himself. In Bonaventure's words, to contemplate God we must "pass through his vestiges . . . enter into our soul . . . [and] go beyond to what is eternal, most spiritual, and above us."[8] While loosely following this path, my own itinerary will differ from Bonaventure's in two main ways. First, the Seraphic Doctor's second step moves from the sensible world to the interiority of the soul, a traditionally Augustinian way of approaching the image of God.[9] Rather than moving inward, my second step will draw upon the more recent attempts to articulate what can be called a relational anthropology, one that sees the image of God not only in the interior faculties but in the communion of human persons with one another. Second, while Bonaventure drew upon the theological and philosophical works standard to his time—for instance, those

6. Ibid., 10.

7. Francis, *Evangelii gaudium*, 27.

8. Bonaventure, *The Soul's Journey into God* 1.2 (trans. Cousins, 60).

9. Some caution is in order here since, for Augustine, the interior faculties of the human person are not the *imago Dei* in its fullness; rather, only when the person remembers God, knows God, and loves God is the Trinity truly imaged.

of Pseudo-Dionysius, Augustine, and Anselm (all of which are perennially rewarding)—I will contextualize Pope Francis's thoughts by way of more recent scholarly resources. I have in mind especially the work of Francis's last two predecessors, Pope St. John Paul II and Pope Benedict XVI. With this itinerary in mind, I first turn to the world of sensible things, and in particular, non-human creation.

The Message of Creation

In the second chapter of *Laudato si'* Pope Francis brings the light of faith to bear on the environment in speaking of what he calls the "Gospel of Creation." The phrase implies that creation has a message of Good News to speak to all men and women of goodwill.

For the pope, we encounter the beginning of this "gospel" in Genesis. Francis bypasses modern debates about the literal sense of the biblical accounts and takes for granted the Christian tradition of interpretation. Translations of Genesis render the first verse of the Bible variously. The Revised Standard Version translates the verse in accord with the Septuagint: "In the beginning, God created the heavens and the earth." The New American Bible Revised Edition, on the other hand, reads: "In the beginning, when God created the heavens and the earth . . ." The first rendering fits the Christian belief in a God who creates *ex nihilo* neatly; the second is indebted to modern historical scholarship and implies the preexistence of something from which God fashioned the world. Francis's reflections follow the more traditional interpretation.[10]

This position has held pride of place in Christianity because of the way it accords with the Christian understanding of God and the value it places upon the created world. In the Christian view, God is not one being amidst the world but is *ipsum esse subsistens*, subsistent being itself. If God is one being among many, even if he is the highest being, he would, in some

10. While some modern biblical scholars might critique Francis's interpretive stance on the basis of the literal sense, I think this would be misguided for two reasons. First, it would be difficult to claim that the author's intention was to promote the factual existence of something like preexistent matter. Second, and more to the point, the biblical author stands as part of an interpreting and worshiping community of belief, one that saw the Genesis text not simply as a record of the past but as a "beginning" that points forward to and helps explain the present. As Reno explains, "A decision in favor of a substantive beginning . . . sets the interpretive agenda for the Bible as a whole. Creation is for the sake of something prior and more fundamental: the divine project or plan. In the beginning, God subjected all things to his final purpose, just as an archer strings a bow in order to pull it back and load it with a force that strains forward toward its target (Rom 8:20–21)." See Reno, *Genesis*, 38.

sense, compete for space with the other beings that exist. So, too, would it be difficult to even properly speak of such a being as "God," since this being would be subject to the limitations imposed by the already existing world. The ultimate form of being, therefore, cannot simply be the most dominant or powerful being in a given setting but must be the very foundation from which the setting and the beings within it come. Thus the Christian claim is that God is transcendent; he is existence itself.[11]

The significance of creation follows from this: for if creation is not simply the handiwork of a higher being but is the coming into existence of all things from nothing, then everything that has being is willed, indeed, is *held in existence* by the will of God. "The creating word expresses a *free choice*," Francis tells us, reflecting upon the words of the Psalmist.[12] Every being, in this sense, is chosen by God. God, who is existence itself, has no need of creation; his free choice to create adds nothing to his *esse* since he is the very perfection of *esse*. But for the creature, who is utterly contingent and in every way dependent on God for existence, creation is everything.[13] A creature's existence is the movement from nothingness to something. Mathematically, such a perfection is quantitatively infinite.

Francis's reflection upon this Christian understanding of creation leads him to see all of creation as a manifestation of God's love. God has no need of creatures, yet he wills their existence. "Every creature," the pope explains, "is thus the object of the Father's tenderness, who gives it its place in the world. Even the fleeting life of the least of beings is the object of his love, and in its few seconds of existence, God enfolds it with his affection."[14] In short, "Creation is of the order of love."[15]

This Christian understanding of creation is the coming together of philosophy and theology in a deeply contemplative vision and, while elevating God by removing him from the world, it unexpectedly results in the elevation of creation as well: "The world came about as the result of a

11. In Francis's words, "There is an infinite distance between God and the things of this world." See *Laudato si'*, 88. For more on this subject, see the incisive and educative prose of Sokolowski in *The God of Faith and Reason*, especially the chapter, "The Metaphysics of Christian Belief."

12. Francis, *Laudato si'*, 77, referencing Ps 33:6; emphasis mine. Here Francis echoes the words of Benedict XVI during his installation Mass: "We are not some casual and meaningless product of evolution. Each of us is the result of a thought of God. Each of us is willed, each of us is loved, each of us is necessary." See Benedict XVI, *Homily*, Sunday 24 April 2005.

13. St. Thomas Aquinas thus describes God's relation to creation as "logical," while the creature's relation to God is "real." See *Summa theologiae* I, q. 13, ad. 7.

14. Francis, *Laudato si'*, 77.

15. Ibid.

decision, not from chaos or chance, and this exalts it all the more."[16] Still, this elevation is clearly not like that of other religions that would claim the world itself is divine.[17] Biblical religion is not pantheistic; nor does it see the workings of nature, whether bountiful or disastrous, as a result of the pleasure or displeasure of the gods.[18] Rather, the Christian understanding of God, Francis explains, brings with it the demythologizing of nature.[19] Two things are noteworthy in this regard. First, as has become increasingly recognized today, this demythologizing of nature provided the necessary foundation for the birth of modern science.[20] Only if the world is not divine can it be approached as an object for study.

Second, the claim that God is metaphysically set apart from the world should not be confused with a deistic view that would see God as standing aloof from what he has made. Creation is not like a clock that has been wound up and let go. God's undergirding of existence means that creation cannot be confined to a moment, even the first moment, of the past. It is an ongoing reality, fully dependent on God's sustaining will. St. Augustine long ago realized that this transcendence of God brings with it an unexpected fruit: because he does not compete with created beings for space within the world but is the foundation for their existence, he can also be intimately close to them. "You were more intimately present to me than my innermost being," Augustine confessed, and yet "higher than the highest peak of my spirit."[21]

These reflections act as a prerequisite for Pope Francis's critique of what he calls a "tyrannical anthropocentrism," one that would see the world

---

16. Ibid.

17. See *Laudato si'*, 90, where Francis explains that the Christian understanding of creation does not "imply a divinization of the earth."

18. Modern biblical scholarship has emphasized the similarities between the creation account of Genesis 1 and those of other ancient near eastern peoples, such as the Bablyonian *Enuma Elish*. Yet, as Joseph Ratzinger explains, these similarities serve as a common ground from which the Israelites expressed the distinctiveness of biblical faith. Whereas the *Enuma Elish* depicts creation as a result of the violence of deities who exist in the world, Genesis presents the God of Israel as the one God who has control over all of creation and who exercises dominion over the idols of other nations. See Ratzinger's *In the Beginning*, 12–14.

19. See Francis, *Laudato si'*, 78.

20. See, for instance, the chapter "God's Handiwork: The Religious Origins of Science," in Stark, *For the Glory of God*, 121–200.

21. *Confessions* 3.6.11 (trans. Boulding, 61). Or, as Francis explains in *Laudato si'*, 80, "God is intimately present to each being, without impinging on the autonomy of his creature."

as an object to be dominated.[22] Here Francis follows the train of thought of his predecessor in a homily Joseph Ratzinger originally preached in 1981 and subsequently published. In the homily, Ratzinger notes:

> What we had previously celebrated—namely, that through faith in creation the world has been demythologized and made reasonable . . . has become an accusation against Christianity. Christianity is said to have transformed all the powers of the universe, which were once our brothers and sisters, into utilitarian objects for human beings, and in so doing it has led them to misuse plants and animals and in fact all the world's powers for the sake of an ideology of progress that thinks only of itself and cares for itself.[23]

Similarly, Francis writes of the "charge that Judeo-Christian thinking, on the basis of the Genesis account which grants man 'dominion' over the earth (cf. Gen 1:28), has encouraged the unbridled exploitation of nature by painting him as domineering and destructive by nature."[24] Both Francis and Ratzinger respond to this charge by arguing for the proper interpretation of Scripture. The dominion declared by the first creation account can only accurately be seen in relation to the second account's command to humanity regarding the earth, "to till it and keep it" (Gen 2:15).

Francis's reading of this command once again embraces a more traditional hermeneutic, one that sees both accounts in light of each other:

> We must forcefully reject the notion that our being created in God's image and given dominion over the earth justifies absolute domination over other creatures. The biblical texts are to be read in their context, with an appropriate hermeneutic, recognizing that they tell us to "till and keep" the garden of the world (cf. Gen 2:15). "Tilling" refers to cultivating, plowing, or working, while "keeping" means caring, protecting, overseeing, and preserving. This implies a relationship of mutual responsibility between human beings and nature.[25]

Ratzinger similarly recognizes that tilling and keeping "signifies that the world is to be used for what it is capable of and what it is called to, but not for what goes against it."[26] Thus, rather than negating a view of the world

---

22. Francis, *Laudato si'*, 68.

23. Ratzinger, *In the Beginning*, 34.

24. Francis, *Laudato si'*, 67.

25. Ibid.

26. Ratzinger, *In the Beginning*, 34.

which would see all creatures as brothers and sisters, the proper Christian understanding of creation encourages precisely this fraternal vision.

And yet one final point remains. Restoring the proper vision of creation must mean more than recognizing the great responsibility of tilling and keeping the earth. That Francis speaks of the "gospel" of creation implies that the earth itself has a message to speak to its human inhabitants. Even the "stones will cry out," Luke 19:40 reminds us.

"The word 'creation' has a broader meaning than 'nature,'" the pope explains, "for it has to do with God's loving plan in which every creature has its own value and significance. Nature is usually seen as a system which can be studied, understood, and controlled, whereas creation can only be understood as a gift from the outstretched hand of the Father of all, and as a reality illuminated by the love which calls us together into universal communion."[27] The proper understanding of creation therefore not only elevates the meaning of the world, but it raises the minds and hearts of those who are able to perceive this meaning to creation's source.

This is similar to a teaching of the late Pope St. John Paul II who, like Francis, recognized creation's character as a "gift." For John Paul, the biblical creation accounts must be read through what he calls the "hermeneutics of the gift."[28] "Yet, at the same time," John Paul explained, "the concept of 'giving' cannot refer to nothing. It indicates the one who gives and the one who receives the gift, as well as the relation established between them."[29] This movement from gift to Giver was something of which he spoke powerfully, even before his pontificate, as the Cardinal Archbishop of Krakow:

> Throughout the description of Genesis the heart can be heard beating. We have before us not a great builder of the world, a demiurge: we stand in the presence of the great heart! No cosmogony, no philosophical cosmology of the past, no cosmological theory of the present day can express a truth like this truth. We can find it only in the inspired pages of Genesis: revelation of the love that pervades the whole earth to its very core, revelation of the Fatherhood which gives creation its full meaning, together with the covenant which gives rise to the creation of man in the image of God.[30]

Both John Paul and Francis thus call us to a proper vision of creation, but this vision is merely partial if it remains fixed on the surface level of

27. Francis, *Laudato si'*, 76.

28. John Paul II, *Man and Woman*, 179.

29. Ibid., 180.

30. Wojtyła, *Sign of Contradiction*, 22.

the world around us. In keeping with our Bonaventurian itinerary we can say that creation's message raises our vision to its source. When Pope Francis willingly embraces the language of his namesake, whose Canticle of Creation invokes the sun as "brother" and moon as "sister," it is more than sentiment. Our "fraternity" with creation implies a common Father.[31] Moreover, this movement upwards—from creation to Creator and from fraternity to the Father—does not leave the world behind. In the human movement to God, because we are both spirit and matter, we are the mediators of redemption for the rest of the material world. All creation "groans" in labor pains, Paul taught, as it waits for the redemption of the children of God (cf. Rom 8:19–23). In the Scriptural view, the consummation of time involves a "new heavens and new earth."[32] Though we must be chaste in our speculations on what this may mean, it is clear that the redemption won by Christ must necessarily have effects upon non-human creation.[33] "All creatures are moving forward with us and through us towards a common point of arrival, which is God, in that transcendent fullness where the risen Christ embraces and illumines all things. Human beings, endowed with intelligence and love, and drawn by the fullness of Christ, are called to lead all creatures back to their Creator."[34]

Ultimately, then, creation proclaims a message that all that exists is dependent on a common source. All beings are signs of God's gratuitous love, and these signs point toward the communion in God that is our final end.

The Image of God as Trinity

In the second stage of our itinerary we move from sensible, non-human beings to a reflection upon the pinnacle of creation, to the human person who is made in "the image and likeness of God" (Gen 1:26). Though Francis recognizes humanity's fraternal communion with the world, "this is not to put all living beings on the same level," he explains, "nor to deprive human beings of their unique worth."[35]

31. Francis quotes a large section of the Canticle in *Laudato si'*, 87. On his use of universal "fraternity," see 92, 221, and 228.

32. See Isa 65:17–18 and Rev 21:1–4. Cf. Matt 19:28, Gal 6:15, and 2 Pet 3:10–13.

33. On this subject, see O'Callaghan's chapter, "The New Heavens and the New Earth" in *Christ Our Hope*, 115–29.

34. Francis, *Laudato si'*, 83. See also *Catechism of the Catholic Church*, 358: "God created everything for man, but man in turn was created to serve and love God and to offer all creation back to him."

35. Francis, *Laudato si'*, 90. At the same time, we should keep in mind Francis's critique of a "tyrannical anthropocentrism" mentioned above. Francis repeatedly cautions

The Christian tradition has consistently held that humankind holds pride of place in creation, that as bearers of the divine image, human beings have an incomparable dignity. So, too, is this dignity directly connected to the creation and existence of human beings as *persons*. Quoting the Catechism, Francis explains that the human being "is not just something, but *someone*. He is capable of self-knowledge, of self-possession, and of freely giving himself and entering into communion with other persons."[36] This description takes for granted the Church's long tradition of defining the *imago Dei* in terms of rationality, that is, the human faculties of reason and free will. Yet it also displays the more recent attempt to define the image by way of a human vocation to communion.

In a certain sense, both views of the *imago Dei* stem from the thought of St. Augustine. In terms of the more classical view, Augustine's reading of Genesis led him to see the image in rational human nature. We should be careful to avoid oversimplification, however, since recognizing the superiority of human beings over the rest of the world in terms of reason and free will would be a position mostly indebted to philosophy and not revelation. Augustine, rather, sought a *Trinitarian* image of God within the person, resulting in the much-discussed "psychological analogies" found in his work, *De Trinitate*, those such as memory, intellect, and will, as well as the mind and its abilities to know and to love.[37] For the bishop of Hippo, these analogies are not simple pedagogical metaphors, something akin to the legend of St. Patrick and the shamrock, but are attempts to understand the epistemology of faith. In other words, Augustine meditates upon the faculties of rational human nature precisely because he is seeking an understanding of how humans come to know and love God. For Augustine, if humans are able to know and love the Trinity, then there must be a Trinitarian structure within human knowing and loving.

The result of Augustine's study is that the image of God is not merely found in human nature, but in its capacity, when empowered by grace, to know and love God. Reflecting upon the faculties of memory, intellect, and will, Augustine writes: "The trinity of the mind is not the image of God because the mind remembers *itself*, understands *itself*, and loves *itself*, but because it can also remember, understand, and love *Him* by whom it was made."[38] The true Augustinian doctrine of the image is, thus, dynamic;

---

against an elevation of the human person that is "tyrannical," (68), "distorted," (69), "excessive," (116), or "misguided" (118, 119, and 122).

36. Ibid., 65, quoting *Catechism of the Catholic Church*, 357; emphasis mine.

37. See *De Trinitate* 9.5.8 and 10.11.15.

38. *De Trinitate* 14.12.15, in Augustine, *The Trinity*, 432; emphasis mine.

nevertheless, it has been consistently proposed by the tradition in its more simplified and static form.

The more recent attempts to see the image in terms of communion also stem from the teachings of Augustine, though, ironically, he denied that the image could be found in the coming together of three human persons. He believed that such an understanding ran counter to Nicaea—three separate human persons could not be consubstantial like memory, intellect, and will (as faculties of one mind) could.[39] Nevertheless, it is not Augustine's teachings on the *imago Dei* that form the backdrop for modern relational anthropology but rather his thoughts about the divine persons of the Trinity.

The Trinity is, of course, the most foundational of Christian doctrines and yet simultaneously the most mysterious. How could the Father, the Son, and the Holy Spirit be distinct and yet one God? Augustine attempted to explain the threeness of God vis-à-vis Arian critics who used the philosophy of Aristotle to challenge Christian orthodoxy. These critics called upon the Aristotelian distinction between *substance*—literally, that which "stands under" and is therefore unique in a given being—and *accidents*—characteristics which, in some sense, are secondary to a being and can be shared by others. In a sense, the question posed by the Arians was: "Are the Persons of the Trinity distinct by way of substance or accident?" The second option was untenable, for God's essence allows for no accidents—there is nothing accidental in God. Likewise, the first was, by Augustine's account, the errant position of his opponents and undergirded their argument for the subordination of the Son. Choosing not to be backed into a corner, the bishop of Hippo harnessed a third category, *relation*, to explain what was distinct in God.[40] While all three divine persons shared the same divine substance, the Father could be identified by the relation of begetting, the Son by the relation of being begotten, and the Holy Spirit by the relation of proceeding from the Father and the Son. Augustine therefore introduced the category of relation into the meaning of personhood. At least on the divine level, to be a person was to be a relation.

Yet this is precisely where the seeming incongruence between divine and human personhood emerges. Augustine rejected the coming together of three human persons as an image of God because, in such a case, each person stands as a separate substance. A given human person is related to other beings and can form further relationships but, in the end, he or she remains, at core, a substance. To speak of the divine persons of the Trinity,

---

39. See *De Trinitate* 12.6.8—12.7.9. Following Augustine, St. Thomas calls this idea of the image in several persons "manifestly absurd." See *Summa theologiae* I, q. 93, a. 6, ad. 2.

40. See *De Trinitate* 5.5.6. See also Kelly, *Early Christian Doctrines*, 274–75.

however, is to speak of their relations, even if these relations are consubstantial. Because of this incongruence and its perceived exacerbation by subsequent theology, several modern theologians have called for a renewed theological anthropology that would see both divine and human persons as primarily relational.

The proponents of this relational anthropology are varied but chief among them, I believe, is Pope Benedict XVI. In a seminal lecture delivered while still a cardinal and later published in the journal *Communio*, Ratzinger lamented the original Augustinian rejection of the social image of the Trinity and especially its later reinforcement in the theology of St. Thomas. Such an anthropology, Ratzinger claimed, defined humans as too narrowly individualistic, leaving the person-as-relation of divine personhood to be a "theological exception."[41] Rather, it is ultimately "relativity toward the other [that] constitutes the human person. The human person is the event or being of relativity."[42] This was a position he advanced, though more cautiously, as pope in his encyclical *Caritas in veritate*: "The Christian revelation of the unity of the human race presupposes a *metaphysical interpretation of the 'humanum' in which relationality is an essential element*."[43]

It remains unclear what role remains for substance in this more starkly relational view of the human person. A different course of action, and one that I find more theologically viable, was offered by Karol Wojtyła in his earlier philosophical works and developed further in the teachings of his papacy. For Wojtyła, there is equal fault to be found in an individualism that would sever the human person from the necessity of community and in a collectivism that would eliminate the dignity of the individual person. Thus he explains that "only the individual people—the personal subjects—who are members of [a] society are substantial subjects (*supposita*), each of them separately, whereas the society itself is simply a set of relations, and therefore an accidental being."[44] Moreover, for Wojtyła, "the subject as a person has a distinctive priority in relation to community. Otherwise it would be impossible to defend not just the autoteleology of the human self, but even the teleology of the human being."[45] For Wojtyła, the substance of the person retains a certain metaphysical priority over his relations with other persons. At the same time, however, the person remains unfulfilled if he does not give himself to others in the free act of self-giving love. In

41. Ratzinger, "Concerning the Notion of Person," 449.

42. Ibid., 452.

43. Benedict, *Caritas in veritate*, 55; emphasis in the original.

44. Wojtyła, "The Person: Subject and Community," 238.

45. Ibid., 252.

the Thomistic view Wojtyła espouses, a substance exists for the sake of its operations. The substance of the person has priority, but the person is only perfected by acts of love which form community.[46] This is one of the foundational principles of the catecheses he delivered that are more commonly known as the Theology of the Body: Adam's loneliness in the garden (what John Paul II calls *original solitude*) is an indication that he is made for the communion he finds in Eve (*original unity*). Yet this is a teaching that can be traced all the way back to John Paul's first papal document, the encyclical *Redemptor hominis*: "Man cannot live without love. He remains a being that is incomprehensible for himself, his life is senseless, if love is not revealed to him, if he does not encounter love, if he does not experience it and make it his own, if he does not participate intimately in it."[47]

Whether one espouses Ratzinger's view that the person is essentially relational or Wojtyła's claim that the person is a substance ordered to and fulfilled by communion with others, it is clear that recent popes have tried to emphasize the relational character of human beings. This necessarily brief and truncated overview of the theological concept of person forms the backdrop for the anthropology put forth by Pope Francis in *Laudato si'*. For Francis, relationality is an essential part of the *imago Dei*. In his words, it is precisely "our openness to others, each of whom is a 'thou' capable of knowing, loving, and entering into dialogue [that] remains the source of our nobility as human persons."[48] And because the redemption of creation necessarily presupposes the redemption of humankind, "we cannot presume to heal our relationship with nature and the environment without healing all fundamental human relationships."[49]

In Francis's view, because all that exists shares a common Father, *communion* is essential to the original integrity of creation. The creation accounts of Genesis "suggest that human life is grounded in three fundamental and closely intertwined relationships: with God, with our neighbor, and with the earth itself"; moreover, "according to the Bible, these three vital relationships have been broken, both outwardly and within us. This rupture is sin."[50]

A significant portion of *Laudato si'* is dedicated to Francis's diagnosis of present-day society and culture as infected by this sinful tendency

46. Wojtyła consistently drew inspiration from the teaching of *Gaudium et spes*, 24: "Man, who is the only creature on earth which God willed for itself, cannot fully find himself except through a sincere gift of himself."

47. John Paul II, *Redemptor hominis*, 10.

48. Francis, *Laudato si'*, 119.

49. Ibid.

50. Ibid., 66.

to disunity. In a particularly interesting section, he critiques modern city planning for its tendency to produce oversaturation and overstimulation, leading to a lack of communion among urban dwellers.[51] So, too, does he claim that humanity has embraced a "technocratic paradigm," one which "exalts the concept of a subject who, using logical and rational procedures, progressively approaches and gains control over an external object."[52] The result of this paradigm is the substitution of relationship, whether with the environment or our fellow human beings, for confrontation. Both the world and human beings are treated like objects. Thus, this technocracy engenders a "practical relativism" that uses persons for convenience or economic gain and then discards them.[53]

Despite the widespread character of the infection, Francis sees the signs of hope within humanity. Even the "asphyxiation" brought about by over-crowdedness and the deep poverty of cities is "countered if close and warm relationships develop, if communities are created, if the limitations of the environment are compensated for in the interior of each person who feels held within a network of solidarity and belonging. In this way, any place can turn from being a hell on earth into the setting for a dignified life."[54] By this, Francis does not imply that the conversion of social institutions themselves is unnecessary. He explains that the rebuilding of relationships is a duty that extends from the most intimate of societal institutions—the family—to ever greater circles of society.[55] As such, the entirety of chapter 5 of *Laudato si'* advocates for ecological (both environmental and human) dialogue on local, national, and international levels. This pursuit of the common good is also diachronic for Francis—solidarity must reach across generations.[56] The healing of relationships, then, is not only pertinent to the present but, in a sense, extends across time.

In the previous section I mentioned that our understanding of Francis's vision of creation is incomplete if it does not see in the gift of created beings a path to the Creator. Similarly, our understanding of Francis's call to personal relationship is incomplete if it does not move from the image of human communion to that infinitely more perfect divine communion which it resembles. That human beings are persons, endowed with the capacity to love and to receive another "thou," speaks to their ultimate end,

---

51. See ibid., 149–53.

52. Ibid., 106.

53. Ibid., 122–23.

54. Ibid., 148.

55. Ibid., 142.

56. See ibid., 159–62.

in which they are addressed by and called to relationship with the divine "Thou."[57] Through grace, human beings are offered a share in the divine life of God, who is a communion of love. As Francis explains, "The human person grows more, matures more, and is sanctified more to the extent that he or she enters into relationships, going out from [him or herself] to live in communion with God, with others and with all creatures."[58] Our itinerary thus draws us through an encounter with creation to solidarity with other human persons, and finally to an encounter with the communion of persons that is the Holy Trinity.

The Proclamation of the Trinitarian God

Having explored Francis's vision of creation and his understanding of the relational character of human beings, we are in a better position to see how these first two stages of our itinerary prepare us for the third: the proclamation of the Trinitarian God.

The guiding thread throughout our reading of *Laudato si'* has been the notion of relationship, communion, or we might even say, dependence. Creation exists in utter dependence on God, and the human vocation to love is dependent upon loving communion with other persons. Yet how can the concept of dependence evangelize a culture marked by individualism and whose watchword is autonomy?

Pope Francis wisely recognizes that the growing concern for the environment is a first foothold by which all men and women of goodwill can begin to make the ascent to God. By this I do not mean that Francis is merely using environmental concern as a façade for his own evangelistic purposes. Rather, in his view, the environment is only fully understood as the work of creation, and thus it is ineluctably bound up with humanity as creation's pinnacle and caretaker and with God as its source and end. In other words, the one who cares for the environment, if she is to find ultimate success in her endeavors, must eventually ascend from a recognition of the truth and goodness of the world, to the truth and goodness of human persons, to the truth and goodness of God. Environmental degradation is, at its core, marked by the separation and disunity caused by sin. To dominate the world is to see oneself as over and above the world instead of as a part of it, related to all things within it because all things share a common source. This is the

---

57. See ibid., 81.

58. Ibid., 240.

hidden idolatry of the "throwaway culture," for only God is truly over and above the world (while remaining intimate to it as its source of existence).[59]

Healing this rift, then, will take more than human efforts at the local, national, and international levels, though of course it must involve these. The healing of sin is a work of grace. Bonaventure writes of the ascent to God: "So our soul could not rise completely from these things of sense to see itself and the Eternal Truth in itself unless Truth, assuming human nature in Christ, had become a ladder, restoring the first ladder that had been broken in Adam."[60] The encounter with Christ, in his revelation of the Father and sending of the Spirit, remains the sole remedy for the sin that breaks the communion of human beings with God and the world. A recognition of our dependence, on the world and on each other, can be the preliminary step that prepares the way for the Church's proclamation of God in Jesus Christ and the communion that he shares with the Father and the Spirit. Francis's quotation of the Catechism is telling in this regard: "God wills the interdependence of creatures. The sun and the moon, the cedar and the little flower, the eagle and the sparrow: the spectacle of their countless diversities and inequalities tells us that no creature is self-sufficient. Creatures exist only in dependence on each other, to complete each other, in the service of each other."[61] The very multiplicity of creatures in this interdependence, Francis notes, following St. Thomas, is an indication of God's glory being incapable of being represented by one creature alone.[62] In a more Franciscan key, the pope adds that "each creature 'testifies that God is three.'"[63]

To proclaim the Trinitarian God is, therefore, to proclaim the one who can heal the disunity of sin. In a world marked by individualism, technocracy, and division, the pope turns our eyes to the example of St. Francis. The poor man of Assisi is admired by religious and non-religious people alike for his radical love for the poor and care for the earth. Yet, Francis tells us, this harmony with human and non-human creatures can only truly be understood as a sign of the "healing of that rupture" that is sin, as a sign of the workings of grace offered in Jesus Christ.[64]

So, to understand the example of St. Francis we must understand the God he loved, and to understand the teachings of the pope who took his

---

59. Ibid., 16.

60. *The Soul's Journey into God* 4.2 (trans. Cousins, 88).

61. *Laudato si'*, 86, quoting the *Catechism of the Catholic Church*, 340.

62. See ibid., 86, referencing *Summa theologiae* I, q. 47, a. 1.

63. Ibid., 239, quoting Bonaventure's *Disputed Questions on the Mystery of the Holy Trinity* 1.2.

64. Ibid., 66.

name we must do the same. For Francis, the saint and the pope, the consummation of a rightful concern for the world is an encounter with the one who leads us into the communion of God.[65]

Bibliography

Augustine, Saint. *The Confessions*. Translated by Maria Boulding. San Francisco: Ignatius, 2012.

———. *The Trinity*. Translated by Stephen McKenna. Washington, DC: Catholic University of America Press, 1963.

Benedict XVI, Pope. *Caritas in veritate*. http://w2.vatican.va/content/benedict-xvi/en/encyclicals/documents/hf_ben-xvi_enc_20090629_caritas-in-veritate.html.

———. *Homily*. Sunday 24 April 2005. https://w2.vatican.va/content/benedict-xvi/en/homilies/2005/documents/hf_ben-xvi_hom_20050424_inizio-pontificato.html.

Bonaventure, Saint. *The Soul's Journey into God*. In *Bonaventure*, translated and edited by Ewert Cousins, 51–116. New York: Paulist, 1978.

Catechism of the Catholic Church. 2nd ed. Washington, DC: United States Catholic Conference—Libreria Editrice Vaticana, 1997.

Francis, Pope. *Evangelii gaudium*. https://w2.vatican.va/content/francesco/en/apost_exhortations/documents/papa-francesco_esortazione-ap_20131124_evangelii-gaudium.html

———. *Laudato si'*. http://w2.vatican.va/content/francesco/en/encyclicals/documents/papa-francesco_20150524_enciclica-laudato-si.html.

John Paul II, Pope. *Man and Woman He Created Them: A Theology of the Body*. Translated by Michael Waldstein. Boston: Pauline, 2006.

———. *Redemptor hominis*. http://w2.vatican.va/content/john-paul-ii/en/encyclicals/documents/hf_jp-ii_enc_04031979_redemptor-hominis.html.

Kelly, J. N. D. *Early Christian Doctrines*. Rev. ed. San Francisco: HarperSanFrancisco, 1978.

O'Callaghan, Paul. *Christ Our Hope: An Introduction to Eschatology*. Washington, DC: Catholic University of America Press, 2011.

Ratzinger, Joseph. "Concerning the Notion of Person in Theology." *Communio* 17 (1990) 439–54.

———. *In the Beginning: A Catholic Understanding of the Story of Creation and the Fall*. Translated by Boniface Ramsey. Grand Rapids: Eerdmans, 1995.

Reno, R. R. *Genesis*. Grand Rapids: Brazos, 2010.

Sokolowski, Robert. *The God of Faith and Reason: Foundations of Christian Theology*. Washington, DC: Catholic University of America Press, 1995.

Second Vatican Council. *Gaudium et spes*. http://www.vatican.va/archive/hist_councils/ii_vatican_council/documents/vat-ii_const_19651207_gaudium-et-spes_en.html.

65. In this light, Francis describes an integral ecology as eucharistic in *Laudato si'*, 236: "In the Eucharist, fullness is already achieved; it is the living center of the universe, the overflowing core of love and of inexhaustible life . . . The Eucharist joins heaven and earth; it embraces and penetrates all creation. The world which came forth from God's hands returns to him in blessed and undivided adoration."

Stark, Rodney. *For the Glory of God: How Monotheism Led to Reformations, Science, Witch-Hunts, and the End of Slavery*. Princeton, NJ: Princeton University Press, 2004.

Thomas Aquinas, Saint. *Summa Theologiae*. 5 vols. Translated by the Fathers of the English Dominican Province. Allen, TX: Christian Classics, 1948.

Wojtyła, Karol. "The Person: Subject and Community." In *Person and Community: Selected Essays*, translated by Theresa Sandok, 219–61. New York: Lang, 1993

———. *Sign of Contradiction*. Translator unknown. New York: Crossroad, 1979.

CHAPTER 6

Serene Attentiveness to the Creator and Creation

—Terrence Ehrman, CSC

Abstract:

Since the Enlightenment, Christian belief in God the Creator has been eclipsed and increasingly alienated from belief in Jesus Christ the Redeemer. In short, creation was reduced to nature, the domain of science whose discoveries have become, for many, an obstacle to faith. The eclipse of creation is also partly the reason behind Lynn White, Jr.'s 1967 indictment that Christianity is the root cause of the ecological crisis. Pope Francis's call for ecological conversion to care for our common home is not only an indirect refutation of White's claim but also integral to Francis's New Evangelization. Francis seeks to enliven faith by a rediscovery of God as Creator through a "serene attentiveness" to creation. He attempts to anneal creation and redemption back into the single divine economy. The dialogue between science and theology, then, becomes fertile ground for evangelization, rendering Francis's project a modern parallel to St. Basil's fourth-century preaching by which he attempted to lead the faithful to God the Creator through a guided encounter with creation. In this chapter, I analyze and discuss Pope Francis's project in relation to St. Basil with evidence from the praxis of serene attentiveness and its promise for the New Evangelization.

Introduction

What does a Blue Dasher dragonfly have to do with Jesus Christ? Many people, Christians included, might think "nothing," in a way analogous to the response in the second century when North African theologian Tertullian asked his rhetorical question about the relation of reason (Greek philosophy) and faith (theology) in his quip, "What does Athens have to do with Jerusalem?" Another way of asking the dragonfly-Christ question is what does creation have to do with redemption? The reflexive difficulty many have today in seeing an immediate and essential connection between the two results not only from the experience of so many people living in urban centers surrounded by a technological bubble that isolates them from experiencing the natural world. It also results from an ideological perspective which is caught up in the alienation of science and religion that reaches back to the Enlightenment. Since the Enlightenment, belief in God the Creator was alienated from belief in Jesus Christ the Redeemer. Concurrent with this rupture, creation was reduced to nature which became the domain of scientific investigation and discovery. Faith and religion turned their gaze away from the natural world and focused primarily on the human person and redemption in Jesus Christ. We currently live in an age dominated by a scientific materialistic worldview that presumes that science and religion necessarily conflict with each other such that science and its discoveries have become, for many, an obstacle to faith. But this need not and should not be the case.

Pope Francis seeks to enliven faith today by a rediscovery of God as Creator through a "serene attentiveness" to creation. He attempts to reunite creation and redemption back into a single divine economy of God's plan for salvation. This reunion also necessarily reconciles science and religion that have been estranged on false pretenses. In the United States, 53 percent of scientists have no religious affiliation, 34 percent are atheists, and 30 percent agnostic.[1] Fertile ground for the New Evangelization are these scientists and those Christians who have a diminished understanding of God as Creator and of nature as God's creation because of claims of conflict between science and faith. St. Paul encountered others publicly in the agora, and the Church needs modern Pauls to be apostles to the agora of science and to the Church itself regarding nature and science. The wondrous encounter of God in and through creation elevates and refreshes the spirit and enlivens faith. Such an encounter of God and of creation, however, often requires today an expert guide to lead one to God and into creation. Pope Francis is doing

---

1. Ecklund, *Science vs. Religion*, 15–16.

just that. In this chapter, I will examine 1) the claim of Lynn White, Jr., that Christianity is to blame for the ecological crisis; 2) the historical origin of the separation of creation and redemption (and of science and religion); 3) Pope Francis's push for the rediscovery of the Creator and the single divine economy of creation/redemption; and 4) St. Basil the Great's preaching as a model for Pope Francis's call for serene attentiveness, ecological conversion, and renewal of faith.

Christianity and the Ecological Crisis

March 2017 marks the fiftieth anniversary of historian, Lynn White Jr.'s, provocative yet overstated indictment of medieval Christianity as the root of the contemporary ecological crisis.[2] White wrote at a time of alarming concern about and initial social response to human degradation of the environment. In the decade prior, Barry Commoner's study and documentation of the absorption of radioactive strontium-90 from nuclear fallout into the food chain and ultimately into the bones and teeth of pre- and post-natal children led to the Nuclear Test Ban Treaty of 1963, and Rachel Carson's 1962 book, *Silent Spring*, stirred the nation to action by alerting it to the dangers the petrochemical DDT posed to the biotic community, including human health and life.[3] Both scientists helped awaken an ecological or environmental consciousness in society. Commoner wrote that until he learned about the environment from his work with nuclear fallout, he, "like most people . . . had taken the air, water, soil, and . . . natural surroundings more or less for granted."[4] White blamed Christianity for this general indifference toward and misuse of the environment.

The divine command to subdue and dominate the earth, hope in an eschatological future, and the practices of science and technology, two fruits of Christianity itself, all interact, he argued, to form Christians with an anthropocentric indifference to human degradation of the natural world. Created as superior to nature and to exploit it, humans looked with contempt upon the world that was created to serve their very needs. Furthermore, Christian belief and worship of one God de-mythologized the world of its nature gods. This exorcism of trees, rocks, and water animated by personal spirits reduced nature to impersonal material objects to be used whimsically by humans, but it also was the necessary condition for the reasoned, and later, scientific study of nature. Science was yoked to technology, which

2. White Jr., "The Historical Roots of Our Ecological Crisis," 1203–7.

3. Reiss, "Strontium-90 Absorption by Deciduous Teeth"; Carson, *Silent Spring*.

4. Commoner, *Closing Circle*, 45.

itself manifested human superiority over nature, and together since the Industrial Revolution, they have provided humankind with an "out of control" power that has radically altered the ecology of the planet.[5]

White, however, overstated his case from both an erroneous interpretation of Genesis 1:28—"fill the earth and subdue it"—and from assuming that religious views solely determine one's relationship to nature. As a result, he overlooked other factors that shape one's view of nature and are causes of ecological destruction, such as the Enlightenment, Cartesian dualism and mechanization of nature, the Industrial Revolution, democracy, capitalism and individual resource ownership, urbanization, increased population, and secularization.[6] Though White overstated his case by neglecting to consider the effects of philosophical modernity listed above, other non-Christian religions and their ecological destruction, and, perhaps most significantly, sin, his critique spurred Christians to re-examine their understanding of Scripture and to (re)develop theological perspectives on creation with the knowledge gained from the relatively young field of ecology.

The Origin of the Separation of Creation and Redemption

White confounded the actual behavior of individual Christians with normative Christian dogma and belief. He did not address the reality that many Christians act in a way that is not Christian. The ecological crisis is not the result of Christians obediently following the Gospel or divine decree but is more so the result of sin and a neglect or ignorance of both the divine will and our identity and mission as creatures made in God's image. White accurately described the *praxis* of Christians over the last several centuries who have selfishly exploited the earth, thereby forcing the extinction of species and damaging ecosystems, but he wrongly attributed this to what is proper to Christianity. Are these Christian actions and attitudes expressive of belief in God the Creator and our relationship to God's creation? Pope Francis notes that "some committed and prayerful Christians . . . tend to ridicule expressions of concern for the environment" (§217). What happened that Christians would and do act so indifferently toward creation that White would think this normative?

---

5. White Jr., "The Historical Roots of Our Ecological Crisis," 1206.

6. Moncrief, "The Cultural Basis of our Environmental Crisis," 31–42; Whitney, "The Lynn White Thesis," 313–31.

The Turn to the Subject

Since the Enlightenment, Christian belief in creation and of God as its Creator has been practically eclipsed. Though Christians even today continue to recite the first article of the fourth-century Nicene-Constantinopolitan creed—"I believe in God the Father Almighty, maker of heaven and earth"—such a profession of faith is often more notional than real, and many Christians possess a deistic view of God who does not interact with the natural world. The roots of this distancing of the Church from creation and Creator are found in the soil of the Enlightenment: Cartesian dualism, Kantian epistemology, and Friedrich Schleiermacher's theological turn to the Church.

René Descartes (1596–1650), called the father of modern philosophy, radically departed from Aristotle's idea of the soul as the form of a body or organizing principle of matter. His anthropology is a true substance dualism divided into physical, material substances and mental, immaterial substances. Cartesian dualism separated mind and body into opposing poles with mind being more valuable than material, inanimate bodies. Living beings, seen as machines, were more prone to devaluation.

A century later, the epistemology of Immanuel Kant (1724–1804) would lead to a further conceptual distance between the human person and nature. Kant divided reality into two realms: phenomena which are appearances experienced by us and noumena which are things-in-themselves and non-sensible objects of understanding. We cannot truly say what nature is nor have knowledge of things-in-themselves, such as God or the soul. We can only know a world of appearances. Nature is a construct of the transcendental ego and can only be understood in relation to the human subject who is at the center of all things. The effect of Kant's epistemology was that God was removed from the world of appearances to an unknowable realm of things-in-themselves.

Friedrich Schleiermacher (1768–1834), as the pioneer of liberal Protestantism and modern theology, set the course for the next century as he continued this turn to the subject and interiority and away from the world. His Archimedean principle of religion was not God or faith but an interior, subjective feeling of absolute dependence. This feeling manifests itself as a need for redemption in Jesus Christ who is the perfect and unique model of God-consciousness for sinful humans who lack such awareness. Only the Christian community communicates Jesus's perfect God-consciousness and fulfills human self-actualization. Schleiermacher's turn to the subject is also a theological turn to the church.[7] His thought influenced the succeeding

7. See Dupré, *Religion and the Rise of Modern Culture*, 95–104; Healy, "Three Ways of Engaging Theologically with Modernity," 177–87.

century of theologians such that Claus Westermann pointed to Schleiermacher and his successors' turn to the church and focus on the redemption of
the human person as the primary cause of theology's detachment from the
Creator.[8] God the Father as Creator was eclipsed by Christ the Redeemer.
With the theologians limiting their domain to salvation history and human
redemption, nature as God's creation was abandoned to the hands of the
scientists, many of whom were predisposed toward conflict with religious
perspectives.

The Scientific Revolution

In 1833, a year before Schleiermacher died, Anglican priest and polymath,
William Whewell, coined the word "scientist." Modern science arose in the
nineteenth century in tandem with secularism and even atheism. This association is not essential but was a deliberate decision on the part of some
scientists at the time, two of whom were ardent promoters of Darwinian
evolution: Thomas Huxley and Ernst Haeckel. Huxley explicitly sought to
exclude undesirable categories of people—one being clergy—and associated
religious dogma from emerging scientific societies.[9] Haeckel (1834–1919),
German biologist, used his defense of Darwinian evolution as a vehicle
to advance his own virulent anti-theism. Historians of science today now
identify the essential conflict between science and religion as a myth. The
works of Andrew Dickson White (1832–1918), *A History of the Warfare
of Science with Theology in Christendom* (1896) and John William Draper
(1811–1882), *History of the Conflict between Religion and Science* (1875),
entrenched the warfare myth deeply into the culture that it thrives today
as the dominant view. Their examples of conflict have been shown to be
concocted or taken out of context.[10]

The conflict between science and religion was further complicated by
the ill-conceived response of nineteenth-century theologians to the increasingly secular community and practice of science. Appropriating a Cartesian mechanistic view of nature, the physico-theologians, such as John Ray
(1627–1705) and William Paley (1743–1805), attempted to refute atheism
by pointing to design in nature as an argument for God's existence, but in
the process they reduced God to a univocal cause in the world in competition with natural causes. Organisms understood as machines required a
mechanic to design and make them. Paley famously argued that just as a

8. Westermann, *Creation*, 2–3.

9. Harrison, *Territories of Science and Religion*, 162–63.

10. Harrison, *Territories of Science and Religion*, 172.

pocket watch in its complexity and design points to a human designer, so too organisms in their complexity and design require a designer, namely God. Trying to defend God's existence, the physico-theologians greatly erred and unwittingly contributed to a further alienation of science and theology.

Their error was to reduce divine causality to the order of nature. God the mechanic working on machine-organisms becomes, in effect, another cause in the world. As a result, divine and natural causes compete with one another at the same ontological level. The physico-theologians, thus, had a univocal view of God as equivalent to natural things. But what if a natural cause could explain the design? Charles Darwin's theory of evolution by natural selection offered such a natural explanation that eliminated the need for a divine cause for design. Richard Dawkins is the torchbearer for Darwin today, arguing in his book directed at Paley's doomed argument, *The Blind Watchmaker*, against the existence of God because natural selection has made the need for God as a designer redundant.[11]

Dawkins, however, himself makes a critical philosophical error, when he presumes that having a natural cause precludes the need for a divine cause. He, like the physico-theologians, presumes a univocal view of God where divine and natural causation are in competition and mutually exclusive. Dawkins's rejection of God is on the order of rejecting imaginary or mythic gods that exist in the taxonomy of things in the world: a teapot, the tooth fairy, Flying spaghetti monster, Zeus, Baal, Thor, and Wotan. But this is not what all call God, certainly not Thomas Aquinas.

One final cause of purported conflict between science and faith is the view that rational science alone begets truth while irrational and superstitious religion does not. Science as the only begetter of truth, however, is not science but scientism. Scientism is also science embedded in a philosophical commitment to naturalism—that all that exists is nature. Science uses a method of naturalism; by self-definition, science does not look for divine causes to explain natural phenomena. However, scientists err in making the jump from methodological naturalism to a metaphysics of naturalism. Just because they have limited themselves to natural causes does not mean that all that exists is nature to the exclusion of the divine. The conflict between science (actually scientism) and religion further pushes apart creation and redemption by reinforcing religion's turn to the subject and by scientists' claiming exclusive rights to knowing the truth about the natural world. Those of faith are allowed to dabble in mythical areas such as redemption, but reality, the natural world, is where scientists operate. Confronting this false science and religion narrative is essential for the New Evangelization.

11. Dawkins, *Blind Watchmaker*.

Rediscover the Creator

Pope Francis's foremost remedy to restore humankind's proper relationship to God and the world is a recovery of knowing and worshipping God
the Father specifically as Creator (§75).[12] Humankind's indifference to and
despoiling of our common home reflects a people who "think and live hori-
zontally" and "have drifted away from God."[13] Insightfully, Pope Francis immediately ties this diminished sense of the transcendence to humankind's
no longer reading God's signs in nature. A rediscovery of the transcendent
God is simultaneously an encounter with God immanently present in the
world that the Christian should encounter as creation and not just as nature.

Rediscovery of the Creator is an encounter with the Trinity. Francis's
theological vision of creation is Trinitarian. All of creation comes to be in
and through the Word of God (§77, 99) who became Incarnate of the Virgin
Mary and takes to himself "part of the material world" (§235). The Holy
Spirit, the giver of life, "possesses an infinite creativity" and is "intimately
present to each being" (§80). The encounter with God requires a freedom
from idolatrous imaginings. Idolatry is either the reduction of God to another univocal thing in the world or the elevation of a thing in the world to
an object of worship. Francis clearly recognizes and proclaims that "there
is an infinite distance between God and the things of this world" (§88). If
one were to make an inventory of everything that exists in the universe,
including the universe itself—quarks, atoms, molecules, bacteria, rocks, paper clips, cars, people, Sequoia trees, planets, galaxies—God would not be
another thing on the list. God is not that kind of "thing" or "being," rather
God is existence or being itself. Every created thing has a nature, a way of
being. The nature of a human being is to be a rational animal. The nature of
God is to be to-be.[14] God is more like a verb than a noun. God transcends
human categories to even speak directly about God.

God's transcendence as Creator brings about a fundamental distinction between God and what God creates. Creation is not just the universe
and everything in it. Creation is fundamentally a relationship of dependence of all that is upon God for existence. God is the cause of existence; all
things have being by participating in God's being. God, however, in no way
depends upon creation. Creation did not have to be at all. It is contingent
upon God's free, generous, and loving decision. God freely creates out of
nothing (*ex nihilo*). Important conceptually, creation is not a change. Only

---

12. Pope Francis, *Laudato si'*, 75. All subsequent references to *Laudato si'* will be
indicated parenthetically.

13. Pope Francis, *General Audience*, June 5, 2013.

14. Burrell, *Aquinas: God in Action*, 48.

something that exists can undergo change. To go from nothing to something is not a change. Furthermore, creation is not a temporal event that took place at some point in the past. God continues to create (*creatio continua*) and to bestow existence on what is. If God ceased holding everything in existence, it would fall into nothingness. God's transcendence as Creator does not remove God to some distant realm but allows God's immanence. God is intimately interior to each thing that is as the cause of its existence. God is in everything through His power and presence.

God's transcendence and immanence as Creator means, then, that creation is much more than nature, and this has important consequences in understanding the relationship of divine and natural causation. Pope Francis distinguishes nature as that "system which can be studied, understood and controlled whereas creation can only be understood as a gift from the outstretched hand of the Father of all, and as a reality illuminated by the love which calls us together into universal communion" (§76). Creation is a metaphysical and theological category and not a scientific one. No scientist studies creation but only nature which is the realm of changes. Scientists study the changes in nature over time, but creation is not a change; it is a relationship of dependence upon God for existence. This ontological relationship is not within the domain or range of science to study. Because of this, divine and natural causes exist at different, non-conflicting levels.

God is not only the cause of existence, but He is also the cause of all causes. God endows created things with natures that operate in certain ways. The lilac bush flowers each spring because its nature is directed toward that end. A botanist can study the physiological and anatomical dimensions of that flowering and derive natural causes; however, this does not eliminate God as the cause of the lilac flowering. Divine causes and natural causes operate at different metaphysical levels that do not conflict but act in concert. God is the primary cause as the cause of existence that allows secondary (=natural) causes to operate which can be studied by scientists. Science only studies secondary causes and not primary cause. Thus, scientific and theological explanations are never in conflict with one another as Paley and Dawkins contend with their univocal view of God as another cause in the natural order.

Pope Francis also directly critiques scientism. "It cannot be maintained that empirical science provides a complete explanation of life, the interplay of all creatures and the whole of reality" (§199). Scientism would invalidate art, poetry, and "reason's ability to grasp the ultimate meaning and purpose of things." With science operating within its proper epistemological boundaries, humans are freed from the blindness imposed by scientism that obscures the divine. In faith, nature can be seen as creation, as God's book.

With eyes of faith, Christians can read God's book of creation and recognize nature as "God's art" (§80). Nature is not only a source of wonder and awe but "a continuing revelation of the divine" (§85). Because God is in all things, all creation has a "mystical meaning" (§233). Pope Francis points to his namesake, St. Francis, as the exemplar who praised God through creation (§10–12). St. Francis's affection for all things natural was intimately and inseparably tied to his passion for Christ crucified. St. Francis should not be reduced to the sentimental bird-bath figure of backyards. Nor should his love of creatures be thought of as "a kind of pantheistic harmony with the forces of the cosmos."[15] St. Francis's delight of creatures was tied to their being related to the Word of God who became incarnate of the Virgin Mary and was crucified on the Cross. Pope Francis expresses this strongly Christological understanding of creation. He writes that "all the creatures of the material universe find their true meaning in the incarnate Word, for the Son of God has incorporated in his person part of the material world, planting in it a seed of definitive transformation" (§235).

St. Francis possessed contuition—or wisdom—that enabled him to see creation as transparent to the Word through whom all creation came to be. The sensible world is a mirror that reflects the divine author. Pope Francis calls Christians to see as St. Francis did and thus to recover a semiotic metaphysics that sees the created world as revelatory of the Creator. All is created in and through the Word of God and all returns to God in and through the Incarnate Word of God—the Risen Christ. Pope Francis writes that "creatures no longer appear under merely natural guise because the risen One is mysteriously holding them to himself and directing them towards fullness as their end . . . [All is] imbued with his radiant presence" (§100). By their very existence, all creatures give glory to God and "convey their message to us" (§34).

Rediscovery of God as Creator and nature as creation reanneals the separated strands of creation and redemption into a single unity of God's economy. The Blue Dasher dragonfly has a direct relationship to Jesus Christ, the Incarnate Word. All of creation came into being in and through the Word of God and all is restored through Christ's death and resurrection. Resurrection is not something that happened only to the corpse of Jesus. The resurrection has cosmic consequences. The resurrection of the Incarnate Word takes place within the larger ambit of creation. Creation is not discarded as an ejected rocket stage, rather the resurrection transforms the first gift of creation. Pope Francis directs the reader's attention to this

---

15. Pope Francis, *Homily*, October 4, 2013.

eschatological fulfillment of creation. The "ultimate destiny" of all of creation is found in the bodily risen Jesus (§83).

Creation and redemption have been reunited, science and theology are not only free from belligerence but are set free for dialogue and integration, and nature is conceptually restored as creation that is revelatory of the Creator. However, these conceptual advances can be empty without Christians who actually encounter the created world. Urban life and technology can so fascinate Christians that they neglect or ignore creation.

Serene Attentiveness and Ecological Conversion

Pope Francis embeds creation and our relationship to it within the proclamation of the Good News. Christians are to understand and interpret creation within the "rhythm of the love story between God and [humankind]."[16] Creation is of the same order of redemption, namely the order of love (§77). So, how are Christians to encounter the gift of creation in this divine love? Pope Francis wants to lead Christians back to an encounter with creation through "serene attentiveness." Concomitant with a movement away from a worldly lifestyle and mindset is a serene attentiveness to God's creation. In this, Pope Francis revitalizes the pastoral practice of St. Basil the Great in the fourth century.

St. Basil preached a series of nine homilies on the six days of creation—the *Hexaemeron*—and his overarching goal was to lead his listeners on a guided tour of the amphitheater of God's creation so that they might recognize the Creator through the wondrous spectacle of that creation. He wanted Christians to be able to see themselves as belonging to God's single divine economy that encompasses both the cosmos and history. They were participants in God's drama. One obstacle to this goal was the Christians' fascination with their own world. Basil wanted to wean them from their infatuation with the theater of their own activities (e.g., magic shows, sensual entertainment, horse races), and to take his listeners by the hand and lead them into the natural world of creation—"the mysterious marvels of this great city of the universe"—so that they can lift their minds to God.[17] Those who lifted their minds to the invisible God by their encounter with the visible world of creation Basil called "well prepared auditors" who could hear and participate in the amphitheater of creation.[18] St. Basil speaks his heart's desire for the Christian community, "I want creation to penetrate you with

16. Pope Francis, *General Audience*, June 5, 2013.

17. St. Basil, *Hexaemeron* 6.1.192; 1.6.133.

18. St. Basil, *Hexaemeron* 6.1.192.

so much admiration that everywhere, wherever you may be, the least plant may bring to you the clear remembrance of the Creator."[19]

The attention to creation that makes possible an encounter with God requires "supreme wisdom" that transcends the "worldly wisdom" of those who study the natural world—natural philosophers in Basil's time and scientists in ours. Basil was acutely aware that mere sight of the visible world did not suffice to lead one to God. He drew attention to the Greek natural philosophers, who he said "made much ado to explain nature", but were blind to a Creator, "deceived," he wrote, "by their inherent atheism."[20] For all their "worldly wisdom", the natural philosophers discovered everything except that God is the Creator of the world they studied.[21] Basil cites St. Paul's teaching to the Christians in Rome that the invisible God can be understood through the visible world (Rom 1:20). Their failure to perceive God from their study of the world, Basil sharply condemns, is because, "they have willfully shut their eyes to the knowledge of the truth."[22]

Pope Francis revitalizes Basil's project. We have already seen how Pope Francis, like Basil, addresses the relationship of science and faith and the need for theological wisdom above worldly wisdom. Francis also, like Basil, explicitly quotes from Romans 1:20 and its Old Testament precursor, Wisdom 13:5 (§12). What remains is how one can attend to the actual created world and recognize it as "a joyful mystery to be contemplated with gladness and praise" (§12). Francis, like Basil, wants to wean contemporary Christians from their fascination with the urban and technological world. Today, many Christians are immersed in a lifestyle of "rapidification" (§18) and a throwaway culture of production and consumption (§22) accompanied by urban visual pollution (§44) and informational and digital mental pollution (§47). The pope understands that people are "attracted by things that are *faster and faster*: rapid Internet connections, speedy cars and planes, instant relationships."[23] All of these are modern analogs of fourth-century Christians' immersion in the theater of human affairs. Instead of this distracted self-absorption, Pope Francis proposes a prophetic and contemplative lifestyle marked by an attitude of serene attentiveness to the other. "To be serenely present to each reality, however small it may be, opens us to much greater horizons of understanding and personal fulfilment" (§222). He recognizes the "desperate need for calmness . . . and slowness"[24], and so

19. St. Basil, *Hexaemeron* 5.2.180.

20. St. Basil, *Hexaemeron* 1.2.128–29.

21. St. Basil, *Hexaemeron* 1.4.131.

22. St. Basil, *Hexaemeron* 1.4.131.

23. Pope Francis, *Meeting with the Bishops of Brazil*, 3.

24. Ibid., 3.

calls for a life integrated with ecology that includes "taking time to recover a serene harmony with creation, reflecting on our lifestyle and our ideals, and contemplating the Creator who lives among us and surrounds us, whose presence 'must not be contrived but found, uncovered.'"[25] This would help restore an attitude of "wonder, of contemplation, and of listening to creation" that has been neglected.[26]

Serene attentiveness to creation and to God opens one to transformed relationships with God, oneself, others, and the natural world. It awakens Christians to their identity and evangelical mission that is intimately related to creation and ecology. In the Garden of Eden, humankind's fall from grace disrupted these fourfold relationships such that we were alienated from God, ourselves, others, and the natural world (§66). Jesus Christ has come to reconcile us to God and to restore these broken relationships. The Resurrection of Jesus Christ has inaugurated the new creation, and participation in the life of Christ in the Sacraments, especially the Church's communal celebration of the Eucharist on Sunday, the Lord's Day, "heals our relationships with God, with ourselves, with others and with the world" (§237). The encounter with Jesus Christ calls the human person to conversion. For the Christian, it calls for "'ecological conversion,' whereby the effects of their encounter with Jesus Christ become evident in their relationship with the world around them. Living our vocation to be protectors of God's handiwork is essential to a life of virtue; it is not an optional or a secondary aspect of our Christian experience" (§217).

Connected to this is Pope Francis's implicit critique of Lynn White, Jr.'s thesis. Both recognize that Christianity de-mythologized nature, but for Francis, this only emphasizes the creaturely status of nature and human responsibility for a fragile world entrusted to our care by God (§78). He implicitly rejects White's claim that de-mythologization necessarily objectifies nature for a divine command to exploit it. White, like many Christians, have incorrectly interpreted the divine command to "have dominion" over the earth (Genesis 1:28) as encouraging humankind's "unbridled exploitation" of nature (§67). Countering claims of absolute human domination, Pope Francis offers a brief exegesis focused on the two verbs of Genesis 2:15—to till and keep the garden—that is more appropriate to the biblical context. These verbs have the broader meaning of "to cultivate, care for, protect" that places humankind and creation in a relationship of mutual responsibility. Developing this beyond what Pope Francis has written, "till" and "keep" are used throughout the Old Testament in reference to Israel's relationship

---

25. Pope Francis, *Evangelii gaudium*, 71.

26. Pope Francis, *General Audience*, June 5, 2013.

to God, particularly the priest's cultic worship. "Till" is connected to the Hebrew words "work", "worship", and "service", and so Israel is to "[s]erve the LORD with gladness" (Ps 100:2). David instructs his son, Solomon, to "keep" God's statutes, commandments, and ordinances (1 Kings 2:2–3).[27] The parallel between creation (=Eden) and redemption (Law and the Temple) casts humans as priests serving in the cosmic temple of creation.

Though Pope Francis does not use this image explicitly, a constellation of other images expresses a similar reality. The vocation of steward for creation has priestly overtones for humans are to "thank God" for creation, "implore his help" for its protection, and ask "pardon for the sins committed against the world."[28] Humans have a unique identity capable of dialogue with God (§81) and "endowed with intelligence and love, and drawn by the fullness of Christ, are called to lead all creatures back to their Creator" (§83), the mediating role of a priest. Francis's institution of the World Day of Prayer for the Care of Creation in 2015 joins Christian responsibility for creation to the Church's liturgy, which is a participation in the priestly office of Christ.[29]

As priests and stewards, Christians do not cease being creatures themselves, though this is the constant temptation, namely, to be autonomous of God and his creation. The sin of pride is fundamentally a denial of creatureliness. An integral end of ecological awareness and conversion is the recognition of one's "ecological citizenship" (§211). Humans are not and cannot be independent of their ecological situation. Our existence depends upon the abiotic factors and biotic communities of Earth's varied ecosystems. An ecological identity wherein "everything is interconnected" fittingly reflects the inner relational life of the Trinity (§240). A serene attentiveness to creation should blossom into a "loving awareness that we are not disconnected from the rest of creatures, but joined in a splendid universal communion" (§220). God creates all things in his love, gazing on each thing with tenderness and "enfolding it with his affection" (§77). Do Christians do the same?

This does not mean that we must only gaze contemplatively upon creation and not touch it, for we need to eat to survive and were created with a "vocation to work" and to transform the world through our creativity and labor (§128). Our treatment of the world, however, should be from an awareness of our true identity and not from a false anthropocentrism and claims to absolute ownership (§67). In the ecological amphitheater of God's

27. Beale, *The Temple and the Church's Mission*, 66–80.

28. Pope Francis, "Show Mercy to Our Common Home," September 1, 2016.

29. Pope Francis, *Letter for the Establishment of the "World Day of Prayer for the Care of Creation*," August 6, 2015.

creation, we participate in a divine drama that plays out over evolutionary time. Taxonomists have named 1.5 million of the other cast members with whom we share the stage. Pope Francis cites St. Thomas Aquinas's insight that only the diversity of species, and not one kind alone, fittingly represents God's goodness (§86). Before the Fall, God brought all the animals to Adam so that he could name them. This naming was not an act of domination and ownership but of knowing that comes from intimacy and communion. Do we explore the world with childlike excitement, eagerly learning what some unidentified creature is? Knowing the name of another creature not only brings familiarity and communion, but we share in the prelapsarian ono-mastic joy of Adam whose naming the animals connected him to the divine mind of God who created them. Encountering creation with contuition is not only to "read reality in a Trinitarian key" (§239), but it is to encounter the Trinity.

Christian priestly identity not only transforms the Christian's relation-ship with creation, but it also transforms one's relationship to God by offer-ing a sacrifice of praise to God. The priestly identity of being stewards of creation is manifest in the praise of God for creation. Francis added "care for our common home" to the lists of the spiritual and corporal works of mercy. As a spiritual work, we are called to a "grateful contemplation of God's world."[30] Indifference to creation indicates a lack of faith that God has created the world whose final end is the "fullness of God" himself (§83). A faithful encounter of creation, contemplating "with wonder the universe in all its grandeur and beauty" demands that "we must praise the whole Trin-ity" (§238). Twenty-first century Christians are not accustomed to praising God for the sun, the Andromeda galaxy, the Blue Dasher dragonfly, or the yellow wood-sorrel that grows prostrate among rocks. Every other Sunday morning, however, Christians pray, in the Liturgy of the Hours, the canticle of Daniel (Daniel 3:57–88, 56) in which all living beings, celestial objects, and elements bless and praise God. Creation is an essential part of God's economy of salvation, and the "memory of the faithful, like that of Mary, should overflow with the wondrous things done by God."[31] This does not ex-clude creation, but joins creation to the saving events of God in Jesus Christ as part of God's single divine economy. The "God who liberates and saves is the same God who created the universe, and these two divine ways of acting are intimately and inseparably connected" (§73). The sacramental order of the Church manifests this unity, especially in the Eucharist wherein creation finds its "greatest exaltation" as an "act of cosmic love" for God (§236).

30. Pope Francis, "Show Mercy to Our Common Home," 5.

31. Pope Francis, *Evangelii gaudium*, 142.

Conclusion: New Evangelization

If one is properly prepared, serene attentiveness to creation opens one to an encounter with God the Creator. This preparation, however, requires a formation in philosophical and theological wisdom, the latter of which requires an encounter with God. Conversion always begins with God's initiation. Both the scientific community, the majority of whom are either atheistic or agnostic, and the Christian community itself, many of whom can be suspicious of science or who do not see a connection between creation and redemption, are fertile ground for the Good News of the Gospel. Pope Francis's attention to ecology and the environment has potent possibilities for evangelization of these communities. Christians should not fear science and its discoveries. Rather, they should be encouraged to not only encounter the Creator through creation but to also study the natural world and have intimate knowledge of how it works—its secondary causes. Science is the modern agora for the proclamation of the Gospel.

The basis for this missionary proclamation is an encounter with God. "Only the beauty of God can attract. God's way is through enticement which attracts us . . . He reawakens in us a desire to call our neighbours in order to make known his beauty. Mission is born precisely from this divine allure, by this amazement born of encounter."[32] Christians are to share this amazement even with other Christians. For Christians who already believe, but for whom nature is opaque to God and creation has been dislodged from its union with redemption, St. Basil or Pope Francis's guiding hand is needed for serene attentiveness to the overlooked theater of creation that can be seen with new eyes of faith as transparent to the divine. Serene attentiveness to nature, born of an encounter with God, rediscovers nature as creation and reunites creation into God's single economy of salvation.

Bibliography

St. Basil the Great. *The Treatise De Spiritu Sancto and The Nine Homilies of the Hexaemeron.* Edited by Paul Böer Sr. Edinburgh: T. & T. Clark, 2012.

Beale, G. K. *The Temple and the Church's Mission: A Biblical Theology of the Dwelling Place of God.* Downers Grove, IL: InterVarsity, 2004.

Burrell, David. *Aquinas: God and Action.* Scranton, PA: University of Scranton Press, 2008.

Carson, Rachel. *Silent Spring.* Boston: Houghton Mifflin Harcourt, 2002.

Commoner, Barry. *The Closing Circle.* New York: Bantam, 1974.

Dawkins, Richard. *The Blind Watchmaker.* New York: Norton, 1996.

---

32. Pope Francis, *Meeting with the Bishops of Brazil,* July 28, 2013, 1.

Dupré, Louis. *Religion and the Rise of Modern Culture*. Notre Dame, IN: University of Notre Dame Press, 2008.

Ecklund, Elaine. *Science vs. Religion: What Do Scientists Really Believe?* Oxford: Oxford University Press, 2010.

Francis, Pope. "Show Mercy to Our Common Home." September 1, 2016. The Holy See Web Site. http://w2.vatican.va/content/francesco/en/messages/pont-messages /2016/documents/papa-francesco_20160901_messaggio-giornata-cura-creato. html (accessed September 2, 2016).

————. "Letter for the Establishment of the 'World Day of Prayer for the Care of Creation.'" August 6, 2015. The Holy See Web Site. http://w2.vatican.va/content/ francesco/en/letters/2015/documents/papa-francesco_20150806_lettera-giornata-cura-creato.html (accessed June 6, 2016).

————. *Laudato si'*. Huntington, IN: Our Sunday Visitor, 2015.

————. *Evangelii gaudium*. November 24, 2013. The Holy See Web Site. http:// w2.vatican.va/content/francesco/en/apost_exhortations/documents/papa-francesco_esortazione-ap_20131124_evangelii-gaudium.html (accessed June 6, 2016).

————. "Meeting with the Bishops of Brazil." July 28, 2013. The Holy See Web Site. http://w2.vatican.va/content/francesco/en/speeches/2013/july/documents/papa-francesco_20130727_gmg-episcopato-brasile.html (accessed August 3, 2013).

————. "General Audience of 5 June 2013." The Holy See Web Site. http://w2.vatican. va/content/francesco/en/audiences/2013/documents/papa-francesco_20130605_ udienza-generale.html (accessed June 16, 2016).

————. "Homily: 4 October 4 2013." The Holy See Web Site. http://w2.vatican.va/ content/francesco/en/homilies/2013/documents/papa-francesco_20131004_ omelia-visita-assisi.html (accessed June 6, 2016).

Harrison, Peter. *The Territories of Science and Religion*. Chicago: University of Chicago, 2015.

Healy, Nicholas. "Three Ways of Engaging Theologically with Modernity." *New Blackfriars* 94 (2013) 177–87.

Moncrief, Lewis W. "The Cultural Basis of our Environmental Crisis." In *Western Man and Environmental Ethics: Attitudes toward Nature and Technology*, edited by Ian Barbour, 31–42. Reading, MA: Addison-Wesley, 1973.

Reiss, Louise Z. "Strontium-90 Absorption by Deciduous Teeth: Analysis of Teeth Provides a Practicable Method of Monitoring Strontiun-90 Uptake by Human Populations." *Science* 134 (1961) 1669–73.

Westermann, Claus. *Creation*. Philadelphia: Fortress, 1974.

White, Lynn, Jr. "The Historical Roots of Our Ecological Crisis." *Science* 155 (1967) 1203–7.

Whitney, Elspeth. "The Lynn White Thesis: Reception and Legacy." *Environmental Ethics* 35 (2013) 313–31.

Doctrinal Encounters

CHAPTER 7

Doctrine and Praxis in Pope Francis's Approach to Evangelization

—Melanie Susan Barrett

Abstract:

In contrast to Pope John Paul II's conceptual use of doctrine, Pope Francis utilizes doctrine primarily to animate practice. In so doing, he turns outwardly to the world first—focusing on the concrete needs of those who are poor, broken, or lost—so that the parameters of their existential situation can dictate the shape of the Church's response. While some critics worry that Francis's approach results in a deterioration of doctrine—by replacing settled moral teachings with a form of situation ethics—such concerns are unwarranted. Francis's principal aim is not to dismantle the Church's fundamental moral doctrine, but rather to preserve the proper balance between doctrine and practice, insofar as doctrine exists above all for the salvation of souls. Francis explicitly delineates this pastoral strategy—along with its underlying rationale—in *Evangelii gaudium*, which is explored fruitfully according to four aspects: (1) what challenges Francis takes to be the most pressing; (2) which strategies for pastoral care he rejects as either ineffective or not authentically Christian; (3) which aspects of doctrine he deems central to the Church's mission; and (4) what this implies about Francis's methodological approach to evangelization in general.

S aint Pope John Paul II, in his 1990 encyclical, *Redemptoris missio*, acknowledged a widespread problem in which "entire groups of the baptized have lost a living sense of the faith, or even no longer consider themselves members of the Church, and live a life far removed from Christ and his Gospel."[1] To facilitate the return of these disaffected members, John Paul proposed a "new evangelization" that is "new" in its ardor, methods, and expression.[2] This agenda took shape during his pontificate by means of dynamic personal appearances (in events such as World Youth Day), as well as creative developments in the presentation of doctrine, particularly in the area of moral theology.

These developments interwove key philosophical insights (from classical Thomism and contemporary phenomenology) with several of Vatican II's theological emphases (on the centrality of scripture, the universal call to holiness, and the need for a Christ-centered anthropology): culminating in a comprehensive exposition of the profound and inviolable dignity of the human person—along with its relevant social implications—against the backdrop of the contemporary culture of death.[3] By reforming the Church's internal, conceptual framework for thinking about theology along these lines, the pope conjectured, the Church could better confront a fallen world with the good news of the Gospel.

Moving forward in history to the pontificate of Pope Francis, we observe a similar concern: to evangelize "the lukewarm and the non-practicing" through "new avenues . . . new paths of creativity . . . different forms of expression, more eloquent signs and words with new meaning for today's world," so as to recover the Gospel's "original freshness."[4] Also, like John Paul, Francis evangelizes both by means of deeply symbolic gestures and personal encounters, and through novel articulations of Church teachings in the service of pastoral need.

---

1. John Paul II, *Redemptoris missio*, 33.

2. Address of John Paul II to the assembly of CELAM (Episcopal Conference of Latin American nations), March 9, 1983.

3. The relevant texts from Vatican II are *Optatam totius*, 16, and *Gaudium et spes*, 22 and 24. My use of the term "doctrine" includes teachings found both in John Paul II's major papal documents pertaining to moral theology (*Veritatis splendor, Redemptor hominis, Evangelium vitae, Familiaris consortio, Centesimus annus, Sollicitudo rei socialis*, and *Salvifici doloris*) and his Wednesday papal audiences on the theology of the body. For the definitive English translation of the latter, see John Paul II, *Man and Woman He Created Them*. Throughout this essay, I use the term "doctrine" to indicate exercises of the ordinary papal teaching office. Obviously, the weight of authority given to the teaching in an individual document should be assigned using the accepted methods of interpretation.

4. Francis, *Evangelii gaudium*, 11.

However, in contrast to John Paul II's conceptual use of doctrine, Francis utilizes doctrine primarily to animate practice. In so doing, he turns outwardly to the world first—focusing on the concrete needs of those who are poor, broken, or lost—so that the parameters of their existential situation can dictate the shape of the Church's response. While some critics worry that Francis's approach results in a deterioration of doctrine—by replacing settled moral teachings with a form of situation ethics—I believe that such concerns are unwarranted. Francis's principal aim is not to dismantle the Church's fundamental moral doctrine, but rather to preserve the proper balance between doctrine and practice, insofar as doctrine exists above all for the salvation of souls.[5] I will demonstrate this argument by illuminating and analyzing key passages from *Evangelii gaudium*, Francis's 2013 apostolic exhortation on evangelizing the modern world.

Pope Francis does not confront the world's ills as a soldier armed with doctrine, in search of suitable targets where the greatest impact can be made in the spiritual struggle between good and evil. Rather, he begins by immersing himself in a particular context, and then querying which aspects of doctrine can heal the specific type of brokenness that he encounters. The end result is a set of overarching guidelines for pastoral care, within which some diverse methodological approaches can be regarded as valid. Francis does not worry that this will engender confusion regarding Church teaching. Instead, he expresses confidence that this will open greater space for the Holy Spirit to operate in the lives of the faithful and those they seek to evangelize.

Francis explicitly delineates this pastoral strategy—along with its underlying rationale—in *Evangelii gaudium*. In order to sketch the precise contours of Francis's approach, I will dissect and evaluate the document in order to ascertain: (1) what challenges Francis takes to be the most pressing; (2) which strategies for pastoral care he rejects as either ineffective or not authentically Christian; (3) which aspects of doctrine he deems central to the Church's mission; and (4) what this implies about Francis's methodological approach to evangelization in general.

(1) Pressing Challenges

Francis commences *Evangelii gaudium* by singling out "extreme consumerism" as the great danger plaguing our contemporary world. A heart that is covetous yet complacent tends to pursue frivolous pleasures—and do so

---

5. See, for example, the 1983 *Code of Canon Law* (c 1752), which states that "the salvation of souls . . . must always be the supreme law in the Church."

feverishly—causing one's conscience to become blunted. This blocks out not only God but also other people, especially the poor. Francis observes that believers also can fall prey to this temptation, causing them to become resentful, angry, listless, and unfulfilled rather than joyful and filled with the Holy Spirit.[6]

Audiences ripe for evangelization include: (1) Christians who possess deep faith (which they express in various ways) but who rarely attend mass, (2) baptized Christians who lack faith entirely, and (3) individuals who either do not know Jesus or always have rejected him. Francis declares that the third group is most in need of missionary activity, but throughout the document he advances ecclesial prescriptions intended to benefit all three groups.[7]

In the second chapter, he isolates two factors that will restrain or weaken the desire for missionary renewal *from a pastoral perspective*. Those that *threaten the life and dignity of God's people* include (but are not limited to): extreme poverty, present unemployment coupled with no future possibilities for work, disease, fear, desperation, no joy for life, disrespect for others, and violence.[8] Such ills stem from complex structural causes, such as the idolatry of money, an unquenchable thirst for power and possessions, large-scale economic inequality, an impersonal economy that reduces human beings to mere consumers, a throwaway culture (in which many people are not just exploited or oppressed but entirely excluded), and globalized indifference (in which we no longer feel compassion for the poor and suffering, but instead regard them as someone else's responsibility).[9]

Also problematic are a deterioration of cultural roots, overexposure to mass media and its concentration on entertainment, a diminishment of traditional values (especially with regard to marriage and family), individualism, and secular rationalism.[10] Rather than providing a comprehensive antidote to these ills, religion has been plagued by its own difficulties: persecutions of Christians, attitudes and policies that relegate religion entirely to the private sphere, fundamentalism, new religious movements that promise spirituality without God, widespread religious indifference, moral relativism, and a weakened sense of sin (both personal and collective).[11]

6. *Evangelii gaudium*, 2.

7. Ibid., 15.

8. Ibid., 52–53.

9. Ibid., 53–56.

10. Ibid., 62–63.

11. Ibid., 61.

A second set of factors *negatively affect those involved in the work of evangelization*, most notably: (1) an overemphasis on freedom and relaxation, rather than viewing ecclesial work as a constitutive part of one's identity; and (2) fixating one's spiritual life on a few exercises that are personally comforting but not outward-directed (toward encounters with others or passionate engagement with the world). Though prayerful, such workers become individualistic, experience a crisis of identity, and eventually discover that their initial zeal for evangelization has faded.[12]

This problem is exacerbated when they are further tempted to "relativize or conceal their Christian identity and convictions" in order to feel accepted by the broader culture (of intellectual and media elites) which is skeptical and cynical regarding Church teaching. Desiring to be "like everyone else" and to possess "what everyone else possesses," the joy of mission gradually becomes stifled. Even if they continue to work in evangelization, such work feels burdensome so they contribute only minimal time and energy. The end result is a practical relativism— "acting as if God did not exist, making decisions as if the poor did not exist, setting goals as if others did not exist, working as if people who have not received the Gospel did not exist" —which Francis deems "even more dangerous than doctrinal relativism." He observes that even the person with "solid doctrinal and spiritual convictions" can fall prey to this malady if his or her desire for money, power, or glory eclipses the importance of serving others.[13]

With this framing of the context in mind, Francis then proceeds to map out his policy prescriptions: certain dangerous pitfalls the Church unwittingly has fallen into (in the past) and must cautiously endeavor to avoid (in the future); along with overarching guidelines for pastoral work, within which a diverse set of approaches are permitted and even encouraged, so that the Spirit might work actively and creatively in the Church.

(2) Strategies Rejected

In my reading of *Evangelii gaudium*, the approaches to evangelization—and pastoral work in general—that Francis overtly rejects coalesce around four sets of concerns: (1) ecclesial structures that overvalue administrative results at the expense of personal encounters necessary for true conversion; (2) the temptation to become self-enclosed; (3) immanentism and the temptation to spiritual worldliness; and (4) preaching that is ineffective because it fails to convey the Gospel's central message.

12. Ibid., 78.
13. Ibid., 80.

First, Francis excoriates Church workers for being mere administrators—focused primarily on self-preservation—rather than missionaries.[14] He speculates that this could result from bad structures in the Church, or from good structures not undergirded by the life of the Spirit, both of which hamper evangelization.[15] Either way, many parishes have become "a useless structure out of touch with people or a self-absorbed group made up of a chosen few."[16] Ecclesial communities are unable to fill the gap because many lose contact with their local parish, or focus their ministry on only part of the Gospel.[17]

Church leadership also can contribute to the problem, for many bishops do not listen to everyone—only those who tell them what they would like to hear—and those who work for the Vatican, as well as the papacy itself, do not always hear God calling them to their own pastoral conversion.[18] The end result is that many parishes and communities are unwelcoming, or focus only on administering the sacraments (at the expense of other evangelizing efforts), or deal with people's problems bureaucratically to such an extent that "an administrative approach prevails over a pastoral approach."[19]

Second, many in the Church are tempted to become self-enclosed, so their evangelization efforts either are diminished or are not rooted in charity. Francis quotes Benedict XVI, who proclaims that "being a Christian is not the result of an ethical choice or a lofty idea, but the encounter with an event, a person," namely Jesus Christ, "which gives life a new horizon and a decisive direction."[20] Without the life of the resurrected Christ animating one's actions, however, one's faith life is neither joyful nor fruitful. Francis conjectures that "Christians whose lives seem like Lent without Easter" not only lack the internal motivation for sustained mission-work, they also cannot witness the faith to others in a way that is attractive and compelling.[21]

If evangelizing activity is undertaken "as a joyful response to God's love," then it will be both productive and personally fulfilling; even working too hard will produce "a content and happy tiredness." By contrast, engaging in such work without adequate spiritual motivation will cause one to feel anxious, burdened, unsatisfied, and unbearably fatigued—perhaps

14. Ibid., 25 and 27.
15. Ibid., 26.
16. Ibid., 28.
17. Ibid., 29.
18. Ibid., 31–32.
19. Ibid., 63.
20. Ibid., 7, citing Benedict XVI, *Deus caritas est*, 1: AAS 98 (2006), 217.
21. Ibid., 6.

even to the point of illness. Francis characterizes this deleterious state of affairs as "pastoral acedia," and traces it to unrealistic goals and a lack of patience (that is, anxiously trying to separate the wheat from the weeds—instead of trusting in God—resulting in discouragement, defeatism, and sterile pessimism); or approaching the work in a depersonalized way; or being unable to tolerate criticism or failure.[22] Such workers gradually develop "a tomb psychology"; like mummies in a museum they can no longer "radiate light and communicate life" but instead become disillusioned, sad, and bereft of hope.[23]

Rather than being creative in pastoral work, one continues to do things the way they always have been done.[24] This is an easy trap to fall into, because structures can provide a false sense of security, rules can make one into a harsh judge, and habits can make one feel safe, altogether destroying the motivation to reach out to those in one's midst who are spiritually starving.[25] When dealing with those who are weak or imperfect, one is tempted to close oneself off, become rigid and defensive, and retreat into one's own security in order to avoiding getting one's shoes soiled by the mud of the street.[26] One's conscience might be deeply troubled by people who fail to follow procedures, yet remain unmoved by the deeper spiritual needs of those who lack friendship with Jesus, a community of faith to support them, and a meaningful, goal-oriented life.[27]

Along with the temptation to self-enclosure, believers also can be seduced by an immanentist attitude that ultimately bears fruit in spiritual worldliness. In the broader culture, immanentism (the rejection of God's transcendence) can lead either to false autonomy (in which God is entirely absent) or a spiritual consumerism tailored to an unhealthy individualism. Rather than explicitly rejecting God by embracing atheism, people acknowledge their thirst for God but then seek to satiate it with inauthentic spiritualities—such as "a disembodied Jesus who demands nothing of us with regard to others"—which are not life-giving and cannot engender true healing, freedom, or peace.[28]

Such immanentism is inherently anthropocentric. One's own self—rather than God—becomes the center of one's faith life. Within the Church,

22. Ibid., 82 and 85.
23. Ibid., 83.
24. Ibid., 33.
25. Ibid., 49.
26. Ibid., 45.
27. Ibid., 49.
28. Ibid., 89.

immanentism can manifest itself as an attraction to gnosticism—whereby faith is essentially subjective, and one seeks to consume discrete experiences of consolation and enlightenment but without the concomitant experience of personal conversion. Or immanentism can lead to a "self-absorbed promethean neopelagianism" in which one trusts only in one's own powers and "[feels] superior to others" because one "[observes] certain rules or [remains] intransigently faithful to a particular Catholic style from the past." Rather than evangelizing others, one "analyzes and classifies" them; rather than helping them to experience God's grace, one "exhausts his or her energies in inspecting and verifying," culminating in "a narcissistic and authoritarian elitism."[29] The Church is essentially reduced to a "tollhouse" in which its members serve as arbiters rather than facilitators of grace.[30]

Francis contends that even if such gnostic or neopelagian attitudes are coupled with adherence to Church doctrines, regular practice of Church disciplines, and outwardly professed piety and love for the Church, they still can fuel a spiritual worldliness in which one seeks to advance one's own interests rather than Christ's: "not the Lord's glory but human glory and personal well-being."[31] One becomes overly concerned about being seen by others; captivated by the prospect of social and political gain; obsessed with self-help/self-realization programs; unduly fixated on liturgy, doctrine, or the church's prestige; or simply self-congratulatory about one's practical management skills and caught up in a business mentality that principally benefits the institutional Church rather than "those who are distant or the immense multitudes who thirst for Christ." As a consequence, the Church dwindles to a mere museum piece, or it becomes the exclusive property of a small elite; in either case, "the mark of Christ, incarnate, crucified and risen" is nowhere to be found.[32]

When this occurs, both one's interior spiritual growth and the Church's exterior efforts at evangelization are undermined simultaneously. Preoccupied with self-interest, one becomes obsessed with external appearances; fixates on other people's mistakes; cannot learn from one's own sins; is not truly open to forgiveness; and tends to battle with those Christians who impede one's personal quest for money, power, pleasure, or prestige by "[stoking] a spirit of exclusivity" and forming an inner circle of elites rather than belonging to the whole church.[33] Instead of seeking to accomplish great

29. Ibid., 94.
30. Ibid., 47.
31. Ibid., 93.
32. Ibid., 94–95.
33. Ibid., 97–98.

works on the Church's behalf, one becomes satisfied with a mere "modicum of power," for vainglory leads one to favor "[being] the general of a defeated army [rather] than a mere private in a unit which continues to fight."[34]

A fourth set of pitfalls that impede effective evangelization involves ineffective preaching. One issue pertains to style, which always should be chosen with the hearer's needs in mind, because specific formulations either can enhance or impede one's ability to grasp the substance of what is being communicated. To this end, Francis criticizes preachers who rely heavily on an orthodox language that is alien to their listeners, arguing that it hinders their ability to receive the Gospel (despite being technically accurate).[35]

However, Francis's chief concern with regard to homiletics pertains to content: Does the homily (or other forms of public proclamation) convey the Gospel's central message? Or does it fail to do so? To preach moral teachings separate from the foundational context that makes them meaningful will prove ineffective, Francis cautions, because it typically causes the Church's message to be identified with its secondary aspects. Only the heart of Christ's teaching—"the beauty of the saving love of God made manifest in Jesus Christ who died and rose from the dead"—renders these secondary teachings both meaningful and beautiful in the first place. Not all listeners possess the requisite background, or can make the necessary conceptual connections to the core of the Gospel on their own.[36]

Accordingly, Francis criticizes those homilists who preach "certain doctrinal or moral points based on specific ideological options" rather than the fullness of the gospel; or who are personally "obsessed with the disjointed transmission of a multitude of doctrines to be insistently imposed," rather than focusing on the essentials of Christian faith: that which is "most beautiful, most grand, most appealing and at the same time most necessary."[37]

Similarly problematic is preaching that focuses more frequently on secondary issues than core issues: for example, discussing law more than grace; temperance more than justice or charity; the Church more than Christ; or the Pope more than God's Word. When preachers do this, avers Francis, Christian morality comes across merely as "a form of stoicism, or self-denial, or merely a practical philosophy or a catalogue of sins and faults." Not only is the message no longer fresh; to make matters worse, "the

---

34. Ibid., 96.
35. Ibid., 41.
36. Ibid., 34 and 36.
37. Ibid., 35 and 39.

edifice of the Church's moral teaching risks becoming a house of cards" which, in Francis's estimation, "is our greatest risk."[38]

In sum, from Francis's perspective, ineffective preaching focused on secondary topics, immanentism resulting in spiritual worldliness, being self-enclosed rather than outward-focused, and being overly bureaucratic, all constitute dangerous snares that the Church must strenuously avoid if it wishes to improve future mission effectiveness.

(3) Core Doctrinal Principles

In *Evangelii gaudium*, Francis offers more than a list of flawed strategies to reject. He also provides some overarching guidelines for pastoral work, within which a diverse set of approaches are permitted and even encouraged, so that the Spirit might work actively and creatively in the Church. Consequently, he avows explicitly that the papal magisterium should not offer "a definitive or complete word on every question which affects the Church and the world," not only because dialogue with other disciplines (such as philosophy and the social sciences) is necessary for a full understanding of truth, but also because he firmly believes that the pope should not "take the place of local bishops in the discernment of every issue which arises in their territory."[39]

Corresponding to this desire "to promote a sound decentralization," Francis's positive guidelines, like his critiques, emerge more as observations gleaned from his examination of the current situation than as a conceptual set of fundamental principles.[40] Nevertheless, I will systematize them according to that which he focuses on most concertedly.

First and foremost, Francis maintains that evangelizers should concentrate their efforts on communicating the core message. He reminds his readers that both the dogmas of faith, and the Church's moral teachings, comprise a hierarchy of truths in which some are more important than others. By focusing on the essentials—those which directly express the heart of the Gospel— "the message is simplified, while losing none of its depth and truth, and thus becomes all the more forceful and convincing."[41]

By teaching people about the God of love who saves them, we can help bring them into relationship "not with vague spiritual energies or

---

38. Ibid., 39.
39. Ibid., 40, 132–33, 182, 238, and 242–43.
40. Ibid., 40.
41. Ibid., 35–36.

powers, but with God, with Christ, with Mary, with the saints."[42] This may be accomplished not only through discursive reasoning but also through genuine forms of popular piety—such as those praised by the Aparecida Document—which express the content of the faith symbolically.[43] Related to this, Francis urges us to re-examine both beautiful customs that no longer communicate the heart of the Gospel, and rules or precepts that are no longer useful for directing and shaping people's lives. He also cautions us not to burden the faithful with too many precepts, because it could make religious practice appear as a form of servitude.[44]

Notably, although Francis distinguishes primary from secondary teachings of the faith, and underscores the necessity of focusing on that which is primary, he does not intend thereby to dismiss other teachings. He explicitly asserts that just as there exists a unity of virtues in which all are crucial, so too the entire Gospel message is essential. "All of the truths are important and illumine one another," hence no truth may be denied or the Gospel message will be deformed.[45] Francis's supreme goal remains to pass on the faith in its integrity. At the same time, "the centrality of certain truths" must clearly be evident in order for the Christian message to be conveyed as a harmonious totality.[46]

Accordingly, when preaching or teaching about morality, Francis proposes that we bear in mind the following: (1) virtues are more central than the acts that proceed from them; (2) among the virtues, faith working through love is the most important; (3) among human acts, love of neighbor is the most essential; and (4) among virtues pertaining to external acts, mercy is paramount.[47]

---

42. Ibid., 39 and 90.

43. Ibid., 90 and 124.

44. Ibid., 43.

45. Ibid., 39.

46. Ibid., 39. Citing the teaching of the Second Vatican Council concerning the hierarchy of truths in Catholic doctrine (*Unitatis redintegratio*, 11), Francis states that "all revealed truths derive from the same divine source and are to be believed with the same faith, yet some of them are more important for giving direct expression to the heart of the Gospel . . . This holds true as much for the dogmas of faith as for the whole corpus of the Church's teaching, including her moral teaching" (*Evangelii gaudium*, 36). This is the proper lens through which to interpret Francis's comments in *Evangelii gaudium*, paragraph 34 and following, contrasting "secondary" aspects of the faith with those at the "heart" or "core" of the Gospel.

47. Ibid., 37. Francis cites Gal 5:6, and Thomas Aquinas, *Summa theologiae*, I–II q.66, a.4–6 (on equality among the virtues); I–II q.108, a.1 (on external acts in relation to the New Law); II–II q.30, a.4 (on mercy as the greatest virtue pertaining to our neighbor); and II–II q.30, a.4, ad 1 (on mercy as the most pleasing sacrifice to God).

Second, the Gospel has a social aspect; it encourages face to face encounters.[48] We are meant to respond to God by opening our hearts to divine love, seeing Christ in others, desiring their happiness as God does, and then actively going out of ourselves to seek their good.[49] The different virtues are meant to facilitate this loving response.[50] Rather than being self-enclosed, we should engender fraternity and solidarity with others.[51] Francis insists that this is not an option but a veritable demand of discipleship, because "a personal and committed relationship with God . . . at the same time commits us to serving others."[52]

It also constitutes an indispensable component of the work of salvation, for as Francis reminds us, we are not saved by ourselves, individually, or by our own efforts. Rather, "God attracts us by taking into account the complex interweaving of personal relationships entailed in the life of a human community."[53] Consequently, pastoral activity always should aim to increase interpersonal bonds.[54] If those to whom we reach out subsequently respond with ingratitude, or unjustly attack us, Francis exhorts us to accept suffering within the "embrace of the crucified Jesus" rather than fleeing back into solitude.[55]

Third, all the baptized are called to evangelize: not only clergy, lay ministers, or those who possess certain charisms. Every individual Christian—and every Christian community—is called by Jesus to go forth from their comfort zone in order to reach the peripheries.[56] Furthermore, the Gospel must be preached to everyone—in all places and "without hesitation, reluctance, or fear"—and through both word and deed. Francis proclaims that we can take the initiative with others boldly, because God first did so for us.

Fourth, in addition to faith working through love—which is paramount—some additional virtues are fundamental to mission work.[57] We must be willing to humble ourselves, "touching the suffering flesh of Christ in others," by metaphorically (or perhaps even literally) washing the feet of

48. Ibid., 88.

49. Ibid., 39 and 92.

50. Ibid., 39.

51. Ibid., 87.

52. Ibid., 91.

53. Ibid., 113.

54. Ibid., 67.

55. Ibid., 39 and 91.

56. Ibid., 19–20.

57. Ibid., 37.

those in need.[58] God's love gives meaning to life, and giving to others fulfills us in turn.[59] Yet we always must bear in mind that the primary actor in evangelization is God, not us.[60] Christians can sustain hope within the various "spiritual deserts" found in our families, workplaces, and communities, through being for others a living source of water, but this water is not our own; it is given to us from the side of Christ.[61]

Along with humility, we need both patience and endurance. Accordingly, Francis counsels us to focus on the fruit of our mission work, but without overreacting to the weeds; to be creative and accept even imperfect fruit; and to be willing to be a martyr, though without ever striving to make enemies.[62]

In sum, effective evangelization (1) focuses on communicating the core message of the Gospel; (2) seeks out face-to-face encounters and endeavors to increase interpersonal bonds; (3) is a mandate for all Christians, and is meant for all people in all places; and (4) necessitates several virtues: most notably, faith working through love, humility, patience, and fortitude.

(4) Characterizing Francis's Methodology

As I have demonstrated thus far, Francis's approach to evangelization is in no way deductive. He does not begin with certain doctrinal principles, and then apply them to various cases. Rather, he begins squarely with praxis: the diversity of concrete situations that the Church engages in its pastoral work on a daily basis. Within this praxis, he makes judgments about which needs are most pressing, which pastoral strategies have failed to address those needs, and which approaches are most likely to be effective. It seems reasonable to conclude that such judgments are shaped by Francis's own experience in pastoral ministry, as well as his personal existential commitment to what he terms the "core" or "heart "of the Gospel: God's saving love for us, manifested in Jesus who died and rose from the dead.

Insofar as Francis draws on specific doctrines, he does so primarily to illuminate praxis. We could perhaps characterize this as a *practical* use of doctrine rather than a *conceptual* use of doctrine. One advantage of such an approach is that it provides tremendous flexibility and adaptability in dealing with complex, real-world situations. For example, in urban areas

58. Ibid., 23–24.
59. Ibid., 8–9.
60. Ibid., 12.
61. Ibid., 86.
62. Ibid., 24.

that suffer from grave social injustices (such as human trafficking, the drug trade, the abuse of minors, neglect of the elderly, corruption, and criminal activity), multicultural tensions, isolation, distrust, and a lack of fraternal connectedness, a one-size-fits-all program for evangelization would likely be too "uniform and rigid" to be effective.[63]

One disadvantage of Francis's method is that a lack of conceptual precision regarding *which* doctrines ought to illuminate *which* situations could lead to different moral evaluations of the same case. In Francis's estimation however, such disagreements are not inherently problematic: "For those who long for a monolithic body of doctrine guarded by all and leaving no room for nuance, this might appear as undesirable and leading to confusion. But in fact such variety serves to bring out and develop different facets of the inexhaustible riches of the Gospel."[64]

Francis expresses confidence that as long as the differing approaches to theology, philosophy, and pastoral practice are guided by the Spirit, then the Church will benefit from each of them. In fact, a certain amount of diversity is to be expected because individuals receive reality and the Gospel only partially, and therefore need to complement one another in order for the truth to emerge in its fullness.[65] Nevertheless, the deposit of faith does not itself change, although truth sometimes needs to be expressed in new forms to facilitate greater understanding.[66]

Accordingly, while some critics interpret Francis's emphasis on praxis as signaling an endorsement of situation ethics, this clearly is not the case.[67] Although Francis asserts that the Word is free to the point of unpredictability and unruliness, he also commends the United States Bishops for having "rightly pointed out" that there exist "objective moral norms which are valid for everyone," in response to their moral relativist critics who critique the church for hindering individual freedom.[68]

63. Ibid., 67.

64. Ibid., 40.

65. Ibid., 40 and 40n44.

66. Ibid., 41. Here Francis cites John XXIII, *Address for the Opening of the Second Vatican Council*: AAS 54 (1962), 792; and John Paul II, *Ut unum sint*, 19: AAS 87 (1995), 933.

67. According to Joseph Fletcher's 1966 book, *Situation Ethics*, certain acts traditionally judged by the Church to be objectively evil (such as lying, adultery, premarital sex, or murder) can become morally good in certain situations: "All laws and rules and principles and ideals and norms, are only contingent, only valid if they happen to serve love" in the concrete circumstance. See Fletcher, *Situation Ethics*, 30. For an official critique of this position, see Supreme Sacred Congregation of the Holy Office, *Instruction on "Situation Ethics" contra Doctrinam*, 144; and John Paul II, *Veritatis splendor*, 59.

68. *Evangelii gaudium* 22 and 64.

Furthermore, in counseling how clergy ought to deal with sinners, Francis proposes a balanced approach. He declares that the confessional "must not be a torture chamber but rather an encounter with the Lord's mercy which spurs us on to do our best," and asserts that for a person experiencing great difficulties, even a small step can be greatly pleasing to God. He cites John Paul II's *Familiaris consortio* to contend that accompaniment in personal, spiritual growth must proceed "with mercy and patience" yet *"without detracting from the evangelical ideal."*[69]

As justification, Francis invokes the traditional teaching of the Church—which stipulates that even when one performs an act that is gravely evil in an objective sense, one's subjective culpability might be reduced, such that the sin is not mortal—by citing the *Catechism of the Catholic Church*: "Imputability and responsibility for an action can be diminished or even nullified by ignorance, inadvertence, duress, fear, habit, inordinate attachments, and other psychological or social factors."[70] It is with this caveat in mind that Francis goes on to express optimism that God's saving love "is mysteriously at work in each person, above and beyond their faults and failings," for "whenever perfection is not possible," the Gospel can still bring goodness and light *"without renouncing the truth."*[71]

In conclusion, Francis utilizes doctrine primarily to animate practice. He turns first to the world—especially to those on the margins—so that the parameters of their existential situation can dictate the shape of the Church's response. Francis's principal aim is not to dismantle the Church's fundamental moral doctrine, by collapsing it into situation ethics, but rather to preserve the proper balance between doctrine and practice, insofar as doctrine exists above all for the salvation of souls. This methodological trajectory, set forth in Francis's 2013 apostolic exhortation, *Evangelii gaudium*, provides a helpful lens for interpreting his later writings and public pronouncements.

Bibliography

Catechism of Catholic Church. Washington, DC: United States Catholic Conference, 1997.

Code of Canon Law. Vatican City: Libreria Editrice Vaticana, 1983. http://www.vatican.va/archive/ENG1104/_INDEX.HTM.

Fletcher, Joseph. *Situation Ethics: The New Morality*. Louisville: Westminster John Knox, 1997.

---

69. Ibid., 44. See also John Paul II, *Familiaris consortio*, 34; italics added for emphasis.

70. *Evangelii gaudium*, 44; and *Catechism of the Catholic Church*, 1735.

71. *Evangelii gaudium*, 44–45; italics added for emphasis.

Francis, Pope. *Evangelii gaudium: The Joy of the Gospel.* New York: Random House, 2014.

———. *Amoris laetitia: The Joy of Love.* Vatican City: Libreria Editrice Vaticana, 2016.

———. *Laudato si': On Care for Our Common Home.* Vatican City: Libreria Editrice Vaticana, 2015.

John Paul II, Pope. Address to the assembly of CELAM (Episcopal Conference of Latin American nations). March 9, 1983. In *Compendium on the New Evangelization: Texts of the Pontifical and Conciliar Magisterium, 1939-2012,* edited by Pontifical Council for the Promotion of the New Evangelization, 124–26. Washington, DC: United States Conference of Catholic Bishops, 2015.

———. *Centesimus annus: On the Hundredth Anniversary of Rerum Novarum.* Washington: United States Catholic Conference, 1991.

———. *Evangelium vitae: The Gospel of Life.* Boston: Pauline, 1995.

———. *Familiaris consortio: The Role of the Christian Family in the Modern World. Acta Apostolicae Sedis* 74 (1982) 81–191. Boston: Pauline, 1981.

———. *Man and Woman He Created Them: A Theology of the Body.* Translated by Michael Waldstein. Boston: Pauline, 2006.

———. *Redemptor hominis: The Redeemer of Man.* Boston: Pauline, 1979.

———. *Redemptoris missio: On the Permanent Validity of the Church's Missionary Mandate.* 1990.   http://w2.vatican.va/content/john-paul-ii/en/encyclicals/documents/hf_jp-ii_enc_07121990_redemptoris-missio.html.

———. *Salvifici doloris: On the Christian Meaning of Human Suffering.* Boston: Pauline, 1984.

———. *Sollicitudo rei socialis: On Social Concern.* Boston: Pauline, 1987.

———. *Veritatis splendor: The Splendor of Truth.* Boston: Pauline, 1993.

Rourke, Thomas R. *The Roots of Pope Francis's Social and Political Thought: From Argentina to the Vatican.* Lanham, MD: Rowman & Littlefield, 2016.

Supreme Sacred Congregation of the Holy Office. *Instruction on "Situation Ethics" contra Doctrinam.* February 2, 1956. *Acta Apostolicae Sedis* 48 (1956).

Vatican II. *Unitatis redintegratio: Decree on Ecumenism.* 1964. http://www.vatican.va/archive/hist_councils/ii_vatican_council/documents/vat-ii_decree_19641121_unitatis-redintegratio_en.html

———. *Gaudium et spes: Pastoral Constitution on the Church in the Modern World.* Boston: Pauline, 1965.

———. *Optatam totius: Decree on Priestly Training.* 1965. http://www.vatican.va/archive/hist_councils/ii_vatican_council/documents/vat-ii_decree_19651028_optatam-totius_en.html

Pope Francis and Christian Credibility

—GLENN B. SINISCALCHI

Abstract:

A lively and outspoken pontiff, Pope Francis takes up frequently the credibility of Catholic and, indeed, Christian faith. Three years after his election in March 2013, we can glean from his encyclicals (*Lumen fidei* and *Laudato si'*), apostolic exhortations (*Evangelii gaudium* and *Amoris laetitia*), and other writings clear lines in his apology for faith. Because many commentators have misinterpreted several of the pope's actions and statements, it might be profitable for theologians to delineate his teachings on the credibility of Christian faith. No theologian or religious scholar has discussed the different motives of credibility in the writings of Pope Francis.[1] Such an endeavor should be paramount for the Christian faithful, especially given the biblical mandate to evangelize the world. How does Francis understand the case for Christian faith in the modern world? This chapter will focus exclusively on Francis's writings to answer this question.

Remaining faithful to Scripture and Tradition, the Pope maintains the importance of answering modern challenges to the Church's teaching in fresh new ways: "We need to develop a new synthesis capable of over-

---

1. See, e.g., Kasper, *Pope Francis' Revolution of Tenderness and Love*; Faggioli, *Pope Francis*; Gaillardetz and Rausch, *Go into the Streets!*

coming the false arguments of recent centuries. Christianity, in fidelity to its own identity and the rich deposit of truth which it has received from Jesus Christ, continues to reflect on these issues in fruitful dialogue with changing historical situations. In doing so, it reveals its eternal newness."[2] Sensitive to new circumstances and cultural contexts, the pope highlights several motives for believing in Jesus Christ. These motives span the theoretical and the existential, stressing the need for (1) theoretical apologetics, (2) the experience of discipleship and unconditional love, and (3) the meaning of Catholic doctrine.

Pope Francis as Apologist

One of the central beliefs of Catholic Christianity is the omnibenevolence of God. By accepting God's love in Jesus Christ, every believer is called to love those whom God loves. Since we are called to love *everyone*, it follows that disciples will speak the truth to the beloved.[3] For, love speaks—and therefore defends—the truth, especially when the surrounding context calls for it. Therefore we ought to recognize the importance of developing the skill of articulating the reasons for and against the Gospel. In *Lumen fidei*, Francis observes: "Those who have opened their hearts to God's love, heard his voice and received his light, cannot keep this gift to themselves."[4] By definition, the one who loves goes beyond him or herself for the betterment of others.

The enterprise of giving reasons for faith clashes with the philosophies of relativism and indifferentism.[5] Such philosophies make it difficult to take Christian faith as a viable world-view. Be that as it may, Francis affirms the necessity of providing reasons in support of the Gospel: "Theology . . . must be at the service of the faith of Christians, [and] work humbly to protect and deepen the faith of everyone, especially ordinary believers."[6] For Francis, the very practice of theology is concerned with defending the faith. "The Church," he states, "must offer abundant signs of God's presence and closeness."[7] Part of what it means to be a disciple is to provide reasons in support of the Gospel.

2. Francis, *Laudato si'*, 121.

3. Francis, *Lumen fidei*, 27, 34, 47.

4. Ibid., 37.

5. Francis, *Evangelii gaudium*, 61.

6. Francis, *Lumen fidei*, 36.

7. Francis, *Message of his Holiness Pope Francis for the Thirty First World Youth Day*, 2016, 1.

If an evangelist's interlocutors can at least apprehend the rationale for the Christian faith, apologetics might become a useful tool. In his Apostolic Exhortation, *Evangelii gaudium*, the Pope declared:

> Proclaiming the Gospel message to different cultures also involves proclaiming it to professional, scientific and academic circles. This means an encounter between faith, reason and the sciences with a view to developing new approaches and arguments on the issue of credibility, a creative apologetics which would encourage greater openness to the Gospel on the part of all. When certain categories of reason and the sciences are taken up into the proclamation of the message, these categories then become tools of evangelization; water is changed into wine.[8]

This passage is significant in the corpus of postconciliar teaching documents because the controversial term "apologetics" is employed. John Paul II, for instance, stressed the importance of reason in matters of faith, but he only spoke of "fundamental theology."[9] Moreover, we see that "apologetics" is supposed to be used within the broader context of "professional, scientific and academic circles." This means that apologetics is appropriate for evangelists and their dialogue partners when both parties can at least *think* through the reasons in support of the Gospel.

At the same time, Francis does not shy away from urging all Christians to be actively engaged in defending the faith at some level: "all Christians," he observes, are encouraged "to demonstrate [the Christian message] by their words."[10] The ability to use words in providing a case for the gospel and Church teaching is correlated with the development of one's mind.

No matter the surrounding context of the encounter between evangelists, apologists, and their interlocutors, there should be no such thing as an apologetics that seeks to "win an argument." Rather, an authentic witness seeks to meet doubters' needs with respect: "It is true that in our dealings with the world, we are told to give reasons for our hope, but not as an enemy who critiques and condemns. We are told quite clearly: 'do so with gentleness and reverence' (*1 Pet* 3:15) and 'if possible, so far as it depends upon you, live peaceably with all' (*Rom* 12:18)."[11]

Now that we have seen that apologetics has a significant role in the Catholic Church, we can turn to the different ways in which Francis defends

---

8. Francis, *Evangelii gaudium*, 132.

9. John Paul II, *Fides et ratio*, 67. I have never seen the word "apologetics" used in conciliar or postconciliar teaching documents.

10. Francis, *Evangelii gaudium*, 258.

11. Ibid., 271.

the faith. The most important examples include the following: an evidential approach to Jesus, the defense of moral truth within the broader context of Catholic social ethics, and the natural knowability of God. When I speak of "Francis's apologetics," I am speaking of his defense of the pillars of faith that are accessible to natural reason. "Because God is trustworthy," he writes, "it is reasonable to have faith in him, to stand fast on his word."[12]

The first theme is centered on the use of evidence for the historical Jesus. If Jesus was "God in the flesh," then his existence, words, and deeds are in principle open to historical investigation. Quite naturally, using the historical approach may—with the guidance of the Holy Spirit—help to produce new converts. Some of the Christological signs include Jesus's miracles and his death on the cross (including the theological meaning assigned to the crucifixion by the earliest Christians). Says Francis: "The clearest proof of the reliability of Christ's love is to be found in his dying for our sake."[13] How, then, does one know that God is with us in daily struggles that life presents? One can point to the fact of Jesus's slow torture and execution upon a Roman cross.

Likewise, it is only natural for human beings to search for clues in history that can answer questions about the final destiny of humanity. The search for these answers about what lies beyond the grave can be satisfied by the historical fact of Jesus's resurrection. Thus the post-mortem appearances of Jesus (see (1 Cor 15:3–7) are interpreted as evidence for the emergence of the disciples' faith in the resurrection. In his encyclical *Lumen fidei*, we read:

> Christ's death discloses the utter reliability of God's love above all in the light of his resurrection. As the risen one, Christ is the trustworthy witness, deserving of faith (cf. *Rev* 1:5; *Heb* 2:17), and a solid support for our faith. 'If Christ has not been raised, your faith is futile,' says Saint Paul (1 Cor 15:17). Had the Father's love not caused Jesus to rise from the dead, had it not been able to restore his body to life, then it would not be a completely reliable love, capable of illuminating also the gloom of death. When Saint Paul describes his new life in Christ, he . . . presumes that Jesus himself is worthy of faith, . . . Precisely because Jesus is the Son, because he is absolutely grounded in the Father, he was able to conquer death and make the fullness of life shine forth.[14]

As with the case for the historicity of the crucifixion, the resurrection of Jesus is presented as a credible event. Similar to the case for the resurrection,

12. Francis, *Lumen fidei*, 23.

13. Ibid., 16.

14. Ibid., 17.

Francis references the apologetic import of Jesus's miracles: "Seeing the signs which Jesus worked leads at times to faith, as in the case of the Jews who, following the raising of Lazarus, 'having seen what he did, believed in him' (*Jn* 11:45)."[15]

The second area of rational apologetics centers on the defense of Catholic ethical positions. Today there is an urgent need to defend life (from conception to natural death), human dignity, natural rights, moral duties, the welfare of the poor, the legitimate right to private property, the common good, and the integrity of the environment. Pope John Paul II once said: "the Church's Magisterium has spoken out with increasing frequency in defence of the sacredness and inviolability of human life."[16] It is noteworthy to observe that the terms "defend" and "safeguard" are used more in reference to human life, dignity, natural rights, and responsibilities than any doctrine or moral practice in the Church.[17]

Francis continues this tradition of defending the human person with a renewed conviction. The pontiff's celebrated encyclical on the environment, *Laudato si'*, repeatedly testifies to the defense of several themes in Catholic social ethics.[18] In the pope's words: "Those who are committed to defending human dignity can find in the Christian faith the deepest reasons for this commitment."[19] Elsewhere, we read: "Living our vocation to be protectors of God's handiwork is essential to a life of virtue; it is not an optional or a secondary aspect of our Christian experience."[20] Francis is heavily concerned with global indifference, the consumer mentality, and other forces that sap the enthusiasm for and defensibility of Christian faith.[21]

---

15. Ibid., 30.

16. John Paul II, *Evangelium vitae*, 57.

17. The popes have frequently emphasized the need to defend life, natural rights, human dignity, and rights and duties. See John XXIII, *Princeps pastorum*, 24, *Ad petri cathedram*, 129, 139, *Grata recordatio*, 15, *Mater et magistra*, 1, 15, 16, 20, 22, 37, 85, 89, 103, 108, 109, 111, 179, 249, *Pacem in terris*, 9, 14, 24, 50, 56, 68, 56, 60–63, 65, 77, 104; Paul VI, *Mense maio*, 8, *Populorum progressio*, 39, 42, *Humane vitae*, 20, 23; John Paul II, *Redemptor hominis*, 10, 12, 13, 17–18, *Dives in misericordia*, 1, 11, *Laborem exercens*, 8, 13, 20, *Slavorum apostoli*, 9–10, *Redemptoris missio*, 60, *Centesimus annus*, 3, 6, 7, 13–15, 22, 24, 29, 30, 36, 46, 55, 61, *Veritatis splendor*, 34, 51, 101, *Evangelium vitae*, 1, 2, 5–6, 27, 34, 41–42, 48, 55, 57, 60, 62–63, 71, 77, 81, 82, 90–91, 93, 101, 104, *Ut unum sint*, 74, 76, *Fides et ratio*, 60, 90, 102, *Ecclesia de eucharistia*, 20; Benedict XVI, *Deus caritas est*, 28, *Caritas in veritate*, 11, 22, 34, 29, 43, 55–56, 61–62, 68, 70, 75–76.

18. Francis, *Laudato si'*, 65, 90, 93, 157, 201, 217, 232.

19. Ibid., 65.

20. Ibid., 217.

21. Pope Francis, *Church of Mercy*, 61, 107, 113.

The third example of rational apologetics is the doctrine of the natural knowledge of God. God the creator can be known by simply exercising human reason and opening ourselves to the world before us. Echoing the natural theology of Thomas Aquinas (1225–1274), the Pope said: "The universe as a whole, in all its manifold relationships, shows forth the inexhaustible riches of God . . . Aquinas wisely noted that multiplicity and variety 'come from the intention of the first agent.' . . . The sun and the moon, the cedar and the little flower, the eagle and the sparrow: the spectacle of their countless diversities and inequalities tells us that no creature is self-sufficient."[22]

Francis's exposition of the existence of God is unique among postconciliar Catholic teachings.[23] To be sure, no pope ever spoke about beauty as a natural path to God. But, for Francis, nature is a "magnificent book in which God speaks to us and grants us a glimpse of his infinite beauty and goodness. 'Through the greatness and the beauty of creatures one comes to know by analogy their maker' (Wis 13:5) . . . For this reason, [Saint] Francis asked that part of the friary garden always be left untouched, so that wild flowers and herbs could grow there, and those who saw them could raise their minds to God, the Creator of such beauty."[24]

Given the nod toward Aquinas's philosophical theology, Francis also affirmed the traditional divine attributes.[25] Nowhere does he depart from the theological definition of God as defined at Vatican I (1869–1870). He speaks of the "infinite distance between God and the things of this world, which do not possess his fullness."[26] Uncontroversially, God is "omnipotent"[27] and characterized by "infinite love."[28] Unlike many modern theologians, whose work in the dialogue between science and religion is characterized by the interaction between God and creation, Francis is not a pan-en-theist or a theistic personalist. This should serve as a corrective to drifts toward

---

22. Francis, *Laudato si'*, 86. See also 12, 85, 87, 88, 221.

23. For postconciliar passages that speak about the natural knowability of God, see John XXIII, *Mater et magistra*, 63, 208, 215, 217, *Pacem in terris*, 6, 38, 47, 49–50; Paul VI, *Ecclesiam suam*, 49, 104, *Populorum progressio*, 42, *Humanae vitae*, 10; John Paul II, *Dives in misericordia*, 2, *Dominum et vivificantem*, 36–37, *Centesimus annus*, 37, *Veritatis splendor*, 2, 9, 36, 39–41, 43, 45, 60, 84, 99, etc, *Evangelium vitae*, 21, *Fides et ratio*, 4, 9, 19, 22, 24, 36, 53, 67, 76, 83, 84; Benedict XVI, *Spe salvi*, 30, *Caritas in veritate*, 45, 68, 74, 75.

24. Francis, *Laudato si'*, 12.

25. Francis, *Laudato si'*, 73–75, 243, 246.

26. Ibid., 88.

27. Francis, *Amoris laetitia*, 311.

28. Ibid., 59

theological views on the nature of God that depart from the tenets of classical theism.

Credibility and Human Experience

Above we saw that the Pope maintains that theoretical apologetics has a role to play in the Church's attempt to evangelize the world. Apologetics can also help sustain the Church in keeping the faith in the middle of serious doubts. Be that as it may, Francis acknowledges that the primary motive of credibility is found within the experiential realm, especially as it pertains to an encounter with Spirit-filled disciples: "Jesus wants evangelizers who proclaim the good news not only with words, but above all by a life transfigured by God's presence."[29] "It is not only with words but also and above all with a practical witness in our life that we are teachers and educators of our people."[30] All effective evangelization begins with prayer.[31] Most conversions are therefore triggered by supra-rational encounters with believers, which go above mere evidential approaches. Francis says that the "new evangelization calls on every baptized person to be a peacemaker and a credible witness to a reconciled life."[32]

Simply put, one cannot understand the pope's theology of credibility without highlighting the various existential means that individuals might take in coming to faith. Francis does not settle for philosophical, historical and sociological defenses of the Gospel. To reduce the enterprise of evangelization to a theoretical defense would be woefully shortsighted. By contrast, experiences with united Christians in various ways can serve as a compelling reason to believe in Jesus.

Conversely, unpleasant experiences can turn people away from Christianity in general and the Church in particular.[33] As Giuliano Vigini has noted: "Pope Francis keeps sending out warnings that heavy-handedness, intransigence, hypocrisy, and other shortcomings need to be abolished because they undermine Christian credibility."[34] Furthermore, "Inconsistency on the part of pastors and the faithful between what they say and what

29. Francis, *Evangelii gaudium*, 259.

30. Pope Francis, *Church of Mercy*, 88.

31. Ibid., 82, 123.

32. Francis, *Evangelii gaudium*, 239.

33. Pope Francis, *The Name of God Is Mercy*, 71.

34. Vigini, preface in *Church of Mercy*, xiii.

they do, between word and manner of life, is undermining the Church's credibility."[35]

When Francis thinks of the witness of hospital workers, counselors, teachers, social activists, and those who care for the elderly their witness, for example, he is comforted and sustained in his own efforts to overcome selfishness in the struggle to follow Jesus. In Francis's words:

> The pain and the shame we feel at the sins of some members of the Church, and at our own, must never make us forget how many Christians are giving their lives in love. They help so many people to be healed or to die in peace in makeshift hospitals. They are present to those enslaved by different addictions in the poorest places on earth. They devote themselves to the education of children and young people. They take care of the elderly who have been forgotten by everyone else. They look for ways to communicate values in hostile environments. They are dedicated in many other ways to showing an immense love for humanity inspired by the God who became man. I am grateful for the beautiful example given to me by so many Christians who joyfully sacrifice their lives and their time. This witness comforts and sustains me in my own effort to overcome selfishness and to give more fully of myself.[36]

His experience of pastoral workers therefore gives him the strength to become a better disciple. In other places, the pope showcases the kinds of experiences that help doubters come to faith: happiness, beauty, joy, eloquence of life, religious conviction, and enthusiasm. Observing the ways that people heed the call to enter religious life, the pope once again stresses an experiential path: "The consecrated life will not flourish as a result of brilliant vocation programs, but because the young people we meet find us attractive, because they see us as men and women who are happy!" He continues the same line of argument: "Similarly, the apostolic effectiveness of consecrated life does not depend on the efficiency of its methods. It depends on the eloquence of your lives, lives which radiate the joy and beauty of living the Gospel and following Christ to the full."[37]

Following the convictions of Catholic ecumenical theologians, the experience of Christian unity can be understood as a movement in experiential credibility.[38] "Those wounded by historical divisions," he observes,

---

35. Pope Francis, *Church of Mercy*, 56.

36. Francis, *Evangelii gaudium*, 76.

37. Francis, *To All Consecrated on the Occasion of the Year of Consecrated Life*, II.1.

38. Francis, *Evangelii gaudium*, 100, 244.

"find it difficult to accept our invitation to forgiveness and reconciliation, since they think that we are ignoring their pain or are asking them to give up their memory and ideals. But if they see the witness of authentically fraternal and reconciled communities, they will find that witness luminous and attractive."[39] Notice that the encounter with ecclesiastical unity can prompt individuals to take seriously the Church's teaching.

Only an authentic disciple can become an effective witness to Jesus. "The Church," he writes, "does not evangelize unless she constantly lets herself be evangelized . . . God's word, listened to and celebrated, . . . strengthens Christians, enabling them to offer an authentic witness to the Gospel in daily life."[40] Or again: "The more Christians immerse themselves in the circle of Christ's light, the more capable they become of understanding and accompanying the path of every man and woman towards God."[41] An encounter with disciples who are genuinely united is closely linked to the experience of holiness. Catholic teaching never characterizes the Church as sinful; it is always marked with the sign of holiness. An encounter with saints can therefore draw both insiders and outsiders closer to Christ and the Church.

Likewise, the proper response to suffering does not typically lie within the province of natural theologians. Rather, as evangelizers we must become compassionate toward those who are suffering; we must be present with those who experience injustice: "God does not provide arguments which explain everything; rather, his response is that of an accompanying presence, a history of goodness which touches every story of suffering and opens up a ray of light. In Christ, God himself wishes to share this path with us and to offer us his gaze so that we might see the light within it."[42] Most of the time our actions as disciples will speak louder than our words.

Lastly, because faith makes a moral difference in the lives of believers, it follows that entire cultures that have been affected by Christianity will be positively changed.[43] Such a change can also trigger conversions in those who witness such Christian cultures. Because Jesus Christ is the light of the nations, His presence, work, and message can be apprehended by outsiders through the nature the Church. A major motif in credibility in Catholicism has to do with the positive impact of Christianity upon those cultures where the Gospel is faithfully lived and taught. In the corpus of scholastic litera-

39. Ibid., 100
40. Ibid., 174.
41. Francis, *Lumen fidei*, 35.
42. Ibid., 57.
43. Ibid., 21.

ture this argument was known as the *via empirica*. The Church, insofar as she remains faithful to the Gospel, can serve as a sign of credibility. Francis provides one example of how the *via empirica* might be cast:

> Nor is the light of faith, joined to the truth of love, extraneous to the material world, for love is always lived out in body and spirit; the light of faith is an incarnate light radiating from the luminous life of Jesus. It also illumines the material world, trusts its inherent order and knows that it calls us to an ever widening path of harmony and understanding. The gaze of science thus benefits from faith: faith encourages the scientist to remain constantly open to reality in all its inexhaustible richness. Faith awakens the critical sense by preventing research from being satisfied with its own formulae and helps it to realize that nature is always greater. By stimulating wonder before the profound mystery of creation, faith broadens the horizons of reason to shed greater light on the world which discloses itself to scientific investigation.[44]

Today historians of science recognize that a Catholic mindset was partially responsible for cultivating the necessary intellectual soil in Europe for the sudden emergence of the scientific revolution.[45] Correlatively, as Catholicism continues to devolve in different parts of the West, various cultures will in fact become confused about morality in different ways and begin to suffer.[46] When the Catholic faith has had a positive impact, it becomes easier for doubters to believe in Jesus.

Charity and Credibility

Undoubtedly, the most important experiential motive of credibility is found through love.[47] "The topic of mercy," says Walter Kasper, "has now become the key word of his pontificate, a topic that, from the very first day, he addresses over and over again in countless speeches."[48] So powerful is the role of love in the thought of Pope Francis that he sees it as a major hermeneutical

44. Ibid., 34.

45. Hodgson, *Theology and Modern Physics*, 19–40, 207–22.

46. Francis, *Lumen fidei*, 55, 57.

47. Vigini, preface in *Church of Mercy*, xi, "How these nets should be cast is the focus of Pope Francis' apostolic preaching and mission . . . The keyword of his program, which signposts the way, is sealed in the title: *mercy*." See also Francis, *Lumen fidei*, 16–17; *Evangelii gaudium*, 266; *Misericordiae vultus*, 12.

48. Kasper, *Pope Francis' Revolution of Tenderness and Love*, 31.

key for interpreting and implementing the Second Vatican Council (1962–1965). How should the Church's mission be advanced given the reforms of the Council? He answers: "Errors were condemned, indeed, because charity demanded this no less than did truth, but for individuals themselves there was only admonition, respect and love. Instead of depressing diagnoses, encouraging remedies; instead of direful predictions, messages of trust issued from the Council to the present-day world."[49]

Love exceeds and makes sense out of the propositional statements that are used to formulate doctrine. Love goes above and beyond the rational, but is definitely not against it. Thus, care and compassion for the human person takes precedence over his or her beliefs. As Kasper recognized, the Pope "is a man of encounter and praxis, who is averse to every limited ideology. For him reality takes primacy over idea . . . [His approach] is indebted not to theological books, but to his great pastoral experience as spiritual advisor, provincial, and bishop in the midst of the culture of Buenos Aires."[50]

Francis takes up the original posture of the Council in various ways to further the cause of Christ. This can be seen in several of his writings. In the papal bull of indiction, *Misericordiae vultus*, the Pope repeatedly testifies to the evidential power of supernatural love: "[The Church's] life is authentic and credible only when she becomes a convincing herald of mercy. The Church is called above all to be a credible witness to mercy."[51] When the Church loves the people of the world, She is in fact following the voice of the Lord.

Although some commentators might think that Francis has initiated a major change within the Church by stressing unconditional love as a means to evangelize and/or dialogue with the world, it should be noted that many other popes have emphasized the apologetical potential of charity.[52] Moreover, Jesus himself was the great revolutionary of love. Hence the emphasis on love should not be considered a radical break from the past, but is the Pope's concentrated attempt to implement a vision that has already been provided. Massimo Faggioli has keenly observed: "The Argentine Jesuit

---

49. Francis, *Misericordiae vultus*, 4.

50. Kasper, *Pope Francis' Revolution of Tenderness and Love*, 19.

51. Francis, *Misericordiae vultus*, 25. See also 9, 10, 14, 17.

52. John XXIII, *Princeps pastorum*, 26, 37, *Mater et magistra*, 1, 239, *Aeterna dei sapientia*, 75–76, 79; Paul VI, *Ecclesiam suam*, 63, 103, *Sacerdotalis caelibatus*, 24, 26, 45, 56, *Humanae vitae*, 29; John Paul II, *Dives in misericordia*, 3, 6, 12–14, *Slavorum apostoli*, 9–11, *Sollicitudo rei socialis*, 42, 48, *Redemptoris missio*, 42–43, 70, 89, 91, *Centesimus annus*, 57, *Veritatis splendor*, 3, 20, 26, 89, 95, *Evangelium vitae*, 63, 77, 81, 86–88, 99, *Ut unum sint*, 36, 93; Benedict XVI, *Deus caritas est*, 8, 17, 19, 24, 28, 30, 32–33, 40, 42, *Spe salvi*, 28, 38–39, *Caritas in veritate*, 1, 2, 4–5, 78.

Bergoglio perceives Vatican II as a matter not to be reinterpreted or restrict-ed, but implemented . . . Francis represents an opportunity for a resumption of dialogue not *on* Vatican II, but *from* Vatican II in the life of the Church."[53]

Therefore, Francis's concern is to help motivate believers to take on the "smell of the sheep."[54] In other words, he envisions a Church that will accompany the world in the journey toward the eschaton. Pleading with members of the Church, he averred: "I would prefer a thousand times over a bruised Church to an ill Church! A Church, a catechist, with the courage to risk going out, and not a catechist who is studious, who knows everything but is always closed—such a person is not well. And sometimes he or she is not well in the head."[55]

Francis turns to the historical figure of Jesus to illustrate the true meaning of love and discipleship. Nowhere is the witness of love made more evident than in the life of Jesus. By reaching human beings on their grounds, the One who is Eternal Love became a tangible and visible reality. That concrete reality provides evidence for love itself: "Love, after all, can never be just an abstraction. By its very nature, it indicates something con-crete: intentions, attitudes, and behaviours that are shown in daily living."[56] Since God is love, it makes sense He will reach out to human beings to save and sanctify them: "The signs [Jesus] works, especially in favour of sinners, the poor, the marginalized, the sick, and the suffering, are all meant to teach mercy. Everything in him speaks of mercy."[57] In his book *The Name of God is Mercy*, Francis remarked:

> Jesus moves according to a different kind of logic. At his own risk and danger he goes up to the leper and he restores him, he heals him. In so doing, he shows us a new horizon, the logic of a God who is love, a God who desires the salvation of all men. Jesus touched the leper and brought him back into the com-munity. He didn't sit down at a desk and study the situation, he didn't consult the experts for pro and cons. What really mat-tered to him was reaching stranded people and saving them, like the Good Shepherd who leaves the flock to save one lost sheep. Then, as today, this kind of logic and conduct can be shocking, it provokes angry mutterings from those who are only ever used to having things fit into their preconceived notions and ritual

53. Faggioli, *Pope Francis*, 34, 40.

54. Ibid., 12–13.

55. Pope Francis, *Church of Mercy*, 19.

56. Francis, *Misericordiae vultus*, 8.

57. Ibid., 8.

purity instead of letting themselves be surprised by reality. By a
greater love or a higher standard.[58]

Extending the theology of credibility as displayed in the life and teachings
of Jesus, marriage and family life also serve as concrete signs of God's love;
married couples therefore serve as signs of Christ's love for the Church.
Thus the apostolic exhortation, *Amoris laetitia*, urges the reader to seriously
consider the evangelical witness of married couples.[59] The couples' "mutual
belonging is a real representation, through the sacramental sign, of the same
relationship between Christ and the Church . . . they are for one another and
for their children witnesses of the salvation in which they share. Marriage is
a vocation, inasmuch as it is a response to a specific call to experience conjugal love as an imperfect sign of the love between Christ and the Church."[60]

Since the sacraments are signs of Christ's love for humanity, matrimony is a clue for apprehending the truth of supernatural realities. Correlatively, the sacrament of matrimony bestows a special grace on couples
that enables them to live evangelistically in the world.[61]

Hence, "By their witness as well as their words, families speak to others
of Jesus. They pass on the faith, they arouse a desire for God and they reflect
the beauty of the Gospel and its way of life. Christian marriages thus enliven
society by their witness of fraternity, their social concern, their outspoken-
ness on behalf of the underprivileged, their luminous faith and their active
hope. Their fruitfulness expands and in countless ways makes God's love
present in society."[62]

Catholicism and Other Religions

Pope Francis shows an interest to explicate the uniqueness of Jesus along
with maintaining the real possibility of salvation outside the Church. Such a
contention is faithful to the teachings of Vatican II.[63] There is a substantive
difference between knowing Jesus and being cognitively unaware of him.
The positive impact of knowing Jesus is life-changing and immediate:

> It is impossible to persevere in a fervent evangelization unless
> we are convinced from personal experience that it is not the

58. Pope Francis, *The Name of God is Mercy*, 65–66.

59. Francis, *Amoris laetitia*, 44, 61, 63, 71–73, 87, 121, 123, 134, 162, 184, 213, etc.

60. Ibid., 72.

61. Ibid., 73.

62. Ibid., 184.

63. O'Collins, *The Second Vatican Council on Other Religions*.

same thing to have known Jesus as not to have known him, not the same thing to walk with him as to walk blindly, not the same thing to hear his word as not to know it, and not the same thing to contemplate him, to worship him, to find our peace in him, as not to. It is not the same thing to try to build the world with his Gospel as to try to do so by our own lights. We know well that with Jesus life becomes richer and that with him it is easier to find meaning in everything. This is why we evangelize.[64]

Not to be overlooked, members of the other world religions can in fact be saved.[65] How can this candid admission regarding the salvation of the formal outsiders be reconciled with Jesus's unique status as savior of the world? Further, does interfaith dialogue trump the salvific work of Jesus? The Pope answers these questions decisively in *Evangelii gaudium*:

> In this dialogue, ever friendly and sincere, attention must always be paid to the essential bond between dialogue and proclamation, which leads the Church to maintain and intensify her relationship with non-Christians. A facile syncretism would ultimately be a totalitarian gesture on the part of those who would ignore greater values of which they are not the masters. True openness involves remaining steadfast in one's deepest convictions, clear and joyful in one's own identity, while at the same time being "open to understanding those of the other party" and "knowing that dialogue can enrich each side." What is not helpful is a diplomatic openness which says "yes" to everything in order to avoid problems, for this would be a way of deceiving others and denying them the good which we have been given to share generously with others. Evangelization and interreligious dialogue, far from being opposed, mutually support and nourish one another.[66]

In his language about dialogue and proclamation, Francis picks up the document issued in 1991 by the Pontifical Council for Interreligious Dialogue and the Congregation for the Evangelization of Peoples.[67] Continuing the traditional teaching of the Church, evangelization takes precedence over the notion of interfaith dialogue, but Christians can grow in the Lord by

---

64. Francis, *Evangelii gaudium*, 266.

65. Francis, *Lumen fidei*, 35, 54.

66. Francis, *Evangelii gaudium*, 251.

67. Pontifical Council for Interreligious Dialogue, *Dialogue and Proclamation*, 75, 82.

listening to the voice of the Spirit which can be found in the lives of the religious others.[68]

Given the work of the Spirit outside the formal boundaries of the Church, evangelists should seek common ground with the religious others for the mutual benefit of everyone in the dialogue, but the former should help to bring the latter to fulfillment in Jesus Christ. For, everyone has the right to hear and respond to the Good News: "All peoples and cultures have the right to be helped from within their own traditions to enter into the mystery of God's wisdom and to accept the Gospel of Jesus, who is light and transforming strength for all cultures."[69] Although the "outsiders" should accept the Gospel, the "insiders" recognize that the ongoing attraction of eternal Love calls them to continuously surrender their lives over to Jesus Christ.

By understanding the "signs of the times," Catholic evangelists can anticipate the kinds of objections that doubters may have, and then remove obstacles for these people to perceive the truth of the Gospel. The Gospel is never heard in a vacuum, but is always heard against the backdrop of the culture we live in. It follows that one of the sacred duties of evangelists is to clarify the meanings of the terms that they use in the explication of controversial doctrines.

Conclusion

One of the salient features of Catholic theology is that there are different ways to understand or implement the Gospel in a changing world. There is a legitimate pluralism within the bounds of orthodoxy. Different challenges will call for different responses from the Church. The same must be said for Francis's theology of credibility.

Typically, doubters come to faith because of an encounter with authentic disciples. Perhaps the best thing that evangelists can do in the middle of someone's doubts or emotional struggles is to be present in his or her life. Love is the ultimate apologetic, for it reaches the entire person. People are awakened in the faith by the presence of caring individuals. Conversely, too many unbelievers and lukewarm believers see the sterile lifestyles of the Church and flippantly believe that there is no supernatural component to Catholicism.

Even so, some doubters are persuaded by academic reasons for faith. To be sure, part of "living out the faith" will consist of doing apologetics. "Once again let us ask ourselves: Are we missionaries by our words, and

---

68. Francis, *Evangelii gaudium*, 254.

69. Cf. Francis, *Message of Pope Francis for World Mission Day 2015*, 1.

especially by our Christian life, by our witness? Or are we Christians closed in our hearts and in our churches—sacristy Christians? . . . We should all ask ourselves: How do I bear witness to Christ through my faith?"[70] Regardless of the circumstances, Christians must bear witness to Jesus and the Church in dialogue with the world with kindness and respect.

Bibliography

Benedict XVI, Pope. *Caritas in veritate*. http://w2.vatican.va/content/benedict-xvi/en/encyclicals/documents/hf_ben-xvi_enc_20090629_caritas-in-veritate.html.

———. *Deus caritas est*. http://w2.vatican.va/content/benedict-xvi/en/encyclicals/documents/hf_ben-xvi_enc_20051225_deus-caritas-est.html.

———. *Spe salvi*. http://w2.vatican.va/content/benedict-xvi/en/encyclicals/documents/hf_ben-xvi_enc_20071130_spe-salvi.html.

Faggioli, Massimo. *Pope Francis: Tradition in Transition*. New York: Paulist, 2015.

Francis, Pope. *Amoris laetitia*. https://w2.vatican.va/content/dam/francesco/pdf/apost_exhortations/documents/papa-francesco_esortazione-ap_20160319_amoris-laetitia_en.pdf.

———. *The Church of Mercy*. Chicago: Loyola, 2014.

———. *Evangelii gaudium*. http://w2.vatican.va/content/francesco/en/apost_exhortations/documents/papa-francesco_esortazione-ap_20131124_evangelii-gaudium.html.

———. *Laudato si'*. http://w2.vatican.va/content/francesco/en/encyclicals/documents/papa-francesco_20150524_enciclica-laudato-si.html.

———. *Lumen fidei*. http://w2.vatican.va/content/francesco/en/encyclicals/documents/papa-francesco_20130629_enciclica-lumen-fidei.html.

———. "Message of his Holiness Pope Francis for the Thirty First World Youth Day, 2016." http://w2.vatican.va/content/francesco/en/messages/youth/documents/papa-francesco_20150815_messaggio-giovani_2016.html.

———. "Message of Pope Francis for World Mission Day 2015." https://w2.vatican.va/content/francesco/en/messages/missions/documents/papa-francesco_20150524_giornata-missionaria2015.html.

———. *Misericordiae vultus*. https://w2.vatican.va/content/francesco/en/apost_letters/documents/papa-francesco_bolla_20150411_misericordiae-vultus.html.

———. *The Name of God is Mercy*. New York: Random House, 2016.

———. "To All Consecrated on the Occasion of the Year of Consecrated Life." https://w2.vatican.va/content/francesco/en/apost_letters/documents/papa-francesco_lettera-ap_20141121_lettera-consacrati.html.

Gaillardetz, Richard, and Thomas Rausch, eds. *Go into the Streets!: The Welcoming Church of Pope Francis*. New York: Paulist, 2016.

Hodgson, Peter E. *Theology and Modern Physics*. Burlington, VT: Ashgate, 2013.

John XXIII, Pope. *Princeps pastorum*. http://w2.vatican.va/content/john-xxiii/en/encyclicals/documents/hf_j-xxiii_enc_28111959_princeps.html.

———. *Mater et magistra*. http://w2.vatican.va/content/john-xxiii/en/encyclicals/documents/hf_j-xxiii_enc_15051961_mater.html.

———. *Ad petri cathedram*. http://w2.vatican.va/content/john-xxiii/en/encyclicals/documents/hf_j-xxiii_enc_29061959_ad-petri.html.

---

70. Pope Francis, *Church of Mercy*, 38, 56.

————. *Aeterna Dei sapientia*. http://w2.vatican.va/content/john-xxiii/en/encyclicals/documents/hf_j-xxiii_enc_11111961_aeterna-dei.html.

————. *Pacem in terris*. http://w2.vatican.va/content/john-xxiii/en/encyclicals/documents/hf_j-xxiii_enc_11041963_pacem.html.

————. *Grata recordatio*. http://w2.vatican.va/content/john-xxiii/en/encyclicals/documents/hf_j-xxiii_enc_26091959_grata-recordatio.html.

John Paul II, Pope. *Centesimus annus*. http://w2.vatican.va/content/john-paul-ii/en/encyclicals/documents/hf_jp-ii_enc_01051991_centesimus-annus.html.

————. *Dives in misericordia*. http://w2.vatican.va/content/john-paul-ii/en/encyclicals/documents/hf_jp-ii_enc_30111980_dives-in-misericordia.html.

————. *Dominum et vivificantem*. http://w2.vatican.va/content/john-paul-ii/en/encyclicals/documents/hf_jp-ii_enc_18051986_dominum-et-vivificantem.html.

————. *Ecclesia de eucharistia*. http://www.vatican.va/holy_father/special_features/encyclicals/documents/hf_jp-ii_enc_20030417_ecclesia_eucharistia_en.html.

————. *Evangelium vitae*. http://w2.vatican.va/content/john-paul-ii/en/encyclicals/documents/hf_jp-ii_enc_25031995_evangelium-vitae.html.

————. *Fides et ratio*. http://w2.vatican.va/content/john-paul-ii/en/encyclicals/documents/hf_jp-ii_enc_14091998_fides-et-ratio.html.

————. *Laborem exercens*. http://w2.vatican.va/content/john-paul-ii/en/encyclicals/documents/hf_jp-ii_enc_14091981_laborem-exercens.html.

————. *Redemptor hominis*. http://w2.vatican.va/content/john-paul-ii/en/encyclicals/documents/hf_jp-ii_enc_04031979_redemptor-hominis.html.

————. *Redemptoris missio*. http://w2.vatican.va/content/john-paul-ii/en/encyclicals/documents/hf_jp-ii_enc_07121990_redemptoris-missio.html.

————. *Slavorum apostoli*. http://w2.vatican.va/content/john-paul-ii/en/encyclicals/documents/hf_jp-ii_enc_19850602_slavorum-apostoli.html.

————. *Sollicitudo rei socialis*. http://w2.vatican.va/content/john-paul-ii/en/encyclicals/documents/hf_jp-ii_enc_30121987_sollicitudo-rei-socialis.html.

————. *Veritatis splendor*. http://w2.vatican.va/content/john-paul-ii/en/encyclicals/documents/hf_jp-ii_enc_06081993_veritatis-splendor.html.

————. *Ut unum sint*. http://w2.vatican.va/content/john-paul-ii/en/encyclicals/documents/hf_jp-ii_enc_25051995_ut-unum-sint.html.

Kasper, Walter. *Pope Francis' Revolution of Tenderness and Love*. New York: Paulist, 2015.

O'Collins, Gerald. *The Second Vatican Council on Other Religions*. Oxford: Oxford University Press, 2013.

Paul VI, Pope. *Ecclesiam suam*. http://w2.vatican.va/content/paul-vi/en/encyclicals/documents/hf_p-vi_enc_06081964_ecclesiam.html.

————. *Humanae vitae*. http://w2.vatican.va/content/paul-vi/en/encyclicals/documents/hf_p-vi_enc_25071968_humanae-vitae.html.

————. *Mense maio*. http://w2.vatican.va/content/paul-vi/en/encyclicals/documents/hf_p-vi_enc_29041965_mense-maio.html.

————. *Populorum progressio*. http://w2.vatican.va/content/paul-vi/en/encyclicals/documents/hf_p-vi_enc_26031967_populorum.html.

————. *Sacerdotalis caelibatus*. http://w2.vatican.va/content/paul-vi/en/encyclicals/documents/hf_p-vi_enc_24061967_sacerdotalis.html.

Pontifical Council for Interreligious Dialogue, *Dialogue and Proclamation*.

CHAPTER 9

The Unity of the Virtues in a Missionary Key

—Andrew Kim

Abstract:

The thesis of the unity of the virtues—one must possess all of the virtues to possess even one of them—was upheld in different forms by Plato, Aristotle, Augustine, and Aquinas. However, contemporary moralists almost universally decry this thesis as distorting the nature of virtue as it is materialized in the lives and actions of ordinary people. Unfortunately, academic discourse regarding the unity of the virtues has tended to be either entirely theoretical or narrowly limited to particular individuals or groups as "test cases" regarding the validity of the thesis. It is both significant and reinvigorating, therefore, that in his apostolic exhortation, *Evangelii gaudium*, Pope Francis evokes the thesis of the unity of the virtues as pivotal to the task of evangelization. The purpose of the current essay is to reevaluate the merit and practical applicability of the unity of the virtues in light of the "missionary option" as proposed by Pope Francis.

The unity of the virtues, often referred to as the unity thesis, holds that in order to possess a single virtue one must possess them all. Contemporary moralists almost universally decry the unity thesis as distorting the reality of virtue as it manifests in the lives of those who possess it. However, I have argued that the Thomistic version of the unity thesis illuminates the reality of virtue in a manner that attends to the objections raised by critics of the thesis more coherently than the alternative defini-tions of virtue proposed by the very same critics.[1]

In *Evangelii gaudium*, Pope Francis establishes a new frontier for this ongoing debate by defining the "organic unity of the virtues" as an indis-pensable criterion for authentic evangelization.[2] This raises the issue of whether the vision for evangelization put forward by Francis is subject to the kinds of objections that are commonly brought to bear upon the unity thesis. Primarily at issue here is whether Francis, by employing the unity thesis as a criterion, has defined "authentic evangelization" in a manner that puts the task of evangelizing out of reach for ordinary or even extraordinary individuals. In this chapter, I argue that by utilizing a Thomistic version of the unity thesis as a criterion for authentic evangelization, Francis is not only responsive to the objections just mentioned but also shines new light upon the radical distinctiveness of the Thomistic unity thesis considered within a theological framework.

The argument of the current chapter unfolds in three sections. The first section examines two primary and interrelated objections to the unity thesis. The next section offers a close read of select passages from *Evangelii gaudium* for the purpose of demonstrating that Francis employs the unity of the virtues as a criterion for authentic evangelization, thus raising the issue of whether the understanding of evangelization he puts forward is suscep-tible to the criticisms of the first section. This section then goes on to eluci-date the manner in which the objections of the first section may be applied to authentic evangelization as characterized by Francis. The final section distinguishes between the Thomistic version of the unity thesis employed by Francis in *Evangelii gaudium* and the Stoic version of the unity thesis Francis rejects in the same paragraph, and in so doing, makes clear that Francis's utilization of the unity of the virtues as a criterion for authentic evangelization is capable of being responsive to the concerns which ani-mate the objections derived from the second section. This final section then concludes by reiterating the thesis of this chapter by drawing from the prior sections as well as key passages in *Evangelii gaudium* in order to show that by contextualizing the Thomistic unity thesis as a criterion for authentic evangelization, Francis is able to shed new light upon the radical distinctive-ness of the same thesis evaluated within a theological framework.

---

1. Kim, "Thomas Aquinas on the Connection of the Virtues."

2. Pope Francis, *Evangelii gaudium* (*EG* hereafter).

I. Two Common Objections to the Unity Thesis

The purpose of this section is to clarify and assess two interrelated but importantly distinct objections to the unity thesis. The first objection contends that if the unity thesis is true, then those who possess virtue are "capped off" and thus unable to grow in the moral life.[3] I refer to this as the "impossibility of growth objection." The second objection argues that if the unity thesis is true, then those who lack virtue will only be able to attain it by a dishearteningly demanding and astonishingly abrupt transition from lacking virtue entirely to possessing it completely. I refer to this as the "impossibility of transition objection." Both objections share the unexamined assumption that to affirm the unity of the virtues is to define virtue as a range quality rather than a scalar quality.[4] Also, both objections operate on the basis of a perceived binary conflict between virtue considered as an abstract ideal and virtue as manifested in the lives of actual people. In this view, the former creates an unrealistic and unattainable standard for virtue which is then arbitrarily employed to discount the latter. Those who reject the unity of the virtues on this ground, therefore, regard the unity thesis as a hindrance to an accurate understanding of character in general and virtue in particular.[5]

To begin, the impossibility of growth objection decries the unity thesis for discounting virtue as embodied in the lives of actual people. According to this view, the unity thesis operates on the false premise that there exists such a thing as "*complete* human virtue" or a "*fully* good human life if that means a human life that could not be improved in any way."[6] This objection, then, regards definitions of virtue rooted in the unity thesis to be profoundly distorted.

The impossibly of growth objection is particularly useful with regard to assessing the unity thesis inasmuch as it invites us to scrutinize fundamental

3. Here I borrow a term used by McInerny. See *Difficult Good*.

4. See Rawls, *Theory of Justice*, 506. Also see Waldron's discussion of this topic in *Species and the Shape of Equality*, 76–82. I employ the concepts of a "range" property versus a "scalar" property to delineate between competing definitions of virtue.

5. For example, see Doris, *Lack of Character*. For a critique of the metaphysical assumptions underlying situationist psychology as articulated by Doris, see my "Have the Manicheans Returned?" For a broader discussion of this topic see Miller, "Should Christians Be Worried about Situationist Claims in Psychology and Philosophy?" Miller affirms the general premise of my just mentioned article insofar as he insists upon the need for Christian ethicists to take the claims of situationist psychology more seriously than they currently are (49). However, more relevant to the current chapter, Miller upholds the definition of virtue espoused by situationist psychology as more in keeping with Christian faith than idealized definitions. As we shall see, the current chapter disagrees with this claim.

6. Adams, *Theory of Virtue*, 173.

questions regarding the manner in which one defines virtue. More precisely put, this objection, though employing different terminology than I use here, helps us to clarify the important distinction between virtue considered as a "range" quality versus virtue understood as a "scalar" quality. According to the manner in which I use the concepts here, a "range" quality is a quality that exists in an absolute state and is therefore not subject to gradation. For example, one is either a citizen of France or not. Living in Paris as opposed to Marseille does not make one either more or less French as "being French" is a range quality. One either is or is not. A "scalar" property, on the other hand, is a property that is subject to gradation and may, as a result, be possessed by different individuals to varying degrees. For instance, one may be able to speak French with varying degrees of fluency.

Now, a major assumption implied but not examined by the impossibility of growth objection is that to uphold the unity thesis is to understand virtue as a range quality. It is certainly true that one can find historical examples of groups that understand virtue as a range quality and affirm the unity thesis. For instance, the link between the unity thesis and virtue as a range quality is on full display in Stoic thought about virtue. Diogenes Laertius (ca. 250 AD) reports that the Stoics repudiate the Peripatetic view that there exists a "middle state" in which one might be understood as "progressing" toward virtue without yet possessing it. The moral absolutism of the Stoics is summarily expressed in a striking metaphor:

> For just as those who are submerged in the ocean cannot breathe, whether they are so close to the surface that they are just about to emerge or they are down deep . . . so too whoever is making little progress toward the habit of virtue is no less in misery than one who has not progressed at all.[7]

The Stoics, then, appear to understand virtue as a range property. Virtue denotes a state of moral perfection that does not admit of degrees. Such a view when combined with the unity thesis leads to the conclusion that to accurately attribute any virtue to an individual, one most attribute all of the virtues in an absolute state to that same individual. If we do not want to attribute all of the virtues in an absolute state to an individual, then we cannot attribute any virtue to her or him at all. We see here how the impossibility of growth objection functions on the basis of what I referred to earlier as a perceived binary conflict between virtue as an abstract ideal and virtue as manifested in the lives of actual people. This objection seems particularly

---

7. Cicero, *De finibus* 3.14.48.

apt with regard to Stoic thought. J. M. Rist helps to clarify the underlying logic of Stoic thought in the following passage:

> If the concept of moral goodness admits of degrees, who can say that it could reach a term? If Smith is better than Jones, who is better than Thomas, how can any man be said to be perfect? Could not some moral improvement be imagined? In other words, how could there be a sage or wise man? The Stoics in fact reject a form of the ontological argument in advance. For them, if there are degrees of moral goodness, there cannot be a good, only a relative good.[8]

Herein lies precisely the view against which the impossibility of growth objection responds. If virtue is a range quality, and if one must possess all of them to possess even one of them, then not only is it the case that there exists such a thing as "*complete* human virtue" or a "*fully* good human life," it would also hold that, by definition, the virtuous person has no need of and is indeed impervious to moral growth whereas those lacking virtue lack it absolutely.[9] The enormous canyon between those possessing virtue and those lacking it, then, forms the basis for the second objection of the current section to which I now turn.

The impossibility of transition objection recognizes that if virtue is a range quality and if the unity thesis is true, then there must be only two kinds of people: those with all of the virtues, and those with none of them. Whereas the previous objection concerns the impossibility of growth for those in Group A, the current objection is concerned with the situation of those in Group B. In short, if Group A is "capped off" in moral perfection and Group B utterly deprived of virtue, then there would not exist a common space in which members of Group A could assist members of Group B. A representative sample of this objection may be found in the work of Alasdair MacIntyre

MacIntyre associates the unity thesis with virtue understood as a range quality and argues that virtue so understood renders moral progress impossible for Group B who would lack a "point of moral contact" with Group A. MacIntyre explains his view through a thought experiment involving a courageous and temperate Nazi:

> Consider what would be involved, what was in fact involved, in the moral re-education of such a Nazi: there were many vices that he had to unlearn, many virtues about which he had to

---

8. Rist, *Stoic Philosophy*, 84.
9. Adams, *Theory of Virtue*, 173.

learn. Humility and charity would be in most ways, if not quite in every way, new to him. But it is crucial that he would not have to unlearn or relearn what he knew about both coward-ice and intemperate rashness in the face of harm and danger. Moreover, it was precisely because such a Nazi was not devoid of the virtues that there was a *point of moral contact* between him and those who had the task of re-educating him, that there was something on which to build. To deny that that kind of Nazi was courageous or that his courage was a virtue obliterates the distinction between what required moral re-education in such a person and what did not. Thus, I take it that if any version of moral Aristotelianism were necessarily committed to a strong thesis concerning the unity of the virtues (as not only Aquinas, but Aristotle himself were) there would be a serious defect in that position.[10]

Hence, even if there were a Group A, it is imperative, in MacIntyre's view, that those who lack certain virtues not be conceived of as "devoid of the virtues." Group A must accurately assess the condition of Group B in order to "re-educate" Group B. Thus, MacIntyre appears to regard "a strong thesis concerning the unity of the virtues" as a corollary of the view that virtue is a range quality. When combined, these two views, in MacIntyre's assessment, would place an implacable divide between Group A and Group B. Further-more, if someone were to transition from the latter to the former, however mysteriously, this transition would need be, as John Langan has observed, "surprisingly sudden and implausibly difficult."[11]

In conclusion, this section has evaluated two prominent objections to the unity thesis. Both objections imply that if the unity thesis is true, then no one possesses virtues. The impossibility of moral growth argument con-tends that if the unity thesis is true, then those who, in theory, possess virtue are "capped off" and thus invulnerable to growth in the moral life. Finally, the impossibility of transition objection regards the unity thesis as negat-ing the possibility of attaining virtue for those who lack it. Both objections

---

10. MacIntyre, *After Virtue*, 180; my italics. For a critique of MacIntyre's view as put forward in *After Virtue*, see Lutz, "Is MacIntyre's Theory of Tradition Relativistic?" MacIntyre later revised his view. See MacIntyre, *Whose Justice? Which Rationality?* One might observe how the objection considered here corresponds with MacIntyre's work regarding the possibility of dialogue across moral traditions. For more on this topic, see Fowl, "Could Horace Talk with the Hebrews?"; Hare, *Language of Morals*; Hauerwas, "The Church as God's New Language"; Stout, *Ethics After Babel*.

11. Langan, "Augustine on the Unity and the Interconnection of the Virtues," 89. Kent has also explored the "acquiring the virtues all at once problem." See Kent, "Re-thinking Moral Dispositions: Scotus on the Virtues."

infer a causal link between the unity thesis and virtue understood as a range quality. Having summarized these critiques, then, we may now advance to an examination of the unity thesis as a criterion for authentic evangelization as expounded by Francis in *Evangelii gaudium*.

II. The Unity of the Virtues as a Criterion for Authentic Evangelization

This section scrutinizes select passages from *Evangelii gaudium* for the sake of making clear that Francis employs the unity of the virtues as a criterion for authentic evangelization in a manner that raises the issue of whether the program for evangelization he proposes is susceptible to the objections of the preceding section. As we shall see, a cursory read of the passages that follow could lead one to raise objections structurally similar to those just considered. This section concludes, then, by discerning the shape of these objections as applied to Francis's presentation of authentic evangelization. Having accomplished this, we will then be in position to assess these objections.

In *Evangelii gaudium*, Francis constructs a dichotomy between two groups which I shall again refer to as "Group A" and "Group B." Those in Group A have encountered Jesus, accepted "his offer of salvation," and thus been "set free from sin, sorrow, inner emptiness, and loneliness." In addition to the characteristics just mentioned, those in Group A also lead lives that are "dignified and fulfilled," because they are rooted in "the life in the Spirit which has its source in the heart of the risen Christ." Hence, the most distinctive feature of Group A is that they possess a "joy that is constantly born anew."[12]

Distinctive characteristics of Group B include the following: "the desolation and anguish born of a complacent yet covetous heart, the feverish pursuit of frivolous pleasures, and a blunted conscience" as well as a caved in "interior life" marred by selfishness, an inability to hear God's voice or feel God's love, apathy for the poor, and indifference with regard to doing good. Apparently, a large portion of those in Group B wrongly imagine themselves to be in Group A when, in reality, they also have succumbed to the aforementioned selfishness and are thus, according to Francis, "resentful, angry, and listless." I refer to this group as "Subgroup B." The purpose of Francis's exhortation, then, is to commend a method of evangelization informed by

12. *EG* 1–2.

the kind of joy possessed by Group A in a manner that will forge "new paths for the Church's journey in years to come."[13]

Since they possess a "joy that is constantly born anew," Francis "invites" those in Group A "to a renewed personal encounter with Jesus Christ, or at least an openness to letting him encounter them." Francis implores Group A to "do this unfailingly each day" by saying to Jesus as follows: "Lord, I have let myself be deceived; in a thousand ways I have shunned your love, yet here I am once more, to renew my covenant with you. I need you. Save me once again, Lord, take me once more into your redeeming embrace." Failure to constantly renew this covenant places one into the earlier mentioned Subgroup B, that is, the "resentful, angry, and listless . . . Christians whose lives seem like Lent without Easter."[14]

Francis recognizes that there may exist a set in Group A mired in "grief" and "great suffering" but reaffirms nonetheless that it is incumbent upon this set to allow the "joy of faith to slowly revive them." Francis states that this joy is regained through a "renewed encounter with God's love" that enables one's faith to persevere through "detachment and simplicity." The great barrier to receiving God's love, according to Francis, is the "slow suicide" of self-absorption.[15]

In Francis's view, then, it follows that in order for evangelization to be fruitful, it must be rooted in the distinctive kind of joy possessed by Group A which turns out, upon further examination, to be but a corollary of encountering God and receiving God's love. It is, therefore, a fundamental duty of those in Group A to continually accept this love. Thus, for Francis, receiving God's love and evangelizing are axiomatic, since to receive love is to share it.[16]

In addition to being a duty, then, evangelizing is also the means to a paradoxical and transcendental self-fulfillment achieved only by the emptying of self. Thus, "when the Church summons Christians to take up the task of evangelization, she is simply pointing to the source of authentic personal fulfilment" and thereby witnessing to "a profound law of reality: that life is attained and matures in the measure that it is offered up in order to give life to others. This is certainly what mission means." In Francis's view, it is unlikely that those in Group B will be drawn into the good news of the Gospel by evangelizers who are "resentful, angry, and listless . . . Christians whose lives seem like Lent without Easter," and who evangelize in a manner

13. *EG* 1–3.

14. *EG* 1–6.

15. *EG* 6–7; 272.

16. *EG* 8.

that is "dejected, discouraged, impatient or anxious." Indeed, it appears as though one of Group A's chief obstacles to evangelizing emerges from the activities of Subgroup B.[17]

Francis seems to think that those in Subgroup B exist at opposite poles of a dialectical tension. At the one extreme are those who, failing to recognize the primacy of God in mission, regard evangelizing as a "heroic individual undertaking" and thereby close themselves off from "the newness which God himself mysteriously brings about and inspires, provokes, guides and accompanies in a thousand ways." At the extreme opposite end of the dialectical tension are those who make an idol of newness itself and thus cut themselves off from "the living history which surrounds us and carries us forward." Authentic evangelization seems to require advancing beyond these two poles into a higher synthesis.[18]

To specify in a more concrete manner, Francis explains that Group A consists of "the faithful who regularly take part in community worship and gather on the Lord's day to be nourished by his word and by the bread of eternal life." Group A also includes "those members of the faithful who preserve a deep and sincere faith, expressing it in different ways, but seldom taking part in worship." Subgroup B is comprised of "the baptized whose lives do not reflect the demands of Baptism." Though they have been baptized, they "lack a meaningful relationship to the Church and no longer experience the consolation born of faith." Group B also includes "those who do not know Jesus Christ or who have always rejected him."[19]

The evangelization efforts of Group A are primarily ordered to Group B and then secondarily to Subgroup B. Put another way, if Group A is to reach Group B, then the latter must be protected from Subgroup B. Therefore, in order to authentically evangelize Group B, the Church must continually undergo a missionary transformation of its own whereby it renews the faith of those within its own ranks whose actions do not reveal, but rather conceal, God's presence in the world. It is for this reason that Francis urges "each particular Church to undertake a resolute process of discernment, purification and reform."[20]

Francis maintains that failure to undergo the missionary conversion of which he speaks on both the individual and collective level causes the central meaning of the Gospel to be distorted. While Group A accepts that "all revealed truths derive from the same divine source and are to be believed

17. *EG* 10.

18. *EG* 11–13.

19. *EG* 14.

20. *EG* 30; Also see *Gaudium et spes*, 19–20.

with the same faith," they also are aware that one must prioritize certain truths over others if one is to give "direct expression to the heart of the Gospel." The central message of the Gospel moves the mind beyond mere propositions to a direct experience with the "beauty of the saving love of God made manifest in Jesus Christ who died and rose from the dead." It is this message, above all else, that the members of Group A desire to communicate with the members of Group B.[21]

The members of Subgroup B, on the other hand, are "obsessed with the disjointed transmission of a multitude of doctrines to be insistently imposed." They are careless with the Gospel causing what are in reality secondary aspects of Christ's message to be prioritized over the central message. This doubly harms Group B inasmuch as the central message of the Gospel is not communicated to them at all while the secondary aspects are communicated to them in an alien context rendering those aspects into unintelligible propositional assertions lacking in substance and meaning.[22]

In addition to correctly prioritizing the Gospel message, those in Group A also recognize the role one's actions play in evangelizing. Thus, the actions of Group A embody "faith working through love." These "works of love directed to one's neighbor [are] the most perfect external manifestation of the interior grace of the Spirit." In addition to faith and love, then, the members of Group A also possess mercy which "is the greatest of the virtues, since all the others revolve around it and, more than this, it makes up for their deficiencies." Their mercy flows from God's mercy which reveals God's omnipotence "to the greatest degree." Alternatively, the members of Subgroup B prioritize "the law above grace, the Church above Christ, and the Pope above God's Word."[23]

Those in Group A realize that a Christian morality not rooted in the Gospel is not a Christian morality at all. Since the "Gospel invites us to respond to the God of love who saves us," and since "all of the virtues are at the service of this response of love," it follows that a truly Christian morality must affirm "the organic unity existing among the virtues." There exists, then, in Francis's view, a kind of symbiosis between "the harmonious totality of the Christian message" and the harmonious totality of the group or individual from which that message emanates. Absent this harmonious totality, Christian morality is distorted into "a form of stoicism, or self-denial, or merely a practical philosophy or a catalogue of sins and faults," and the

21. *EG* 34–36.

22. *EG* 35.

23. *EG* 37–38, referencing Aquinas, *Summa theologiae* (*ST* hereafter) IIa IIae q. 30 a. 4.

Gospel itself is reduced "to certain doctrinal or moral points based on specific ideological options."[24]

The unity of the virtues, then, is a criterion for authentic evangelization. The "joy of the Gospel" is nothing other than a "renewed encounter with God's love." In order for this love to achieve its end, it utilizes all of the virtues. In Thomistic terms, charity needs the other virtues to be perfect in act, since actions ordered by charity are much more than mere expressions of charity. Aquinas held that charity cannot achieve its end without the moral virtues, because it is through the moral virtues "that man performs each different kind of good work."[25] Therefore, charity would be unable to achieve its end of loving God without the other virtues, yet the other virtues also require charity in order to be true and perfect.

Having explicated the key role played by the unity thesis in *Evangelii gaudium*, we may now proceed to discern the shape of the objections of the prior section as applied to Francis's presentation of authentic evangelization. In order to do so, we must first make clear two distinctive features of the version of the unity thesis endorsed by Francis. First, Francis is referring to infused virtues. Second, Francis is employing a Thomistic version of the unity thesis insofar as he prioritizes the formal and final cause in understanding virtue.[26] We must, therefore, consider whether the objections of the first section are applicable to the unity thesis so understood.

At this point, we may benefit from Jean Porter's analysis of the unity thesis employing Martin Luther King, Jr. as a counterexample to the unity of the virtues.[27] One may derive the central argument of Porter's essay from the following passage:

> There *are* counterexamples to the [unity] thesis which are . . . difficult to address, precisely because they call attention to people who apparently combine real and even heroic virtues with equally real and crippling vices in one character and one lifetime. King . . . offers such an example. Together with his heroic

24. *EG* 39.

25. *ST* Ia IIae q. 65 a. 3.

26. For more on the distinction between infused and acquired virtue, see McKay-Knobel's "Two Theories of Christian Virtue." For a recent defense of what Knobel refers to as "unification theory," see Mattison, "Can Christians Possess the Acquired Virtues?"

27. Porter, "Virtue and Sin." For a critique of Porter's argument, see Titus, "Moral Development and Connecting the Virtues." For a critique of both views, see my "Progress in the Good." Some have taken issue with my argument regarding the distinctiveness and value of the Thomistic version of the unity thesis. For example, see Murray, "Wandering Virtues," 35. Others, however, have found the argument compelling. For instance, see Fitzgerald, "No Woe to You Lawyers."

and saintly virtues, he displayed clear weakness, particularly through repeated extramarital affairs which he clearly regretted, yet could not forswear.[28]

Porter's argument takes the objections of the previous section up a notch as she not only contrasts an abstract ideal of unified virtue with an equally, and ironically, abstract notion of "the average individual" but with an actual human being who is generally regarded as having possessed heroic virtue. If the unity thesis is true, according to Porter, then the courage and justice of King would not qualify as virtue. If the virtue of King cannot pass muster, then whose can? In Porter's judgment, then, it is only a seriously flawed definition of virtue that would be unable to account for the virtues of an individual who, like King, seemed to possess a character capable of seamlessly and repeatedly moving between displays of heroic virtue at one moment and serious sin the next.

Furthermore, Porter's essay is directly responsive to the issue of whether the infused virtues, particularly as understood within a Thomistic framework, may be able to overcome the problem of moral conflict as existing in individuals such as King. The problem with Aquinas's understanding of acquired virtue, according to Porter, is that it "seems to imply that anyone whose life is marked by a pattern of serious moral struggle, in any respect, is therefore not a person of true virtue."[29] Thus, the courage of King would have to be placed in the same category as the brave bank robber, and she thinks "there must be something wrong with that conclusion."[30]

Porter acknowledges, then, that objections to the unity thesis need to account for important differences in the kind of unity thesis under review. To illustrate, Porter clarifies that for Aquinas "the normal context for the development and exercise of the virtues is the life of grace."[31] According to Aquinas, those who partake of this life have all of the virtues infused into them directly by God through charity.[32] However, such a person may continue to experience moral conflict and struggle due to "the effects of past habits or some other cause."[33] Thus, Aquinas's thesis "can account for the possibility that someone who is truly virtuous is nonetheless also morally

28. Porter, "Virtue and Sin," 528; her italics.

29. Ibid., 529.

30. Ibid.

31. Ibid.

32. *ST* Ia IIae q. 65 a. 3.

33. Porter, "Virtue and Sin," 530; *ST* Ia IIae q. 65 a. 3 ad. 2.

flawed in some ways."[34] This Thomistic view, then, could explain individuals such as King who seem to exhibit moral heroism despite moral struggles.

Ultimately, however, Porter argues that the Thomistic thesis fails because it can only account for "moral flaws" that "are not *too* serious."[35] In Porter's view, "repeated infidelity" implies a persistent and severe "kind of callousness" that even the Thomistic thesis is unable to harmonize with the life of grace.[36] Drawing from Porter's analysis, then, we may now consider the shape of the objections of the preceding section as applied to Francis's presentation of authentic evangelization.

Beginning with the impossibility of growth objection, it would not be difficult to read a definition of virtue as a range quality into the passages from *Evangelii gaudium* referenced earlier. For example, characteristics belonging to Group A such as having accepted Jesus's "offer of salvation," being "set free from sin," and possessing a "joy that is constantly born anew" could be interpreted as absolute states not subject to gradation.[37] One has either accepted Jesus's offer of salvation, or one has not. One has either been set free from sin, or one has not. One either is constantly born anew, or one is not.

In keeping with Porter's just mentioned critique, one may also observe that the characteristics possessed by those in Group B seem to be mutually exclusive from the characteristics possessed by those in Group A such that one could not possess both at the same time. It is difficult, for example, to imagine an individual who is endowed with the capacity to transmit the "beauty of the saving love of God made manifest in Jesus Christ who died and rose from the dead," while simultaneously remaining "obsessed with the disjointed transmission of a multitude of doctrines to be insistently imposed."[38] It is, again, hard to imagine one and the same person evangelizing in a manner informed by love and selflessness while remaining "dejected,

---

34. Porter, "Virtue and Sin," 532.

35. Ibid.; Porter's italics.

36. Ibid. This is why Porter argues that Aquinas's thesis is "inadequate." See Porter, "Virtue and Sin," 537. In my view, Porter's argument takes insufficient notice of Aquinas's view which, while acknowledging that charity can be lost through a single act, also makes clear that charity can "be restored through a single act of repentance: An act of repentance is, by virtue of grace, able to destroy a vicious habit that has been generated. That is why if someone has the vice of intemperateness, when he repents it no longer remains there alongside the infused virtue of temperance in the character of a vice. Rather, it is already in the process of being destroyed, and has become instead a sort of tendency. However, a tendency is not the contrary of a perfected habit." *De virt. comm.* a.10 ad. 16.

37. *EG* 1–2.

38. *EG* 34–36.

discouraged, impatient or anxious."[39] More concretely, perhaps, one either possesses a "deep and sincere faith" in Jesus, placing her or him in Group A, or "does not know Jesus, or rejects Jesus," placing her or him in Group B.[40]

This brings us to the impossibility of transition objection as applied to Francis's presentation of authentic evangelization. This objection is particularly salient here as evangelization by its very nature is directed to the other. Thus, if an implacable divide exists between Group A and Group B, then all attempts at evangelization would turn out to be nothing other than self-referential, tendentious, and vain endeavors.

As MacIntyre observes, if there is no "point of moral contact" between those in Group A and those in Group B, then no improvement can take place. Further, to apply MacIntyre's argument to the issue here under review, if Group A is utterly perfect in virtue and suffer from no serious sin, while Group B is "devoid of virtue" and mired in sin, then there would, it seems, be no such point of contact. The question, then, is whether the infused virtues can bridge the chasm between Group A and Group B in a manner that the acquired virtues cannot.

John Langan has argued that rooting the unity thesis in Christian faith and charity leads to a version of the unity thesis that causes more problems than it solves as it "produces a double standard in the evaluation of Christian and non-Christian persons." Langan rightly recognizes that Augustine's version of the unity thesis is able to account for the "possibility that virtue and sin can coexist in the individual agent" while at the same time "giving a gradualist account of the development of the life of true virtue." However, Langan criticizes Augustine's thesis for denying non-Christians not only "the moral virtues which classical antiquity regarded as the height of human achievement," but also "the theocentric virtues of faith and charity."[41] This "double standard" arising from Christian versions of the unity thesis, then, is particularly relevant in light of MacIntyre's critique insofar as it would amount not just to unfairness but the impossibility of moral communication and growth. When considered in reference to evangelization, then, these observations become quite troubling. If this view is correct, then, as I said before, evangelization would be at best a fool's errand and at worst delusional vanity.

39. *EG* 10.

40. *EG* 15.

41. Langan, "Augustine on the Unity and the Interconnection of the Virtues," 95. What Langan refers to as a "gradualist account" is, I think, much more significant than Langan recognizes. How one evaluates the unity of the virtues is contingent on whether one presumes an understanding of virtue as a range quality or scalar (gradualist in Langan's language).

III. Scalar Virtue

The purpose of this final section is to assess the objections to the unity thesis heretofore considered both in and of themselves and as applied to Francis's understanding of authentic evangelization. In order to do so we first need to make clear that the unity thesis does not axiomatically imply that virtue is a range quality and examine the implications of this. Having accomplished this task, we may then advance to a more accurate evaluation of Francis's understanding of authentic evangelization. In this way, I maintain that Francis's view overcomes the objections of the previous section while also casting new light upon the radical distinctiveness of the Thomistic unity thesis considered within a theological framework.

Christian accounts of the unity of the virtues generally follow the Augustinian move of defining virtue as a scalar quality. Were it not for Protagoras and Aristotle, one might even trace the historical emergence of this definition back to Augustine's critique of the Stoics:

> It seems to me that the Stoics are wrong in refusing to admit that the man who is increasing in wisdom has any wisdom at all, and insisting that he has it only when he is absolutely perfect in it; not that they refuse to admit the increase, but for them he is not wise in any degree unless he suddenly springs forth into the free air of wisdom after coming up and, as it were, emerging from the depths of the sea.[42]

Repudiating the Stoic definition of virtue as a range quality, Augustine likens the attainment of virtue to emerging from a dark cave and gradually adjusting to the light.[43] Defining virtue as a scalar quality, then, Augustine argues that virtue is achieved by degrees (*progrediendo*). Additionally, as mentioned earlier, Augustine transposes the unity thesis into a distinctively Christian framework as may be observed from the following:

> To sum up briefly the general view I have about virtue so far as relates to right living: Virtue is the charity by which what ought to be loved is loved. This charity exists more in some, less in others, and in some not at all; but the greatest charity, which admits no increase, exists in no human living on earth. So long as it admits of increase, what makes it less than it ought is due surely to vice.[44]

---

42. Augustine, *Epist.* 167.2.4.

43. Ibid.

44. Ibid. See Houser, *Cardinal Virtues*, 215.

Aquinas follows not only Augustine but also Aristotle in defining virtue as a scalar quality noting that, for the philosopher, "virtue is the tendency of something complete towards what is best. However, someone can be more disposed or less disposed towards what is best; accordingly, he has virtue to a greater or lesser degree."[45] Aquinas borrows the Augustinian move of differentiating his scalar quality definition from the range quality definition of the Stoics who erred when they said "that no one possesses a virtue without possessing it supremely." According to Aquinas, the Stoic position "does not seem to follow from the character of a virtue, because there is such a variety of ways in which people share in a virtue."[46]

Obviously Aristotle, Augustine, and Aquinas did not recognize an intrinsic conflict between the unity thesis and virtue defined as a scalar quality. Indeed, as demonstrated earlier, the Stoic view was a critique of the Aristotelian view while the Augustinian and Thomistic views are, in several ways, a critique of the Stoic view. It makes sense, then, that there would be noteworthy differentiation here. However, the question still remains of how the unity thesis operates when joined to an understanding of virtue as a scalar quality. Daniel McInerny examines this issue in the following passage:

> While admitting that no one said the virtuous life was going to be easy, we should add that no one ever said (except the Stoics) that the virtuous life had to be capped off in order to be fully virtuous. There are, in other words, degrees of perfection and of unity in attainment of the virtues, and it is reasonable to suppose that we can achieve a certain level of perfection and unity in the life of virtue without having yet achieved absolutely perfect unity of the virtues. Accordingly, the virtuous life might most realistically be described as the life devoted to achieving perfect unity of the virtues, with the recognition built-in that we are always on the way towards that perfect unity.[47]

This view harmonizes with Francis's reference to the Thomistic notion of mercy as "the greatest of the virtues, since all the others revolve around it and, more than this, it makes up for their deficiencies."[48] It wouldn't make much sense for Aquinas to simultaneously assert that virtue does not admit of deficiency and also that mercy "makes up" for the deficiencies of certain

---

45. *De virtutibus communis* a. 11 ad 15.

46. *De virtutibus cardnalibus* a. 3. Francis seems importantly aware of this distinction as he warns against distorting Christian morality into "a form of stoicism" as referenced earlier.

47. McInerny, *Difficult Good*, 85.

48. *EG* 37-38, referencing Aquinas *ST* IIa IIae q. 30 a. 4.

virtues. That mercy is able to do this would indeed be an untenable position if virtue is a range quality but is congruous with virtue understood as a scalar quality.

While defining virtue as a scalar quality attends to the impossibility of growth objection, it does not, in and of itself, respond to the impossibility of transition objection. Even were one to recognize the possibility of "true but imperfect virtue" there still remains the possibility that the individual who is virtuous to degree X might be so far removed from the person who is virtuous to degree Y that there does not exist a "point of moral contact" between the two.[49] Brought back into the realm of authentic evangelization as put forward by Francis, then, there would still be the problem of evangelization achieving its end. Envisioning virtue and the moral life in a scalar context enables Francis to characterize Group A's interactions with Group B not as demanding "surprisingly sudden and implausibly difficult" transitions but rather as accompanying others "with mercy and patience" as one transitions between multiform gradations "of personal growth as these progressively occur."[50] This "accompaniment" language is of fundamental importance, because "in every activity of evangelization, the primacy always belongs to God, who has called us to cooperate with him and who leads us on by the power of his Spirit."[51] It is God alone who "gives the growth."[52]

In addition to being responsive to the objections heretofore considered, then, Francis's utilization of the unity thesis as a criterion for virtue also sheds new light upon the radical distinctiveness of the Thomistic unity thesis considered within a theological framework. By making God's mercy communicated to us through Christ, the impetus of the moral life, Francis reminds us that theological versions of the unity thesis must be sufficiently theological. More precisely put, the Augustinian and Thomistic versions of the unity thesis are not merely the Platonic and Aristotelian theses wearing theological hats. Rather, the respective theses of Augustine and Aquinas differ from those of Plato and Aristotle not only in degree but in kind. The

---

49. *De virtut. card.*, a. 2. Also see *ST* Ia IIae q. 65 a. 2. "It is therefore clear from what has been said that only the infused virtues are perfect, and deserve to be called virtues simply: since they direct man well to the ultimate end. But the other virtues, those namely, that are acquired, are virtues in a restricted sense, but not simply, for they direct man well in respect of the last end in some particular genus of action, but not in respect to the last end simply."

50. *EG* 44.

51. *EG* 12.

52. Ibid., referencing 1 Cor 3:7.

latter root virtue in human effort alone, while the former root virtue in a response to the God who "has loved us first."[53]

Notwithstanding, there remain several issues interrelated to but importantly distinct from the arguments of this chapter that require serious reflection. One main issue, in my view, may be gleaned from Langan's contention that the very notion of distinctively Christian virtue creates "a double standard" which is problematic for any moral system, but particularly problematic with regard to moral systems, "whether philosophical or theological," that wish "to be universal." Langan views this as exceptionally troublesome for "Christians who live in a world that is characterized by both religious pluralism and secular unbelief."[54] On one level, Francis seems resigned to a sectarian view of Christianity as he admits that Christians "will never be able to make the Church's teachings easily understood or readily appreciated by everyone. Faith always remains something of a cross; it retains a certain obscurity which does not detract from the firmness of its assent." Moreover, Francis does not seem to think that reason can play a decisive role in addressing the just mentioned problem since "some things are understood and appreciated only from the standpoint of this assent, which is a sister to love, beyond the range of clear reasons and arguments."[55] In view of this problem, Francis urges us to "remember that all religious teaching ultimately has to be reflected in the teacher's way of life, which awakens the assent of the heart by its nearness, love and witness."[56] Such a way of life, in Francis's view, would subsist in a soul possessing all of the virtues and, by the power of the Spirit, be communicated to others in a "missionary key."[57]

Bibliography

Adams, Robert Merrihew. *A Theory of Virtue*. Oxford: Clarendon, 2006.

Aquinas, Thomas. *Summa Theologica*. Translated by the English Dominicans. 3 volumes. New York: Benziger, 1912–36.

———. *Questions on Virtue: Quaestio disputata de virtutibus in communi, Quaestio disputata de virtutibus cardinalibus, de fraterni correctionis*. Edited by E. M. Atkins and Thomas Williams. Translated by E. M. Atkins. Cambridge: Cambridge University Press, 2005.

53. *EG* 12, referencing 1 John 4:19.

54. Langan, "Augustine on the Unity and the Interconnection of the Virtues," 95.

55. *EG* 42. For a Thomistic reply to the sectarian problem, see my "Aquinas and Hauerwas on the Religious and the Secular."

56. *EG* 42.

57. *EG* 33. It seems, then, that more attention to the role of the virtues in evangelization in general and dialogue in particular is needed. For more on this topic, see my "Dialogue and Communion."

Doris, John M. *Lack of Character*. Cambridge: Cambridge University Press, 2002.

Fowl, Stephen. "Could Horace Talk with the Hebrews? Translatability and Moral Disagreement in MacIntyre and Stout." *The Journal of Religious Ethics* 19, no. 1 (1991) 1–20.

Fitzgerald, John J. "No Woe to You Lawyers: A Virtue-Based Approach to Happiness Within the Legal Profession." *Journal of Moral Theology* 4, no. 2 (2015) 89–120.

Francis. *Evangelii gaudium*: Apostolic Exhortation of the Holy Father Francis to the Bishops, Clergy, Consecrated Persons, and the Lay Faithful on the Proclamation of the Gospel in Today's Word. Vatican City: Libreria Editrice Vaticana, 2013.

Gaudium et spes, Pastoral Constitution on the Church in the Modern World. Translated by Austin Flannery. Dublin, Ireland: Dominican, 1996.

Hare, R. M. *The Language of Morals*. Oxford: Oxford University Press, 1952.

Hauerwas, Stanley. "The Church as God's New Language." In *The Hauerwas Reader*, edited by John Berkman and Michael Cartwright, 142–65. Durham, NC: Duke University Press, 2001.

Houser, R. E. *The Cardinal Virtues: Aquinas, Albert, and Philip the Chancellor*. Toronto: Pontifical Institute of Mediaeval Studies, 2004.

Kent, Bonnie. "Rethinking Moral Dispositions: Scotus on the Virtues." In *The Cambridge Companion to Duns Scotus*, edited by Thomas Williams, 352–54. Cambridge: Cambridge University Press, 2003.

Kim, Andrew. "Thomas Aquinas on the Connection of the Virtues." PhD diss., Catholic University of America, 2013.

———. "Have the Manicheans Returned? An Augustinian Alternative to Situationist Psychology." *Studies in Christian Ethics* 26, no. 4 (2013) 451–72.

———. "Progress in the Good: A Defense of the Thomistic Unity Thesis." *Journal of Moral Theology* 3, no. 1 (2014) 147–74.

———. "Aquinas and Hauerwas on the Religious and the Secular." *New Blackfriars* 96, no. 1063 (2015) 311–25.

———. "Dialogue and Communion." *Journal of Moral Theology* 5, no. 2 (2016) 179–83.

Knobel, Angela McKay. "Two Theories of Christian Virtue." In *America Catholic Philosophical Quarterly* 84, no. 3 (2010) 599–618.

Langan, John P. "Augustine on the Unity and the Interconnection of the Virtues." *Harvard Theological Review* 72, no. 1 (1979) 81–95.

Lutz, Christopher Steven. "Is MacIntyre's Theory of Tradition Relativistic?" In *Tradition in the Ethics of Alasdair MacIntyre: Relativism, Thomism and Philosophy*, edited by Christopher Steven Lutz, 65–109. Plymouth, UK: Lexington, 2004.

MacIntyre, Alasdair. *After Virtue*. Notre Dame: University of Notre Dame Press, 1981.

———. *Whose Justice? Which Rationality*. Notre Dame: University of Notre Dame Press, 1988.

Mattison III, William C. "Can Christians Possess the Acquired Virtues?" *Theological Studies* 72 (2011) 558–85.

McInerny, Daniel. *The Difficult Good: A Thomistic Approach to Moral Conflict and Human Happiness*. New York: Fordham University Press, 2006.

Miller, Christian B. "Should Christians Be Worried about Situationist Claims in Psychology and Philosophy?" *Faith and Philosophy* 33, no. 1 (2016) 48–73.

Murray, Alan Christopher. "Wandering Virtues: Modesty, Patience, and Loyalty in Clinical Medicine." PhD diss., Vanderbilt University, 2016.

Porter, Jean. "Virtue and Sin: The Connection of the Virtues and the Flawed Saint." *Journal of Religion* 75, no. 4 (1995) 521–39.

Rawls, John. *A Theory of Justice.* Oxford: Oxford University Press, 1971.

Rist, J. M. *Stoic Philosophy.* Cambridge: Cambridge University Press, 1969.

Stout, Jeffrey. *Ethics after Babel: The Language of Morals and Their Discontents.* Boston: Beacon, 1988.

Titus, Craig Steven. "Moral Development and Connecting the Virtues: Aquinas, Porter and the Flawed Saint." In *Ressourcement Thomism: Sacred Doctrine, the Sacraments, and the Moral Life,* edited by Reinhard Hütter and Matthew Levering, 330–52. Washington, DC: Catholic University of America, 2010.

Waldron, Jeremy. *Species and the Shape of Equality.* Cambridge: Cambridge University Press, 2002.

Marriage as Mundane Participation in the Divine Sacrifice of Love

The Sacramental Realism of Amoris laetitia

—TIMOTHY P. O'MALLEY

Abstract:

Reactions to *Amoris laetitia* have focused primarily upon the possibility of admitting divorced and re-married Catholics to Communion. Such an approach militates against a more robust reading of the apostolic exhortation's treatment of the sacrament of marriage. In this essay, I argue that Pope Francis is articulating a sacramental account of married love as a mundane participation in God's Paschal sacrifice, and in the process, moving beyond an over-emphasis of sexual intimacy and procreation discernable in John Paul II's *Theology of the Body*. The argument proceeds in four steps. First, through a reading of John Paul II's *Theology of the Body*, I argue that the late pontiff over-emphasizes sexual union within marriage at the expense of the mundane aspects of married love. Second, I show how this lacuna is corrected by Marc Cardinal Ouellet, who provides a liturgical-sacramental account of marriage in which sexual intimacy is only one part. Third, I note how this broader liturgical-sacramental approach to marriage is discernable in *Amoris laetitia*. Lastly, I suggest ways that this approach to marriage might be integral to the New Evangelization.

Among Catholic commentators, reactions to Pope Francis's apostolic exhortation *Amoris laetitia* (AL), have dealt primarily with the admittance of divorced and remarried Catholics to the Eucharist. Chapter 8 of the exhortation, while referencing John Paul II's teaching on continence in *Familaris consortio* (FC), 84, leaves open the possibility that those in this irregular situation may be readmitted to Eucharistic communion while still engaging in sexual intercourse (AL, 296–300). In the conventional world of papal documents, where one affirms the teachings of one's predecessors, Pope Francis's comments on the irregular situation of divorced and remarried Catholics is a seeming rejection of John Paul II's magisterial teaching on the need for continence for Eucharistic participation among the divorced and remarried.

Such tensions in magisterial teaching, rather than being viewed as the overthrow of one regime by another, should serve as an occasion for theologians to discern opportunities for theological development. In this essay, I seek to integrate John Paul II's call for continence within marriage for divorced and remarried Catholics with Pope Francis's theological realism in *Amoris laetitia*. I argue that continence within a second union of a divorced and remarried Catholic requires a sacramental theology of marriage that does not place an ideal at the center of the nuptial mystery. Pope Francis's theological realism, relative to matters of marriage and family life, particularly as related to spiritual fertility among the infertile in *Amoris laetitia,* is better situated to foster the discipline of continence among divorced and remarried Catholics.

John Paul II on Sex in the Sacrament of Marriage

John Paul II's *Theology of the Body* has been described as a revolution in theological thought and method.[1] His contribution to a more robust understanding of the nuptial mystery is discernable both in his treatment of the male and female body as a theological sign, as well as in his account of what it means to be created in the "image of God." This *Theology of the Body,* beginning from the primordial sacrament of matrimony in the Garden of Eden, responds to the reduction of the human person to an object. As Cardinal Scola comments about the effect of calculating, objectifying thought in late modern life: "Man spends his existence in the calculated search of how affections and work, in which the invisible I-thou relation takes its everyday form, can satisfy desire, generate pleasure, and limit (if possible,

---

1. Cahall, *Mystery of Marriage,* 11–13.

eliminate) pain."[2] The modern imagination, formed in this debilitating calculation, cannot perceive on its own the existence of the world itself as gift let alone human sexuality.[3]

For John Paul II and those who followed him, Christian marriage and family life functions as a sacramental medicine for a world grown astigmatic to love. Christianity reveals to man and woman that:

> God is love and in Himself He lives a mystery of personal loving communion. Creating the human race in His own image and continually keeping it in being, God inscribed in the humanity of man and woman the vocation, and thus the capacity and responsibility, of love and communion. Love is therefore the fundamental and innate vocation of every human being (FC, 11).

The contours of John Paul II's *Theology of the Body* are discernable in this passage from *Familaris consortio*. God is a Trinity, a communion of persons, who creates human beings in the image of God. Men and women are made to participate in this *ecstasis* of divine love. In marriage, men and women live out this vocation of love in mutual self-gift through their very embodied existence including in the act of sex. Procreation is intrinsic to the act of sex because this original communion of man and woman results in life. The family (including mother, father, and child) then becomes an icon of this communion of love within human history. As Cardinal Marc Ouellet notes, "[A] Trinitarian anthropology of the family opens a new horizon of meaning for conjugal and familial love, situating it already in an eschatological perspective, as a service to the Glory of God understood as an exchange between the divine Persons."[4] The family, for this reason is integral to the transformation of the world into a site of divine love in the new evangelization.[5]

What is the function of human sexuality for John Paul II in creating this communion of love? In both Karol Wojtyła's *Love and Responsibility*, and John Paul II's *Theology of the Body*, one discerns an elevation of human sexuality noticeably absent from earlier philosophical and theological

---

2. Scola, *Nuptial Mystery*, 111–12.

3. On the role of "gift" in the thought of John Paul II, see Kupczak, *Gift & Communion*, 93–136.

4. Ouellet, *Divine Likeness*, 71.

5. "The Christian Family to the extent it succeeds in living love as communion and service as a reciprocal gift open to all, as a journey of permanent conversion supported by the grace of God, reflects the splendor of Christ in the world and the beauty of the divine Trinity" (Benedict XVI, "The Domestic Church, Evangelized and Evangelizing," 1337).

accounts of sex within Christian thought. In his phenomenological examination of love and sex, Wojtyła writes:

> True love, love that is interiorly full, is one in which we choose a
> person for his own sake; thus in it a man chooses a woman and
> a woman a man not merely as a 'partner' for sexual life, but as a
> person to whom he or she wants to give his or her life. The sexual values, so vibrant in sensual and affective lived-experiences,
> accompany this decision and contribute to its psychological
> vividness, but they do not determine its depth. The very 'core'
> of choosing a person must be personal, not merely sexual. Life
> will test the value of the choice and the true greatness of love.[6]

Although it may seem that Wojtyła is de-emphasizing sex in love, in fact, he is elevating it. He notes earlier in the same chapter that all decisions about love will necessarily involve sexual value: "this love is to have its sexual overtone, which is to constitute the basis of the whole interaction between persons of different sex."[7] The term "sexual value" (*stosunek seksualny*) is essential to grasping Wojtyła's phenomenological account of spousal love. Sexual desire is a value insofar as it manifests to the one loving the intrinsic beauty of the beloved. As Dietrich Von Hildebrand notes about the value response of love, "Love in all its forms . . . involves this consciousness of the preciousness of the beloved person, and of a value datum so closely united with the person that the person stands before me as valuable, beautiful in himself, deriving all his attractive power and delightfulness from his preciousness and beauty."[8] By speaking about a sexual value, Wojtyła is treating sex not as an idol of pleasure unto itself but an icon that reveals to the properly disposed person the intrinsic goodness of the beloved.[9]

Wojtyła is by no means Pollyannaish about the ease through which a man or a woman learns to perceive this sexual value. He deals well with the reality of concupiscence in human sexuality. Concupiscence of the flesh in *Love and Responsibility* is the devolution of sexual value into mere desire: "[I]nterest in the sexual value 'linked with the body' so easily changes into another, i.e., into bodily desire."[10] It is this power of sex, which can deform the will that properly describes what is meant by concupiscence.

---

6. Wojtyła, *Love and Responsibility*, 115–16.

7. Ibid., 114.

8. Hildebrand, *Nature of Love*, 19.

9. Here, value is closely linked to Marion's account of the idol and the icon, particularly in love. See Marion, "The Intentionality of Love," 71–101.

10. Wojtyła, *Love and Responsibility*, 131.

Still, for Wojtyła, not all hope is lost. Concupiscence can be healed through the virtue of chastity, "a form of self-possession that makes sexual and other forms of self-donation possible."[11] This formation into chastity is not simply the exercise of the raw, naked will. Instead, it is that virtue that continually affirms the fundamental dignity of the beloved at every moment: "The essence of chastity lies precisely in 'keeping up' with the value of the person in every situation and in 'pulling up' to this value every reaction to the value of the 'body and sex.'"[12] There is a need for a sexual education that is not about the technology of sex but a formation into the virtue of chastity:

> The most important point of this education is to shape the following conviction: *the other person is more important than I.* This conviction will not appear all of a sudden and out of nothing, purely on the basis of bodily intercourse alone. It can be only and exclusively a result of integral education in love. *Sexual intercourse alone does not teach love, but love, if it is a true virtue, will also turn out to be such in conjugal sexual intercourse.*[13]

If this education is formative of human identity, then sex within the context of marriage becomes integral to perceiving the value response of love. For in the sexual act when carried out in this virtuous manner, man and woman give themselves entirely to one another, not just physically, but spiritually (FC, 11). Human sexuality can mediate an encounter with the value response of love.

For John Paul II, this sexual education is provided most fully within the context of a Christian account of the nuptial mystery. In his *Theology of the Body,* the ferocity of concupiscence is acknowledged: "Flaring up in man, this invades his senses, excites his body, involves his feelings and in a certain sense takes possession of his heart. Such passion, originating in carnal concupiscence, suffocates in his heart the most profound voice of conscience, the sense of responsibility before God."[14] This disease of concupiscence is caused by a separation of the human gaze from awareness of the original nuptial dimension of the human body.[15]

This original nuptial dimension is the foundation of John Paul II's later discussion of the medicinal quality to the sacrament of marriage itself. Adam and Eve, before the Fall, discovered in each other's maleness and femaleness the vocation toward communion that all humanity is called toward:

11. Grabowski, *Sex and Virtue,* 86.

12. Wojtyła, *Love and Responsibility,* 155.

13. Ibid., 259.

14. John Paul II, *Theology of the Body,* 145.

15. Ibid., 147.

"the meaning of man's original unity, through masculinity and femininity, is expressed as an overcoming of the frontier of solitude."[16] This vocation to communion is itself an act of the body, expressed through the bodily givenness of being created male and female:

> The body, which through its own masculinity or femininity right from the beginning helps both to find themselves in communion of persons, becomes, in a particular way, the constituent element of their union, when they become husband and wife. This takes place, however, through a mutual choice. This choice establishes the conjugal pact between persons, who become one flesh only on this basis.[17]

It is important to notice that John Paul II is not simply talking about sexual union here. Instead, he is noting that the communion of persons takes place fundamentally through the gift of the will as both men and women discover in each other a desire for completion. Such a desire is related to human sexuality but is not reducible to sexuality.

Nonetheless, human sexuality as expressed in this conjugal gift becomes a sign of this communion of personhood. As John Paul II writes:

> The body which expresses femininity manifests the reciprocity and communion of persons. It expresses it by means of the gift of the fundamental characteristic of personal existence. This is the body—a witness to creation as a fundamental gift, and so a witness to Love as the source from which this same giving springs. Masculinity and femininity—namely, sex—is the original sign of a creative donation and an awareness on the part of man, male-female, of a gift lived in an original way. Such is the meaning with which sex enters the theology of the body.[18]

Prelapsarian sex would have pointed humanity toward a vision of the created order as gift. Human sexuality would have been understood as an act of co-creation whereby the human person would give fully of oneself through the sign of his maleness or her femaleness for the flourishing of human society.

Although human beings fell from this original vision of gift, human sexuality can still become this kind of sign through the gift of the sacrament of marriage. It is within the Christian salvific economy of marriage whereby one receives an education away from concupiscence. In this sacrament, one

16. Ibid., 45.
17. Ibid., 50.
18. Ibid., 62.

learns to read the body aright: "[M]an, in a real way, is the author of the meanings whereby, after having reread in truth the language of the body . . . is also capable of forming in truth that language in the conjugal and family communion of the persons."[19] For in the rite of marriage itself, human sexuality is taken up into that great mystery of redemption that is Christ and the Church: "The liturgy . . . elevates the conjugal path of man and woman, based on the language of the body reread in truth, to the dimensions of mystery. At the same time it enables that pact to be fulfilled in these dimensions through the language of the body."[20] Human sexuality, in its unitive and procreative dimensions, can become itself a sign of the mystery of divine love embodied in the Incarnation and continued in the Church.

Allowing one's sexuality to become a sign of the divine mystery itself requires a life-long formation. Here, few adequately recognize that John Paul II's *Theology of the Body* is not fundamentally about the goodness of human sexuality alone. For John Paul II, there is no return to Paradise. But through the practice of continence, there is the possibility for restoring in a sacramental modality the original communion that human beings were called to. Conjugal love, for John Paul II, is not reducible to sexual intercourse. In consecrated life, there is an expression of one's conjugality through virginity. And marriage itself must keep virginal continence as central to expressions of human sexuality: "Perfect conjugal love must be marked by that fidelity and that donation to the only Spouse (and also of the fidelity and donation of the Spouse to the only Bride), on which religious profession and priestly celibacy are founded."[21] In marriage, the couple seeks to give oneself not simply to one's husband or wife but to the single Spouse, who makes possible the effective salvific union of man and woman in the first place.[22] In other words, it's not sex in marriage that is intrinsically holy. It is, instead, the giving of oneself in marriage through the icon of the spouse to the Spouse, Jesus Christ.

As such, continence within marriage ensures that human sexuality will not become the central activity of nuptial love. Married continence enables the union of *eros* and *agape* integral to a Christian approach to love.[23] Con-

19. Ibid., 367.

20. Ibid., 378.

21. Ibid., 277.

22. "This solemn union is not only contracted with the spouse; it also concerns Christ to whom both partners belong as members of His Mystical Body. The conclusion of marriage, therefore, becomes a consecration to God which may be likened to a religious vow. It does not only mean that both spouses give themselves to each other in God; they give themselves anew to Christ in the other" (Hildebrand, *Marriage*, 50).

23. John Paul II, *Theology of the Body*, 374.

tinence, as called for by *Humanae vitae* as a way of planning one's family, "has the essential task of maintaining the balance between the communion in which the couple wish to mutually express only their intimate union and that in which . . . they accept responsible parenthood."[24] Through periodic continence, the couple learns to treat each other as gift, developing affection that is not reducible to human sexuality. Continence ensures that the spouse always remains an icon, not just an idol of the concupiscent person.

John Paul II's discussion, thus, of marriage and divorce in *Familaris consortio* has to be understood in the context of his rather robust account of marriage and continence. Divorce within Catholicism remains for John Paul II an impossibility because of the radical sign of marriage, which manifests the union of Christ and the Church. Yet, he is aware that the pastoral situation in the modern world complicates what has been revealed by Christ: "[T]here are those who have entered into a second union for the sake of the children's upbringing, and who are sometimes subjectively certain in conscience that their previous and irreparably destroyed marriage had never been valid" (FC, 84). The Church has a responsibility to minister to divorced and remarried Catholics, who although unable to approach the altar may nonetheless experience the grace of life within the Church.

But John Paul II goes even further than simply acknowledging that divorced and remarried Catholics are still in the Church. Instead, he writes:

> Reconciliation in the sacrament of Penance which would open the way to the Eucharist, can only be granted to those who, repenting of having broken the sign of the Covenant and of fidelity to Christ, are sincerely ready to undertake a way of life that is no longer in contradiction to the indissolubility of marriage. This means, in practice, that when, for serious reasons, such as for example of the children's upbringing, a man and a woman cannot satisfy the obligation to separate, they "take on themselves the duty to live in complete continence, that is, by abstinence from the act proper to married couples" (FC, 84).

John Paul II is aware that it is often impossible in the modern world to simply end a second union. The collateral for many of these unions would be harmful to children, who would be ripped away from those whom they have called father or mother. Although John Paul II does not discuss other instances where a union would continue in continence, it is not difficult to consider situations in which sharing common finances would make it nearly impossible to separate without harm to both the man and the woman. In such instances, one is called to practice continence, which described

24. Ibid., 413.

above is not simply an absence of sex. It is instead an elevation of human affection so that both the man and the woman can recognize the gift of the other person.

While there is extraordinary mercy in this teaching, it is also not the easiest to offer to divorced and remarried Catholics. Partially, this may be John Paul II's idealistic view of human relationships in his theological anthropology. Although he notes that human beings cannot return to the Garden, he frequently himself returns to a consideration of that original relationship in Genesis, before the Fall, as an icon of the original sacrament. And in this ideal relationship, human sexuality is fundamentally unitive and procreative.

Grounding his account of the sacrament of marriage in a theological anthropology based in human sexuality, it becomes difficult to imagine human communities that do not come into existence through the self-gift of sexual union. For this reason, John Paul II's theological account of infertility in married life is weak. In *Familaris consortio*, he argues that even though a couple may be infertile, human sexuality is still unitive. And the couple, through their sexual union, may offer "important services to the life of the human person, for example, adoption, various forms of educational work, and assistance to other families and to poor or handicapped children" (FC, 14). But what does sexuality become in a relationship in which there is no longer the possibility of procreation? What does infertility reveal about the self-gift of the human person to another?

In his account of family life, one either "participates" in the Trinitarian communion of family life made possible through procreation or one is continent. If marriage and procreation (as well as virginity) are not the only ways of being a body in the world, what are the others? How would a man and a woman living as brother and sister in a family manifest this Trinitarian love to the world without sexual union? What about a homosexual person who experiences attraction not to someone of an opposite sex? Such questions are not critiques of John Paul II's overall account of the *Theology of the Body*. But they reveal one of the difficulties of implementing John Paul II's description of continence among divorced and remarried Catholics. A theology of marriage and family life cannot simply be constructed through the ideal situation, but also in the exceptions that make up those concrete historical signs in which one manifests this communion of personhood.[25]

In this sense, John Paul II offers to the Church one possibility in which divorced and remarried Catholics may live together in union with one another as brother and sister. Yet, his account of human sexuality does not

---

25. See Rubio, *Christian Theology of Marriage and Family*.

adequately provide a theological and spiritual formation in which such an irregular situation may manifest to the world the vocation of humanity as created in the image and likeness of God. It is in Pope Francis's *Amoris laetitia* that such an account may be found.

The Sacramental Realism of *Amoris laetitia*

Pope Francis's *Amoris laetitia* has been read as a critique of John Paul II's *Familaris consortio*. Such a reading ignores the dependency of Pope Francis upon John Paul II's account of married love and family life. In the earliest paragraphs of the document, Pope Francis articulates an account of nuptial and Trinitarian communion, quoting his predecessor:

> The triune God is a communion of love, and the family is its living reflection. Saint John Paul II shed light on this when he said, "Our God in his deepest mystery is not solitude, but a family, for he has within himself fatherhood, sonship, and the essence of the family, which is love. That love, in the divine family, is the Holy Spirit." The family is thus not unrelated to God's very being. This Trinitarian dimension finds expression in the theology of Saint Paul, who relates the couple to the "mystery" of the union of Christ and the Church (cf. *Eph* 5:21-33) (AL, 11).

While the document is expressive of Pope Francis's earthy rhetoric, it finds its theological grounding in the theology of marriage and family life emerging from Pope John Paul II.

Yet, there are distinctions in the document worth attending to, besides the possibility of divorced and remarried Catholics entering into Eucharistic communion in the Church through the internal forum. Although Pope Francis is frequently presented in the media as an optimist of the highest order, his own magisterium may be characterized by a profound realism about the effects of sin and death in the world. In his *Evangelii gaudium* (EG), the same Holy Father who playfully reminds Christian pastors not to live as if there is only Lent without Easter (EG, 6), also diagnoses the Church with a "spiritual worldliness, which hides behind the appearance of piety and even love for the Church . . . seeking not the Lord's glory but human glory and personal well-being" (EG, 93).

Such Christian realism is at the heart of his *Laudato si'* (LS). Readers looking to encounter a manifesto expressing the gift of creation will also discover in this encyclical a text that is critical of the technological paradigm itself. As the Holy Father writes:

> It can be said that many problems of today's world stem from the tendency, at times unconscious, to make the method and aims of science and technology an epistemological paradigm which shapes the lives of individuals and the workings of society. The effects of imposing this model on reality as a whole, human and social, are seen in the deterioration of the environment, but this is just one sign of a reductionism which affects every aspect of human and social life. We have to accept that technological products are not neutral, for they create a framework which ends up conditioning lifestyles and shaping social possibilities along the lines dictated by the interests of certain powerful groups. Decisions which may seem purely instrumental are in reality decisions about the kind of society we want to build (LS, 107).

In this sense, *Laudato si'* is not simply a document written to people of good will, encouraging them to take better care of the environment. Rather, it is a radical critique of a culture in which technological knowing has become the primary lens through which human beings interact with the world and one another. It is not enough to simply become "better stewards" of environmental resources. Human beings must experience a radical conversion toward communion.

This kind of realism also marks *Amoris laetitia*. In chapter two of the text, he critiques the Church's often less than realistic approach to theological ideals relative to marriage:

> At times we have also proposed a far too abstract and almost artificial theological ideal of marriage, far removed from the concrete situations and practical possibilities of real families. This excessive idealization, especially when we have failed to inspire trust in God's grace, has not helped to make marriage more desirable and attractive, but quite the opposite (AL, 36).

This second chapter of *Amoris laetitia* deals concretely with the obstacles toward communion that married couples experience. Such obstacles include radical poverty, pornography, insufficient housing, constant work, migration, drug use, legal restrictions, domestic violence, and misogyny. This laundry list of obstacles may seem pessimistic but they deal with the concrete reality in which the sacramental sign of marriage will be lived.

Chapter 4's spiritual commentary upon 1 Corinthians 13:4–7 is a further adaptation of Pope Francis's theological realism. In this chapter, he describes married love not simply as the fulfillment of a vocation toward a communion of persons but as a series of concrete practices (not simply sexual) whereby this communion of love is established. For example, he cautions married couples:

> Married couples joined by love speak well of each other; they try to show their spouse's good side, not their weakness and faults. In any event, they keep silent rather than speak ill of them. This is not merely a way of acting in front of others; it springs from an interior attitude. Far from ingenuously claiming not to see the problems and weaknesses of others, it sees those weaknesses and faults in a wider context" (AL, 113).

Pope Francis is focusing on an account of marriage not simply as the sexual union of persons, creating a kind of Trinitarian communion in the family. Instead, married love is that concrete place where divine love is practiced in human society. Here, Pope Francis seemingly returns to an earlier account of Christian love as fulfilled not in sexual union but in the creation of a society of friendship.[26] Later in the same chapter, drawing on Thomas Aquinas, he notes that "conjugal love is the 'greatest form of friendship.'" It is a union possessing all the traits of a good friendship: concern for the good of the other, reciprocity, intimacy, warmth, stability and the resemblance born of a shared life" (AL, 123). This friendship does result in sexual union that is both unitive and procreative for Pope Francis; but sex itself can become a form of escapism that causes one to "renounce the beauty of conjugal union" (AL, 155).

Pope Francis's theological realism relative to the sacrament of marriage is most clear in his discussion of infertility. He notes that some couples cannot have children, and therefore the Church must have a clearer account of fruitfulness in marriage that is not simply the result of sexual procreation. Adoption, as the Holy Father notes, "is a very generous way to become parents . . . Those who accept the channel of adopting and accepting someone unconditionally and gratuitously become channels of God's love" (AL, 179). Fruitfulness in marriage is never simply sexual; it is always an expansion of that conjugal union into society for the caring of all of those on the margins. In this sense, it is not simply infertile couples who must have a broader sense of fruitfulness: "Even large families are called to make their mark on society, finding other expressions of fruitfulness that in some way prolong the love that sustains them. Christian families should never forget that 'faith does not remove us from the world but draws us more deeply into it'" (AL, 181). A family that sees itself as withdrawn from the world, even one that is large, does not yet understand the gift of conjugal fruitfulness.

26. See Burns, "Martial Fidelity as a *remedium concupiscentiae*: An Augustinian Proposal."

Much more could be said about the manner in which Pope Francis's theological realism informs his robust account of love in married and family life. Yet, it is chapter 8, specifically his discussion of divorced and remarried Catholics, which has generated the most heat. Pope Francis's discussion of divorce and remarriage begins with an account of pastoral sensitivity to the diversity of situations that any priest would deal with. Pope Francis's pastoral realism recognizes that making judgments relative to marriage and family life cannot simply be the application of universal rules to every situation: "It is a matter of reaching out to everyone, of needing to help each person find his or her proper way of participating in the ecclesial community" (AL, 297).

So too among divorced and remarried Catholics, there are a diversity of situations. There are those in "a second union consolidated over time, with new children, proven fidelity, generous self giving, Christian commitment, a consciousness of its irregularity and of the great difficult of going back without feeling in conscience that one would fall into new sins" (AL, 297). There are also those relationships in which one spouse was permanently abandoned by the other.

Pastoral care for the divorced and remarried cannot be a univocal fit. In pastoral counseling, bishops and priests should lead divorced and remarried persons in:

> an examination of conscience through moments of reflection and repentance. The divorced and remarried should ask themselves: how did they act towards their children when the conjugal union entered into crisis; whether or not they made attempts at reconciliation; what has become of the abandoned party; what consequences the new relationship had on the rest of the family and the community of the faithful; and what example is being set for young people who are preparing for marriage . . . What we are speaking of is a process of accompaniment and discernment which "guides the faithful to an awareness of their situation before God. Conversation with the priest . . . contributes to the formation of a correct judgment on what hinders the possibility of a fuller participation in the life of the Church" (AL, 300).

The goal of the conversation is not simply to allow the divorced and remarried person to enter fully into Eucharistic communion. While footnote 336 acknowledges that there may be occasions in which such discernment leads to a recognition that "in a particular situation no fault exists" (in which case, an annulment could be asked for with ease), Pope Francis does not foreclose the possibility that continence may be called for in this relationship in order to participate fully in the Eucharistic life of the Church. Further, the account of marriage and family life in the rest of the document makes it possible to propose a robust sense of continence whereby a divorced and remarried couple abstains from sexual union yet experiences the genuine fruits of marriage in raising a family together, as well as letting their love transform the created order. It also allows for the possibility that the Church welcomes the couple fully into her life even though they remain sexually active, not allowing Eucharistic communion at the present time, all the while ministering to the couple so that they might be a communion of love for the world.

Thus, it's not that Pope Francis rejects the magisterial teaching of John Paul II. Instead, he nuances it in the context of his theological and pastoral realism, providing the kind of spirituality that could sustain a divorced and remarried Catholic who has courageously chosen to be continent with his or her spouse. Spiritual fruitfulness is possible in any relationship, even in irregular ones.

Conclusion

Thus, Pope Francis's theological and pastoral realism enables the possibility of authentic Trinitarian communion unfolding even in the midst of irregular situations such as infertility, as well as divorced and remarried Catholics. Because John Paul II places so much emphasis upon human sexuality functioning as a sign of the image and likeness of God, he never develops the proper spirituality that would be required for a couple to abstain from sexuality while living under the same roof, raising a family.

Pope Francis's theological and pastoral realism ironically provides a fruitful possibility for implementing John Paul II's proposal of continence for divorced and remarried Catholics. John Paul II's account of married love as restoring the human being toward authentic personhood is integral to the renewal of marriage in Catholic life. Pope Francis is himself dependent upon John Paul II's magisterial teaching.

Yet as a phenomenology of married love, there is a sense in which John Paul II's *Theology of the Body* offers an ideal that exists apart from particular situations. This is not to dismiss John Paul II, as some may be prone to do. It is simply to acknowledge that the concrete historical sign of individual marriages must be measured against the proposal that John Paul II makes. And that John Paul II's *Theology of the Body* is itself a theological proposal that must be developed by theologians, not simply excepted as magisterium.

Pope Francis, by looking through a lens of sacramental realism at marriage, de-emphasizes the centrality of human sexuality to marriage. He acknowledges that sex is not simply for procreation. He notes that sex can lead to a fruitful spiritual life among the couple. But he is also aware that aberrations in sexual life, in fertility, and among divorced and remarried Catholics may not mean the end of spiritual fruitfulness. One can live with a spouse without engaging in sexual union and still participate in the fruitfulness of married love. One can fruitfully transform the created order not through sexual activity but through radical self-gift toward the world.

Perhaps, then, one could read Pope Francis's *Amoris laetitia* less as a rejection of John Paul II and more as a nuanced return to a Christian theology of marriage that places not sex, but the indissoluble, sacramental bond of fidelity, as the supreme good of matrimonial life.[27] Marriage is about friendship and only secondarily about sex. The true sanctity of married love is not above all in the conjugal act but in the mundane participation in the divine sacrifice of love in family life. This transfiguration of the mundane is precisely how marriage and family life are integral to the new evangelization in our era.

Bibliography

Benedict XVI, Pope. "The Domestic Church, Evangelized and Evangelizing." In *Compendium on the New Evangelization: Texts of the Pontifical and Conciliar Magisterium 1939–2012.* Washington, DC: USCCB, 2015.

Burns, J. Patout. "Martial Fidelity as a *remedium concupiscentiae*: An Augustinian Proposal." *Augustinian Studies* 44, no. 1 (2013) 1–35.

Cahall, Perry J. *The Mystery of Marriage: A Theology of the Body and the Sacrament.* Chicago: Hillenbrand, 2016.

Cavadini, John C. "The Sacramentality of Marriage in the Fathers." *Pro Ecclesia* 17, no. 4 (2008) 442–63.

Grabowski, John S. *Sex and Virtue: An Introduction to Sexual Ethics.* Washington, DC: Catholic University of America Press, 2003.

Hildebrand, Dietrich von. *Marriage: The Mystery of Faithful Love.* Manchester, NH: Sophia Institute, 1997.

———. *The Nature of Love.* Translated by John F. Crosby with John Henry Crosby. South Bend, IN: St. Augustine's, 2009.

John Paul II, Pope. *The Theology of the Body: Human Love in the Divine Plan.* Edited and translated by Michael Waldstein. Boston: Pauline, 1997.

Kupczak, Jarosław. *Gift & Communion: John Paul II's Theology of the Body.* Translated by Agatha Rottkamp, Justyna Pawlak, and Orest Pawlak. Washington DC: Catholic University of America Press, 2014.

27. See Cavadini, "The Sacramentality of Marriage in the Fathers."

Marion, Jean-Luc. "The Intentionality of Love." Translated by Stephen E. Lewis. In *Prolegomena to Charity*, 71–101. New York: Fordham University Press, 2002.

Ouellet, Marc Cardinal. *Divine Likeness: Toward a Trinitarian Anthropology of the Family*. Translated by Philip Milligan and Linda M. Cicone. Grand Rapids: Eerdmans, 2006.

Rubio, Julie Hanlon. *A Christian Theology of Marriage and Family*. Mahwah, NJ: Paulist Press, 2003.

Scola, Angelo Cardinal. *The Nuptial Mystery*. Translated by Michelle K. Borras. Grand Rapids: Eerdmans, 2005.

Wojtyła, Karol. *Love and Responsibility*. Translated by Grzegorz Ignatik. Boston: Pauline, 2013.

Cultural and
Political Encounters

CHAPTER 11

The Movement of Intercessory Prayer and the Openness to Encounter

—Leonard J. DeLorenzo

Abstract:

Beginning on the first night of his pontificate, Pope Francis has both practiced and prescribed a low-stakes form of encounter: the exchange of intentions in prayer, or, in an even lower-stakes form, the exchange of good wishes. In this essay I ruminate on this simple gesture as a key to understanding the particular style of Francis's Petrine ministry (one which has a remarkably Pauline spirit) and his method for pursuing the goals of the New Evangelization, especially to the extent that those goals are oriented towards opening spaces for personal encounters. By way of examination, I will look to both his opening address from the balcony of St. Peter's and his blessing from the balcony of the U.S. Capitol Building, reading both of these moments in light of his treatment of St. Paul in *Evangelii gaudium*, his teaching on the practice of love in the home from chapter 4 of *Amoris laetitia*, and even his address to the members of the U.S. Congress. The study of Francis's promotion of the spiritual and even political practice of intercessory prayer will give form to his unrelenting preference for the "concrete Catholic thing" over what might otherwise remain in abstraction as the "idea of the thing."

In his first encounter with the city and the world, Pope Francis bowed his head for a blessing before offering his own blessing in return. The moment was stunning in its simplicity and yet, in retrospect, it was the first move in a style of evangelization that, at times, utilizes low-stakes invitations for encountering others. On that first night, Francis practiced what he would go on to preach: that making room in oneself for the needs of others is necessary for realizing our common good in Jesus Christ.

For those who pray, this action of making room is done as intercessory prayer; for those who do not pray, this action may take the form of sending good wishes. Disciples, in their manner, imitate the missionary spirit of St. Paul while those of good will who are not (yet) disciples participate in the same movement in the way they are able. When one allows the needs and joy of another to enter into his or her own heart, the Gospel is already present: the Good News of Jesus Christ is that we are made one in the love of the Father. With his simple practice and prescription, Francis does not demand that belief come before action but rather acknowledges that action may later lead to belief. The whole point of the Gospel is to heal what ails us and bring us to completion as one in Christ. What Francis believes is that "we achieve fulfillment when we break down walls and our hearts are filled with faces and names!"[1]

In this essay, I will attend to Francis's emphasis on intercessory prayer, both explicit and implicit, which is both a way of pursuing the mission of evangelization and a fruit of it. I will begin with Francis repeating his opening act when standing on another balcony—this time in Washington, D.C.—and then consider his message to the U.S. Congress and the United Nations from that perspective. I will root these words and actions in his missionary vision as primarily found in *Evangelii gaudium*, with a special eye to both the witness of St. Paul and the maternal love of the Blessed Mother. In the third section, I will attend to the fourth chapter of *Amoris laetitia* where Francis provides commentary on St. Paul's hymn of love from 1 Corinthians 13. In the practice of love, the choreography of the Gospel becomes routine as divine concern is translated in human terms, especially in the family. In the end, I argue that Francis's repeated recommendation and exercise of the movement of intercessory prayer heralds the graced human ability to participate in the act of creation, whereby space and time is afforded to the other for his or her own good.

A More Perfect Union

As the first pontiff in history to address a joint session of the U.S. Congress, Pope Francis's speech on September 24, 2015, was historic, but what he said

---

1. Francis, *Evangelii gaudium*, 274.

and did on the balcony of the U.S. Capitol immediately afterwards was revolutionary. Most revolutions have a violent or dramatic flare to them—this one was unassuming, in the spirit of the "revolution of tenderness"[2] he calls for elsewhere. While facing the people, Francis united his petition to God with a request for his audience:

> Father of all, bless these. Bless each of them. Bless the families. Bless them all. And I ask you all please to pray for me. And if there are among you any who do not believe or cannot pray, I ask you to please send good wishes my way.

Looking out on those gathered before him and beyond them to the rest of the U.S. citizenry, Francis makes a claim on them and invites them to make a claim on him. In directing his prayer to the "Father of all," he claims all people as children of God and thus addresses those to whom he speaks as his brothers and sisters. In asking these brothers and sisters to pray for him, he invites them to practice doing for him what he seeks to do for them: consider the good of another and begin to desire that good.

To pray for him as he is praying for others is the most complete form of reciprocal caring since the one who prays for him would also call upon the God whose children Francis claims we all are, thereby making the intercession an act done by one who relates himself or herself to Francis as brother or sister. Yet with the caveat he adds at the end, Francis makes room for those who do not or cannot pray, who would otherwise consider the request for prayers as not addressed to them. To ask these whom he himself also claims as his brothers and sisters to send good wishes his way, he issues an invitation for them to share in the communal action without first having to muster the belief that underlies it. A request to send good wishes does not ask too much, though it does ask that one consider the good of another as important and worthy of attention. This is a way of acting *as if* we all were brothers and sisters who share responsibility for one another without having to pledge oneself to the belief in the one God and Father of all who makes us one as his children in Christ, as Francis himself believes.

This act of respect for the condition of his non-believing brothers and sisters is reminiscent of the generosity and the affection Francis showed at the end of his first press briefing in 2013, when he invited the members of the press into a moment of silent reflection. He expressed his reverence for the consciences of those who are not Christian or do not believe in God, and then, in inviting them join together in silence rather than prayer, he honored them as valued and full of dignity, "knowing that each one of you is

---

2. Ibid., 88.

a child of God." As later on the balcony of the U.S. Capitol, he makes a claim on all even as he seeks to give each person the proper space and means to seek out the good of others. In both instances, Francis asks that all begin to act as if children of the same family.

Representing the Common Good

Francis's claim and request may seem to lack drama when spoken from balconies addressing those who have gathered willingly, where common courtesy would suggest that each person consider not just his or her own needs but also the needs of others. The revolutionary nature of his balcony blessings becomes more apparent, however, when we recognize this same claim and request in one of the places in which mutual enmity, duplicity, and competitiveness are more likely the norm than the unfortunate exception: the chambers of Congress. At the heart of his address to the elected representatives of the American people and, through them, to the very people he later blessed from the balcony, Francis issued the salutary challenge to practice seeing and acting for each other as brothers and sisters:

> The contemporary world, with its open wounds which affect so many of our brothers and sisters, demands that we confront every form of polarization which would divide it into these two camps [of good vs. evil, righteous vs. sinners]. We know that in the attempt to be freed of the enemy without, we can be tempted to feed the enemy within. To imitate the hatred and violence of tyrants and murderers is the best way to take their place. That is something which you, as a people, reject . . . We must move forward together, as one, in a renewed spirit of fraternity and solidarity, cooperating generously for the common good.[3]

In a nation founded upon the principle of "liberty and justice for all"—even if the meaning of liberty and justice is widely disputed—one thing at least to which all can and do agree is the rejection of tyrannical forces that seek to replace the good of the many with the self-interests of the few and the powerful. Of course, it is much easier to reject the rule of the few and the powerful when you are not one of them and quite a bit harder to reject forms of tyranny when these happen to serve one's own narrow self-interest. What Francis is saying to those who have been vested with certain powers belonging only to the few is that in their mutual opposition to external forces of oppression and dehumanization, they must not seek to villainize those

---

3. Francis, "Address to Congress."

within their own nation and halls of government who disagree with them or even those who directly oppose them. Should these elected representatives give in to that reactionary form of violence, then they come to imitate that which they also reject: the lust for self-interest and the attempt at dominion of others. Instead, Francis says, they ought to practice caring for those who disagree with and oppose them, seeking the others' good along with their own good. In like fashion, this posture of strength in humility must begin with exercising care and concern for one another, accepting even those who disagree with or oppose you as brothers and sisters within the household of one's own nation. In other words, he is instructing the members of Congress to look across the aisle and, in place of the pathology of suspicion and enmity, practice mutual concern. And if they can do nothing else, then try sending good wishes.

Even if this is idealistic, especially in the contemporary climate, Francis is claiming that this is the form of true governance. Standing before Congress, he asks for nothing less than for those who sit before him to allow their own hearts to become open to the cares and the good of the people they represent. To do this, each representative must also accept the cares and recognize the good of those who disagree with and oppose them from within their own governing body—those who are likewise responsible for seeking the good of their own constituents. In Francis's words of counsel:

> Politics is an expression of our compelling need to live as one, in order to build as one the greatest common good: that of a community which sacrifices particular interests in order to share, in justice and peace, its good, its interests, its social life . . . In a word, if we want security, let us give security; if we want life, let us give life; if we want opportunities, let us provide opportunities.[4]

In the halls of power, sacrificing one's own interests to heed the interests of others is a sign of weakness and a recipe for defeat—both legislatively and likely electorally. Francis is advocating a revolution of the notion of power: that the strength of resistance to the enemies of the common good who press in from outside of the nation be matched with a strength of resistance to allow oneself to become the enemy of the common good within the nation. The place for the elective representative to begin exercising this reimagined power in service of the common good is within the congressional body where the offering of good wishes for other members and those they represent will begin to heal the chronic rivalrousness that corrupts from within. Even this small act of sending good wishes is, in such a setting, an

4. Ibid.

act of sacrifice in which one suspends one's claim to superiority in recogniz-ing the legitimacy of the needs and values of others.

The Voice of the Poor

On the very next day Francis switched roles from addressing a body of representatives to speaking as a representative himself before the General Assembly of the United Nations. Whereas in his speech to Congress he was prescribing the action of intercessory prayer—or the exchange of good wishes—as a foundation for building up the common good, his speech to the U.N. revealed the fruits of intercessory prayer. When he stood before the representatives of the nations of the world, he stood as the willing represen-tative of the poor, whose needs and concerns he carried in himself because the Church prays regularly for them.

In recognizing the mission of the United Nations to promote the com-mon good and to protect the human dignity of all,[5] Francis spoke first to the sickness of the natural environment. While some critiqued Francis for not speaking more about issues that they deem as directly threatening the dignity of human beings, it is important to heed the perspective from which the pope considered ecological issues. From the perspective of the poor, he argued that "any harm done to the environment *is* harm done to humanity."[6] The misuse of natural resources and the inequitable commerce of goods and profit (for the wealthy) and waste (for the poor) perpetuate systemic exclusion whereby the few live comfortably at the expense of the many. By way of self-interest wielded over the environment, the tyrannical forces of the few and the powerful pin down the wellbeing of the disenfranchised. Francis sums up his reading of the environmental crisis as a specifically *hu-man* crisis in the following section of the speech:

> The poorest are those who suffer most from such offenses, for three serious reasons: they are cast off by society, forced to live off what is discarded and suffer unjustly from abuse of the environment. They are part of today's widespread and quietly growing "culture of waste". The dramatic reality [of] this whole situation of exclusion and inequality with its evident effects has led me, in union with the entire Christian people and many oth-ers, to take stock of my grave responsibility in this regard and

---

5. See preamble of the "UN Charter."
6. Francis, "Address to United Nations"; emphasis added.

> to speak out, together with all those who are seeking urgently-
> needed and effective solutions.[7]

To see the "evident effects" of the "culture of waste," one cannot look from the perspective of the economically prosperous and financially secure. Such effects are not evident to those such as these, who do not suffer the cost of the very system from which they benefit. Rather, in order to see these effects Francis is testifying to a revolution of perspective, whereby those who learn to see from the perspective of those who are suffering become capable of seeing the absence of good that afflicts the poor. In the voice of the poor, Francis argues that for those who are most vulnerable to the degradation of the environment, the unjust distribution of goods and wealth, and systemic practices of exclusion, there is no debate about whether or not the ecological threat is real. From the perspective of the poor, the effects are evident.

Francis goes on to claim that the urge to commodify the natural goods that justly belong to all is translated through social and economic manifestations into the commoditization of human beings: "human trafficking, the marketing of human organs and tissues, the sexual exploitation of boys and girls, slave labor, including prostitution, the drug and weapons trade, terrorism and international organized crime."[8] What blinds the powerful from knowing the human cost of the "culture of waste" is the inability or unwillingness to see the situation from the perspective of those who suffer. The vision necessary for true peace and the cultivation of the common good is acquired through the practice of considering the good of the other and then learning to desire that good.[9]

Francis's speech at the United Nations originated not in himself but in those he represents. He spoke to the powerful on behalf of the poor so that his voice becomes their voice in a place where they might otherwise remain in silence. Francis ceded the space of his authority to the needs of the neediest and proclaimed that it is only from their perspective that any one can truly understand the common good in which all are called to participate:

> The common home of all men and women must continue to
> rise on the foundations of a right understanding of universal
> fraternity and respect for the sacredness of every human life,
> of every man and every woman, the poor, the elderly, children,
> the infirm, the unborn, the unemployed, the abandoned, those

7. Francis, "Address to United Nations."

8. Ibid.

9. Near the conclusion of his encyclical letter, Francis comments on the approach to suffering in relation to the vision of faith, especially in light of the witness of the saints, see Francis, *Lumen fidei*, 105.

considered disposable because they are only considered as part of a statistic.[10]

Rejecting the reduction of human beings to statistics and to reclaim them as, at the very least, worthy of attention and concern and, at most, beloved children of the one God and Father of Jesus Christ *is* an evangelizing effort, even when not conducted in the mission of evangelization. To see the faces and hear the names of those otherwise neglected and forgotten recognizes their indisposable dignity and awards a fuller share of humanity to those who did not heed them previously. Even for those who do not (yet) have the gift of faith to believe, acting as if others are one's brothers and sisters favors the promotion of the kind of good that is non-exclusionary and held in common. This action is already the beginning of the Gospel.

The Evangelizer's Prayer

In the apostolic exhortation *Evangelii gaudium*, Francis proclaimed as fundamentally true of the Gospel what he later demonstrated in his blessings and speeches during his visit to the United States. Positively stated, Francis attests that the Gospel belongs to everyone, that it is our *common* good. Negatively stated, he argues that there can be no joy in the Gospel—no *Good* News—where there are attempts to protect what is good for oneself at the expense of sharing what is good with others. What the Gospel of Jesus Christ discloses and inaugurates is that the sharing of concern, the willful identification with the condition of others, and the action of willing the good of others are intrinsic to the good of the human person as created, redeemed, and sanctified in Christ. To be "in thrall to an individualistic, indifferent and self-centered mentality"[11] is incompatible with the joy of the Gospel because it denies the Gospel's premise: that what is truly good for each person is the holistic promotion of the good of all. According to that peculiar logic of the Gospel, to seek to hoard the good for oneself is to lose the good, whereas to seek the good of others is to gain the good for oneself.

The task of the Gospel and the work of evangelization is "to desire, seek, and protect the good of others,"[12] and in the desire for the good of others, one refreshes the desire for what is, in fact, good for oneself. Seeking out the good of others as what is truly good for oneself is a difficult and painful process for those bent towards pursuing self-interests and harbors of secu-

10. Francis, "Address to United Nations."

11. Francis, *Evangelii gaudium*, 208.

12. Ibid., 178.

rity, as is typical in a world under the twin myths of the scarcity of goods and the rivalry of claimants. It is with "small steps", then, that the refreshment of seeking what is truly good comes about, "in the midst of great human limitations."[13] In sum, the distinctive and holistic common good to which the Gospel calls us "presumes the creation of a new mindset which thinks in terms of community and the priority of the life of all over the appropriation of goods by a few."[14] It is by way of the renunciation of claims to private possessiveness at the expense of others, the reconsideration of the needs of others, and the recalibration of desires and intentions in willful harmony with others that the movement of evangelization proceeds, "beyond all our preferences and interests, our knowledge and motivations . . . for the greater glory of the Father who loves us."[15]

Before turning at the end of *Evangelii gaudium* to Mary as the Mother of Evangelization and Star of the New Evangelization, Francis gives his attention to St. Paul as the model of the missionary power of intercessory prayer. In Paul—the first truly universal evangelizer—Francis glimpses how concern for the wellbeing others is intimately connected to the mission of evangelization. As Francis recognizes, Paul's prayer "was full of people" as he witnesses to the union of love of God and love of neighbor: "I constantly pray with you in every one of my prayers for all of you . . . because I hold you in my heart" (Phil 1:4, 7).[16] He admires how Paul's vision, "far from being suspicious, negative and despairing . . . is a spiritual gaze born of deep faith which acknowledges what God is doing in the lives of others. At the same time, it is the gratitude which flows from a heart attentive to others."[17] Paul's heart is healthy.

In and through intercessory prayer, Paul made his heart a space for what *Gaudium et spes* would later call "the joys and hopes, the grief and anguish of the people of [his] time, especially those who [were] poor or afflicted."[18] Francis finds "missionary power" in intercessory prayer because far from competing with or standing apart from contemplation of the love of God, contemplating the needs and good of others in prayer is a privileged way to participate in God's love and concern for these others who each, like the one at prayer, has a face and name. They are neither statistics nor rivals but brothers and sisters of the same God and Father. To offer prayer

13. Ibid., 44.

14. Ibid., 188.

15. Ibid., 267.

16. Ibid., 281.

17. Ibid., 282.

18. *Gaudium et spes*, 1.

in service of their good is to enter into the space of Christ's Sacred Heart, where the needs and concerns of those he loves find a home (see John 17).

If the Christian is to cling to and adore Christ, then the Christian becomes drenched in Christ's intentions. As Francis puts it, "when we stand before Jesus crucified, we see the depth of his love which exalts and sustains us, but at the same time, unless we are blind, we begin to realize that Jesus's gaze, burning with love, expands to embrace all his people. We realize once more that he wants to make use of us to draw closer to his beloved people."[19] The power of prayer is its cultivation of an interior space reserved for the presence of God, and the distinctive power of intercessory prayer is in populating that space with the names and faces of those whom God loves.[20]

In an attempt to grasp more fully the intimate union of love of God and love of neighbor that is forged in part through intercessory prayer—where one's attention is given over to the needs of others—it is worthwhile to consider the consummate point of Simone Weil's elegant and direct essay on prayer and attention. In her own words and style, she captures in compelling fashion what Francis perceives in the witness of St. Paul and proclaims as the way of the Gospel:

> Not only does the love of God have attention for its substance; the love of our neighbor, which we know to be the same love, is made of the same substance. Those who are unhappy have no need for anything in this world but people capable of giving them their attention. The capacity to give one's attention to a sufferer is a very rare and difficult thing; it is almost a miracle; it *is* a miracle. Nearly all those who think they have this capacity do not possess it. Warmth of heart, impulsiveness, pity are not enough . . . The love of our neighbor in all its fullness simply means being able to say to him: "What are you going through?" It is a recognition that the sufferer exists, not only as a unit in a collection, or a specimen from the social category labeled "unfortunate," but as a man, exactly like us, who was one day stamped with a special mark by affliction. For this reason it is enough, but it is indispensable, to know how to look at him in a certain way. This way of looking is first of all attentive. The soul empties itself of all its own contents in order to receive into itself the being it is looking at, just as he is, in all his truth.[21]

19. Francis, *Evangelii gaudium*, 268.

20. See ibid., 262.

21. From the essay, "Reflections on the Right Use of School Studies with a View to the Love of God," in Weil, *Awaiting God*, 64–65; emphasis in original text.

To be sure, giving attention to the needs and good of others is an expression and fruit of the love of God. At the same time, though—and this seems to be very much the point of Francis's low-stakes evangelizing tactic—practicing paying attention to the needs of others or simply sending "good wishes" their way forms the disposition necessary for the love of God. Since, in the end, the encounter with the love of God cannot be separated from the encounter with those whom God loves, Francis is willing to clear a small path to evangelization on the side of working to love the brother or sister whom one *can* see whenever one is not ready or willing to work on loving the God whom one cannot see (1 John 4:20). The path of love of neighbor merges with the love of God, in the end, and vice versa.

Evangelization's Choreography in *Amoris laetitia*

Both *Evangelii gaudium* and the earlier *Lumen fidei* end with reflections on and prayers to the Blessed Mother. In *Lumen fidei*, Francis presents her as "the perfect icon of faith" who "treasured in her heart all that she had heard and seen, so that the word could bear fruit in her life."[22] Jesus's mother accompanies her Son to the cross, "whence her motherhood will extend to each of his disciples."[23] In her complete and unbroken fidelity to the Word of God, she receives as her inheritance the gift of motherhood for all those whom her Son loves. Her love of God finds its fruit in love of neighbor.

In *Evangelii gaudium*, Francis presents Mary from the other direction, going from love of neighbor to love of God. "With the Holy Spirit," Francis begins, "Mary is always present in the midst of people." In Jesus's great love for us, he gave us Mary as our mother from the cross "because he did not want us to journey without a mother"[24] and "as a true mother, she walks at our side, she shares our struggles and she constantly surrounds us with God's love."[25] Here with Mary, the more familiar love of a mother opens a path to the compassion and concern of the love of God.

In Mary, Christ's twin commandments are fulfilled: love of God and love of neighbor become one. In Francis's preaching, either side of that love may offer the first steps for evangelization as he trusts that, in and through the prayer of Mary, the one love will yield the other. This fullness of love is the fullness of the Gospel: the mission and gift of Jesus Christ himself. In this love alone is the fullness of joy, for in him the divine plan is made complete:

22. Francis, *Lumen fidei*, 58.

23. Ibid., 59.

24. Francis, *Evangelii gaudium*, 285.

25. Ibid., 286.

*that they may all be one; even as you, Father, are in me, and I in you, that they
also may be in us, so that the world may believe that you have sent me* (John
17:21, RSV). From Mary, in whom the fullness of Christ's joy first dawns,
and from St. Paul, who broadcast this joy to the ends of the earth, Francis
seeks to learn and to teach the divine choreography that is translated into
human terms in and through the exercises of mutual concern that that are
practiced most of all in the setting of the family. From the family as the fount
of renewal for the Church and the world, the invitation to encounter others
that will echo from blessings on balconies and in speeches given in the halls
of power begins to sound as those who share kinship practice creating space
and time for the other person to be and to become.

In the fourth chapter of *Amoris laetitia*, Francis follows St. Paul's great
hymn on love from the First Letter to the Corinthians (13:4–7). Francis
names the practice of love as the basis of family life. Moreover, the family
itself is one of the Church's primary agents of evangelization for the world.[26]
In seeking to discover the neglected richness of the overused and under-
considered meaning of "love," Francis provides a short exegesis on each of
the attributes that Paul identifies. The first pair of attributes—that love is
"patient" and "kind"—establishes the basic rhythm of love's dynamic and
guides the rest of Paul's four-verse reflection. The key to renewing the imagination about love from these attributes is giving ourselves over to learning
what they mean within the economy of Scripture rather than interpreting
them through our previous assumptions.

The Greek term translated as "patience" is, as Francis notes, *makro-
thyméi*. This Greek term itself is used to translate the Hebrew term *'erek
'appayim*, which is identified as a divine attribute in Exodus 34:6: *The Lord
passed before [Moses], and proclaimed, "The Lord, the Lord, a God merciful
and gracious, slow to anger ['erek 'appayim], and abounding in mercy and
faithfulness"* (cf. Numbers 14:18, Wisdom 11:23, 12:2, 15:1; Psalms 86:15,
145:8). In the very first word that Paul employs to describe love, something
more than the translation of Hebrew to Greek is occurring. Paul is teaching
that in and through the one who practices love as being "slow to anger,"
a divine attribute is taking flesh as it is translated in human terms. When
God reveals himself to Moses as the one who is "slow to anger," the Lord's
patience is leaving open the possibility of the sinner's repentance—or, in
this case, the repentance of the sinful nation. In one sense, this patience is
a withholding of power, leaving open time and space for the heart of the
sinner to turn, to heal, and to grow. In divine terms, patience is primarily
power and freedom—the power of willful restraint when domination is not

---

26. See especially Francis, *Amoris laetitia*, 289–90; cf. ibid. 223.

only possible but even justified, and the freedom from the compulsion of the situation so as to wait upon future possibilities.[27]

When translated into human terms as it takes flesh in the one who loves, this "patience" is exercised as restraining oneself in opportunities to assert dominance—even when the circumstances seem to justify such a move—and the active willingness to wait for and to wait with the other for whom the possibilities for change and growth always abound. As Francis reads Paul, the patience of love is proper to a creature who, in humility, is called to "recognize that other people also have a right to live in this world, just as they are . . . even when he or she acts differently than I would like."[28] This posture of "patience" is a form of willed passivity—of active restraint— in the interest of the other person's good and in recognition of one's own status as creature rather than Creator.

Having secured the discipline of withholding force with the first attribute of love, the other half of Paul's opening pair then describes the proactive complement to patience. This next word, "kind", is only used here in the whole of the Bible: in Greek, chrestéuetai. The root word, chrestos, denotes a good person—that is, "one who shows his goodness by his deeds."[29] While waiting on the other, the one who loves does not simply leave the other to his or her own devices, but rather discerns how to be of assistance and readily acts upon what the other needs. In so doing, the space and time that the one who loves opens up for the beloved is given a positive charge: it becomes an environment in which, as Dorothy Day always remembered Peter Maurin saying, "it is easier to be good."[30]

In the pairing of "patience" and "kindness," Paul establishes the basic rhythm of love as the readiness to refrain from asserting one's will at the expense of another and the action of giving assistance to the other, for his or her own wellbeing. What would obstruct such simple and elegant choreography would be the clunky and untimely steps of "jealousy" that makes you regret the good fortune of another, "boastfulness" and "arrogance" that puff you up and make you into a pushy know-it-all, "rudeness" that reinforces preexisting negative attitudes, "irritableness" that grows from hidden indignations, and "resentfulness" that keeps account of wrongs and refuses to grant the possibility of an open future.[31] To wait with and to act for the

27. Ibid., 91.

28. Ibid., 92.

29. Ibid., 93.

30. Day, *Thérèse*, 31; cf. Day, *The Long Loneliness*, 170, 280; and Day, *By Little and By Little*, 43, 98, 126.

31. See Francis, *Amoris laetitia*, 94–104.

one in need sets the horizon of the lover's heart: the one who loves learns to desire the prize of rejoicing in what is right, a desire that casts out that "toxic attitude" that delights in the other's misfortune because the other is seen as a competitor. "In other words," Francis writes, "we rejoice at the good of others when we see their dignity and value their abilities and good works."[32]

In the end, the Pauline understanding of love has to do with the development of a loving character, which is strong, open, positive, and stable. There is a magnanimity to this character, which "bears all things" by seeing faults and weaknesses in the wider context of a good that may be shared in common rather than claimed individually.[33] This is the kind of character inclined toward giving the benefit of the doubt to the other person, "believing all things" in openness rather than habitually distrusting in suspicion. It is a character that need not control outcomes but "hopes all things," reckoning with the fact that things will change and expectations will often go unmet. At bottom, this is a character that "endures all things," which means that it beholds a stable disposition of seeking the good, finding dignity, siding with the other, and being continually cleansed of obsessive self-regard.[34]

The Marian character of this choreography is held in those two elegant steps of patience and kindness, steps that hide the careful discipline of one who routinely avoids missteps and regularly practices her art. In Mary, love is made perfect as she waits with all her children as she waited on the Word and, while sharing our struggles, offers to that space and time of waiting the fruit of her prayer to help us become worthy of the promises of Christ, in whom joy is made complete.[35] While it is seemingly a very long way from the mundane movements of a home and a mother's or spouse's or sibling's love to the chambers of the U.S. Congress and the assembly of the United Nations, the very courtesy that Francis calls for in diverse, public settings is born, reared, and perfected in the private, interpersonal setting of those who live together.

While the setting and circumstances affect the style of the proclamation, what Francis proclaims consistently bears that Pauline style of reaching

---

32. Ibid., 109.

33. "Thanks to magnanimity, we can always look at the horizon from the position where we are. That means being able to do the little things of every day with a big heart open to God and to others. That means being able to appreciate the small things inside large horizons, those of the kingdom of God" (Francis and Spadaro, "A Big Heart Open to God").

34. See Francis, *Amoris laetitia*, 111–18. In the book that Francis said "did me such good," Kasper writes that "love creates and grants space to the beloved, in which he or she can become themselves" (Kasper, *Mercy*, 92).

35. See again Francis, *Lumen fidei*, 58; and *Evangelii gaudium*, 286.

out for the good of others as you welcome the faces and names of others into your own heart. If this form of communion is the goal of evangelization and intercessory prayer is particularly suited to that goal, then both the way and the end are practiced and cherished most of all within the life of the family: "The family is the primary setting for socializaton, since it is where we first learn to relate to others, to listen and share, to be patient and show respect, to help one another live as one."[36] For those who do not (yet) see themselves living as brothers and sisters with others, Francis would have them simply try listening and sharing, being patient and showing respect, and attempting to help one another.

A Big Heart Open to God and Others

The words Francis spoke from the balcony of St. Peter's or, especially, the balcony of the U.S. Capitol, may very well sound to most as courteous words from a generally kind man, who is just asking for the modest help of positive intentions sent his way. When we contemplate those words more deeply, however, and allow them to lead us back to St. Paul and Mary, and into the home as the domestic studio of love itself, we might come to realize the audacity of his request and witness. Far more than saying "let me be" or even "wish me luck," he is asking others to make a space in their hearts for him and he promises to make a space in his for them. Through intercessory prayer offered to the Father of all on behalf of others, what makes the prayer efficacious is the sacrifice of the privacy of one's heart. Within the heart of the one who prays for others the space for encounter comes to be. It is a genuine act of creation: what was not, comes to be. The sacrifice of privacy brings about its own reward as no one is alone anymore when you allow names and faces to fill your heart. Mary pondered this truth from the start and Paul learned it through the obedience of his prayer. Francis is inviting others to sacrifice loneliness for the sake of joy.

To those who do not or cannot pray, Francis is willing to accommodate his message. He invites them, at minimum, to desist from speaking and filling the space of their minds and hearts with narratives that tend to run on loop about themselves and others. Just sit here in silence with me for a moment, he seems to say, so together we can practice the discipline of not taking up too much space. If, however, you find yourself able and willing, join me in the practice of sending good wishes to others, maybe even those whom we are used to distrusting or reviling. Francis is willing to bet that this exercise is healthy, refreshing, and, if practiced even with minimal

36. Francis, *Amoris laetitia*, 276.

devotion, gently persuasive. It is a small path that, in the end, will not only lead to the discovery of the good of the other as inextricably connected to one's own good, but also to the discovery of God as the true fount and fulfillment of all love.

Bibliography

Day, Dorothy. *By Little and By Little: The Selected Writings of Dorothy Day*. Edited by Robert Ellsberg. New York: Knopf, 1984.

———. *The Long Loneliness*. San Francisco: HarperCollins, 1952.

———. *Thérèse: A Life of Thérèse of Lisieux*. Notre Dame, Indiana: Fides, 1960.

Flannery, Austin. "Gaudium et Spes: Pastoral Constitution on the Church in the Modern World." In *Vatican Council II: Constitutions, Decrees, Declarations (Vatican Council II)*, edited by Austin Flannery, 163–282. Rev. ed. Northport, NY: Costello, 1996.

Francis, Pope. *Amoris Laetitia: The Joy of Love*. 2016. https://w2.vatican.va/content/dam/francesco/pdf/apost_exhortations/documents/papa-francesco_esortazione-ap_20160319_amoris-laetitia_en.pdf.

———. *Evangelii Gaudium: The Joy of the Gospel*. Washington, DC: United States Conference of Catholic Bishops, 2013.

———. *Lumen Fidei*. San Francisco: Ignatius, 2013.

———. "Meeting with the Members of the General Assembly of the United Nations Organization: Address of the Holy Father." Presented at the Apostolic Journey of His Holiness Pope Francis to Cuba, to the United States of America and Visit to the United Nations Headquarters, New York, September 25, 2015. https://w2.vatican.va/content/francesco/en/speeches/2015/september/documents/papa-francesco_20150925_onu-visita.html.

———. "Visit to the Joint Session of the United States Congress: Address of the Holy Father." Presented at the Apostolic Journey of His Holiness Pope Francis to Cuba, to the United States of America and Visit to the United Nations Headquarters, Washington, DC, September 24, 2015. https://w2.vatican.va/content/francesco/en/speeches/2015/september/documents/papa-francesco_20150924_usa-us-congress.html.

Francis, Pope, and Antonio Spadaro. "A Big Heart Open to God." *America Magazine*. Accessed September 22, 2015. http://americamagazine.org/pope-interview.

Kasper, Walter. *Mercy: The Essence of the Gospel and the Key to Christian Life*. Translated by William Madges. New York: Paulist, 2014.

"United Nations Charter." June 6, 1945. http://www.un.org/en/sections/un-charter/un-charter-full-text/index.html.

Weil, Simone. *Awaiting God: A New Translation of "Attente de Dieu and Lettre a Un Religieux."* Translated by Bradley Jersak. Maywood, CT: Fresh Wind, 2013.

CHAPTER 12

The Time of Encounter in the Political Theology of Pope Francis

—Joseph S. Flipper

Abstract:

In *Evangelii gaudium*, Pope Francis insists on the priority of time over space in achieving peace within human societies. He contrasts the priority of space—the attempt to possess "spaces of power and self-assertion"—with the priority of time—the initiation of processes and the acceptance of limitation. In *Laudato si'* and *Amoris laetitia* Francis reiterates "time is greater than space" in discussions of environmental policy and teaching on the family. I trace the development of the Pope's understanding of the priority of time, beginning from his pastoral work in Argentina, during which he navigated a period of Argentine state terrorism, and his critical engagement with theologies of liberation. I then turn to his writings as Jorge Bergoglio, including *Reflexiones en esparanza* (1992) and *Ponerse la patria al hombro: memoria y camino de esperanza* (2003), *La Nación por construir: utopía, pensamiento y compromiso: VIII Jornada de Pastoral Social* (2005), and his encyclicals as Pope Francis. Embedded in his writings is a critique of the spatialization of Christian social life under colonization and its aftermath. The priority of time represents a recovery of a Christian political theology with profound implications for pastoral practice.

In his 2013 apostolic exhortation, *Evangelii gaudium*, Pope Francis names four broad principles for building a just and peaceful society: "time is greater than space"; "unity prevails over conflict"; "realities are more important than ideas"; and "the whole is greater than the part."[1] He explains, these principles are derived from the four "pillars" of Catholic social doctrine, which the *Compendium of the Social Doctrine of the Church* lists as the "permanent principles of the Church's social doctrine": "the dignity of the human person," "the common good," "subsidiarity," and "solidarity"[2] On close examination, the two series do not precisely align. The four principles Francis describes in *Evangelii gaudium* are clearly distinct from those of the *Compendium*. They are broader and do not target a particular institution.[3]

His first principle—"time is greater than space"—is the most abstract. In *Evangelii gaudium*, he contrasts the priority of space—the attempt to possess "spaces of power and self-assertion"—with the priority of time—the initiation of processes and the acceptance of limitation. In *Laudato si'* and *Amoris laetitia* Francis reiterates that "time is greater than space" in discussions of environmental policy and teaching on the family. A survey of Francis's writings indicates that the principle "time is greater than space" is diffused throughout his papal writings. This principle is found in his writings and addresses as Jorge Bergoglio, during the time he was a religious superior and archbishop, including *Reflexiones en esparanza* (1992) and

---

1. Pope Francis, *Evangelii gaudium*, 222. Ivereigh claims that Jorge Bergoglio "would deduce from a letter [Juan Manuel de] Rosas wrote to Quiroga his own principles of good government, not least that 'reality is superior to the idea.'" Ivereigh, *Great Reformer*, 5.

2. Pontifical Council for Justice and Peace, *Compendium of the Social Doctrine of the Church*, 160.

3. There may be a parallel between the *Compendium*'s "solidarity" and Francis's "the whole is greater than the part": both suggest an orientation of the individual or groups toward the social whole. There may be a parallel between the *Compendium*'s principle of the "common good" and Francis's "unity prevails over conflict": each points to shared goods within a unified social order. Francis's list lacks even a remote parallel to "the dignity of the human person" or "subsidiarity." His four principles do not appear to translate or to re-describe the four principles of Catholic social doctrine. They function differently. The four principles of Catholic social doctrine concern regulating relationships between institutions: the individual's relationship to the social body, specifically the nation-state, and the role of smaller communities within the social body. Francis's principles concern the way in which we, as individuals and communities, engage processes. Whereas the Catholic social teaching principles are conceived for relatively static and normative institutions (individual, family, mediating institutions, church, local government, national government), Francis's axioms are conceived for people in the midst of flux, changing social institutions, and the emergence of new social practices. As a result, Francis's axioms appear abstract insofar as they do not target any particular institution.

Ponerse la patria al hombro: memoria y camino de esperanza (2003), *La Nación por construir: utopía, pensamiento y compromiso: VIII Jornada de Pastoral Social* (2005). In these writings, Bergoglio embeds a critique of the spatialization of Christian social life under colonization and its aftermath. The priority of time constitutes the lens through which Pope Francis assesses the challenges of the present age and constitutes the framework by which he develops a particularly Jesuit integration of spiritual discernment, encounter, and action. The priority of time represents a recovery of a Christian political theology with profound implications for pastoral practice.

The Priority of Time in the Writings of Pope Francis

Pope Francis's axiom "time is greater than space" forms part of a wide-ranging reflection on the mystery of God in human life, pastoral practice, and political intervention. Austen Ivereigh refers to it as a "sapiential" axiom, grounded in personal experience and reflection.[4] Its first appearance in a major papal document is found in the encyclical letter *Lumen fidei* on June 29, 2013, four months after Francis's election as Pope. *Lumen fidei* was to be the third of a trilogy planned by Pope Benedict XVI, following *Deus caritas est* (2005) and *Spe salvi* (2007). With Benedict XVI's retirement in 2013, the manuscript was passed to Francis. In *Lumen fidei*, Francis credited Pope Benedict XVI with nearly finishing the initial draft and minimized his own work on the manuscript, referring to a "few contributions of my own."[5] A section entitled "God Builds a City for Them" reflects on the role of faith in human societies. In a sub-section entitled "Consolation and strength amid suffering," Francis explains that the virtue of hope implies that Christians should be neither frustrated by obstacles nor be lured by false solutions to challenges:

> In union with faith and charity, hope propels us towards a sure future, set against a different horizon with regard to the illusory enticements of the idols of this world yet granting new momentum and strength to our daily lives. Let us refuse to be robbed of hope, or to allow our hope to be dimmed by facile answers and solutions which block our progress, "fragmenting" time and changing it into space. Time is always much greater than space. Space hardens processes, whereas time propels towards the future and encourages us to go forward in hope.[6]

4. Ivereigh, *Great Reformer*, 142–43, 211.

5. Pope Francis, *Lumen fidei*, 7.

6. Ibid., 57.

Francis makes two claims that will appear repeatedly in his papal writings. First, hope provides a new "horizon" for human life. The horizon is the extent of sight and constitutes the space and time in which realities appear. The same realities, he claims, can take on a new dimension if understood in light of their past and future, that is, within a new horizon. Second, Francis claims that gravitating toward easy solutions is to arrest time and change it into space, hardening process. Francis's contrast between time and space has become a recurring theme throughout his writings and interviews.

Building on *Lumen fidei*, in *Evangelii gaudium* (2013) Pope Francis reflects on the temporal horizon of human existence. Expounding the principles of building just societies named above, he describes the first in a section entitled "Time is greater than space":

> A constant tension exists between fullness and limitation. Fullness evokes the desire for complete possession, while limitation is a wall set before us. Broadly speaking, "time" has to do with fullness as an expression of the horizon which constantly opens before us, while each individual moment has to do with limitation as an expression of enclosure. People live poised between each individual moment and the greater, brighter horizon of the utopian future as the final cause which draws us to itself. Here we see a first principle for progress in building a people: time is greater than space.[7]

Francis describes the human condition as a tension between the experience of limitation and contingency, on the one hand, and possession and fulfillment, on the other. *Fullness* refers to the experience of possibility, of potential limitlessness. *Limitation* is the experience of finiteness, whether in terms of physical limits, fragility, or finite power and control. Both fullness and limitation are essential to the human condition. Every moment reveals the limits of human action—since we can only do one thing at a time in a particular place—yet opens up to the potential for future and eschatological fulfillment. "Time is greater than space" summarizes a reflection on the existential condition of humanity and points to a way of thinking about political action.

The principle "time is greater than space" suggests that an authentic politics is built, not from the exercise of control, but the creation of realities that can perdure. Francis explains:

> One of the faults which we occasionally observe in sociopolitical activity is that spaces and power are preferred to time and

---

7. *Evangelii gaudium*, 221.

processes. Giving priority to space means madly attempting to keep everything together in the present, trying to possess all the spaces of power and of self-assertion; it is to crystallize processes and presume to hold them back. Giving priority to time means being concerned about initiating processes rather than possessing spaces. Time governs spaces, illumines them and makes them links in a constantly expanding chain, with no possibility of return. What we need, then, is to give priority to actions which generate new processes in society and engage other persons and groups who can develop them to the point where they bear fruit in significant historical events.[8]

According to Francis, postmodern humanity exists in a vacillation between fullness and limit, and, therefore, between a Promethean technological drive and despair. In terms of political life, Francis suggests that we vacillate between the attempt to possess and control using the technologies at our disposal, or alternatively give into despondency when we experience the limits of our power. The politics Pope Francis advocates is one of "generating processes of people-building."[9] He frequently refers to "generating processes": developing capacities, creating lines of communication, inclusion in decision-making, opening spaces. Francis contrasts concern for process with the concern for results, usually driven by short-term thinking. It would be inadequate to think of this as merely an opposition between long-term versus short-term goals. Rather, it is an opposition between dynamic, temporally extended social realities and static systems. Processes of "people-building" have no precise end term. Francis explains that the principle "time is greater than space" "invites us to accept the tension between fullness and limitation, and to give a priority to time."[10]

Sociopolitical engagement—person-centered and open to time—is similar to evangelization. In *Evangelii gaudium*, Francis uses the same language to describe evangelization that he uses to describe building just societies.[11] In contrast to the "fragmentation" of time characterizing the accumulation of power, accompanying others on the journey to Christ requires development of relationships through time. Introducing others to the mystery of God requires an authentic accompaniment of others and a "genuine spiritual encounter" with others.[12] For Francis, accompaniment

8. Ibid., 223

9. Ibid., 224.

10. Ibid., 223.

11. See ibid., 225.

12. Ibid., 171.

requires discernment, patience, and time. "Time is God's messenger," he states.[13] The advancement of the Gospel occurs through the media of personal encounter and the relationships built upon that encounter. By implication, the advancement of the Gospel requires ongoing engagement over a long period of time. Both political activity and evangelization must be sustained by the virtue of hope. This is why, describing political activity, Francis alludes to Jesus's counsel to the disciples that they must await the spirit (John 16:12–13). He also refers to the parable of the weeds and the wheat (Matthew 13:24–30), in which the weeds and wheat, evil and good, grow side-by-side until the harvest.

The axiom, "time is greater than space," finds concrete examples in other documents. The Pope's encyclical *Laudato si'* (2015) speaks of the need for developing long-term environmental policy and regulation. Obstructing it is a consumerist model of economics with its attendant prioritization of "immediate results" leading to a gridlock. The ineffective politics within nations results from the stratification and hostility between interests:

> The myopia of power politics delays the inclusion of a far-sighted environmental agenda within the overall agenda of governments. Thus we forget that "time is greater than space," that we are always more effective when we generate processes rather than holding on to positions of power. True statecraft is manifest when, in difficult times, we uphold high principles and think of the long-term common good. Political powers do not find it easy to assume this duty in the work of nation-building.[14]

"Nation-building" of political processes parallels "people-building." Both require a sustained presence and engagement. Both need means to open up spaces in which there are competing interests to processes through which problems can be resolved.

Francis's axiom also appears in his writings on the family in *Amoris laetitia*, the post-synodal apostolic exhortation (2016). First, he quotes *Evangelii gaudium*'s "time is greater than space" when speaking of doctrinal and moral issues in the church. Many issues, he says, do not have to be resolved by papal intervention. Appealing to John 16:13 ("the spirit guides us toward the entire truth"), Francis explains that the differences of cultures and the incompleteness of human understanding lead us to allow for a diversity of practices.[15] Second, speaking of the difficulty of raising children, he repeats this axiom as a counsel for parents:

13. Ibid., quoting Peter Faber.

14. Pope Francis, *Laudato si'*, 178.

15. Pope Francis, *Amoris laetitia*, 3.

It is more important to start processes than to dominate spaces. If parents are obsessed with always knowing where their children are and controlling all their movements, they will seek only to dominate space. But this is no way to educate, strengthen and prepare their children to face challenges. What is most important is the ability lovingly to help them grow in freedom, maturity, overall discipline and real autonomy. Only in this way will children come to possess the wherewithal needed to fend for themselves and to act intelligently and prudently whenever they meet with difficulties. The real question, then, is not where our children are physically, or whom they are with at any given time, but rather where they are existentially, where they stand in terms of their convictions, goals, desires and dreams.[16]

The relationship between children and parents gives a concrete form for Francis's outlook. Children's growth takes place through an incubation in the family, during which they discover their authentic selves, their true callings, and gradually take a rightful independence. This growth must take place in freedom. It cannot take place through absolute control. Here, Francis sounds like an advocate of "free range children." Indeed, he understands that fearful paroxysms of contemporary parenthood must be balanced through the virtues of patience and hope.

In an interview with fellow Jesuit, Antonio Spadaro, Pope Francis links this principle of *time* to the vision embedded in the vision of Ignatius of Loyola. Ignatius's saying, "*Non coerceri a maximo, sed contineri a minimo divinum est* [Not to be limited by the greatest and yet to be contained in the tiniest—this is the divine]."[17] The saying of Ignatius impacts how Francis thinks of his papal ministry. He explains, "it is important not to be restricted by a larger space, and it is important to be able to stay in restricted spaces."[18] Restricted space implies restricted scope of action, using "weak means" and local influence.[19] Considering the role of the popes in recent history, his suggestion is surprising. He continues, "we can always look at the horizon from the position of where we are. That means being able to do the little things of every day with a big heart open to God and to others. That means being able to appreciate the small things inside large horizons, those of the kingdom of God."[20] While purposefully restricting the *space* of ministry, Francis suggests that change for the better requires *time* to discern and to

16. Ibid., 261.

17. Spadaro, "A Big Heart Open to God," 12.

18. Ibid., 12–13.

19. Ibid., 13.

20. Ibid.

develop. In the interview, he goes on to explain that he tries not to make decisions hastily and is usually suspicious of the first decision he arrives at. In this way, the Ignatian "time of discernment" is implicit in the exercise of Francis's papal ministry.[21]

Ultimately, Francis's vision of ministry depends on his discernment of the economy of salvation, that is, how God acts within the world for salvation. He explains that while God is in the past and in the future,

> the 'concrete' God, so to speak, is today . . . God is to be encountered in the world of today. God manifests himself in historical revelation, in history. Time initiates processes, and space crystallizes them. God is in history, in the processes. We must not focus on occupying the spaces where power is exercised, but rather on starting long-run historical processes. We must initiate processes rather than occupy spaces. God manifests himself in time and is present in the processes of history. This gives priority to actions that give birth to new historical dynamics. And it requires patience, waiting.[22]

Francis's dependence upon Ignatian discernment, and the soteriological grounds for that discernment are clear. God acts in the world by acting through history; God's presence in the processes of history are salvific. As a result, we discover God's presence within our own lives and in the flow of the moment. Francis links this notion of God's presence in history to Ignatian discernment, being sensitive to the actions of God in time, and being sensitive to our "affection toward things and situations."[23] It is all premised on the real action of God with us in the world.

The axiom, "time is greater than space," is diffuse throughout Pope Francis's writings and has wide-ranging application. When it comes to human relationships, the diachronic outlook prevails over the synchronic. It seeks something more powerful than temporary control. Instead, it seeks to put into motion processes and ways of being in the world, in such a way that cannot entirely be controlled. The "priority of time" that takes place in relationships in the family and in evangelization can be scaled up when speaking about national and international processes.

21. Ibid.
22. Ibid., 46.
23. Ibid., 47.

The Dialectics of Difference

Pope Francis's theology is developed from eclectic sources and has formed through prayer, discernment, and pastoral ministry. However, before his election as Pope, Jorge Bergoglio drew from Romano Guardini (1885–1968), a German priest of Italian descent, as a source for understanding the dynamics of cultural encounter. Bergoglio especially favored Romano Guardini's books *The Lord* and *The End of the Modern World*, the latter of which he quotes frequently in his papal writings.[24] Bergoglio had once sought to complete a dissertation on Guardini's essay, *Der Gegensatz: Versuch zu einer Philosophie des Lebendig-Konkreten* [*The Contrast: Essay on the Philosophy of Concrete-Living Being*]. For our purposes, two elements from Guardini's work appear in Bergoglio's writings: first, an account of our historical moment, postmodernity, in its challenges and opportunities for the life of faith; second, a dialectic capable of addressing the theological and pastoral challenges of our time.

First, Bergoglio has frequently drawn from Romano Guardini's assessment of postmodernity in *The End of the Modern World*, which gave philosophical orientation to a postwar humanity for whom modern moral and epistemological certainties had been dashed. Guardini claimed that modernity generated a new cosmological vision of the world, which is now transitioning to a postmodern cosmology. The older, medieval cosmology presented a finite delimited world, but one that manifested an "infinity of depth."[25] This infinite depth was secured through a hierarchy of being. Terrestrial realities related symbolically or sacramentally to higher levels of reality.[26] Each thing contained an infinite depth because of its place in God's plan and its symbolic role in the hierarchical scheme of being. Modern cosmology, with its vision of a potentially infinite extension of space and potentially infinite future, flattened the medieval hierarchy. Guardini explains, "As man discovered that the universe extended farther than he had imagined in every direction, these contours were broken . . . Man began to feel that expansion itself was a liberation."[27] In early modern European thought, the infinity of space coincides with the dignity of the human being, whose freedom mirrors God's creation. Guardini says that human beings found themselves in a world with infinite extension. The discovery of this came

24. Francis cites *The End of the Modern World* once in *Evangelii gaudium* (224) and seven times in *Laudato si'* (105, 108, 115, and 203). He cites Guardini's "Von Wesen katholischer Weltanschauung" (1923) once in *Lumen fidei*.

25. Guardini, *End of the Modern World*, 48.

26. Ibid., 48–49

27. Ibid., 50.

with the challenge of orienting oneself in a meaningful universe: "Even as this new world view affirmed a freedom of space, it denied to human existence its own proper place. While gaining infinite scope for movement man lost his own position in the realm of being."[28] The human place in the universe could be regained only by meeting the challenge of extended space. He explains: "For the new man of the modern age the unexplored regions of the world were a challenge to meet and conquer. Within himself he heard the call to venture over what seemed an endless earth, to make himself its master."[29] The religious imagination of the modern age, tied to the infinite extension of space, dovetailed with the colonial enterprise of conquering every part of the earth.

Guardini interprets the end of modernity—postmodernity—as a period of transition and realignment. The modes of thinking in modernity are gone, but nothing has taken its place. The modern problem of extended space does not disappear in postmodernity, rather, it changes and intensifies. The world of today has lost the "modern sense of the infinite" and instead has come to experience the cosmos as finite: "Although science continues to measure distances ever more enormous in scope or more minute in detail, these measurements are always finite."[30] The postmodern universe lacks both the infinite depth of the medieval period and the infinite extent of the modern. More important than the shift in cosmology is the shift in value. We no longer see the universe as the result of God's generosity or of the human soul: "The technological mind sees nature as an insensate order, as a cold body of facts, as a mere 'given,' as an object of utility, as raw material to be hammered into useful shape; it views the cosmos similarly as mere 'space' into which objects can be thrown with complete indifference."[31]

Gaurdini's account of modernity influences Bergoglio's account of the crisis of the postmodern world. According to Bergoglio, postmodern humanity is orphaned (*orfandad*). A primary symptom of spiritual orphanhood is "discontinuity": the "loss or absence of the links in time and the interwoven socio-politics that constitutes a people (*un pueblo*). *We are part of a fragmented society that has cut its community ties.*"[32] In Bergoglio's description, discontinuity is not only a product of the social disruption through globalization and urbanization, but also a disruption of collective

---

28. Ibid., 50.

29. Ibid., 50–51.

30. Ibid., 71–72.

31. Ibid., 74.

32. Bergoglio, *La Nación por construir*, 19. This translation and translations of Spanish-language sources are mine unless otherwise indicated.

memory. It is a "deficit of memory, conceived as the integrating power of our history, and a deficit of tradition, conceived as the riches of the road walked by our elders."[33] The discontinuity of our space compounds the discontinuity of our narratives. The relationship to the human being's "vital space" has been broken, fragmented, and segmented: "The city fills itself with *no-places*, empty spaces submitted exclusively to instrumental logic, deprived of symbols and references that provide for the construction of community identities."[34] Jane Jacobs referred to the "gray areas" of the city, places where social life has broken down.[35] But Bergoglio sees no-places in the central business districts and residential suburbs as well, where space is relegated to merely economic utility. Spatial "rootlessness"—where space is reduced only to utility—is part of a spiritual rootlessness in which the narratives of a people have fallen away. The crisis of modernity is one in which time has become fragmented and in which space and place have lost their existential density.

The second element that Bergoglio draws from Guardini is an analysis of the hegemonic structure of postmodern life and an alternative vision. The dangers of postmodernity do not consist only in the absence of common histories and spaces that conduce to community life. Postmodernity also imposes an overarching order. According to Bergoglio, postmodern life is characterized by hegemonic order that suppresses the distinctive narratives, ways of life, and spaces of communities. Following Romano Guardini, Bergoglio describes postmodernity as a Hegelian resolution of differences, one that creates unity (social, political, ideological) through the annihilation of difference. Though somewhat abstract, Guardini's dialectic provides Bergoglio a method for describing an alternative: a unity that does not suppress difference, but instead maintains a tension between diverse poles of truth, between diverse communities, and among diverse cultures.

Guardini's book *Der Gegensatz* [*The Contrast*], on which Bergoglio began a doctoral dissertation, advanced a dialectic neither Hegelian nor Kierkegaardian in form. Peter Šajda explains that "What Guardini sees as misleading in the Romanic and Hegelian notion of opposition is the over-emphasis on the *relatedness* of the two poles, while what he rejects in Kierkegaard is the over-emphasis on their *difference*."[36] For Hegel, ultimate reality is constituted by the dialectical interplay of opposed realities, not only in concepts but also in history. Historical reality is a process by which

33. Ibid.

34. Ibid., 20

35. Jacobs, *The Death and Life of Great American Cities*, 68.

36. Šajda "Romano Guardini," 55.

realities are posed and opposed, the thesis and the antithesis. The result of the interplay between thesis and antithesis is *Aufhebung*, bearing the simultaneous meaning of *preserving* and *transcending*. Two realities, or poles, are preserved perfectly in the third. Guardini rejected the Hegelian attempt to erase all differences between cultures and epochs in a historical dialectic. He also rejected Søren Kierkegaard's reaction against Hegel, which, preserving the absolute difference between God and humanity and between the Gospel and human culture, conceived the relation between the two poles as "total otherness."[37] According to Guardini, while the Hegelian dialectic loses all transcendence, the Kierkegaardian dialectic loses God's immanence.

Guardini's theory of oppositions or "contrasts" does not so much resolve the tension between contrasts as it preserves them. Opposed poles are not reconciled through synthesis, but instead by holding the poles of opposition in creative tension, not pushing for an ultimate resolution. One might compare Guardini's dialectic to a spider's web, whose structure is maintained through tension.[38] Bergoglio employs Guardini's contrast, not only for theorizing disagreement in church or society and its resolution, but also for theorizing the relationship between different peoples and cultures. For Bergoglio, conflict between points of view are not absolute oppositions in which there must be an absolute winner. Living within the nexus of tension is the key to his thinking. An example of this is found in one of his essays on the religious life as a tensioned pole within the church:

> The framework will be, then, a framework of *tensions*. Thus it must be conceived because it is a framework of life. All tension is between polarities: then, how is it resolved? One tension, for life to be maintained, cannot be resolved by assimilation of one of the poles in detriment to the others, nor by a synthesis (of a Hegelian type) that annuls polarities. The tension (in this case the ecclesial tension) must be resolved on a superior plane, that would not be synthesis, but the resolution that contains virtually the tensioned polarities.[39]

---

37. Ibid.

38. Guardini's contrasts are similar to Henri de Lubac's *paradox*, which he describes as "the search or wait for synthesis. It is the provisional expression of a view which remains incomplete, but whose orientation is ever towards fullness." De Lubac, *Paradoxes of Faith*, 9. For de Lubac, truth is not a self-contained conceptual whole; any conceptual formulation falls short of reality. We experience "paradox," the tension between truths that draws the human mind from its conceptual formulation to the unseen unity that holds them together. The poles of paradox can only be resolved on a transcendent plane.

39. Bergoglio, "La Vida sagrada y su mision en la Iglesia y en el mundo," 204.

In Bergoglio's hands it is not a precise theological method, but a way of seeing things diffusely applied to conflict mediation, to doctrinal development, and to history itself. Tension between poles of opposition is, for Bergoglio, part of life itself. The truth regarding humanity is found imperfectly and concretely in the diverse spectrum of humanity. It requires that differences are not subsumed into a third reality and annulled, but assumed and preserved on another level.

Bergoglio employs the dialectic of oppositions to contrast *internationalism*—that is, hegemonic economic and political systems that dissolve difference— with *universalism*—a relation of differences. In Bergoglio's interpretation, postmodern politics and economics function like colonial rule in that they flatten the particularities of place and culture into the same transactional currency. There is a form of resolving tension that "annuls the virtualities proper to each one of the poles in tension."[40] He explains, in "different *forms of internationalism* . . . The functionality of internationalism comes to fill the spaces that, by a poor resolution of tension, leaves vacant *the sense of the universal*."[41] In internationalism, the mediation of difference takes place through a political economy that organizes all particularities to their utility. By preserving and transcending local differences, "internationalism" exemplifies the Hegelian dialectic: authentic diversity is lost when subsumed in international systems of politics and governance.

Contrasting an "imperial conception of globalization" with a "true globalization," he writes that the former

> is conceived as a perfect sphere, polished. All peoples are fused in a uniformity that annuls the tension between particularities. This globalization constitutes a totalitarianism more dangerous of postmodernity. True globalization must be conceived not as a sphere but as a polyhedron: the facets (the idiosyncracies of [different] peoples) conserve their identity and particularity, but are united—tensioned harmoniously—seeking the common good.[42]

An authentic globalization does not annul the tension between diverse peoples and places but instead seeks to hold difference in tension. Bergoglio proposes an alternative mediation of difference—what he terms "universalist"—that takes place through mutual encounter and ongoing life together. In *universalism*, the tension of differences (of truths, of cultures) is never

40. Ibid., 209.

41. Ibid.

42. Bergoglio, "Prólogo," 10.

resolved through assimilation in one system, but distinct poles are brought into a related tension.

Bergoglio's distinction between internationalism and universalism, or the distinction between "imperial conception of globalization" and "true globalization" parallels the contrast between spatial and temporal logic in the papal writings. In the Hegelian dialectic, internationalisms aim at controlling space, bringing all places into the same transactional system. In contrast, the Guardinian dialectic does not achieve unity through the resolution of difference, but instead finds an incomplete unity by bringing differences into tension, into conversation. For Bergoglio, a Christian universalism is distinctly temporal because a complete unity cannot be found in this life. Universalism depends on the open-endedness of time. It contains an eschatological trajectory.

History, Memory, and Hope

The axiom, "time is greater than space"—along with "unity is superior to conflict" and "the whole is greater than the part"—first appears in Jorge Bergoglio's writings in a 1974 talk given to the Argentine Jesuit provincial congress.[43] Bergoglio presents these axioms as the "most important criteria for directing processes." They constitute his reflections on leadership within the Jesuit order. The meaning of the amplitude of time, however, is explained by his meditations on the nature of time and history. For Bergoglio, the charism of St. Ignatius and the practices of the Jesuits respond to the condition of existential rootlessness by recapturing a sense of history. Ignatian spirituality responds to the fragmentation of postmodern existence by proposing a method by which one might draw these fragments into a whole, according to which one's own experience may be joined to God's temporal action.

For Bergoglio, the primary spiritual challenge facing people today is the fragmented nature of human experience, the inability to discover a narrative whole. In the Jesuit *Spiritual Exercises*, memory unites the fragments of experience with the history of salvation. Bergoglio's understanding of time echoes that of Guardini. From a theological perspective, time is dense with God's presence. A recognition of this presence saves us from the fragmentariness of life: "Our time, the time fecund in God, is what saves us from the slavery of the moment; time inserts us into the 'history' of the holy faithful people making us fecund in our apostolate and freeing us from the sterile 'cartoon' ('historieta') that is surrounded by the contradictions of

---

43. Bergoglio, "Una institución que vive su carisma," 48.

the moment."[44] To have a history requires one to look within the moment to discover the meaning of the moment within the scope of time. "To look at our history is, without doubt, to look through the fragmentariness of our understanding, to travel parcels but envisage the great extended prairies, to see fragments but to contemplate forms." [45] Ignatian spiritual practices aim at the recovery of history. In the *Spiritual Exercises*, the month-long Jesuit retreat, the retreatant relates the events of their own life history to the scope of the history of salvation in the Bible. Ignatius instructed the Jesuits to interrogate their memory, to recollect creation and redemption, and to situate themselves within the story. Bergoglio explains, the memory relates contrary fragments of experience to God's plan: "This Ignatian conception is the possibility of concentrating contraries, of inviting to the common table concepts that apparently cannot be reconciled, because it refers them to a superior plane in which they encounter their synthesis."[46] For Bergoglio, through the *Spiritual Exercises* and daily examination of conscience, memory functions to recognize and to produce a unity of one's life within God's gracious plan.

In Bergoglio's reading of Jesuit spirituality, memory aims not only for a personal unity, but also for the dynamic unity of the Jesuit order itself. Reflecting on the mission of the Jesuits, Bergoglio explains that its primary purpose was to bring about union with God through the "union of souls" among the Jesuits themselves, and, through the Jesuits, all others with whom they came into contact.[47] Because Ignatius envisioned a religious order that would be sent where needed, the primary problem of the Jesuit *Constitutions* was how to a provide for a unity of soul over great distances, which was not a problem in monasticism. The Jesuit *Constitutions* address the problem of preserving unity amidst diverse missions. To be clear, this is a spiritual challenge rather than a challenge of organization or logistics.

According to Bergoglio, hope is prerequisite to unity. As Ignatius of Loyola stated in the *Constitutions*, "In Him alone put hope of preserving and moving forward the Jesuits."[48] Bergoglio explains that Ignatius repeatedly uses the phrase: "and conformed to this hope." This is to say that "all of the means that are used to preserve the wellbeing of, and augment, the Body should take *the form of* hope."[49] Hope

---

44. Ibid., 53.
45. Bergoglio, "Historia y presencia," 17.
46. Ibid., 17–18.
47. Bergoglio, "Esperanza y institución," 200.
48. Ibid., 205.
49. Ibid., 206.

signifies *formalitas* that orders in a referential totality all the particularities of the body. On the other hand, hope has a dynamic hue—of action, of movement—while *giving substance* to things unseen. To refer to it as a foundational virtue has the advantage of underlying *the dynamism* that must exist in the idea (and in the theology) of the preservation and augmentation of the body of the Society, and thus, of the goal of the union of souls.[50]

Embodied in the *Constitutions* of the Jesuits is the notion that God chooses to unite the members of the Society, and God acts in them, and God gives them unique missions: "In this dynamic conception appears implicitly the reality of *diversity*. It will be a union of *diverse* persons, with *diverse* missions, in *diverse* places, with *diverse* modalities." For Ignatius, he writes, "*diversity* is an essential element of the union of souls."[51] Hope constitutes the form of God's still-unseen-plan that orders diversity into a unity. Speaking of the suppression of the Society of Jesus, Pope Francis says the Jesuits, under former Superior General Lorenzo Ricci, "gave priority to history" in an act of hope rather than to succumb to an easy compromise to save the Society.[52]

Bergoglio moves seamlessly from microhistorical to macrohistorical planes, namely from the individual, to the religious order, to society at large. For him, the processes of interrogating one's memory in the *Spiritual Exercises* are essentially the same as the processes of constructing the collective memory, the narrative of the people and of their history.

At its depth, it is a conception of unity that is put into play when Ignatius mentions memory, the power to synthesize the diversity of times in a unity. As it was in our lands: the Jesuits arrived with all the history of sixteen centuries of the Church, with a very clear position before the religious problems debated in Europe during their time, and made a synthesis with the time of the natives. And this synthesis was history. The history that would make the Jesuits would be sealed by a unity embodied by a synthesis of conflicts.[53]

Bergoglio regards the synthesis of personal history envisioned in the *Spiritual Exercises*, and attained practically in the Jesuit order, as a union

50. Ibid., 206; italics allude to Hebrews 11:1.

51. Ibid., 213.

52. Pope Francis, "Celebration of Vespers and Te Deum on the Occasion of the Bicentennial of the Re-Establishment of the Society of Jesus: Address of Pope Francis," line 23. See Bergoglio, "Esperanza y institución," 213.

53. Bergoglio, "Historia y presencia," 18.

of differences.[54] The *Spiritual Exercises* are a microcosm of the dynamics of history and corporate memory in society.

In Bergoglio's presentation, hope constitutes the antidote to the fragmentariness of postmodern existence. Hope orders the diversity of experience towards an eschatological unity. Personal unity requires relating the disparate realities of life to its final goal. Similarly, the Society of Jesus is grounded in the hope that the diverse missions spread across the globe will find a unity in God's plan. Being a people requires that diverse persons with distinctive histories discover a shared narrative, one open to a future we cannot control. This openness to the temporal future, which finds a distinct articulation in the mission of the Jesuits, responds to the fragmentation and self-enclosure of postmodern life. The axiom, "time is greater than space," is a summary of this teaching. He writes, "Only the wisdom of discernment saves us, since this supposes an abandonment to the will of God, with which implies renouncing merely human controls or disciplinary reductions of processes. To make a good decision, Saint Ignatius advises us to consider how we will be in the hour of death: there is clear abandonment to the designs of God, and our fantasies cannot control time."[55]

"Projects of the Heart"

For Bergoglio, the openness to time characteristic of Jesuit spirituality constitutes a model for forging unity without losing diversity. "Time is greater than space" suggests a hope that diverse ideas, people, or missions may be one without the imposition of a hegemonic order, the attempt to control spaces. For Bergoglio, the paradigmatic contrast between an openness to time and the attempt to control space is found in the history of the Jesuit missions in Latin America, in the contest between a Catholic universalism and the colonial project.

On August 27, 1974, Bergoglio penned the principles that guide Universidad del Salvador in Buenos Aires, a Jesuit institution, prior to its transferal to lay oversight. He explains, "It is not strange that the Society confronted the then nascent liberal-bourgeois attempt to homogenize the historical and human reality of the world, through action conjoined to state

54. However, there is ambiguity in his account of unity. He describes the unity of poles of opposition as a unity that attains on a transcendent level. The distinctiveness of cultures and their histories is retained, though they find a point of unity on a transcendent plane. Bergoglio wishes to avoid a Hegelian synthesis that he believes annuls diversity. However, when he speaks of human unity, he speaks concretely of a unity that takes form in time, as a history of people coming together.

55. Bergogio, "Conducir en lo grande y en lo pequeño," 103.

centralism and enlightenment rationalism, to the detriment of the multifaceted richness of creation."[56] The missionary activity of the Jesuits, he says,
sought to preserve human diversity in the face of the colonial project:

> In China as in River Plate, the Society refused to be the reli-
> gious justification of the European expansion, by providing
> the missioned peoples organizational and social elements that
> permitted the free development of their cultural individuality,
> integrating them into the universal through a Faith felt as their
> own. The Society is fundamentally universalist; and, for this,
> contrary to the homogenizing internationalism that, by "reason"
> or by force, denies peoples the right to be themselves.[57]

Bergoglio claims that the Jesuit missions were a project of integration. However, he locates the specific difference between the Jesuit missions and the
colonial project in that the Jesuits discovered a dignity of indigenous life and
sought to preserve the indigenous culture against the colonial onslaught.
His dichotomy, of course, is not a nuanced history, though it provides the
categories by which he reads this history.

For Bergoglio, Spain's efforts to wrest the Andean mission territories
from the Jesuits in the eighteenth century exemplifies the contrast between
universalism and internationalism. The first Jesuits arrived in El Rio de la
Plata ("River of Silver") in 1585. El Rio de la Plata, or "River Plate," as the
English called it, is an estuarial region on the borders of northern Argentina, Paraguay, and Brazil, originally ignored by the Spanish, and where the
Jesuits created missions outside of the Spanish military control.[58] Alonso
Rodríguez, SJ (1598-1628), Juan del Castillo, SJ (1595-1628), and Roque
González de Santa Cruz, SJ (1576-1628) were missionaries in River Plate
killed by the indigenous there. According to Bergoglio, the Jesuit motivation was not to be an adjunct for European dominion, but to allow for the
autonomy of the indigenous people. He argues that the dominant theories
of governance in the Jesuit order at the time derived from Francisco Suárez,
SJ. According to Suárez, the power to rule is derived from God. But the
people themselves have the power to "delegate it in a prince" (as in "princeps," or "principle"). The American continent would witness the inversion
of this right in the Treaty of Permuta: "the prince will no longer seek the
common good, and the life and culture of the people will be betrayed."[59] The

56. Bergoglio, "Principios." Translation indebted to Ivereigh, 64.

57. Ibid.

58. Cordoza-Orlandi and González, *To All Nations from All Nations*, 160

59. Bergoglio, "Proyección cultural y evangelizadora de los mártires rioplantenses,"
293.

1750 Treaty of Permuta tentatively established the boundaries of the Spanish and Portuguese empires in the Americas. The seven Jesuit missions in the River Plate were to pass to Portuguese control. By 1753, war broke out between the Portuguese and the Guaraní, the native people who lived in the Jesuit missions. The result was the Portuguese victory and the enslavement of the Guaraní.

Speaking about accounts written of the River Plate martyrs (*mártires rioplantenses*), Bergoglio writes that "the missionaries were told to *found villages* (living frontiers) . . . [and to] save the people there: to return them to the dignity of the sons of God (who, with other colonizers would be slaves)." He explains that "it was a *project of the heart*," not one of colonization. "It is also the project of the heart of a people that carries the Gospel and knows to open itself—because of justice—to the culture of the people who it evangelizes . . . and at the same time it is the project of the heart of the other people that for its part opens its culture to the seed of the Gospel, and which in these latitudes will flourish equally and distinctly: it will be wheat . . . but from red soil."[60] Using the biblical image of the seed falling on soil (Mark 4; Matthew 13), Bergoglio claims that it is the Gospel that is active in opening the hearts of those within both cultures. The missionary activity of the Jesuits was a "project of the heart" because it was based on mutual encounter and exchange, as well as rooted in human dignity.

In Bergoglio's complex description of the Jesuit project in River Plate, he explains that the "Holy Martyrs" had an attitude of "*fatherhood*" [*la paternidad*] for those they evangelized, a spiritual fatherhood that entailed a love for the people and the "capacity to give them their own life."[61] Bergoglio's language of fatherhood could be taken as paternalism, particularly a paternalism linked to racial and cultural hierarchy. Fatherhood, as he describes it, requires one to be oneself through communion with others. It is a spiritual paternity: "The entire project of paternity entails necessarily a dimension of greatness whose root is the acceptance of transcending oneself."[62] Bergoglio's language of self-transcendence is used to describe the relationship between cultures. To transcend one's own culture is not to leave it behind by adopting another, nor is it one of melding two cultures into a third.

> Since the essence is fatherhood, it is a project definitively opposed to projects . . . that prescind from popular feelings, from sentiments, and from the organization and work of the people.

60. Ibid., 291.
61. Ibid., 295.
62. Ibid.

> They did not implement a process of withdrawal from their own culture (in this case, that of the indigenous) forgetting the destiny of universality of the entire cultural project . . . Neither was it a project that facilitated the easy absorption of the style of life of others, and that rejects conflict so fundamental of being oneself and—at the same time—confirming difference. That type of project marks a lame posture that negates the risk of diversity. The project of the three martyrs is a *project of Christian freedom*, of making people free, and that will be the center in the Reductions.[63]

The fatherhood he describes is not the same as the cultural paternalism brought inevitably by colonization in the Americas, which sought either to make the indigenous Spanish or to make them slaves. But neither is it one in which all parties would remain untouched by the other. It invites the challenge and paradox of going out of oneself and remaining oneself.

According to Bergoglio, the Jesuit missions had preserved the "living frontiers" that permitted an exchange between people, culture, and religion. He contrasts the "living frontiers" [*fronteras vivas*] with the "metropolitan hegemony," the margins and the center. "Living frontiers" refers to frontiers constituted by people rather than merely the lines on the map. In his interview with Antonio Sparado, SJ, he explains, "When I insist on the frontier, I am referring in a particular way for those who work in the world of culture to be inserted into the context in which they operate and on which they reflect. There is always the lurking danger of living in a laboratory. Ours is not a 'lab faith,' but a 'journey faith,' a historical faith. God has revealed himself as history, not as a compendium of abstract truths."[64] In this case, the living frontiers are those of both indigenous and European descent who are presented with the challenge of an encounter through which both peoples would be changed and would have to transcend themselves.

These frontiers were soon gone. In Bergoglio's presentation, the people [*el pueblo*] were caught between a war of ideologies: those of the indigenous medicine men [*los hechiceros*] and those of the European fortune hunters [*bandeiras*]:

> The bandeiras progressively destroyed these living frontiers looking for "Bolivian ore" . . . and a little more than a century later, in 1750, we arrive at the "Treaty of Permuta" in which the prince forgot his people, and Spain traded what was his for what was already his. The Bourbon enlightenment courts culminated

---

63. Ibid., 296–97.

64. Spadaro, *A Big Heart Open to God*, 59.

their process of consolidation in Europe. The Codicil of Isabel I would be supplied by the instructions of S.M. Don Carlos III to the inspector José Gálvez: "to respond to the noble intention of organizing this great kingdom and making uniform its political and economic system with that of the metropolis, of which will result, among many other advantages revealed by time, that its government will be calibrated according to the interior government residing in Spain, and that those who hold office would not have to understand contrary rules, or at least very different than those observed in their country of origin." The fecund universality that integrates and respects differences and idiosyncrasies was replaced by an absorbent metropolitan hegemony of a domineering kind. These lands that were "provinces" of the Kingdom came to be "colonies." No longer was there a place for projects of the heart: it was the epoch of the enlightenment of the mind.[65]

The projects of the heart were crushed under the power of state centralization and domination of the frontier by the capitals of Europe. The encounter between peoples was brought under state control. The "living frontier" was brought under domination by systems: successively the *ecomiendas* and *las reducciones de indios*. In *las reducciones de indios*, Spain sought not just to conquer each territory, but sought a reorganization of indigenous society. It sought to simultaneously civilize the indigenous, Christianize them, and to have them contribute to the colonial economy. *Reducciones* placed the indigenous into towns with uniform governance and economic structure, ordering the indigenous and settlers within the colonial economy. *Reducciones* were laid out with a similar city plan, provided a church and priest, and a governor [*corregidor de indios*]. They sought to create a Spanish civic existence in the colonies.

Bergoglio's narrative of the *reducciones* illustrates the conflict he perceived between giving the priority to time and spatializing Christian life. The Spanish cosmopolitan hegemony organized all civic, religious, and economic life in the space of empire. The projects of the heart—those processes by which a human encounter and exchange could be made—were destroyed by the ordering of all places into a system governable by the courts in Europe and the realization of a uniform economy. In effect, it destroyed the *fronteras vivas*, the places of encounter. South America suffered uniquely from what we might call the spatialization of Christian life under colonial

---

65. Bergoglio, "Proyección cultural y evangelizadora de los mártires rioplantenses," 314–15. Translation indebted to Ivereigh, 63.

rule and beyond. Process was replaced by a system that sought to eliminate all contradiction or difference. Time was fractured into space.

Bergoglio presents the River Plate martyrs as witnesses to an alternative resolution to the meeting between peoples: "Martyrdom was a further step on the road of horizons wider than what had been imposed on these people. They were animated to overcome limits in search of Christian liberty, of evangelical justice, for those children who they loved as sons; they put up with a thousand and one contradictions . . . but, further, they were intimately convinced that *time was theirs*. Men of time with the wisdom to overcome contradictions."[66] For Bergoglio, the martyrdom of the Jesuits was not an escape from the temporal, but indicative of their commitment to living within time and amidst tension. It was a witness to a Christian political alternative, which seeks unity within tension rather than uniformity.

The Political and the Pastoral

In February 2016, returning by plane to Rome from Mexico, Pope Francis fielded questions from reporters. Philip Pullella asked Francis to react to Donald Trump's criticism that the Pope is a "very political person." Francis responded, "Thank God he said I was a politician because Aristotle defined the human person as '*animal politicus*.' At least I am a human person."[67] This humorous and seemingly spontaneous exchange concerned a topic to which Francis had already given considerable reflection. In his conversation with Abraham Skorka, Bergoglio said, "We are all Political animals, with a capital P. We are called to constructive political activity among our people. The preaching of human and religious values has a political consequence."[68] He states that while the church must avoid partisan politics, the Gospel directly impacts the political. Bergoglio did not imagine the political and spiritual as distinct ontological or existential planes. Instead, he describes political activity and spiritual-ecclesial communion using similar language: solidarity, union, and hope.

The political is essential to being human, and political activity is inscribed in ways of being in community. Aiming at a transcendent good, the church fulfills political activity by constituting the nexus of a unity of diverse people. There is, for Bergoglio, a correspondence between politics and pastoral activity, both of which share the goal of human unity. Bergoglio

66. Ibid., 312.

67. Pope Francis, "Full text of Pope Francis' in-flight interview from Mexico to Rome," *Catholic News Agency*, lines 106–26.

68. Bergoglio and Skorka, *On Heaven and Earth*, 136.

interpreted Pope John Paul II's 1998 visit to Cuba and meeting with Fidel Castro, then president of Cuba, as a joint pursuit of truth, "la búsqueda de la verdad."[69] Bergoglio claimed that there is a harmony between the political struggle of the people of the communist island nation and the transcendent aim of the Gospel: "The mission of the Pope and the reception of Fidel Castro converge in the implementation of new methodologies to apply in political transformation, on the one hand, and evangelization, on the other."[70] The church's role is dialogical, "participating to construct the communion between human beings and the church."[71] Though Bergoglio attributed an active role to the church represented by the Pope in "transmitting the word of Christ," he also attributed to the church a passive receptivity of the spirit of the Cuban people. Cuba was the crossroads for the meeting of people from the Americas, Europe, and Africa, and today, it carries the living memory of these diverse origins.[72] The church, he says, rescued the distinct religiosity of various peoples by channeling it toward the faith. The church became the nexus of communion with God and communion between people, though not by homogenization but by receptive inclusion. Bergoglio conceived the universalist impulse of Catholicism not as the imposition of a universal order, but as a willingness to include and incorporate the distinct contributions of all.

Bergoglio describes the integrative role of politics similarly to that of the church. He describes society as "networks of politics" (drawing from Karl Deutsch) and politics as "an *ambit*, a *space* . . . whose function is 'relational'" (from Sheldon Wolin). Political institutions and activities have the specific function to "integrate the discontinuities of group and organizational life in a society of common participation."[73] Politics "converts" other human activities into the social life of the community. He explains that

69. Bergoglio, *Diálogos entre Juan Pablo II y Fidel Castro*, 14. Bergoglio, at the request of the Vatican, produced a compilation of the speeches given by Pope John Paul II and Fidel Castro. His lengthy introduction contextualized the meeting as a historical moment that was also a theology in practice.

70. Ibid.

71. Ibid., 13.

72. Ibid., 56–57. Bergoglio's rhetoric of unity is inspiring, yet unsettling. His lengthy introduction fails to mention—except with a passing reference to enslavement of Africans—either the violence under which the integration of diverse people occurred or the near complete loss of indigenous life on the island due to disease and slavery. The distinction that needed to be made—drawn out elsewhere, but not here—is between the universalist vision embedded in Catholicism and the realities of colonial Catholicism that failed to match that vision and that contributed to human suffering on a grand scale.

73. Bergoglio, "Necesidad de una anthropología política," 260.

political institutions provide a "relational function," namely to "to define political space or place where the tensional forces of society are related, as in a tribunal, a legislature, a political party, etc. Also they serve to define political time, the period within which is the place of decision, the resolution. Political organizations and systems thus provide a framework, inside of which the spatial and temporal activities of individuals, groups, and institutions are linked."[74] Bergoglio is in accord with sources of Catholic social doctrine that speak of the state as a particular and delimited institution within society. Yet, his vision of politics is broader. Many human activities and group activities should be brought into political relation in society, and political institutions help this to occur.

Similar to the terms that Bergoglio uses to describe the church's mission of unity, and specifically the Jesuit charism, he uses terms to describe the task of forming unity in society. He explains that social unity is not made real by an idea or an ideology, but instead

> in a *united* [*solidario*], habitual, constant effort to overcome the momentariness. The fact is politics neither makes sense nor is the pastoral established through the urgency of structural reform, if not through the invitation to political concord or friendship, which can develop itself only rooted in the *free attitude of solidarity* and that does not respond without the aspiration of the encounter with the one Good that unites all people inwardly.[75]

Both pastoral and political actions aspire to something beyond the discontinuity of space and the fragmentation of time, the principal symptoms of the postmodern malaise. Like the encounter of people within the church, an authentic politics is grounded in solidarity. It requires the priority of time: an openness to the ongoing development of relationship, to political process, and to a future we cannot yet see.

Conclusion

In his writings and interviews, Francis frequently describes the politics that can address our current problems as requiring the priority of time over space, that is, open-ended processes over control of territory. Though distilled in a pithy axiom, this principle has wide-ranging application. The priority of time is the antidote to the fragmentation and spatialization

74. Ibid.
75. Ibid., 287.

of postmodern life, the loss of our narratives and intelligible spaces. The priority of time constitutes an element of Bergoglio's theological response, based on his meditations on Jesuit identity and interpreted through the South American experience of colonization and the *reducciones*. Though the Catholic Church imagined its mission inside the spatialized world of modernity and colonialism, Bergoglio proposes an alternative vision drawn by the virtue of hope. The politics of process closely corresponds to what Francis envisions as the role of the church: to establish authentic solidarity and open-ended relationships. Francis cautions us not to be as interested in securing powerful position as were are in creating fruitful processes for dialogue, communion, and common pursuit of the good. Without neglecting the pursuit of structural reforms, Francis's political theology suggests that encounter and solidarity are not only means, but also ends.

Bibliography

Bergoglio, Jorge Mario. *Diálogos entre Juan Pablo II y Fidel Castro.* Buenos Aires: Ciudad Argentina, 1998.

———. "Esperanza y institución, 'y conforme a esta esperanza . . .': Algunas reflexiones acerca de la unión de los ánimos." In *Reflexiones en esperanza*, 199–256. Vatican City: Libreria Editrice Vaticana, 2013. Originally published as *Reflexiones en esperanza*. Buenos Aires: Universidad del Salvador, 1992.

———. "Historia y presencia." In *Meditaciones para religiosos*, 17–21. Bilbao: Ediciones Mensajero, 2014. Originally published as *Meditaciones para religiosos*. San Miguel, Buenos Aires: Provincia SJ, 1982.

———. "Una institución que vive su charisma." In *Meditaciones para religiosos*, 43–60. Bilbao: Mensajero, 2014.

———. *La Nación por construir: Utopía, pensamiento y compromiso: VIII Jornada de Pastoral Social.* Buenos Aires: Clariatana, 2005.

———. "Necesidad de una antropología política: Un problema pastoral" In *Reflexiones en esperanza*, 257–88. Vatican City: Libreria Editrice Vaticana, 2013.

———. "Prólogo." In Guzmán Carriquiry, *Una Apuesta por américa latina: Memoria y destino históricos de un continente*, 7–11. Buenos Aires: Sudamericana, 2005.

———. "Proyección cultural y evangelizadora de los mártires rioplantenses." In *Reflexiones en esperanza*, 289–317. Vatican City: Libreria Editrice Vaticana, 2013.

———. "La Vida sagrada y su mision en la Iglesia y en el mundo." *Teología: Revista de la Facultad de Teología de la Pontificia Universidad Católica Argentina* 66 (1995) 203–12.

Bergoglio, Jorge Mario, and Abraham Skorka. *On Heaven and Earth: Pope Francis on Faith, Family, and the Church in the Twenty-First Century.* Translated by Alejandro Bermudez and Howard Goodman. New York: Image, 2015. Originally published as *Sobre el cielo y la tierra.* Buenos Aires: Sudamericana, 2010.

Cordoza-Orlandi, Carlos F., and Justo L. González. *To All Nations from All Nations: A History of the Christian Missionary Movement.* Nashville: Abigndon, 2013.

Ivereigh, Austen. *The Great Reformer: Francis and the Making of a Radical Pope*. New York: Holt, 2014.

Pontifical Council for Justice and Peace, *Compendium of the Social Doctrine of the Church*. Washington, DC: USCCB 2005.

Pope Francis. *Amoris laetitia*. https://w2.vatican.va/content/dam/francesco/pdf/apost_exhortations/documents/papa-francesco_esortazione-ap_20160319_amoris-laetitia_en.pdf.

———. "Celebration of Vespers and Te Deum on the Occasion of the Bicentennial of the Re-Establishment of the Society of Jesus: Address of Pope Francis, Saturday, 27 September 2014." https://w2.vatican.va/content/francesco/en/speeches/2014/september/documents/papa-francesco_20140927_vespri-bicentenario-ricostituzione-gesuiti.html.

———. *Evangelii gaudium*. http://w2.vatican.va/content/francesco/en/apost_exhortations/documents/papa-francesco_esortazione-ap_20131124_evangelii-gaudium.html.

———. "Full text of Pope Francis' in-flight interview from Mexico to Rome." *Catholic News Agency*. http://www.catholicnewsagency.com/news/full-text-of-pope-francis-in-flight-interview-from-mexico-to-rome-85821/.

———. *Laudato si'*. http://w2.vatican.va/content/francesco/en/encyclicals/documents/papa-francesco_20150524_enciclica-laudato-si.html.

———. *Lumen fidei*. http://w2.vatican.va/content/francesco/en/encyclicals/documents/papa-francesco_20130629_enciclica-lumen-fidei.html.

———. "Principios." Universidad del Salvador. August 27, 1974. www.usal.edu.ar/principios.

Guardini, Romano. *The End of the Modern World: A Search for Orientation*. Translated by Joseph Theman and Herbert Burke. New York: Sheed and Ward, 1956. Originally published as *Das Ende der Neuzeit: Ein Versuch zur Orientierung*. Basel: Hess, 1950.

Jacobs, Jane. *The Death and Life of Great American Cities*. New York: Vintage, 1992.

Lubac, Henri de. *Paradoxes of Faith*. Translated by Sadie Kreilkamp. San Francisco: Ignatius, 1987.

Šajda, Peter. "Romano Guardini: Between Actualistic Personalism, Qualitative Dialectic, and Kinetic Logic." In *Kierkegaard's Influence on Theology Tome III: Jewish and Catholic Theology*, edited by Jon Stewart, 45–74. Burlington, VT: Ashgate 2012.

Spadaro, Antonio. *A Big Heart Open to God: A Conversation with Pope Francis*. New York: HarperOne, 2013.

CHAPTER 13 ————————————————————————

Social Communication as Encounter

—Daniella Zsupan-Jerome

Abstract:

This chapter presents a survey of Pope Francis's vision for social communication. Starting both from theological foundations and from the observation of communication as a fundamentally human relational experience, Pope Francis urges us to avoid approaching social communication in our digital culture as a gadget-driven and instrumental activity. Instead, he proposes that social communication in our digital age remains a human, relational act that has the potential to bring about true encounter with one another. Along these lines he also invites us into the theology of communication, reminding us that God's revelatory work offered in Word and in Spirit (that is, divine communication) is salvific and transformative. In addition to maintaining the dignity of the human aspect of communication, he calls us toward this theological vision as a way to shape our communication practices toward a sense of communion.

The theme of encounter, constitutive of Pope Francis's vision for evangelization, is the backbone of his vision for social communication as well. Focusing particularly on social communication in and through digital media, this chapter examines Pope Francis's thought to bring about true encounter in and through these mediated means. The documents that help break open this question include Pope Francis's "Address to the Participants in the Plenary Assembly of the Pontifical Council for Social Communications" (September 21, 2013), and selections from *Evangelii gaudium* (November 24, 2013), and the 2014, 2015 and 2016 "Message(s) for the World Communications Day." In examining each of these documents, this chapter looks for how communication and true encounter mutually illuminate one another, as they both emphasize a basic call to relationship, with God and with one another.

"Address to the Participants in the Plenary Assembly of the Pontifical Council for Social Communications" (September 21, 2013)

In the chronology of the documents we are examining, Pope Francis's "Address to the Participants in the Plenary Assembly of the Pontifical Council for Social Communications" appears first. In it, he offers three basic points on social communication, all centered around the theme of encounter. In some ways, this brief address is an effective summary statement of his vision on social communication and encounter, a vision he will develop in further detail the "Message(s) for the World Communications Day."

The address moves through three basic points, making the case that 1) the area of communication is de facto important for the Church; 2) the Church should strive to enter into dialogue with men and women today through the practical means of communication at our disposal; and 3) communication should be ordered toward bringing others to meet Christ. Moving along the trajectory of these three points is instructive. First, by making the case that the area of communications is de facto important for the Church, Pope Francis shifts the conversation around communications from an instrumental approach—what medium, platform, technology or gadget to use—to an ecclesiological approach of how communication is constitutive of the Church's identity. Along these lines, he recalls "the Church's solicitude for communication in all its forms which are important tools for the work of evangelization."[1] By casting communication under the umbrella of evangelization, Pope Francis shows how essential and central it is to the identity and mission of the Church. It is not just a cultural or pastoral topic, but a topic at the very heart of the Church, as a community called to go, to proclaim and to make disciples of all nations by the sharing of the Good News (Matthew 28:19; Mark 16:15).

In this first point of the address, Pope Francis notes an important shift in the perception of what communication is. He observes, "In the last few decades the various means of communication have evolved significantly,

---

1. Pope Francis, "Address to the Participants in the Plenary Assembly of the Pontifical Council for Social Communications," 1.

but the Church's concern remains the same, though it assumes new ways of expression. There is a difference between these forms that are functional means of communication and communication itself, which is something else entirely. The world of communications, more and more, has become an 'environment' for many, one in which people communicate with one another, expanding their possibilities for knowledge and relationship."[2] In moving us away from the functional notion of communication as means, to communication as an environment of knowledge and relationships, Pope Francis broadens the conversation so that the Church can enter it more readily. If communication is not reduced to its instruments or media, then it truly is a relational encounter between persons that expands our possibilities for knowledge and relationship. Defined in this sense, communication is a topic replete with theological, spiritual and pastoral significance. Retrieving communication from the captivity of the instrumental, Pope Francis makes space for a much broader conversation.

The second main point of the address further encourages the Church's involvement in the world of communication—that environment of knowledge and relationship that is our context today. To enter this environment, Pope Francis takes the approach of discernment by way of listening and attentiveness to the realities of life today: "I believe that the goal is to understand how to enter into dialogue with men and women of today, to know how to engage this dialogue in order to appreciate their desires, their doubts and their hopes."[3] He calls the Church to accompany people starting with where they are, and to be a Church "that knows how to walk with men and women along the path."[4] This kind of accompaniment allows the Church to enter into the reality of the environment of communication, and to perceive and experience its gifts and challenges. For English speakers, the metaphor of the path and of walking together also might bring to mind another one: to walk a mile in another person's shoes. This kind of accompaniment is dialogical: it genuinely listens and seeks into the experience and perspective of the other. Using these metaphors, Pope Francis teaches that it is important for the Church to carefully consider the environment of communication, but also to experience communication by way of "dialogue, and with discernment, to use modern technologies and social networks in such a way as to reveal a presence that listens, converses, and encourages."[5] His vision of

---

2. Ibid.
3. Ibid., 2.
4. Ibid.
5. Ibid.

the Church engaging communication is ordered toward encounter, both by observation and by the experience of listening and dialogue.

The third main point of Pope Francis's address is to cast all Church communication in this light, as ordered toward encounter with Christ. The challenges we face today, especially in our digital communication environment, find their answer in Christ, whether the challenge is "disorientation, isolation, loss of meaning, inability to connect with a home, or struggle to find meaningful relationships."[6] The Church's task, in many ways is to meet people along the way and help guide them home to Christ. He states it unambiguously: "This is the challenge: to bring the person to Christ."[7] Along these lines, in the third and final section of the address, he reflects briefly on what this encounter might look like. He deepens the image of walking with people by recalling the narrative of the disciples on the road to Emmaus (Luke 24:13-35), and Christ's own model of accompaniment found in this story, that not only broke open the Scriptures for the two travelers, but did so in a way that enkindled their hearts. To emphasize this, Pope Francis refers to beauty: "The challenge is to rediscover, through the means of social communication as well as by personal contact, the beauty that is at the heart of our existence and journey, the beauty of faith and of the beauty of the encounter with Christ."[8] He will expound on what he means by the way of beauty (*via pulchritudinis*) in *Evangelii gaudium*, but here, joined to the road to Emmaus reference, beauty contributes to that which warms the hearts of men and women.[9] In light of this narrative, Pope Francis asks us to examine whether our presence and plans measure up to this, or whether we remain simply technicians.[10] Implied in his question is the warning that if we remain technicians, we stay focused on instruments rather than on human persons. The language of encounter here reiterates the focus on the profound theological and ecclesial meaning of communication as a relational act in an environment of knowledge and relationship, introduced earlier on in this address.

Albeit brief, Pope Francis's "Address to the Participants in the Plenary Assembly of the Pontifical Council for Social Communications" offers a simple, three-point trajectory that leads the Church into the topic of communication as a reality ordered toward encounter with Christ. He calls the

6. Ibid.

7. Ibid., 3.

8. Ibid.

9. Ibid. For Pope Francis's understanding of the "way of beauty" or *via pulchritudinis*, see *Evangelii gaudium*, 167.

10. Pope Francis, "Address," 3.

Church to think about communication theologically, to engage in communication pastorally and dialogically, and to order communication toward Christ—a true and personal encounter with Him. Although he does not spell this out, this trajectory forges a close association between encounter with Christ and the revelation of the Word, and implies that to encounter Christ in and through communication is in fact a return to understanding Him as the Word made flesh, and the fullness of God's self-communication. If our own communication practices do not reveal this reality in some way, there is something amiss. Pope Francis closes his address with this final thought: "It is necessary to be absolutely clear that the God in whom we believe, who loves all men and women intensely, wants to reveal himself through the means at our disposal, however poor they are, because it is he who is at work, he who transforms and saves us."[11] Trusting in the revelatory potential of our communication practices can therefore transform our experience toward a salvific one. If it is God who is at work in our communication, our fundamental and primary objective is one of discernment: to trust, to listen and be open to how God is calling us to authentic communication and encounter with others.

Evangelii gaudium

A comprehensive treatment of Pope Francis's apostolic exhortation, *Evangelii gaudium*, is beyond the scope of the present chapter. Instead, our focus here remains on social communication and encounter, and how Pope Francis clarifies his vision for this through select sections of *Evangelii gaudium*, in particular paragraphs 87–88.[12]

Encounter, essential to Pope Francis's vision for the Church, is introduced as the gate through which to enter into this text. Pope Francis leads off with a powerful call: "I invite all Christians, everywhere, at this very moment, to a renewed personal encounter with Jesus Christ, or at least an openness to letting him encounter them; I ask all of you to do this unfailingly each day. No one should think that this invitation is not meant for him or her, since 'no one is excluded from the joy brought by the Lord.'"[13] This call is all encompassing as it is meant to be constitutive of our identity in Christ. As it is a defining element of being Christian, encounter with Christ

11. Ibid.

12. In *Evangelii gaudium*, Pope Francis treats the topic of the instantaneity of media and communication, and the risk of reducing the meaning of content, in paragraphs 34–35.

13. Ibid., 3.

ought to generate and to be the goal of every effort of evangelization. This includes social communication.

In paragraphs 87–88, Pope Francis makes this connection explicitly. He begins with describing the networked reality of our communication environment as it offers the potential for both chaos and encounter:

> Today, when the networks and means of human communication have made unprecedented advances, we sense the challenge of finding and sharing a "mystique" of living together, of mingling and encounter, of embracing and supporting one another, of stepping into this flood tide which, while chaotic, can become a genuine experience of fraternity, a caravan of solidarity, a sacred pilgrimage. Greater possibilities for communication thus turn into greater possibilities for encounter and solidarity for everyone.[14]

In this description, Pope Francis makes a prophetic claim: that networks and means of human communication, albeit chaotic, can be ordered toward communion with God. Juxtaposing the image of a network with that of a fraternity, the images of caravan and pilgrimage introduce direction and purpose to a concept that could otherwise remain simply an ever-expanding amorphous cloud. In some ways, endless expansion could actually resonate with the image of invitation into mystery, but the Christian sense of mystery is not directionless; rather, it is invitation into an inexhaustible relationship that leads us into the heart of God. By naming the network as fraternity, caravan and pilgrimage, Pope Francis insists on its communal, mystical potential, and reveals it as a way for us to be connected toward communion.

Along with this vision of a network toward communion, Pope Francis also offers us a challenge, and does so explicitly in reference to encounter. He calls us out of ourselves according to the de facto disposition necessary for the Christian ideal. He states: "To go out of ourselves and to join others is healthy for us. To be self-enclosed is to taste the bitter poison of immanence, and humanity will be worse for every selfish choice we make."[15] This disposition to go out of ourselves is in fact key for fulfilling the potential of the network to lead us toward communion. Because our experience of network can be indeed chaotic and overwhelming, we survive in it by retreating into smaller, more manageable circles. Pope Francis challenges one aspect of this otherwise natural human tendency, and calls us to continue to remain open. Our circles, when formed too rigidly can become defined by "suspicion, habitual mistrust, fear of losing our privacy, and all the de-

14. Ibid., 87.
15. Ibid.

fensive attitudes which today's world imposes on us."[16] In some ways, these attitudes help fortify the walls we may erect around our smaller circles, so that we can better understand who is in and who is out, and somehow manage the otherwise overwhelming sense of our belonging to the flow of digital culture. Or, instead of belonging to smaller circles of a particular identity, we may also use the technology itself to build walls: "for just as some people want a purely spiritual Christ, without flesh and without the cross, they also want their interpersonal relationships provided by sophisticated equipment, by screens and systems which can be turned on or off at command."[17] Managing relationships via the screen allows us to more easily connect with or disconnect from others; people can in fact become "just connections" that we manage instead of persons whom we encounter. At the same time, erecting such boundaries need not be the only way to find refuge in the chaos of the network. In lieu of building a fortress either by ideology or by technology, Pope Francis calls us to the stability of the Gospel as our firm footing in the flow of digital culture. It is the Gospel that can enable us best to move from chaos toward order, from a sense of endless data to encounter and communion.

Pope Francis closes this section by reminding us that the "Son of God, by becoming flesh, summoned us to the revolution of tenderness."[18] This point is prophetic: by calling us back to the Incarnation and to a revolution of tenderness, Pope Francis reminds us that even in the network, words (data, image, sound) should lead us back to flesh, meaning that we always remain focused persons connected through digital means. There is always a person behind a screen. The revolution of tenderness is one that insists on the full, embodied personhood of "users" and envisions the network as persons in communion. Tenderness emerges from recognizing not only the personhood but dignity and brokenness of the other through the screen. In this recognition there is also mutuality and potential for relationship. This speaks directly against the challenge of the commodification of the human person in digital culture, as well as to the reality of violent language; both symptoms of a culture that is losing sight of encounter. [19]

Evangelii gaudium, the blueprint of Pope Francis's vision for the Church, thus frames social communication in the digital age as a network environment with potential for the More. To be sure, part of the work of

---

16. Ibid., 88.

17. Ibid.

18. Ibid.

19. For the commodification of the human person in digital culture, see Caccamo, *Let Me Put It Another Way*, 12–14.

evangelization (old or "the new") is to insist on this potential and to transform this aspect of society toward true encounter with Christ and with one another.

"Message(s) for World Communications Day" (January 24, 2014–2016)

"Communication at the Service of an Authentic Culture of Encounter" (2014)

Each year since 1967, on the feast of St. Francis the Sales, the Pope publishes a Message in anticipation for that year's World Communications Day. Pope Francis has offered three such messages, each touching on some aspect of social communication and encounter.[20] His most substantial treatment of encounter is found in his 2014 "Message for the 48th World Communications Day," titled "Communication at the Service of an Authentic Culture of Encounter."[21] In this message, Pope Francis looks through the lens of the parable of the Good Samaritan and asks of us anew, "who is our neighbor," particularly in the networked environment of digital culture. His point is not simply for us to identify who the neighbor is, but to follow the lead of the Good Samaritan, to take responsibility for our neighbor, and to offer mercy, healing and the Good News.

A much-quoted line of Pope Francis comes from this document: "The Internet in particular offers immense possibilities for encounter and solidarity. This is something truly good, a gift from God."[22] Calling the Internet "a gift from God" received some media attention, but focusing only on this misses the overall point.[23] More significant is his overall idea of forming a "culture of encounter" with the help of the media. According to Pope Francis, "a culture of encounter demands that we be ready not only to give but also to receive. Media can help us greatly in this, especially nowadays when the networks of human communication have made unprecedented advances."[24]

20. At the time this chapter was composed, the theme of the 2017 "Message for World Communications Day" had been published as well: "'Fear not, for I am with you': Communicating Hope and Trust in Our Time."

21. Pope Francis, "Message for the 48th World Communications Day." This brief document, as well as the other "Message(s) for World Communications Day," have no paragraph numbers.

22. Ibid.

23. See, for instance, Fung and Boorstein, "Pope Francis Calls the Internet a 'Gift from God.'"

24. Pope Francis, "Message for the 48th World Communications Day."

A culture of encounter then implies not just proximity but actual mutuality between persons, a genuine gift of self and reception of the other in return. Here, Pope Francis resonates closely with the theology of communication as articulated in older ecclesial documents on social communication, including the Pontifical Commission for Social Communication's 1971 document, *Communio et progressio. Communio et progressio* defines communication theologically as a gift of self, offered in love, and rooted in the image of Christ, the Perfect Communicator.[25] Communication is never simply an offering of information, but always implies a relational basis that aims for reciprocity, mutuality, and communion. Pope Francis's culture of encounter builds on the same foundation.

As Pope Francis elaborates on what communication has to do with an authentic culture of encounter, he returns us to the parable of the Good Samaritan (Luke 10). He casts communication as an expression of "neighborliness" and insists that "those who communicate in effect become neighbors."[26] His point in part is to distinguish between the mere fact of a connection and the more intentional, relational posture of authentic communication. He calls us toward the latter: "it is not enough to be passersby on the digital highways, simply 'connected'; connections need to grow into true encounters."[27] As we are still exploring the parable of the Good Samaritan, his reference to being passersby on the digital highway holds a strong challenge. In the parable of the Good Samaritan, the passersby of course were the Levite and the priest, who crossed to the other side of the road instead of stopping to help the battered victim of robbery. As Pope Francis notes: "The Levite and the priest do not regard him as a neighbor, but as a stranger to be kept at a distance. In those days it was rules of ritual purity which conditioned their response. Nowadays there is a danger that certain media so condition our responses that we fail to see our real neighbor."[28] Before we can unpack how this happens in our digital culture today, it is helpful to unpack further the example of the Levite and the priest. The Levite and the priest are no neighbor to the victim of robbery in several ways. We are told that they both see him (Luke 10:31-32), and they do perceive the victim as present, because they make the effort to cross the road in response. However, they perceive him primarily as a problem or hindrance, rather than as a person. There is no sense of mutuality or gift of self offered

---

25. Pontifical Commission for Social Communication, *Communio et progressio*, 11.

26. Pope Francis, "Message for the 48th World Communications Day."

27. Ibid.

28. Ibid.

in any measure, because these characteristics of authentic communication must unfold between persons, rather than between a person and a problem.

When the Samaritan enters the story, he perceives the personhood of the victim: he sees him and takes pity on him (Luke 10:33). The difference between the Good Samaritan and the priest and the Levite is not lack of information: all three see and perceive. But only the Good Samaritan is moved with pity to assist the man in need. As Pope Francis notes: "The Good Samaritan not only draws nearer to the man he finds half dead on the side of the road; he takes responsibility for him. Jesus shifts our understanding: it is not just about seeing the other as someone like myself, but of the ability to make myself like the other. Communication is really about realizing that we are all human beings, children of God. I like seeing this power of communication as neighborliness."[29]

To move beyond sight and perception to taking responsibility for our neighbor is the move toward true encounter, and to commit to this collectively would form a culture of encounter. In digital culture, we too are not lacking for things to see. The screen is replete with information, and we perceive the presence of others through text, sound and image. The question to continue to discern in this context is in what way does the screen reveal or conceal the real presence of the other as a person? Of course, this is up to us; the screen is not some entity with power over us and over our capacity to encounter one another. As Pope Francis reminds us: "the digital world can be an environment rich in humanity; a network not of wires but of people."[30] This means that our communication practices in and through the screen are up to us, even if they are mediated by the screen. Through what we see on the screen, we can still perceive, recognize, and dignify the person behind it whose words, image or sound reveal their real presence to us.

Being neighborly in our digital context does not rest with the recognition of the person behind the screen. Being neighbors means also to take responsibility for one another, and attend to the pain and brokenness of those around us. As Pope Francis points out: "the digital highway is a street teeming with people who are often hurting, men and women looking for salvation and hope."[31] Recognizing the other through the screen means being open to their joys, hopes, pain, and need for the Good News. In response to recognizing especially the woundedness of those around us, the image of the Good Samaritan is once again instructive: "May the image of the Good Samaritan who tended to the wounds of the injured man by pouring oil and

29. Ibid.
30. Ibid.
31. Ibid.

wine over them be our inspiration. Let our communication be a balm which relieves pain and a fine wine which gladdens the heart."[32] This means that our communication practices in and through the screen must be intentional in offering healing, hope and the Good News to those we meet on the digital highway. This is part of the "missionary vocation of the Church."[33]

How we communicate in and through digital culture builds on encounter and heralds the Good News *within* the context of that encounter. Without this necessary context of encounter, the words we offer may not be effective, or may even come across as an assault. "Effective Christian witness is not about bombarding people with religious messages, but about our willingness to be available to others 'by patiently and respectfully engaging their questions and their doubts and they advance in their search for the truth and the meaning of human existence.'"[34] It can be an easy mistake in our digital context to reduce evangelization to a broadcasting of religious messages through social media or other digital platforms, without any attention to entering into dialogue with the intended recipients. Is simply posting a religious meme or sharing an article truly evangelization? Instead of broadcasting to recipients, Pope Francis calls us to think about encountering conversation partners, and to practice communication with them with a sense of deliberateness, calm, silence and listening, patience and understanding.

If *Evangelii gaudium* was Pope Francis's blueprint for the Church, his "Message for the 48th World Communications Day," on "Communication at the Service of an Authentic Culture of Encounter," is perhaps his blueprint for how he understands social communication and encounter today in our digital context. In this brief document, he calls us toward a culture of encounter by attending to neighborliness, healing and life-giving words, and to entering into dialogue with people as conversation partners and fellow seekers of truth and meaning.

"Communicating the Family: A Privileged Place of Encounter with the Gift of Love" (2015)

Pope Francis's second "Message for World Communications Day," published in 2015, intentionally connected to that year's theme, the "Year of the Family." In "Communicating the Family: A Privileged Place of Encounter with the Gift of Love," Pope Francis returns to the fundamental human relational activity of communication, as something we are born with and something

32. Ibid.

33. Ibid.

34. Ibid.

we first learn in the context of family. In lieu of particular communications media, his focus throughout this brief message remains on the basic human activity of communication, and what we can learn from this for forming a culture of encounter. By focusing on the basic human activity of communication, Pope Francis also makes this topic broadly accessible and inclusive. Communication, as rooted in the family, retrieves the topic from the captivity of instruments and technology; communication is no longer about having media literacy or being media savvy, but instead is about how we as human beings can interact with one another as authentically as possible.

We learn to communicate in the family. Along these lines, in "Communicating the Family," Pope Francis maintains a number of key points. Communication is something we first experience in the womb, and first learn in the context of the family. Communication is necessarily bodily and it disposes us to understand it as a gift that we receive before anything else. Communication in the context of the family has the potential to allow us to recognize and to create closeness, and to teach us about forgiveness, prayer and community. As such, before we think about communication in strictly technological or media-related terms, Pope Francis urges us to discover how the human experience of being born and raised in a family already shapes us powerfully in terms of being communicators. As members of a family, we learn listening, language, mutuality, acceptance, gratitude, forgiveness and reconciliation. What we learn in the family about authentic human communication we must retain also for communicating the faith, especially through new media contexts.

Returning once again to encounter in the networked environment of digital culture, Pope Francis names a significant challenge: "the great challenge facing us today is to learn once again how to talk to one another, not simply how to generate and consume information. The latter is the tendency which our important and influential modern communications media can encourage. Information is important but it is not enough. All too often things get simplified, different positions and viewpoints are pitted against one another, and people are invited to take sides, rather than to see things as a whole."[35] He reminds us that communication is a relational act between persons, and thus it must not be commodified into simple exchange of information. By walking us through the dynamics of communication in the family, Pope Francis is showing us that we are capable and called to communication that is much more than the generation and consumption of data, or surface-engagement with oversimplified, flattened information. The full human reality of communication is always more

35. Pope Francis, "Message for the 49th World Communications Day."

complex, contextual, embodied, and relational. When imagining a culture of encounter, the family is held up as an exemplary "environment in which we learn to communicate in an experience of closeness, a setting where communication takes place, a 'communicating community.'"[36] It is a common foundation and resource for us all for thinking about the culture of encounter that Pope Francis envisions.

"Communication and Mercy: A Fruitful Encounter" (2016)

As with the "Message for World Communications Day" of the previous year, Pope Francis couples his 2016 "Message for World Communications Day" with the theme of the year, the "Year of Mercy." In "Communication and Mercy: A Fruitful Encounter," he offers a brief reflection on the potential of communication to build bridges, extend mercy, effect reconciliation, and build relationships.

He begins by re-emphasizing communication as a theological endeavor: "What we say and how we say it, our every word and gesture, ought to express God's compassion, tenderness and forgiveness for all. Love, by its nature is communication; it leads to openness and sharing. If our hearts and actions are inspired by charity, by divine love, then our communication will be touched by God's own power."[37] Our communication, in both content and through the way it is carried out, has the potential to be revelatory. What we say and how we say it can reveal God's love, wisdom, compassion and Good News. This of course does not add to or compromise the Church's public revelation, but rather allows for our own communication to be transformed by God's revelatory Word, in both content and expression. As such, our communication becomes theological, in that through our human words and gestures, it submits to the dynamic of divine revelation itself, and imitates God's act of self-giving love uttered in Word and Spirit to humankind. In communicating compassionately, tenderly and lovingly with all, we model revelation. Building all of our communication on this theological foundation, we trust that it will indeed be touched by God's own power.

Following from this theological foundation, Pope Francis also reasserts that communication is an ecclesial endeavor: "As sons and daughters of God, we are called to communication with everyone, without exception. In a particular way, the Church's words and actions are all meant to convey mercy, to touch people's hearts, and to sustain them on their journey to that

36. Ibid.
37. Pope Francis, "Message for the 50th World Communications Day."

fullness of life which Jesus Christ was sent by the Father to bring to all."[38] If our communication practices can is some way model divine revelation itself, then this cannot be restricted to individual efforts of particular Christians. It must instead begin as an ecclesial task, an appropriate calling for the whole Body of Christ. According to Avery Dulles, the whole life of the Church can be rightly viewed as a communications process, and the Church itself could aptly be labeled as "Communications."[39] As a Church, we are fundamentally called to communicate the Good News of Jesus Christ, this is constitutive of our ecclesial identity. *Evangelii nuntiandi* clearly expresses this as it notes: "Those who have received the Good News and who have been gathered by it into the community of salvation can and must communicate and spread it."[40] As Church, we are called to communicate and to do so expressing God's own loving and merciful self-communication to all.

Given that communication is both theological and ecclesial, what must it look like to authentically express these foundations? Pope Francis here begins with more specific examples: building bridges, enabling encounter and inclusion, offer encouragement and through mercy, listening and creating "a new speech and dialogue."[41] Here, his call is especially healing when thinking about public communication, whether political rhetoric, comment exchanges on public fora, or even online harassment in and through social media, and to what extend violent language plays a regular part of our exchanges.[42] As Pope Francis asserts "our words and actions should be such as to help us all escape the vicious circles of condemnation and vengeance which continue to ensnare individuals and nations, encouraging expressions of hatred."[43] Creating a new speech and a new dialogue can be a radical alternative to verbal violence in all its forms, and fundamentally express Good News and life-giving words in response to words that are violent and destructive. To embrace this radical alternative, we must listen and seek to encounter others in and through communication, "to pay attention, to want to understand, to value, to respect and to ponder what the other person says. It involves a martyrdom or self-sacrifice."[44]

38. Ibid.

39. Dulles, *The Church Is Communications*, 68–69.

40. Pope Paul VI, *Evangelii nuntiandi*, 13.

41. Pope Francis, "Message for the 50th World Communications Day."

42. For specific statistics on the prevalence of online harassment and violent language, see Duggan, "Online Harassment."

43. Pope Francis, "Message for the 50th World Communications Day."

44. Ibid.

"Communication and Mercy: A Fruitful Encounter" thus calls us to show mercy particularly through our acts of communication. How we enter into conversation with another, how we are able to listen and to receive their words, how we are able to dialogue, to privilege the truth, but also to navigate disagreement all can reveal God's love and mercy, and bring about reconciliation.

A Vision of True Encounter

Looking at Pope Francis's thoughts on social communication, his vision for true encounter throughout the documents examined above is closely connected with communication. Authentic communication is theological: it has the potential to reveal God's own self-communication, which is loving self-gift offered abundantly to humankind in Word and in Spirit. It is also ecclesial, a calling and task constitutive of Christian identity to share the Good News of Jesus Christ in the same mode of loving self-gift expressed through word, gesture and witness of life. In order to do this well, communication must always seek to encounter: to engage with and to receive the words of another as a fundamental relational act that takes place between persons. True encounter, then, is a way to emphasize this basic relational foundation of communication, which can otherwise be easily narrowed to an exchange of information or data. True encounter thus serves communication, especially in our digital culture, to remind us of one another as persons in relationship, and persons behind the screen.

Bibliography

Caccamo, James F. "Let Me Put It Another Way: Digital Media and the Future of the Liturgy." *Liturgy* 28, no. 3 (2013) 7–16.

Duggan, Maeve. "Online Harassment." *Pew Research Center Internet, Science and Technology Report.* October 22, 2014. Accessed October 15, 2016. http://www.pewinternet.org/2014/10/22/online-harassment/.

Avery R. Dulles. "The Church Is Communications." *IDOC Internazionale* 27 (1971) 68–82.

Pontifical Commission for Social Communication. Pastoral Instruction *Communio et progressio* (1971) 11. Accessed October 11, 2016. http://www.vatican.va/roman_curia/pontifical_councils/pccs/documents/rc_pc_pccs_doc_23051971_communio_en.html.

Francis, Pope. "Address of the Holy Father Francis to the Participants in the Plenary Assembly of the Pontifical Council for Social Communications." September 21, 2013. Accessed October 10, 2016. https://w2.vatican.va/content/francesco/en/

speeches/2013/september/documents/papa-francesco_20130921_plenaria-pccs. html.

———. Apostolic Exhortation *Evangelii Gaudium: On the Proclamation of the Gospel in Today's World*. November 24, 2013. https://w2.vatican.va/content/francesco/ en/apost_exhortations/documents/papa-francesco_esortazione-ap_20131124_ evangelii-gaudium.html. Accessed October 10, 2016.

———. "Message for the 48th World Communications Day Communication at the Service of an Authentic Culture of Encounter." January 24, 2014. Accessed October 11, 2016. https://w2.vatican.va/content/francesco/en/messages/communications/ documents/papa-francesco_20140124_messaggio-comunicazioni-sociali.html.

———. "Message for the 49th World Communications Day: Communicating the Family: A Privileged Place of Encounter with the Gift of Love." January 24th, 2015. Accessed October 13, 2016. http://w2.vatican.va/content/francesco/en/ messages/communications/documents/papa-francesco_20150123_messaggio- comunicazioni-sociali.html.

———. "Message for the 50th World Communications Day: Communication and Mercy: A Fruitful Encounter." January 24th, 2016. Accessed October 15, 2016. https://w2.vatican.va/content/francesco/en/messages/communications/ documents/papa-francesco_20160124_messaggio-comunicazioni-sociali.html.

Fung, Brian, and Michelle Boorstein. "Pope Francis Calls the Internet a 'Gift from God.'" *The Washington Post*. January 23, 2014. Accessed October 15, 2016. https:// www.washingtonpost.com/news/the-switch/wp/2014/01/23/the-pope-calls-the- internet-a-gift-from-god/.

Paul VI, Pope. Apostolic Exhortation *Evangelii Nuntiandi* 13. 1975. Accessed October 15, 2016. http://w2.vatican.va/content/paul-vi/en/apost_exhortations/ documents/hf_p-vi_exh_19751208_evangelii-nuntiandi.html.

Pontifical Commission for Social Communication. Pastoral Instruction *Communio et Progressio* 11. 1971. Accessed October 11, 2016. http://www.vatican.va/ roman_curia/pontifical_councils/pccs/documents/rc_pc_pccs_doc_23051971_ communio_en.html.

CHAPTER 14

Pope Francis on the Evangelization of Culture

—R. Jared Staudt

Abstract:

Pope Francis continues a trajectory initiated by Pope Leo XIII and crystalized at the Second Vatican Council of defining the importance of human culture and relating it to the work of evangelization. Francis demonstrates continuity with the teaching of *Guadium et spes* and Pope John Paul II on the nature of culture, but also brings a distinctive approach in rooting culture in the encounter of persons. This chapter examines Francis's contributions to the topic of culture under three headings. First, it examines how Francis analyzes contemporary culture through the lens of its transitory nature. This applies to how it views time, money, resources, people, and God. Next, it presents how Francis calls for a movement from a throw away culture to one of encounter. The encounter between people and with God draws the individual beyond himself and enables a genuine culture to emerge through love. Finally, it outlines how Francis calls for an evangelization of culture through inculturation and by facilitating an encounter with God.

Introduction: The Magisterium's Teaching on Culture from Pope Leo XIII to Pope Francis

Culture entered the Catholic Church's vocabulary fairly recently. Pope Leo XIII can be considered the father of the Church's teaching on culture through his initiation of Catholic social teaching.[1] Broadly speaking, Leo began a new focus in engaging the social issues of modern culture. More specifically, he proposed a theology of work, which provides the foundation for understanding how human culture proceeds from and cooperates with God's work of creation. In defending private property, Leo put forth a theological understanding of how humanity shapes nature according to an inward principle.

> Now, when man thus turns the activity of his mind and the strength of his body toward procuring the fruits of nature, by such act he makes his own that portion of nature's field which he cultivates - that portion on which he leaves, as it were, the impress of his personality; and it cannot but be just that he should possess that portion as his very own, and have a right to hold it without any one being justified in violating that right.[2]

Culture arises precisely in the rational ability to shape nature according to the outward needs and inward spiritual capacity of the human race.

The Second Vatican Council's Pastoral Constitution, *Gaudium et spes*, offered the first sustained, direct treatment of the topic of culture in the history of the Church. Chapter II of the Constitution, "The Proper Development of Culture," begins by providing a helpful definition of culture and its importance:

> Man comes to a true and full humanity only through culture, that is through the cultivation of the goods and values of nature ... The word "culture" in its general sense indicates everything whereby man develops and perfects his many bodily and spiritual qualities; he strives by his knowledge and his labor, to bring the world itself under his control. He renders social life more human both in the family and the civic community, through improvement of customs and institutions. Throughout the course of time he expresses, communicates and conserves in his works, great spiritual experiences and desires, that they might be of advantage to the progress of many, even of the whole human family.[3]

Following the Council, the topic of culture arose more frequently in magisterial teaching. For instance, Pope Bl. Paul VI first indicated the crucial role

---

1. The Pontifical Council for Culture released an anthology of the Church's teaching on culture, which begins with the teaching of Pope Leo XIII. See *Fede e cultura*.

2. Pope Leo XIII, *Rerum novarum*, 9.

3. The Second Vatican Council, *Gaudium et spes*, 53.

of culture in the Church's efforts of evangelization: "The split between the Gospel and culture is without a doubt the drama of our time, just as it was of other times. Therefore every effort must be made to ensure a full evangelization of culture, or more correctly of cultures. They have to be regenerated by an encounter with the Gospel."[4] Thus, Vatican II's vision of culture entered into the renewed emphasis on evangelization encouraged by Paul and taken up by Pope St. John Paul II in calling for a New Evangelization.

John Paul II could be considered the "culture Pope," for his own artistic background, frequent use of the theme in his magisterial teaching, and for his creation of the Pontifical Council for Culture. John Paul did not situate culture as an intellectual or artistic ideal, but rather as a way of life by which we express our deepest beliefs. Therefore, he articulated the view that "the synthesis between culture and faith is not only a demand of culture, but also of faith . . . A faith that does not become culture is not fully accepted, not entirely thought out, not faithfully lived."[5] Due to the need for faith to express itself in this way, John Paul called the Church to embark on the task of creating a new culture: "Your vocation, in this turn of the century and of the millennium, is that of creating a new culture of love and of hope inspired by the truth that frees us in Christ Jesus. This is the goal of inculturation, this is the priority for the new evangelization."[6] Throughout his Pontificate, John Paul laid the groundwork for placing the theme of culture at the center of the Church's efforts of engaging and transforming the modern world.

Francis addresses the theme of culture throughout the major documents of his Pontificate, as well as in many audiences, speeches, and addresses. *Evangelii gaudium* examines culture in relation to evangelization, focusing on how contemporary culture presents obstacles to the Church's mission as well as possibilities for inculturating faith in the modern world. *Laudato si'* provides a fundamental vision for culture insofar as it engages the theme of humanity's role in caring for and shaping God's creation. Like *Evangelii gaudium*, it also provides a critique of contemporary culture, particularly through the lens of technology's destructive role on the environment and society. *Amoris laetitia* focuses particularly on the role of relationships in culture, as Francis combats individualistic tendencies. *Lumen fidei*, Francis's first encyclical, was initially drafted by Pope Benedict XVI and bears the mark of the Pontiff Emeritus's thought in many ways, including the danger of secularism in the modern world. I include it my

4. Pope Bl. Paul VI, *Evangelii nuntiandi*, 20.

5. Pope St. John Paul II, "Address to the Italian National Congress of the Ecclesial Movement for Cultural Commitment" (January 16, 1982).

6. Pope St. John Paul II, "Letting the Gospel Take Root in Every Culture" (January 10, 1992), n. 10.

considerations of Francis's writings on culture as it is officially a part of his magisterium. Francis's shorter teachings, usually delivered orally, focus largely on the call to form a new culture of encounter.

The focus of this chapter will be on how Pope Francis has continued the trajectory of engaging the theme of culture, but with his own distinctive approach. Francis deepens Paul's analysis of the split between the Gospel and modern culture, particularly through his description of a throwaway culture. He counters the throwaway culture with a call to form a culture of encounter. Thus, through his analysis of modern culture, the task of evangelizing culture finds a personal grounding, which roots Francis's articulation of how we can renew our cultural environment.

Before articulating the contrast between a throwaway culture and a culture of encounter, it is important to lay out briefly how Francis understands culture in general. His most detailed description of culture comes in his Apostolic Exhortation, *Evangelii gaudium*:

> The concept of culture is valuable for grasping the various expressions of the Christian life present in God's people. It has to do with the lifestyle of a given society, the specific way in which its members relate to one another, to other creatures and to God. Understood in this way, culture embraces the totality of a people's life. Each people in the course of its history develops its culture with legitimate autonomy. This is due to the fact that the human person, "by nature stands completely in need of life in society" and always exists in reference to society, finding there a concrete way of relating to reality. The human person is always situated in a culture: "nature and culture are intimately linked." Grace supposes culture, and God's gift becomes flesh in the culture of those who receive it.[7]

Francis demonstrates continuity with *Gaudium et spes*, particularly by linking culture and nature, but also shows a more personal bent by linking culture to how the members of society relate to one another. Culture expresses the Christian life, as we saw in John Paul, but it also entails a call to meet another: "For culture is always born of reciprocal encounter which seeks to stimulate the intellectual riches and creativity of those who take part in it; this is not only a good in itself, it is also something beautiful."[8] Francis affirms culture's intellectual and creative grounding, but these as-

---

7. Pope Francis, *Evangelii gaudium*, 115. Francis refers the reader to the *Puebla Document* (1979), 386–87, and *Gaudium et spes*, 36. The two quotes are from *Gaudium et spes* 25 and 53.

8. Pope Francis, "Address to the Council of Europe" (Nov. 25, 2014).

pects only emerge from an encounter. In fact, culture arises from the heart of the human person: "We need a contemplative approach that . . . seeks to uncover the foundation of cultures, which at their deepest core are always open and thirsting for God."[9] He continues: "Here is the key. Through testimony we can affect the deepest core, where culture is born. Through testimony the Church sows the mustard seed, but she does so in the very heart of the cultures being generated in the cities."[10] The rebuilding of culture will occur when the inner depths of the person opens up to the transcendent call awaiting within them. The Church draws out this potential through encounter and testimony, which elicit the intellectual and creative potential of the person for culture.

Pope Francis's Analysis of Contemporary Culture

Francis has many ways of describing contemporary culture, linked by a common, core trait of the transitory—the culture of the temporary, the culture of the ephemeral, the culture of waste, a throwaway culture. We find a lack of stability and permanence, an inability to value and care for what is in front of us, as the core trait of our society: "In the prevailing culture, priority is given to the outward, the immediate, the visible, the quick, the superficial and the provisional."[11] Francis recognizes that an uprooting of the foundations of culture has occurred, leading to fragmentation, a breaking of traditional relationships to land, values, other people, and ultimately God. We can put Francis's diagnosis of the overarching crisis of culture into five categories: time, money, resources, people, and God.

First, Francis describes the impact of our culture on time, through our creation of a "culture of the temporary, "which makes it "very hard to make a definitive decision."[12] The transitory nature of this culture undermines our ability to make a commitment, which has personal and societal consequences. Personally, Francis describes how a "culture of the ephemeral" leads to "the speed with which people move from one affective relationship to another."[13] The inability to put down roots and keep to a decision undermines the acceptance of a vocation, including marriage and family life.[14]

---

9. Pope Francis, "Address to Participations at the International Pastoral Congress on the World's Big Cities" (Nov. 27, 2014).

10. Ibid.

11. *Evangelii gaudium*, 62.

12. Pope Francis, "Meeting with Seminarians and Novices" (July 6, 2013).

13. Pope Francis, *Amoris laetitia*, 39.

14. Cf. ibid., 40.

Even things that have seemed stable in society, such as ecosystems and even a whole culture, are subject to change within the rule of the temporary. In *Laudato si'*, Francis notes that, especially for indigenous people, we face "the disappearance of a culture," including the undoing of "the social structures which, for a long time, shaped cultural identity and their sense of the meaning of life and community."[15] The loss of traditional culture leads also to the loss of identity, as Francis points out. Therefore, "we can speak of a massive amnesia in our contemporary world," as we no longer look back in time to ground us in the past.[16] The culture of the temporary undermines society by removing any sense of permanence in the past and consequently takes away the impetus for future commitment.

In large part, Francis roots the instability and ephemeral character of our culture in economic practices. Our global economy overlooks the dignity of the human person and the integrity of local culture: "A consumerist vision of human beings, encouraged by the mechanisms of today's globalized economy, has a levelling effect on cultures, diminishing the immense variety which is the heritage of all humanity."[17] *Evangelii gaudium* provides a sustained critique of consumerism as an obstacle to evangelization. The exhortation explains how "a globalization of indifference has developed . . . The culture of prosperity deadens us; we are thrilled if the market offers us something new to purchase."[18] Francis recognizes that indifference to other people and to God comes from an over attachment to things. The medium for the production of these new goods can be found in technology. Technology adjusts our values, away from the values of traditional culture and the commitment they require, toward the immediate. Technology has produced a new truth for modern culture: "In contemporary culture, we often tend to consider the only real truth to be that of technology: truth is what we succeed in building and measuring by our scientific know-how, truth is what works and what makes life easier and more comfortable."[19]

The economic and technological changes of recent times have created what Francis calls a "throwaway culture" or "culture of waste," a central theme in his engagement of our culture. Although this cultural attitude reaches people, we will first look at how it affects our treatment of things. Our culture's overattachment to things ironically feeds into the culture of the temporary, as things are readily displaced to make way for the new, which

15. Pope Francis, *Laudato si'*, 145.

16. Pope Francis, *Lumen fidei*, 25.

17. *Laudato si'*, 144.

18. *Evangelii gaudium*, 54.

19. *Lumen fidei*, 25.

"quickly reduces things to rubbish."[20] Once again, the cultural shift entails a change in value, creating an insensitivity to people and to the importance of cultural goods in relation to people:

> This culture of waste has also made us insensitive to wasting and throwing out excess foodstuffs, which is especially condemnable when, in every part of the world, unfortunately, many people and families suffer hunger and malnutrition . . . Consumerism has induced us to be accustomed to excess and to the daily waste of food, whose value, which goes far beyond mere financial parameters, we are no longer able to judge correctly.[21]

As we saw in the introduction, Pope Leo XIII grounded the Catholic vision of culture in the right use of land and the resources God has provided us in creation. Culture arises out of our acceptance of these goods as a gift and our fashioning of them. Consumerist culture, with its wastefulness, no longer sees the land and resources as a gift. Francis once again sees indigenous peoples as most vulnerable to this value shift: "For them, land is not a commodity but rather a gift from God and from their ancestors who rest there, a sacred space with which they need to interact if they are to maintain their identity and values . . . Nevertheless, in various parts of the world, pressure is being put on them to abandon their homelands to make room for agricultural or mining projects which are undertaken without regard for the degradation of nature and culture."[22] Land represents the rootedness of culture and the identity of its people, which face attack from the demands of temporary economic gain.

The treatment of created goods provides a sign for the treatment of human beings.[23] The throw away culture reaches people as well: "Human beings are themselves considered consumer goods to be used and then discarded."[24] Viewing human beings as waste does not pertain simply to global economic forces, but has become engrained within the common ethos of society. Francis describes that "this 'culture of waste' tends to become a common mentality that infects everyone. Human life, the person, are no longer seen as a primary value to be respected and safeguarded, especially if they are poor or disabled, if they are not yet useful—like the unborn child—or are

---

20. *Laudato si'*, 22.

21. Pope Francis, "Wednesday Audience" (June 5, 2013).

22. *Laudato si'*, 146.

23. On this point, see Pope Benedict XVI, "Message for the Celebration of the World Day of Peace" (January 1, 2007).

24. *Evangelii gaudium*, 53. See also Pope Francis "Meeting with the Sick and Disabled Children Assisted at the Seraphic Institute" (Oct. 4, 2013).

no longer of any use—like the elderly person."[25] The roots of viewing others from the lens of utility comes from an "extreme individualism," which leads "to the idea that one's personality is shaped by his or her desires, which are considered absolute."[26] When the individual is absolute, it is not possible to maintain a vision of the whole and to situate one's own good in relation to created goods and other persons. Ultimately, it is a crisis of the common good, as Francis explains: "We should recognize how in a culture where each person wants to be bearer of his or her own subjective truth, it becomes difficult for citizens to devise a common plan which transcends individual gain and personal ambitions."[27] Culture fundamentally forms and endures as a social reality, but individualism erodes this core, calling into question one's place within larger social and even spiritual goods.

Ultimately, therefore, the shift in values from traditional culture to that of the temporary comes from throwing away God. Although Francis does not use this exact language, he speaks of God as absent and as not considered relevant. The result is isolation, loneliness, and relativism. The absence of God weakens other relationships as well, as Francis notes in *Amoris laetitia*: "The weakening of faith and religious practice in some societies has an effect on families, leaving them more isolated amid their difficulties. The Synod Fathers noted that 'one symptom of the great poverty of contemporary culture is loneliness, arising from the absence of God in a person's life and the fragility of relationships.'"[28] When society accepts as true only the "subjective truths of the individual . . . valid only for that individual and not capable of being proposed to others in an effort to serve the common good . . . ultimately this means the question of God—is no longer relevant."[29] In this sense, the culture of the temporary reaches its ultimate conclusion of excluding the eternal from consideration. This drastically narrows the horizon of culture, which "reduce[s] the faith and the Church to the sphere of the private and personal," which results in "a growing deterioration of ethics, a weakening of the sense of personal and collective sin," and "a general sense of disorientation."[30] Contemporary culture finds no ultimate bearing beyond the immediate, material gratification of the individual, leading to a lack of commitment to the other—to one's family, neighbor, the good of society, and God.

25. "Wednesday Audience" (June 5, 2013).

26. *Amoris laetitia*, 33, quoting *Relatio synodi* (2014), 5.

27. *Evangelii gaudium*, 61.

28. *Amoris laetitia*, 43.

29. *Lumen fidei*, 25.

30. *Evangelii gaudium*, 64.

From a Throw Away Culture to One of Encounter

Pope Francis offers a devastating critique of modern culture: it is fragmented, superficial, and displaces genuine human values that require commitment and sacrifice. If he only offered a critique, it could lead toward
discouragement. Francis, however, offers a powerful vision of the kind of
culture Christians should build. Rather than turning inward in selfishness
and exclusion, it turns toward the other to meet and to receive. The key
words Francis uses to describe the antithesis of our culture are encounter,
care, and closeness. If a throw away culture focuses on the individual and
the satisfaction of immediate material desires, the culture of encounter
opens the individual to the other in a genuine meeting and dialogue of persons. Throughout speeches, written messages, and more formal magisterial
documents, Francis calls on Catholics and all people of good will to create
a culture of encounter.[31]

First, we see how Francis starkly contrasts his description of our culture with one that he calls us to form in its place. Speaking to people who
work with those with disabilities, he states the sharp contrast between them:
"These are two opposing cultures. The culture of encounter and the culture
of exclusion. The culture of prejudice; because it criticizes and excludes.
Precisely because of their fragility, their limitations, the sick and disabled
can become witnesses of the encounter: the encounter with Jesus, which
opens them to life and faith, and to encounter others, with the community."[32]
It is significant that Francis links the encounter with Jesus to the encounter
with others. A culture which excludes God leads us consequently to exclude
others. He repeats the same contrast with different descriptions of these two
cultures: "I repeat forcefully: it is neither a culture of confrontation nor a
culture of conflict which builds harmony within and between peoples, but
rather a culture of encounter and a culture of dialogue; this is the only way
to peace."[33] Francis recognizes the tension underlying the crisis of contemporary culture and calls us to a different kind of meeting and encounter
with others.

---

31. Francis speaks of the importance of the word encounter for him: "It is important
to be ready for encounter. For me this word is very important. Encounter with others" (Pope Francis, "Address to Ecclesial Movements" [May 18, 2013]). Further, he told
youth: "Be servants of communion and of the culture of encounter! I would like you
to be almost obsessed about this" (Pope Francis, "Homily," Cathedral of San Sebastian,
Rio de Janeiro, July 27, 2013).

32. Pope Francis "Address to Members of the Apostolic Movement of the Blind and
the Little Mission for the Deaf and Mute" (March 29, 2014).

33. Pope Francis, "Angelus" (September 1, 2013).

Most importantly, this new culture will come from the presence of God, filling the infinite void of his absence. Francis tells us that God's love is not "to be found in the beyond, on another level of reality, far removed from our everyday relationships," but rather it is "a love that can be encountered."[34] It is Christ who embodies this encounter with God's love and when we encounter him, we are called to encounter others, to share this love. "Because faith is an encounter with Jesus, and we must do what Jesus does: encounter others. We live in a culture of conflict, a culture of fragmentation, a culture in which I throw away what is of no use to me, a culture of waste . . . [W]ith our faith we must create a 'culture of encounter,' a culture of friendship."[35] In other words, our faith impels us to cherish what others discard, to love the other even if they "think differently" or "hold other beliefs."[36] Forming a culture of encounter is part of Francis's vision for evangelization insofar as it brings the love of God to the other, who may be estranged from society and from him. Speaking at World Youth Day in Brazil, Francis articulated the nature of the Christian life: "I wish to reflect with you on three aspects of our vocation: we are called by God, called to proclaim the Gospel, and called to promote the culture of encounter."[37] We first encounter God, who then calls us to draw others into this encounter with him. From this task of evangelization flows a cultural mission. God wants us not only to proclaim the Gospel, but to embody it in how we encounter others generally within the world, affirming their dignity and witnessing to God's love.

God helps us to overcome individuality and to care for the other and for the resources of the world with love.[38] Francis speaks of this as practicing "the way of love." This way offers a holistic approach to reunifying culture through an integral human ecology, as Francis articulates in *Laudato si'*: "Saint Thérèse of Lisieux invites us to practice the little way of love, not to

---

34. *Lumen fidei*, 17.

35. "Address to Ecclesial Movements."

36. Ibid.

37. "Homily," Cathedral of San Sebastian, Rio de Janeiro. Francis continues: "Have the courage to go against the tide of this culture of efficiency, this culture of waste. Encountering and welcoming everyone, solidarity—a word that is being hidden by this culture, as if it were a bad word—solidarity and fraternity: these are what make our society truly human . . . Dear brothers and sisters, God calls us, by name and surname, each one of us, to proclaim the Gospel and to promote the culture of encounter with joy."

38. Francis addresses the overcoming of individuality through a culture of encounter: "This is a proposal: a culture of closeness. Isolation and withdrawing into one's own interests are never the way to restore hope and bring about a renewal. Rather, it is closeness, it is the culture of encounter" ("Meeting with the Academic and Cultural World" [Sep. 22, 2013]).

miss out on a kind word, a smile or any small gesture which sows peace and friendship. An integral ecology is also made up of simple daily gestures which break with the logic of violence, exploitation and selfishness."[39] Love stands at the center of the culture of encounter. We encounter God's love and then communicate this love in a way "which affects not only relationships between individuals but also 'macro-relationships, social, economic and political ones.' . . . In this framework, along with the importance of little everyday gestures, social love moves us to devise larger strategies to halt environmental degradation and to encourage a 'culture of care' which permeates all of society."[40] If a culture of encounter flows from meeting the love of God, then this love should permeate how one then relates to everything, including the environment. The encountered love of God turns into a way of life that cares for other beings.

The family in particular suffers from the temporary nature of a throwaway culture. It should be the place where we learn to care and to encounter others. In *Amoris laetitia* Francis examines how the nuclear family should extend beyond itself to form companionship and to overcome individualism.[41] In particular, he challenges families to overcome impatience and indifference toward the elderly: "Indeed, 'how I would like a Church that challenges the throwaway culture by the overflowing joy of a new embrace between young and old!'"[42] Although we have seen how encountering the love of God stands as the foundation of the culture of encounter, Francis also looks at the mission of the family in leading one into this encounter. The family should create an environment for encountering God: "A positive experience of family communion is a true path to daily sanctification and mystical growth, a means for deeper union with God. The fraternal and communal demands of family life are an incentive to growth in openness of heart and thus to an ever fuller encounter with the Lord."[43] The family, thus, becomes a model for caring for others in a way that models the love of God. Christians are then called to extend this witness into society more broadly.

---

39. *Laudato si'*, 230.

40. Ibid., 231, quoting Pope Benedict XVI, *Caritas in veritate*, 2.

41. See *Amoris laetitia*, 187. Francis also speaks about forming a culture of relationships: "But for this, drawing on the spiritual sap of the Gospel, it is necessary to imagine and experience a new culture in all spheres of the life of a society: from the family to politics to the economy, also known as a culture of relationships" ("Video Message for the 50th Anniversary of the Founding of the Loppiano International Centre" [April 10, 2014]).

42. *Amoris laetitia*, 191, quoting Pope Francis, "Wednesday Audience" (11 March 2015).

43. *Amoris laetitia*, 316.

The principles of a culture of encounter are not simply meant for the realm of faith and family. Francis speaks of the responsibility of a society to promote integration and dialogue. In *Evangelii gaudium* Francis speaks of how "becoming a people . . . is an ongoing process in which every new generation must take part: a slow and arduous effort calling for a desire for integration and a willingness to achieve this through the growth of a peaceful and multifaceted culture of encounter."[44] He continues, speaking of how the whole people within their culture must form "a social and cultural pact."[45] This culture should "privilege dialogue as a form of encounter," by "building consensus and agreement while seeking the goal of a just, responsive and inclusive society."[46] Francis puts the challenge of creating this kind of culture in challenging terms as a risk that is the only way forward:

> The only way for individuals, families and societies to grow, the only way for the life of peoples to progress, is via the culture of encounter, a culture in which all have something good to give and all can receive something good in return. Others always have something to give me, if we know how to approach them in a spirit of openness and without prejudice . . . Today, either we take the risk of dialogue, we risk the culture of encounter, or we all fall; this is the path that will bear fruit.[47]

Francis clearly lays out his goal for human culture—that it focus on building interpersonal relationships. If the concept of culture has traditionally been related to work, the fashioning of economic products, Francis calls for a shift in emphasis to the human person. The encounter and dialogue of persons should lay the foundation for how politics and economics shape culture today.

The Evangelization of Culture

We have seen Pope Francis's vision for the future of human culture based on encounter and care. The final point of examination concerns how to achieve this culture given the landscape of society. Creating a culture of encounter flows from the Church's mission of evangelization, as the process of transforming culture constitutes an act of evangelization itself. Since the Second Vatican Council, the Church has spoken of the evangelization

44. *Evangelii gaudium*, 220.
45. Ibid., 239.
46. Ibid.
47. Pope Francis, "Meeting with Brazil's Leaders of Society" (July 27, 2013).

of culture through the principle of inculturation. When the Church inculturates the Gospel, it expresses the faith in tangible form, creating a new expression of the Christian life within the life of a particular people: "If the Gospel is embedded in a culture, the message is no longer transmitted solely from person to person . . . The ultimate aim should be that the Gospel, as preached in categories proper to each culture, will create a new synthesis with that particular culture."[48] The process of inculturation must continue even in the midst of traditionally Christian societies, which now experience the secularizing tendencies of the crisis of culture expressed above. Francis does not look toward the Christian past with nostalgia, though he nonetheless recognizes the importance of Christian culture: "The immense importance of a culture marked by faith cannot be overlooked; before the onslaught of contemporary secularism an evangelized culture, for all its limits, has many more resources than the mere sum total of believers. An evangelized popular culture contains values of faith and solidarity capable of encouraging the development of a more just and believing society."[49] Not focusing on the past, Francis rather calls for a new way forward in light of the particular challenges and opportunities of contemporary culture. He relates that "what is called for is an evangelization capable of shedding light on these new ways of relating to God, to others and to the world around us, and inspiring essential values. It must reach the places where new narratives

---

48. *Evangelii gaudium*, 129. Earlier, in paragraph 69, Francis described how this process will look different for each culture: "It is imperative to evangelize cultures in order to inculturate the Gospel. In countries of Catholic tradition, this means encouraging, fostering and reinforcing a richness which already exists. In countries of other religious traditions, or profoundly secularized countries, it will mean sparking new processes for evangelizing culture, even though these will demand long-term planning. We must keep in mind, however, that we are constantly being called to grow. Each culture and social group needs purification and growth."

49. Ibid., 68. Speaking of a time "in which the Church has been the single point of reference for culture," Francis recognizes that "we are no longer in that time. It has past. We are no longer in Christianity, no more. Today we are no longer the only ones who produce culture, nor the first, nor the most listened to. We therefore need a change in pastoral mentality" ("Address to the International Pastoral Conference on the World's Big Cities"). Nonetheless, Francis also notes that in many ways contemporary culture threatens the patrimony of culture we have received from the past: "Together with the patrimony of nature, there is also an historic, artistic and cultural patrimony which is likewise under threat . . . Culture is more than what we have inherited from the past; it is also, and above all, a living, dynamic and participatory present reality, which cannot be excluded as we rethink the relationship between human beings and the environment" (*Laudato si'*, 143). In *Evangelii gaudium* he reflects on the role of education in preserving and advancing Christian culture: "Catholic schools, which always strive to join their work of education with the explicit proclamation of the Gospel, are a most valuable resource for the evangelization of culture" (134).

and paradigms are being formed."[50] In this sense, Christians are called to engage contemporary culture with a creative vision of faith.

Although "we still lack the culture needed to confront" the crisis of modern society, God continues to invite people into an encounter with him.[51] This encounter makes the love of God present, drawing the power of this love into the culture itself. Francis teaches that "whenever a community receives the message of salvation, the Holy Spirit enriches its culture with the transforming power of the Gospel . . . In the Christian customs of an evangelized people, the Holy Spirit adorns the Church, showing her new aspects of revelation and giving her a new face."[52] The Spirit inspires the community to respond to a culture of exclusion with the love of God made present in the world, a love which brings about inclusion. In an address where he speaks of reaching out to the many forms of poverty experienced today, including intellectual poverty, he repeats his famous call for the Church to reach out to the peripheries of culture: "The Church has always been present in places where culture is worked out. But the first step is always the priority for the poor . . . It means we must reach out to the flesh of Jesus that is suffering, but also suffering is the flesh of Jesus of those who do not know it with their study, with their intelligence, with their culture. We must go there! I therefore like using the expression 'to go toward the outskirts,' the outskirts of existence."[53] The inculturation of modern society must include a reintegration and inclusion of the excluded, witnessing to the dignity of every human being.[54]

Another key task for inculturation, taken up at significant length in *Laudato si'*, entails the proper use of technology. Francis calls for the resistance to the technocratic paradigm by viewing technology as a "mere instrument," rather than as a force that dominates human life and culture.[55] The Pope describes how we can use technology in service of the human person.

> We have the freedom needed to limit and direct technology; we can put it at the service of another type of progress, one which is healthier, more human, more social, more integral. Liberation

50. *Evangelii gaudium*, 64.

51. *Laudato si'*, 53.

52. Ibid., 16.

53. Pope Francis, "Address to Participants in the Ecclesial convention of the Diocese of Rome" (June 17, 2013).

54. *Laudato si'* points to the family as the place to rebuild a culture of life, where life is welcomed and where children are taught to "show love and respect for life" (213).

55. Ibid., 108.

from the dominant technocratic paradigm does in fact happen
sometimes, for example, when cooperatives of small producers
adopt less polluting means of production, and opt for a non-
consumerist model of life, recreation and community.[56]

Technology poses a great risk to human culture and even the integrity of
nature and genetics.[57] Francis insists that technology is "not neutral," because of how it conditions those who use it and creates a framework for
social interaction.[58] Nonetheless, we are not constrained by its paradigm
as Francis recognizes how it actually contains the potential to strengthen
human relationships.

The Internet, in particular, the dominant means of communication
in contemporary culture, provides a test case for both the proper use of
technology and inculturation more generally. Francis recognizes that the
Internet holds the potential to help form the culture of encounter he advocates, particularly by fostering dialogue and acceptance. He speaks in very
positive terms of this potential: "The Internet, in particular, offers immense
possibilities for encounter and solidarity. This is something truly good, a
gift from God."[59] This does not mean that Francis does not recognize that
modern communication presents challenges to culture as well.

The Internet is a widespread and complex ever evolving reality, and its development raises the perennially relevant question of the relationship between faith and culture ... Amid
the opportunities and dangers of the Internet, we need to "test
everything," knowing that we will certainly find false coins, dangerous illusions and traps to avoid ... Digital communication
offers a number of possibilities, the most important of which is

---

56. Ibid., 112. In a Wednesday audience on June 5, 2013, Francis hits on the importance of cultivation in culture, in a way that reinforces his emphasis on small producers
in *Laudato si'*. It also hearkens to the foundational vision of Pope Leo XIII. He states:
"The verb 'cultivate' reminds me of the care a farmer takes to ensure that his land will
be productive and that his produce will be shared ... What great attention, enthusiasm
and dedication! Cultivating and caring for creation is an instruction of God which he
gave not only at the beginning of history, but has also given to each one of us; it is part
of his plan; it means making the world increase with responsibility, transforming it so
that it may be a garden, an inhabitable place for us all." See also *Laudato si'*, 94, on the
importance of the possession of land.

57. See *Laudato si'*, 130 ff., for a discussion of new biological technologies.

58. Ibid., 107.

59. Pope Francis, "Message for the 48th World Communications Day" (June 1,
2014). He continues: "A culture of encounter demands that we be ready not only to
give, but also to receive. Media can help us greatly in this, especially nowadays, when
the networks of human communication have made unprecedented advances."

> the proclamation of the Gospel . . . Firstly it means encounter-
> ing real women and men, who are often wounded or lost, in
> order to give them real reasons to hope. Proclamation requires
> authentic human relationships destined to culminate in a per-
> sonal encounter with the Lord.[60]

Although technology offers fundamental challenges to human culture by alienating us from nature and from others in a consumeristic mental-ity, nonetheless it can also overcome sources of division and provide new means of encountering others. In this sense, Francis recognizes how the internet can provide one avenue for turning the technological paradigm on its head. Technology, in providing an opportunity to encounter others, can also further the evangelization of cultures by providing an opportunity to encounter the Lord.

Conclusion

Why does culture matter? The Church began forming its social teaching and engaging the topic of culture in a time when a way of life has arisen in the West in opposition to the traditional way of life formed by the Christian faith. Christians are now torn between conflicting visions of life: modern, secular individualism and their Christian faith. Vatican II initiated a new movement to break through this conflict, bringing Christian faith more in-tentionally in dialogue with modern culture, hoping to transform it through the witness of Christians from the inside. Culture matters, because as John Paul said "Christianity is a creator of culture in its very foundation."[61] Faith must become culture, because it must be translated into the fabric of Chris-tians' daily lives.

Pope Francis has received and advanced the legacy of magiste-rial teaching on culture. He has placed his own stamp upon this tradition through his characterization of contemporary culture as a throw away cul-ture and through his insistence on the need to form a culture of encounter. Modern culture has lost its grounding in personal relationships and has drifted to more ephemeral and passing concerns, using and discarding things and persons for temporary advantage. Although economics remain a central concern to Francis' analysis of culture, he, nonetheless, has shifted the focus of culture to interpersonal interaction. This shift provides a helpful way forward for Christians in the modern world. In the midst of profound

---

60. Pope Francis, "Address to the Pontifical Council for the Laity" (Dec. 7, 2013).

61. Pope John Paul II, "Address to UNESCO: Man's Entire Humanity is Expressed in Culture," (June 2, 1980), n. 10.

challenges, the solution entails actions within the daily grasp of everyone. Francis situates the evangelization of culture within the context of encounter, calling us to recognize God's loving presence in relation to our ability to recognize and meet others within the world today.

Bibliography

Benedict XVI, Pope. *Caritas in veritate.* 2009. http://w2.vatican.va/content/benedict-xvi/en/encyclicals/documents/hf_ben-xvi_enc_20090629_caritas-in-veritate.html.

———. "Message for the Celebration of the World Day of Peace." January 1, 2007. http://w2.vatican.va/content/benedict-xvi/en/messages/peace/documents/hf_ben-xvi_mes_20061208_xl-world-day-peace.html.

Francis, Pope. "Address to Ecclesial Movements." May 18, 2013. http://w2.vatican.va/content/francesco/en/speeches/2013/may/documents/papa-francesco_20130518_veglia-pentecoste.html.

———. "Address to Members of the Apostolic Movement of the Blind and the Little Mission for the Deaf and Mute." March 29, 2014. http://w2.vatican.va/content/francesco/en/speeches/2014/march/documents/papa-francesco_20140329_movimento-ciechi-missione-sordomuti.html.

———. "Address to Participants in the Ecclesial convention of the Diocese of Rome." June 17, 2013. https://w2.vatican.va/content/francesco/en/speeches/2013/june/documents/papa-francesco_20130617_convegno-diocesano-roma.html.

———. "Address to Participations at the International Pastoral Congress on the World's Big Cities." November 27, 2014. https://w2.vatican.va/content/francesco/en/speeches/2014/november/documents/papa-francesco_20141127_pastorale-grandi-citta.html.

———. "Address to the Council of Europe." Nov. 25, 2014. https://w2.vatican.va/content/francesco/en/speeches/2014/november/documents/papa-francesco_20141125_strasburgo-consiglio-europa.html.

———. "Address to the Pontifical Council for the Laity." Dec. 7, 2013. https://w2.vatican.va/content/francesco/en/speeches/2013/december/documents/papa-francesco_20131207_plenaria-laici.html.

———. *Amoris laetitia.* 2016. https://w2.vatican.va/content/dam/francesco/pdf/apost_exhortations/documents/papa-francesco_esortazione-ap_20160319_amoris-laetitia_en.pdf.

———. "Angelus." September 1, 2013. https://w2.vatican.va/content/francesco/en/angelus/2013/documents/papa-francesco_angelus_20130901.html.

———. *Evangelii gaudium.* 2013. http://w2.vatican.va/content/francesco/en/apost_exhortations/documents/papa-francesco_esortazione-ap_20131124_evangelii-gaudium.html.

———. "Homily." Cathedral of San Sebastian, Rio de Janeiro. July 27, 2013. http://w2.vatican.va/content/francesco/en/homilies/2013/documents/papa-francesco_20130727_gmg-omelia-rio-clero.html.

———. *Laudato si'.* 2015. http://w2.vatican.va/content/francesco/en/encyclicals/documents/papa-francesco_20150524_enciclica-laudato-si.html.

———. *Lumen fidei.* 2013. http://w2.vatican.va/content/francesco/en/encyclicals/documents/papa-francesco_20130629_enciclica-lumen-fidei.html.

———. "Meeting with Brazil's Leaders of Society." July 27, 2013. http://w2.vatican.va/content/francesco/en/speeches/2013/july/documents/papa-francesco_20130727_gmg-classe-dirigente-rio.html.

———. "Meeting with Seminarians and Novices." July 6, 2013. https://w2.vatican.va/content/francesco/en/speeches/2013/july/documents/papa-francesco_2013 0706_incontro-seminaristi.html.

———. "Meeting with the Academic and Cultural World." September 22, 2013. https://w2.vatican.va/content/francesco/en/speeches/2013/september/documents/papa-francesco_20130922_cultura-cagliari.html.

———. "Meeting with the Sick and Disabled Children Assisted at the Seraphic Institute." October 4, 2013. https://w2.vatican.va/content/francesco/en/speeches/2013/october/documents/papa-francesco_20131004_bambini-assisi.html.

———. "Message for the 48th World Communications Day." June 1, 2014. https://w2.vatican.va/content/francesco/en/messages/communications/documents/papa-francesco_20140124_messaggio-comunicazioni-sociali.html.

———. "Wednesday Audience." June 5, 2013. https://w2.vatican.va/content/francesco/en/audiences/2013/documents/papa-francesco_20130605_udienza-generale.html.

———. "Video Message for the 50th Anniversary of the Founding of the Loppiano International Centre." April 10, 2014.

John Paul II, Pope. "Address to the Italian National Congress of the Ecclesial Movement for Cultural Commitment." January 16, 1982. https://w2.vatican.va/content/john-paul-ii/it/speeches/1982/january/documents/hf_jp-ii_spe_19820116_impegno-culturale.html.

———. "Address to UNESCO: Man's Entire Humanity is Expressed in Culture." June 2, 1980. https://w2.vatican.va/content/john-paul-ii/fr/speeches/1980/june/documents/hf_jp-ii_spe_19800602_unesco.html.

———. "Letting the Gospel Take Root in Every Culture." January 10, 1992. http://www.vatican.va/roman_curia/pontifical_councils/cultr/documents/rc_pc_cultr_doc_20000126_jp-ii_addresses-pccultr_en.html#9.

Leo XIII, Pope. *Rerum novarum.* 1891. http://w2.vatican.va/content/leo-xiii/en/encyclicals/documents/hf_l-xiii_enc_15051891_rerum-novarum.html.

———. *Fede e cultura : antologia di testi del magistero pontificio da Leone XIII a Giovanni Paolo II.* Vatican City : Libreria editrice vaticana, 2003.

Paul VI, Pope. *Evangelii nuntiandi.* 1975. http://w2.vatican.va/content/paul-vi/en/apost_exhortations/documents/hf_p-vi_exh_19751208_evangelii-nuntiandi.html.

Pontifical Council for Culture. *Fede e cultura: antologia di testi del magistero pontificio da Leone XIII a Giovanni Paolo II.* Vatican City: Libreria editrice vaticana. 2003.

Second Vatican Council. *Gaudium et spes.* 1965. http://www.vatican.va/archive/hist_councils/ii_vatican_council/documents/vat-ii_const_19651207_gaudium-et-spes_en.html.

CHAPTER 15

Winning Converts

John A. O'Brien and the Renewal of Lay Leadership in the Church

—John C. Cavadini

Abstract:

This paper compares the thought of Fr. John A. O'Brien in the first half of the 20th century to that of Pope Francis on the topic of Catholic lay leadership in the work of evangelization, of "missionary discipleship," as Pope Francis calls it, or of "making converts" to the Catholic Faith, as Fr. O'Brien, who won the Laetare Medal in 1973, would call it. Both provide paradigms for lay leadership in the Church that extends beyond "collaboration" with the hierarchy to taking "co-responsibility" for the mission of the Church, to use terminology suggested by Pope Benedict.

In the Department of Theology at the University of Notre Dame there are two current holders of a John A. O'Brien endowed professorship, and two living John A. O'Brien professors emeriti.[1] When I was Chair of the Department, it was explained to me that the original endowment, which had grown to the point where it could fund two professorships, was generated from the proceeds of pamphlets written to explain the teachings of the

---

1. This essay was originally delivered as a contribution to the 2015 Marten Program in Homiletics and Liturgics annual conference, held at the University of Notre Dame, June 22–24, 2015. The theme of the conference was, "'What We Have Seen and Heard': Fostering Baptismal Witness in the World," and the following essay takes up this theme as present both in the work of Fr. John A. O'Brien and in the documents of the contemporary Magisterium.

Catholic faith to outsiders and to insiders alike.[2] They were often sold in the vestibules of Catholic churches for mere pennies. The original endowment most likely also included the proceeds from royalties on the sales of Fr. O'Brien's books, including his wildly successful apologetic masterpiece, *The Faith of Millions*, first published in 1938 and subsequently reprinted 27 times and translated into 10 languages.[3] O'Brien gave the money he made from the sales of pamphlets, this book and others, to Fr. Theodore Hesburgh, longtime President of the University of Notre Dame, to use at his discretion. Why to Hesburgh? Probably because Hesburgh had welcomed him to Notre Dame, appointing him as a "research professor" after he had worked for 22 years at the University of Illinois, where he arrived shortly after his ordination in the Diocese of Peoria in 1916 and started the Newman Foundation. He also earned a PhD in Psychology while serving as chaplain to the Catholic students there. After a year spent at Oxford in 1939, perhaps experimenting with other venues in which to do his work, he was invited by Hesburgh to come to Notre Dame. Hesburgh was impressed, it would seem, by O'Brien's amazing output defending and articulating the Catholic positions on subjects ranging from birth and population control, to priestly celibacy, science and religion, and evolution, with his unique, and uniquely charming, combination of zeal and courtesy on the one hand, and sophistication and popularization on the other hand. He was awarded the Laetare Medal in 1973,[4] seven years before his death at the age of 73 in 1980. Here is the citation on display in the Main Building at Notre Dame: "The first priest to receive the Laetare Medal, Father O'Brien was a popularizer of church renewal before the Second Vatican Council. In addition to numerous articles and pamphlets on Catholic affairs, he wrote more than 25 books and edited another 12. A pioneer of the Newman Club movement, he is most remembered for his ability to translate crucial theological issues into the everyday language of the average Catholic layperson."

The significance of John A. O'Brien's life and activities for a symposium on the lay baptismal witness may not yet be apparent from these

2. It should be noted that, in addition to funding positions in the Department of Theology, the proceeds of O'Brien's outreach now also fund two professorships in the Department of Philosophy, along with one in the Department of Romance Languages and Literature.

3. Many of the details of O'Brien's biography given here are also provided on the webpage of the University of Notre Dame Archives (archives.nd.edu), which preserves the full collection of the John A. O'Brien Papers. The author would like to thank Greg Cruess for his editing and archival assistance.

4. The Laetare Medal has been awarded by the University of Notre Dame since 1883, and is traditionally conferred upon a Catholic "whose genius has ennobled the arts and sciences, illustrated the ideals of the Church and enriched the heritage of humanity."

scant biographical details, but one would not have to look very far to find it. Anyone who had ever spoken to Hesburgh on his own interest in theology would eventually discover that he wrote his doctoral dissertation on the significance of the laity in the Church, a dissertation topic that, he would say, was treated from some quarters at the time with disdain. Hesburgh would also proudly recall, however, that his vindication came at the time of the Second Vatican Council, when he learned that his dissertation had been used as a touchstone for what the Council had to say about the laity in *Lumen gentium* and elsewhere. This may give a further clue as to why Hesburgh would have welcomed O'Brien to campus, although Hesburgh did not specify this as a motive when I asked him about O'Brien a number of years ago. Hesburgh spoke of him in admiring tones and compared his down-to-earth style favorably, both in speech and dress, to other famous priest evangelists of the era. Hesburgh remembered how O'Brien would spend his summers preaching out in the open in the South, trying to attract converts, and he admired the courage of his direct, personal approach. I wish I had recorded what Hesburgh had to say about John A. O'Brien but I did not! In any event, one does not have to dip very far into O'Brien's work to discover that he was a passionate advocate of what some today might call lay evangelism, but what I would like to think of (without any conflict implied) as lay leadership in the Church. Commenting in an essay, "How You Can Win Converts," contributed to a 1948 volume he edited entitled, *Winning Converts,* O'Brien had this to say:

> We have a splendid body of Catholic laity in America. They are earnest, loyal and devoted to the Church. They attend Mass with edifying regularity and receive the sacraments frequently. But thus far we have not worked out a suitable means of harnessing their good will, devotion and tremendous latent power, for missionary efforts, for convert work and for the winning of our beloved America for Christ.[5]

He later refers to the "latent power" he mentioned here as a "Niagara of potential energy" (using one of the scientific metaphors he so loved), and argues that our failure to "harness" that energy "constitutes the greatest loss of the Church in America."[6] One can begin to see why Hesburgh was attracted to Fr. John A. O'Brien, and one could imagine that he took some satisfaction in seeing "University of Notre Dame" as the institutional affiliation supplied, as it was for every writer, under O'Brien's name at the beginning of the essays he contributed. In addition, one can note with pride that the

5. O'Brien, "How You Can Win Converts," 28.
6. Ibid.

imprimatur granted to the volume was given by the Most Reverend John Francis Noll, Bishop of Fort Wayne, famous for his leadership in the pre-conciliar movement to renew catechesis in the Church. And, while we're at it, we can note that one of the essays, perhaps the most elegant one in the volume, was by a laywoman, herself a convert to the Catholic faith, Clare Booth Luce.[7]

To take a step back: to whom in "our beloved America" was all of this convert-making energy to be addressed? The most inclusive answer is, "to anyone interested in listening," but the preponderant focus was not on other believers—though again, anyone was welcome and everyone was treated with courtesy, the "right approach" as Luce argued. Rather, the task was imagined as a great outward movement to convert the unchurched. In his introductory essay to the whole volume, "The Contemporary Scene in America," O'Brien begins with "The Statement of the Problem," and has this to say: "The outstanding problem facing the Church in America today is the winning of the 80,000,000 churchless men and women of our land. In comparison with this, all other problems are secondary."[8] How is that for a statement of priorities! But isn't it correct? Could one not hear an echo of Pope Francis's exhortations in *Evangelii gaudium*?

> John Paul II asked us to recognize that "there must be no less-ening of the impetus to preach the Gospel" to those that are far from Christ, "because this is the first task of the Church." Indeed, "today missionary activity still represents the greatest challenge for the Church" and "the missionary task must remain foremost." What would happen if we were to take these words seriously? We would realize that missionary outreach is *paradigmatic for all the Church's activity.*[9]

O'Brien continues by noting that the achievement of this task of winning over the unchurched "will require concerted action on the part of both clergy and laity. It will demand training, discipline, vision and organization."[10] I wonder if it is too much to hear in these words, though written in a vocabulary that may strike us as old-fashioned, what Pope Francis calls for when he speaks of "The Church's Missionary Transformation,"[11] and when he says, for example, "I dream of a 'missionary option,' that is, a missionary impulse

---

7. Luce, "The Right Approach," 59–70.

8. O'Brien, "The Contemporary Scene," 3.

9. Francis, *Evangelii gaudium*, 15 (citing John Paul II, *Redemptoris missio*, 34, 40, and 86).

10. O'Brien, "The Contemporary Scene," 3.

11. Francis, *Evangelii gaudium*, title of chap. 1.

capable of transforming everything, so that the Church's customs, ways of doing things, times and schedules, language and structures can be suitably channeled for the evangelization of today's world rather than for her self-preservation."[12] Again, Francis notes, "Pastoral ministry in a missionary key seeks to abandon the complacent attitude that says: 'We have always done it this way.' I invite everyone to be bold and creative in this task of rethinking the goals, structures, style and methods of evangelization in their respective communities."[13] Again echoing the words of Pope John Paul II, Francis cautions against falling prey to "a kind of ecclesial introversion."[14]

In this regard, one cannot help but notice that O'Brien almost never talks about "serving the Church," but about responding to Jesus's call for evangelization. He closes his introduction as follows: "In the ear of all who read this book will be echoing the words addressed by our divine Master at Jacob's Well to His disciples, as He saw the Samaritans thronging towards Him: 'Behold, I say to you, lift up your eyes and see the countries; for they are white already to harvest.'" He continues, later in the same (closing) paragraph, "These are the words which the divine Master is addressing to the 25,000,000 Catholic people in America today."[15] Note that although the number 25,000,000 is the number usually associated in O'Brien's essays in this book with the number of the Catholic laity, here he does not make a distinction, as though mobilizing the laity were, in effect, mobilizing the whole Church. The laity serve here as a synecdoche, the part—by far the larger part—for the whole. But isn't this, in a way, what *Lumen gentium*, the Dogmatic Constitution on the Church of the Second Vatican Council, means in speaking of the apostolate of the laity in terms of the threefold vocation of Christ? The theology of the laity, is, in a way, the theology of the Church. By addressing "the Catholic people" in this way, the whole Church is enjoined, as it were, to stop looking inward and instead to look out to those who are bereft of the happiness, solace and joy that knowing the Gospel—and the Gospel in its fullness as represented by the Catholic Church—can bring. O'Brien positions both clergy and people, the whole Church, working together, as poised to convert a culture.

One mark of the non-inward-looking character of John A. O'Brien's exhortations is that, coupled with his reluctance to use the language of "serving the Church," he never speaks of "adding numbers to the Church" or of enlarging the Church, but rather, his preferred expressions are "winning

12. Ibid., 27.

13. Ibid., 35.

14. Ibid., 27.

15. O'Brien, "The Contemporary Scene," 10.

souls for Jesus Christ,"[16] and responding to the "plea of Jesus Christ [in Jn. 10:16]" so that one can win other souls, not of this flock, "for the Good Shepherd."[17] It is Christ, not the Church, that is hungering for souls, and the point is not simply to "get people on our team," which is more like proselytizing as I would understand it, but to increase their happiness by bringing them to the bread that will truly nourish their lives and make them meaningful: "Christ is hungering for the souls of the 80,000,000 of our churchless countrymen—pleading with you to hand them not a stone, but the nourishing bread of divine truth."[18] Listen to this exhortation addressed, in his first chapter titled, "How You Can Win Converts," to the Catholic laity, and thus, *because* to the laity, to the Church as a whole. As we remember, for the mobilization of the laity, we will need "concerted action" involving both laity and clergy, and renewed "organization."[19] Here is the exhortation: "Catholic men and women of America! Christ is calling you to proclaim Him and His teachings from the housetops. He is calling you to go out into the highways and the byways to announce His Gospel of mercy, forgiveness and love. He is asking you to open your eyes and see the fields of America whitening with a harvest for the reaping of which the clergy are all too few."[20] There follows the passage quoted above, "Christ is hungering..." Interesting. No mention of the Church as any kind of beneficiary of this action. And—could we again hear with profit the comparison of a passage from *Evangelii gaudium*? Pope Francis, like John A. O'Brien, emphasizes that the call comes from Christ himself:

> In our day Jesus's command to *go and make disciples* echoes in the changing scenarios and ever new challenges to the Church's mission of evangelization, and all of us are called to take part in this new missionary "going forth." *Each Christian* [my emphasis] and every community must discern the path that the Lord points out, but *all of us* [my emphasis] are asked to obey his call to go forth from our own comfort zone in order to reach all the "peripheries" in need of the light of the Gospel.[21]

Again, from John A. O'Brien:

16. O'Brien, "How You Can Win Converts," 14.
17. Ibid., 15.
18. Ibid.
19. O'Brien, "The Contemporary Scene," 3.
20. O'Brien, "How You Can Win Converts," 15.
21. Francis, *Evangelii gaudium*, 20.

> In this land whitening with a harvest of nearly a hundred mil-
> lion souls, ungathered by any reapers, there is a crying need for
> the lay disciples of Christ to supplement the work of the bish-
> ops and priests who are able to gather but a small fragment of
> the vast harvest. To the 25,000,000 lay Catholics of America,
> Christ is now addressing the words first uttered at Jacob's Well
> in Samaria.[22]

Lay Catholics are here not asked to serve the Church, for the Church is not here to serve herself, but to hear a call addressed to them directly by Christ in the Scriptures, and echoed by Popes and priests alike, such that, "with their eyes open to the vision of the whitening harvest of souls in America and with the divine promises echoing in their minds and hearts, the Catho-lic lay men and women of America will throw themselves into the great-est crusade of the twentieth century—the crusade of winning America for Christ."[23]

What exactly does this involve on the part of the laity? It involves initiative. Pope Francis says that "the Church which 'goes forth' is a com-munity of missionary disciples who take the first step, who are involved and supportive, who bear fruit and rejoice.... Let us try a little harder to take the first step and to become involved."[24] John A. O'Brien never tired of telling stories of ordinary Catholics who, in the words of Pope Francis, "took the first step" to share the Gospel with their neighbor. He tells the story, for ex-ample, of Charles Fisher, an uneducated one-armed laborer who worked for the Illinois Central Railroad, who was not afraid to engage his unchurched fellow workers, to ask them to take a look, with a "simple, human appeal" to think about the meaning of their lives. In the course of his 25 years with the railroad, he was able to "bring 19 men to his pastor for instruction" and every one of them agreed, in time, to embrace the Catholic faith. O'Brien drily remarks, "In contrast to the university students to whom I was min-istering, Mr. Fisher had not completed the elementary school course. Yet I am safe in saying that he had been instrumental in bringing more con-verts into the Church than my entire congregation of a thousand students."[25] Later on, "More than any other individual, this one-armed fisher of men," O'Brien notes, punning on Mr. Fisher's name, "untutored in the things of this world but wise in the things of the spirit, opened my eyes to the hitherto

22. O'Brien, "How You Can Win Converts," 14.

23. Ibid., 16.

24. Francis, *Evangelii gaudium*, 24.

25. O'Brien, "How You Can Win Converts," 17.

unsuspected possibilities in lay convert work."[26] I would call this lay leadership. I think Pope Francis would agree. In section 13 of *Evangelii gaudium*, he says the following, beginning with a quote from Hebrews (13:7): "*Remember your leaders, those who spoke to you the word of God.* Some of them were ordinary people who were close to us and introduced us to the life of faith: *I am reminded of your sincere faith, a faith that dwelt first in your grandmother Lois and your mother Eunice* (2 Tm 1:5)." Francis thus reminds us that this leadership has been present in the Church from the time of Paul and Timothy.

Later in the essay, as if making up for his remark about university students, O'Brien goes on to tell the story of a young professor, George M. Reichle, who was teaching public speaking at Notre Dame when he was drafted into the Army, whose education permitted him not only to "take the first step," but to give the instructions for baptism for those he engaged who were not Catholic, as well as to revitalize the faith of men who had fallen away from the practice of the faith.[27] He worked in tandem with the Catholic priest chaplain, who heard the confessions of those returning to the faith, examined and then baptized those newly evangelized, and celebrated Mass for all. Here is someone else who went out of his comfort zone and "took the first step," took initiative, led the way.

Most poignantly, and perhaps most germane to our conference focused on "Fostering Baptismal Witness in the World," is O'Brien's reminiscence in this essay of a lay street preacher, or rather a series of lay preachers, both young men and women, he heard in Hyde Park the year he was in England. He describes the interchange between the speaker, "mounted on a soap box, . . . a young man of twenty-five," and a heckler who had asked a critical question during his 45-minute oration to a crowd of about 100 people. It is worth quoting the reminiscence at a little length, for O'Brien was obviously very moved by this scene of ardent young lay witness:

> It was a moving spectacle for myself and my priest companion from America, where such sights rarely, if ever, are seen. All afternoon long and well into the evening, at intervals of about an hour, a young man or woman would mount the box to carry on the street preaching.... As we listened to the young man speak with great earnestness and vigor, expressing himself simply and driving his points home with apt illustrations, we found a lump forming in our throats and our hearts burning within us.[28]

26. Ibid.
27. See O'Brien, "How You Can Win Converts," 29.
28. Ibid., 26.

Rev. John A. O'Brien street preaching in Richlands, NC, circa 1950s.

O'Brien then goes on to express his wish that "that scene could be reenacted in every city, town and village in America," and says in addition that "that scene in Hyde Park symbolizes the outstanding need in America today—the need for the enlistment of the 25,000,000 Catholic men, women and children in the divinely appointed task of spreading the religion of Jesus Christ among 80,000,000 of our churchless fellow countrymen."[29] Of course, as O'Brien points out, this is "symbolic" because it does not mean that every lay person needs to become a street preacher, but it is a dramatic, and in itself desirable, example of "taking the first step," of leading in seeking "to carry the knowledge of their holy faith to their nonCatholic acquaintances

29. Ibid., 28.

and friends . . . especially those having no religious affiliation."[30] Pope Francis, it may be remembered, also calls for a "renewal of preaching," and in this context mentions the leaders who in the time of Paul were "ordinary people," and, later on, reminds us that "today, as the Church seeks to experience a profound missionary renewal, there is a kind of preaching which falls to each of us as a daily responsibility,"[31] that of which the street preacher of O'Brien's reminiscence serves as the "symbol," to use O'Brien's phrase. Francis continues:

> It has to do with bringing the Gospel to the people we meet, whether they be our neighbors or complete strangers. This is the informal preaching which takes place in the middle of a conversation, something along the lines of what a missionary does when visiting a home. Being a disciple means being constantly ready to bring the love of Jesus to others, and this can happen in any place: on the street, in a city square, during work, on a journey.[32]

O'Brien's collection of essays includes one about an organization called "Convert Makers of America," written by its founder, Fr. John E. Odou, SJ, and intended to organize the laity for making converts out of the unchurched in just the ways Pope Francis has described. O'Brien's introduction to the essay describes it this way:

> The C.M.O.A. is a young organization, which has already accomplished much, but its potentialities are truly great. It seeks to incorporate a somewhat new idea into the lay apostolate, namely, that a lay person can present the teachings of the Faith to an inquirer. Instead of simply bringing the non-Catholic to a rectory, the C.M.O.A. encourages its members to undertake a good share of the work of instruction. Who would deny them the privilege of making the attempt? Perhaps the instruction would not be couched in the same language as that used by a priest. But that may have its advantages. It is almost certain to be simple, direct, down-to-earth.[33]

The author of the essay describes two kinds of work undertaken by the members of C.M.O.A.: "personal" and "project" work.[34] The former includes

30. Ibid.

31. Francis, *Evangelii gaudium*, 127.

32. Ibid.

33. O'Brien, Foreword to "The Convert Makers of America," 35.

34. Odou, "The Convert Makers of America," 37.

the unexpected "preaching" that Pope Francis mentions which, in the words of Fr. Odou, can take place in trains, hotels, depots, beauty parlors, in business life, at school, at home, in the neighborhood—"almost anywhere."[35] The "project" work is all organized by laity, and includes reading rooms, information centers, and lay organized and delivered talks in private homes for groups of 15 inquirers, by invitation.[36] Wouldn't this correspond to what Pope Francis is talking about when he calls for new structures for evangelization, for going forth into the peripheries?

Two women street preaching with a microphone
from the back of a car, circa 1950s.

In fact, the whole collection of essays was based on a symposium to discuss new modes of organization and mobilization that would empower the whole Church to become what Pope Francis calls "missionary disciples," and what John A. O'Brien called "winners of converts." Perhaps this symposium was held at the University of Notre Dame, but the volume makes no mention of the location. In any event, this symposium took place on approximately the 20th anniversary of an earlier symposium organized by O'Brien, a programmatic conference which took place in 1927 and went by the name of *The White Harvest: A Symposium on Methods of Convert Making*. Though

35. Ibid.
36. Ibid., 39–41.

all the essays but one were written by priests, one of the overarching themes of the conference was the idea of mobilizing the Catholic laity. The emphasis of the 1948 symposium on this theme was intended as a follow-up to the earlier conference. The lone essay written by a layman is especially instructive for our purposes because it is an account of an attempt to systematize lay preaching of the Gospel to all comers, but especially to the unchurched, in early twentieth century America. The author was David Goldstein, a former Socialist and convert from a non-religious Jewish background, and the title of the essay is "Lay Street Preaching."[37] It details the projects of the Catholic Truth Guild, a completely lay initiated project of evangelization with a laywoman as President (Mrs. Martha Moore Avery), and a layman, David Goldstein, as Secretary. Goldstein was a street preacher, and he and Mrs. Avery created a mobile preaching station, an outfitted van, the back of which opened up as a portable pulpit, or soapbox, or whatever one should call it. The van contained all kinds of Catholic evangelical literature to distribute to those interested during or after the talk. The autovan was set up on the Boston Commons, in the home archdiocese of Boston, but it also made its way around the country, and one particular event is recounted in detail, a transcontinental preaching tour that began in San Francisco, and ended, at long length, back home in Boston. Members of the Catholic Truth Guild supported the street preachers and financed the literature, which was made available to all comers either at no charge, or, in the case of books, at a 2/3 discount over the list price. This whole project came about in response to an exhortation issued by Archbishop Ireland of Boston, who appealed, as Fr. O'Brien summed it up in his editorial introduction to the essay, "for an apostolate that would bring the Gospel of Christ to the vast multitudes in the highways and byways, who have been untouched by the saving elements of religious truth."[38] He quotes Archbishop Ireland himself as saying, "It is time we bring back the Gospel spirit, to go out into the highways and byways, to preach on housetops, and in the market place. Erect stately churches if you will. They are grand monuments to religion . . . but if some remain outside, speak to them on the streets or the public road."[39] "Along these lines," Pope Francis says, "the Latin American bishops stated that we 'cannot passively and calmly wait in our church buildings.'"[40]

37. Goldstein, "Lay Street Preaching," 209–38.

38. O'Brien, Foreword to "Lay Street Preaching," 207.

39. Ibid.

40. Francis, *Evangelii gaudium*, 15 (citing the Fifth General Conference of the Latin American and Caribbean Bishops, *Aparecida Document*, 548).

I wonder if we have yet to rise to the vision which was already vigorously represented by John A. O'Brien and the priests and layfolk who were his associates across the range of apostolates represented in the winning converts movement, as the symposia he organized, in turn, represented them. In this context, I'd like to reflect briefly on the vision of the document *CoWorkers in the Vineyard of the Lord*.[41] Where is its vision to be located relative to the "salvation armies" of convert winners that Archbishop Ireland had called for at the very beginning of the last century, and the responses to which the lifelong work of John A. O'Brien direct our attention (not the least including his own)? Or where is it to be located in regard to the vision—which I believe to be very congruent with these earlier achievements and visions—proposed to us by Pope Francis in *Evangelii gaudium?* I was Chair of the Department of Theology when the document was released in 2005 and I oversaw its implementation in our Masters of Divinity program, which had already been functioning in many of the ways recommended in terms of the formation and education of layfolk for ministry. In the same year, I created a new program to form what the document calls "lay ecclesial ministers" in catechetical leadership (the Echo program in the McGrath Institute for Church Life), and both of these programs in formation are very dear to my heart. In that context, I was asked to reflect on the theological foundations of *Co-Workers* for the recent summit on Lay Ecclesial Ministry sponsored by three USCCB committees.[42] I was asked in particular to reflect on the relationship between the lay apostolate in general, and the vocation to serve in the capacity of what the document calls lay ecclesial ministry. As I've already indicated, I am very personally invested in forming such people, and even more so as a result of my reading of O'Brien's work.

So, let me say that I have found the vision of *Co-Workers in the Vineyard of the Lord* to be quite seaworthy in this work of education and formation, of linking lay apostolate and ecclesial service. As *Lumen gentium* argues, echoed later by the apostolic exhortations, *Evangelii nuntiandi* and *Christifideles laici*, and by *Co-Workers* itself, the apostolate of the laity is "secular," meaning that the laity's defining role is in the ordinary life of the world

41. *Co-Workers in the Vineyard of the Lord: A Resource for Guiding the Development of Lay Ecclesial Ministry* is a document that was released in 2005 by the United States Conference of Catholic Bishops (USCCB) primarily as "a resource for diocesan bishops," but also addressed to "all others who are responsible for guiding the development of lay ecclesial ministry in the United States" (5).

42. This was the Lay Ecclesial Ministry Summit, held June 7–8, 2015 in St. Louis, Missouri. It was sponsored by the USCCB Committee on Laity, Marriage, Family Life, and Youth, the Committee on Cultural Diversity in the Church, and the Subcommittee on Certification for Ecclesial Ministry and Service, in partnership with the Committee on Doctrine.

which we work to transform in the light of the Gospel.[43] But, as *Evangelii nuntiandi* puts it, quoted by *Co-Workers*, "the laity can *also* feel called, or in fact be called, to cooperate with their pastors in the service of the ecclesial community . . . through the exercise of different kinds of ministries."[44] It is that word "also" that is the issue here—what do you mean, "also"? Is this the kind of "also" that divides a person, so his or her "lay" witness as *lay* is outside of a ministry which he or she *also* has? Or is this a lay person who isn't really a layperson anymore but isn't ordained either? A *tertium quid*?

Co-Workers nicely explains this "also" on the twin foundations of mission and communion which are intimately related—communion is unto mission and mission is unto communion. Building mission builds communion, and "also" building communion builds mission. They are different aspects of the one identity of the Church which is, in Christ, a *sacrament* of God's love for the world. The Church herself, as it were, is fundamentally secular and "also" fundamentally a communion built not *of* the world but *of* God's love through the sacraments. The "also" of the call of lay persons who remain lay but choose to "cooperate with their pastors" in the service of the ecclesial community, reflects this larger "also" of the Church herself. In a way, the lay minister straddles this larger "also." *Co-Workers* explains this well by distinguishing *relations* within communion, and thus within mission, and it founds these distinctions on its careful precision in the use of the word "ministry." The ministry to which the priest is configured in holy orders belongs "along with the word of God and the sacraments which it serves . . . to the *constitutive elements* of the Church."[45] In other words, the great gift of the ministerial priesthood is that the priest, by acting *in persona Christi capitis*, gives the people of God to *themselves, as* people of God, and not as his own private possession. The ministry of the priest, by mediating the headship of Christ, constitutes and protects the identity of the people of God as God's. Thus "the ministry of the priest is entirely on behalf of the Church; it aims at promoting the exercise of the common priesthood of the entire people of God."[46] It is impossible for a layperson to try to exercise such a constitutive ministry without becoming the "hireling" who steals the flock as a private possession. But it *is* possible for a

43. See Second Vatican Council, *Lumen gentium*, 31; Paul VI, *Evangelii nuntiandi*, 70; John Paul II, *Christifideles laici*, 15; USCCB, *Co-Workers in the Vineyard of the Lord*, 8–10.

44. USCCB, *Co-Workers in the Vineyard of the Lord*, 9 (quoting Paul VI, *Evangelii nuntiandi*, 73); emphasis mine.

45. USCCB, *Co-Workers in the Vineyard of the Lord*, 24 (quoting John Paul II, *Pastores dabo vobis*, 16).

46. Ibid.

non-ordained person to help further those ways of *serving* the communion which the ministry of the ordained uniquely *constitutes*—ways of service, of ministering, which wouldn't even exist without the constitutive function of the ordained ministry. *Co-Workers* accordingly distinguishes that the word "ministry" refers to something different, namely, the common "participation in the threefold ministry of Christ, who is priest, prophet and king," which is proper to *all* the Church's members and *flows from baptism.*[47] The lay ecclesial minister makes use of the ministry he or she has in virtue of the common priesthood to, as *Evangelii nuntiandi* and *Co-Workers* say, "cooperate with their pastors in the service of the ecclesial community, for the sake of its growth and life,"—as an exercise, and as not a renunciation, of their lay state.

The layperson brings to the task all his or her experience of living in the world, with family or as a single person, working for a living, etc., the creation of a set of empathies that builds credibility of witness in a unique lay manner. The lay catechist has credibility, for example, partly because he or she is lay, and speaks out of that specific witness with the unique experiences that go with it. Thus, the common priesthood of one layperson is leveraged for the building up of the common priesthood of the rest of the Church.

In the midst of my awareness of how helpful *Co-Workers in the Vineyard* has been in articulating a vision for educating and forming all the young people who so eagerly come to our programs, I am left with two open questions in my mind, both connected to the admittedly provisional phrase "lay ecclesial ministers." Is this phrase the exact right one? My first question pertains to the fact that it uses the *same* word, "ministry" (which must be heard in two such different senses), to refer at one and the same time to a common shared work and yet to two crucially *different* identities. Is it realistic, over time, to sustain this usage? Pope Francis uses the expression "pastoral workers" as a generic term for similar work that, nonetheless, leaves room for different identities, ordained and lay, only the former of whom are *pastores.*[48] But my second, and *main*, worry is the way the use of the word "ministry" could occlude, not the ministry of the priest, but the common ministry of the laity, which "lay ministry" more narrowly defined, is intended to serve. Despite the clearly stated intentions of the document, can the use of the phrase "lay ecclesial minister" to reflect a professional class of lay ministers cause us to forget the way in which *all* the baptized, and *all* lay persons, are called to evangelize, to proclaim the Gospel in word

47. Ibid., 11.

48. See Francis, *Evangelii gaudium*, 76.

and deed, and to take responsibility for the mission of the Church. We are *all* missionary disciples and "it would be insufficient to envisage a plan of evangelization to be carried out by professionals while the rest of the faithful would simply be passive recipients."[49] *Co-Workers* explicitly warns against creating lay ecclesial ministers as an elite "above or outside the laity."[50] But I wonder if in the long run this balancing act can be sustained without having the effect of making us forget that "lay ministry" and "lay leadership" in the Church may not—or rather, should not—be coinciding sets. It seems to limit lay leadership to a "profession" that, yes, arises from baptism but is "configured to" ordained ministry. But no less than Pius XII, quoted by John Paul II, stated that "the faithful, more precisely, the lay faithful, find themselves on the front lines of the Church's life."[51] And in this spirit, Pope Benedict also said that the Church needs "a change in mindset, particularly concerning lay people. They must no longer be viewed as 'collaborators' of the clergy but truly recognized as 'co-responsible' for the Church's being and action."[52] Just as we are implementing more robust roles for laity in the Church, are we actually, in the long run, making some of the laity more "churchy" instead of expanding our notion of Church? Are we, not by forming what are called lay ecclesial ministers, but by calling them this and working out of theology that is perhaps still a little shaky, making the Church itself more "churchy" instead of, in a way, making the whole church more secular, more "lay," in keeping with its true missionary vocation as Pope Francis has reminded us? Are we actually forming a Church that is more inward turning over time, by focusing on forming lay people who want to work in the Church into a charism that is more properly that of the ordained, that is, the charism of serving the Church instead of turning the Church into a missionary body to serve the world?

I will return to John A. O'Brien to allow his words to sum up what is at stake. In the very opening lines of the introduction to the volume *Winning Converts,* he says the following about his top priority of reaching the 80,000,000 unchurched Americans that he never tired of bringing up:

> No nation can endure half slave and half pagan. Either one or the other will ultimately become the American way of life. It is like being in a boat in midstream with a fast current. There is no such thing as remaining stationary through inactivity. You

49. Francis, *Evangelii gaudium*, 120.

50. USCCB, *Co-Workers in the Vineyard of the Lord*, 26.

51. John Paul II, *Christifideles laici*, 9 (quoting Pius XII, *AAS* 38 [1946], 149).

52. Benedict XVI, "Address on the Opening of the Pastoral Convention of the Diocese of Rome," para. 7.

either row up stream or you are carried downstream by the current. Paganism is the current in the stream of American life today, carrying the bulk of our population—from 80,000,000 to 100,000,000—along with it. The Church founded by Jesus Christ to make the principles and ideals of the Christian religion supreme in the life of mankind is faced with the gigantic task of stemming the drift toward paganism and winning the church-less masses for Christ.[53]

Allowing for the way this is stated in a vocabulary that strikes us as old-fashioned, is it not nevertheless prescient? Don't recent studies show how the "current" in American culture today, the dominant "drift," is to the "None's" in terms of religious preference, and that this is, above all, true of Catholics?[54] In the face of this, are we ready to say with O'Brien, whom Theodore Hesburgh admired so much, that "in comparison with this, all other problems are secondary?" And with Pope Francis, who seems to say much the same thing? Reading through Francis's apostolic exhortation with John A. O'Brien in mind, I have to ask myself, do I really, really believe that "if we succeed in expressing adequately and with beauty the essential content of the Gospel, surely this message will speak to the deepest yearn-ings of people's hearts?"[55] Quoting again John Paul II, he makes his own these words: "The missionary's enthusiasm in proclaiming Christ comes from the conviction that he is responding to [an] expectation" on the part of the hearer based on those yearnings.[56] Do we really believe that, as Pope Francis continues in his own words, "we have a treasure of life and love which cannot deceive, and a message which cannot mislead or disappoint. It penetrates to the depths of our hearts, sustaining and ennobling us. It is a truth which is never out of date because it reaches that part of us which nothing else can reach. Our infinite sadness can only be cured by an infi-nite love."[57] I believe that the phenomenon of the growing drift towards the "None" column in religious preference requires us to ask this question of ourselves—all of us in the Church—and, if the answer is "Yes," to find a way of talking about lay people in the Church that gives rise not simply to a new professional class of pastoral workers called lay ministers, but instead finds a way of mobilizing the Church *as* essentially a "lay" organization. We must

53. O'Brien, "The Contemporary Scene in America," 3.

54. See, for example, Manglos-Weber and Smith, "Understanding Former Young Catholics: Findings from a National Study of American Emerging Adults," 3–8.

55. Francis, *Evangelii gaudium*, 265.

56. Ibid. (quoting John Paul II, *Redemptoris missio*, 45).

57. Ibid.

find a new way of being Church in the face of the problems of the beginning of *this* century, so that "missionary discipleship," in Pope Francis's terms, and "winning converts," in John A. O'Brien's, does in fact become our first priority— above and beyond the culture wars, above and beyond arguments over Church leadership, and, most of all, above and beyond the comfort zone that keeps us from the simple sharing of our faith with someone who does not believe, from taking that first step. This must be as true of the individual lay person, as it is of the Church of which he or she is a synecdoche, the part for the whole.

Bibliography

Benedict XVI, Pope. "Address on the Opening of the Pastoral Convention of the Diocese of Rome." https://w2.vatican.va/content/benedict-xvi/en/speeches/2009/may/documents/hf_ben-xvi_spe_20090526_convegno-diocesi-rm.html.

Francis, Pope. *Evangelii gaudium.* http://w2.vatican.va/content/francesco/en/apost_exhortations/documents/papa-francesco_esortazione-ap_20131124_evangelii-gaudium.html.

Luce, Clare Booth. "The Right Approach." In *Winning Converts: A Symposium on Methods of Convert Making for Priests and Lay People,* edited by John A. O'Brien, 63–76. New York: Kenedy, 1948.

John Paul II, Pope. *Christifideles laici.* http://w2.vatican.va/content/john-paul-ii/en/apost_exhortations/documents/hf_jp-ii_exh_30121988_christifideles-laici.html.

Manglos-Weber, Nicolette, and Christian Smith, "Understanding Former Young Catholics: Findings from a National Study of American Emerging Adults." https://icl.nd.edu/assets/170517/icl_former_catholics_final_web.pdf.

O'Brien, John A. "The Contemporary Scene." In *Winning Converts: A Symposium on Methods of Convert Making for Priests and Lay People,* edited by John A. O'Brien, 1–8. New York: Kenedy, 1948.

———. Foreword to "The Convert Makers of America," by John E. Odou. In *Winning Converts: A Symposium on Methods of Convert Making for Priests and Lay People,* edited by John A. O'Brien, i–xi. New York: Kenedy, 1948.

———. "How You Can Win Converts." In *Winning Converts: A Symposium on Methods of Convert Making for Priests and Lay People,* edited by John A. O'Brien, 9–36. New York: Kenedy, 1948.

Odou, John E. "The Convert Makers of America." In *Winning Converts: A Symposium on Methods of Convert Making for Priests and Lay People,* edited by John A. O'Brien, 37–44. New York: Kenedy, 1948.

Paul VI, Pope. *Evangelii nuntiandi.* http://w2.vatican.va/content/paul-vi/en/apost_exhortations/documents/hf_p-vi_exh_19751208_evangelii-nuntiandi.html.

Second Vatican Council. *Lumen gentium.* http://www.vatican.va/archive/hist_councils/ii_vatican_council/documents/vat-ii_const_19641121_lumen-gentium_en.html.

USCCB. *Co-Workers in the Vineyard of the Lord: A Resource for Guiding the Development of Lay Ecclesial Ministry.* 2005. http://www.usccb.org/upload/co-workers-vineyard-lay-ecclesial-ministry-2005.pdf.

Index